MANUAL OF ZEN BUDDHISM

The Buddha with Sixteen Good Gods of the Prajnaparamita
(Hannya Juroku Zenjin)

MANUAL
OF ZEN BUDDHISM

DAISETZ TEITARO SUZUKI

GROVE WEIDENFELD
NEW YORK

Published by Grove Weidenfeld
A division of Grove Press, Inc.
841 Broadway
New York, NY 10003-4793

ISBN 0-8021-3065-8

Library of Congress Catalog Card Number 60-7637

Manufactured in the United States of America

Printed on acid-free paper

First Evergreen Edition 1960

30   29   28   27   26   25

CONTENTS

5

LIST OF PLATES

LIST OF ILLUSTRATIONS

EDITOR'S NOTE

All references to the Author's *Essays in Zen Buddhism*, Series One and Two, and to his *Introduction to Zen Buddhism*, are to the second edition of these works, published in "The Complete Works of D. T. Suzuki."

PREFACE TO FIRST EDITION

In my *Introduction to Zen Buddhism* (published 1934), an outline of Zen teaching is sketched, and in *The Training of the Zen Monk* (1934) a description of the Meditation Hall and its life is given. To complete a triptych the present *Manual* has been compiled. The object is to inform the reader of the various literary materials relating to the monastery life. Foreign students often express their desire to know about what the Zen monk reads before the Buddha in his daily service, where his thoughts move in his leisure hours, and what objects of worship he has in the different quarters of his institution. This work will partly, it is hoped, satisfy their desire. Those who find my *Essays* too bulky or too elaborate may prefer these smaller works on Zen.

Kyoto
   August 1935

DAISETZ TEITARO SUZUKI

THE THUNDERING SILENCE OF VIMALAKIRTI

Vimalakirti is the hero of the sutra bearing his name. The sutra was translated into Chinese by Kumarajiva, 406 C.E., and ever since has been one of the most popular Buddhist books both in China and Japan. Vimalakirti meaning "Undefiled Fame", is a wealthy householder of Vaisali thoroughly acquainted with the Mahayana teaching and spirit. When he is indisposed, the Buddha wants to send some of his disciples to inquire after him, but no one is forthcoming. When the Buddha asks for the explanation, they have one excuse after another. The main reason is that none of his disciples are equal in the understanding of Buddhism to this householder-philosopher. Finally, the weighty task of calling upon Vimalakirti falls on the Bodhisattva Manjusri. The latter is Prajna incarnate as Samantabhadra, and is Love incarnate. After some preliminary conversations in which Vimalakirti says that he is sick because of all his fellow-beings being sick with greed, anger, and folly, the dialogue between the two great figures of Mahayana Buddhism turns to the discussion of what is meant by the doctrine of non-duality. Manjusri expounds his view and then asks what Vimalakirti thinks of the doctrine. The philosopher does not utter a word, remaining perfectly silent. The Bodhisattva praises him most highly. The drawing here represents this silence of Vimalakirti by the modern father of the Rinzai school of Zen Buddhism in Japan. Hakuin is not a professional painter, and for this reason all the more the spirit of the wise old man of Vaisali is seen quivering in every line of this picture in black and white.

I. GATHAS AND PRAYERS

Gatha is a Sanskrit term meaning "verse" or "hymn". In Buddhist literature it is used to designate the versified portion of the sutras. Chinese scholars have adopted this word for their versified compositions, which are known as *chieh*, an abbreviation of *chieh-t'o*, or as *chieh-sang*, which is the combination of the Sanskrit and the Chinese. The gathas collected here are not exclusively those of the Zen sect; some belong to general Buddhism.

GATHAS AND PRAYERS

I

ON OPENING THE SUTRA

The Dharma incomparably profound and exquisite
Is rarely met with, even in hundreds of thousands of
    millions of kalpas;
We are now permitted to see it, to listen to it, to
    accept and hold it;
May we truly understand the meaning of the
    Tathagata's words!

II

CONFESSION

All the evil karma ever committed by me since of old,
On account of greed, anger, and folly, which have
    no beginning,
Born of my body, mouth, and thought—
I now make full open confession of it.

13

III

THE THREEFOLD REFUGE

I take refuge in the Buddha;
I take refuge in the Dharma;
I take refuge in the Sangha.
I take refuge in the Buddha, the incomparably
honoured one;
I take refuge in the Dharma, honourable for its
purity;
I take refuge in the Sangha, honourable for its
harmonious life.
I have finished taking refuge in the Buddha;
I have finished taking refuge in the Dharma;
I have finished taking refuge in the Sangha.

IV

THE FOUR GREAT VOWS[1]

However innumerable beings are, I vow to save
them;
However inexhaustible the passions are, I vow to
extinguish them;
However immeasurable the Dharmas are, I vow to
master them;
However incomparable the Buddha-truth is, I vow
to attain it.

V

THE WORSHIPPING OF THE SARIRA

We prostrate ourselves in all humbleness before the
holy Sarira representing the body of Sakyamuni, the

---

[1] These vows are recited after every service.

Tathagata, who is perfectly endowed with all the virtues, who has the Dharmakaya as the ground of his being, and Dharmadhatu as the stupa dedicated to him. To him we pay our respect with due deference. Manifesting himself in a bodily form for our sakes, the Buddha enters into us and makes us enter into him. His power being added to us, we attain Enlightenment; and [again] dependent on the Buddha's miraculous power, all beings are benefited, become desirous for Enlightenment, discipline themselves in the life of the Bodhisattva, and equally enter into perfect quietude where prevails infinite wisdom of absolute identity. We now prostrate ourselves before him.

VI

The Teaching of the Seven Buddhas

Not to commit evils,
But to do all that is good,
And to keep one's thought pure—
This is the teaching of all the Buddhas.

VII

The Gatha of Impermanence[1]

All composite things are impermanent,
They are subject to birth and death;
Put an end to birth and death,
And there is a blissful tranquillity.

[1] For the sake of the second half of this gatha the Buddha is said to have been willing to sacrifice his own life. For this reason this is also known as the "gatha of sacrifice".

VIII

THE YEMMEI KWANNON TEN-CLAUSE SUTRA[1]

[Adoration to] Kwanzeon!
Adoration to the Buddha!
To the Buddha we are related
In terms of cause and effect.
Depending on the Buddha, the Dharma, and the
    Sangha,
[Nirvana is possible which is] eternal, ever-blessed,
    autonomous, and free from defilements.
Every morning our thoughts are on Kwanzeon,
Every evening our thoughts are on Kwanzeon.
Every thought issues from the Mind,
Every thought is not separated from the Mind.

IX

PRAYER ON THE OCCASION OF FEEDING THE HUNGRY GHOSTS

If one wishes to know all the Buddhas of the past,
present, and future, one should contemplate the nature of this
Dharmadhatu essentially as the creation of Absolute Mind.

Adoration to the Buddhas in the ten quarters;
Adoration to the Dharma pervading the ten quarters;
Adoration to the Sangha in the ten quarters;
Adoration to Sakyamuni the Buddha who is our Master;
Adoration to Kwanzeon the Bodhisattva, who is the
great compassionate and pitying one, ready to save beings
from afflictions;
Adoration to Ananda the Arhat who is the expounder
of the Teaching.

---

[1] *Yemmei* means "prolonging life"; when one daily recites this short document in ten clauses relating to Kwannon, one's health is assured for doing good not only for oneself but for the whole world.

Namu sabo totogyato boryakite, yen!
Sammola sammola, un!
Namu suryoboya totogyatoya tojito, yen!
Suryo suryo boya suryo boya suryo, somoko!
Namu samanda motonan, ban![1]
Adoration to Hoshin[2] the Tathagata;
Adoration to Taho[3] the Tathagata;
Adoration to Myoshishin[4] the Tathagata;
Adoration to Kohashin[5] the Tathagata;
Adoration to Rifui[6] the Tathagata;
Adoration to Kanroo[7] the Tathagata;
Adoration to Omito[8] the Tathagata.
Namu omitoboya totogyatoya,
Toniyato,
Omiritsubomi,
Omirito,
Shitabomi,
Omirito bigyaratei,
Omirito bigyarato gyamini,
Gyagyano shitogyari,

---

[1] It is difficult to tell how this dharani came to be inserted here. As most dharanis are, it is devoid of sense from the human point of view; but it may not be necessarily so to the hungry ghosts, for whom the prayer is offered. Can this be restored to the original Sanskrit as follows?

Namah sarva-tathagatavalokite! Om!
Sambala, sambala! hum!
Namah surupaya tathagataya!
Tadyatha,
Om, suru[paya], surupaya, surupaya, suru[paya], svaha!
Namah samantabuddhanam, vam!

"Be adored! O all the Tathagatas who are regarded [as our protectors]; Om! Provision, provision! Hum! Adored be the Tathagata Beautifully-Formed! Namely: Om! To the Beautifully-formed One! To the Beautifully-formed One! To the Beautifully-formed One! Hail! Adored be all the Buddhas! Vam!"

[2] "Jewel-excelled (*ratnaketu*).
[3] "Abundant-in-Jewel" (*prabhutaratna*).
[4] "Fine-form-body" (*surupakaya*).
[5] "Broad-wide-body" (*vipulakaya*).
[6] "Freed-from-fear" (*abhayankara*).
[7] "Nectar-king" (*amritaraja*).
[8] "Amida" (*amitabha*).

Somoko.[1]

By the supernatural power of this Dharani the food and drink is purified, and this we offer to the spiritual beings as numerous as the sands of the Ganga. We pray that they shall all be fully satisfied and abandon their greed; that they shall all leave their abodes of darkness and be born in the blissful paths of existence; and further that taking refuge in the Triple Treasure they shall awaken the desire for supreme enlightenment and finally come to the realization of it. The merit they thus attain is inexhaustible and will continue on to the end of time, making all beings equally share in this Dharma-food.

O you hosts of spiritual beings, we make this offering of food to you all, which we pray will fill the ten quarters and that all beings of your kind will partake of it.

By the practice of this meritorious deed we pray that we repay what we owe to our parents, who have done all they could for our sakes. May those who are still alive continue to enjoy their happy and prosperous lives for ever, while those who are no more with us be released from suffering and born in the land of bliss.

We pray that all sentient beings in the triple world who are recipients of the fourfold benefaction, together with those beings suffering in the three evil paths of existence and tormented with the eight kinds of calamities, may repent of all their sins and be cleansed of all their sores, so that they may all be released from the cycle of transmigration and be born in the land of purity.

We pray to all the Buddhas, all the Bodhisattva-Mahasattvas in the ten quarters, of the past, present, and future, and to Mahaprajna-paramita, that by virtue of this merit universally prevailing, not only we but all beings shall equally attain Buddhahood.

---

[1] Namo 'mitabhaya tathagataya! Tadyatha, amritodbhave, amritasiddhe, (?)-bhave, amritavikrante, amrita-vikranta-gamine, gaganakirtikare! Svaha!

"Adored be the Tathagata of Infinite Light! Namely: O Nectar-raising one! O Nectar-perfecting one! [O Nectar-] producing one! O One who makes nectar pervade! O One who makes nectar universally pervade! O One who makes nectar known as widely as space! Hail!"

X

GENERAL PRAYER[1]

By the Bhikshus all present here
The mystic formula of Surangama has been recited
    as above,
Which is now dedicated to all the Nagas and Devas
    who are protectors of the Dharma,
And also to all the holy assemblies of the spiritual
    beings who are guardians of this monastery and
    surrounding district.
May all beings in the three evil paths of existence
    variously suffering the eight kinds of disasters be
    thereby released from the afflictions!
May all beings in the triple world who are recipients
    of the fourfold benefaction thereby participate in
    the merit!
May the state continue in peaceful prosperity with all
    its warlike activities stopped!
May the wind blow in time, the rain fall seasonably,
    and the people live happily!
May the entire congregation sharing in the exercise
    cherish the higher aspirations
To go beyond the ten stages with a eap, and this
    without much difficulty!
May this monastery keep on its quiet life, free from
    disturbances.
And the patrons and devotees grow not only in faith
    but in wisdom and bliss!
[We pray this to] all the Buddhas and Bodhisattva-
Mahasattvas in the ten quarters, of the past, present,
    and future, and to Mahaprajna-paramita!

---

[1] This is read, as can be inferred from the text, after the recitation of the
Surangama dharani.

XI

PRAYER OF THE BELL

Would that the sound of the bell might go beyond our
 earth,
And be heard even by all the denizens of the darkness outside the Iron Mountains (*cakravala*)!
Would that, their organ of hearing becoming pure,
 beings might attain perfect interfusion [of all the
 senses],
So that every one of them might come finally to the
 realization of supreme enlightenment![1]

---

[1] It is customary in the Zen monastery to recite the *Kwannongyo* while
striking the big bell, which is done three times a day. The present gatha is
recited when the striking is finished. As will be seen below, from Kwannon
issues a sound which is heard by those who sincerely believe in his power of
releasing them from every form of disaster. Each sound emitted by the bell
is the voice of Kwannon calling on us to purify our sense of hearing, whereby
a spiritual experience called "interfusion" will finally take place in us. See
under the *Ryogonkyo* and the *Kwannongyo* below.

II. THE DHARANIS

Properly speaking, the dharani has no legitimate place in Zen. That it has nevertheless crept into its daily service is due to the general characteristics of Chinese Buddhism of the Sung dynasty, when the Japanese Zen masters visited China and imported it as they found it then, together with the Shingon elements of Chinese Zen. In China the Shingon did not thrive very long but left its traces in Zen.

Dharani, the root of which is *dhr*, "to hold" or "to convey", is ordinarily translated by the Chinese *tsung-ch'ih*, "general holder", or *neng-ch'ih*, "that which holds". A dharani is considered as holding magical power in it or bearing deep meaning. When it is pronounced, whatever evil spirits there are ready to interfere with the spiritual effect of a ritual, are kept away from it.

In the following pages the three most frequently read dharanis are given. When translated they convey no intelligent signification. They mostly consist of invocations and exclamations. The invocation is an appeal to the higher powers, and the exclamation is to frighten away the evil spirits. That the practical result of these utterances is not to be judged objectively goes without saying.

THE DHARANIS

I

DHARANI OF REMOVING DISASTERS

Adoration to all the Buddhas!
Adoration to the Teaching that knows no obstructions!
Thus:
Om! Khya khya khyahi khyahi (speak, speak)!
Hum hum!
Jvala jvala prajvala prajvala (blaze, blaze)!
Tistha tistha (up, up)!

21

Stri stri (?)!
Sphata (burst, burst)!
One who is quiescent!
To the glorious one, hail!

II

DHARANI OF THE GREAT COMPASSIONATE ONE

Adoration to the Triple Treasure!
Adoration to Avalokitesvara the Bodhisattva-Mahasattva
who is the great compassionate one!
Om, to the one who performs a leap beyond all fears!
Having adored him, may I enter into the heart of the
blue-necked one known as the noble adorable Avalokites-
vara! It means the completing of all meaning, it is pure,
it is that which makes all beings victorious and cleanses
the path of existence.
Thus:
Om, the seer, the world-transcending one!
O Hari the Mahabodhisattva!
All, all!
Defilement, defilement!
The earth, the earth!
It is the heart.
Do, do the work!
Hold fast, hold fast!
O great victor!
Hold on, hold on!
I hold on.
To Indra the creator!
Move, move, my defilement-free seal!
Come, come!
Hear, hear!
A joy springs up in me!
Speak, speak! Directing!

Hulu, hulu, mala, hulu, hulu, hile!
Sara, sara! siri, siri! suru, suru!
Be awakened, be awakened!
Have awakened, have awakened!
O merciful one, blue-necked one!
Of daring ones, to the joyous, hail!
To the successful one, hail!
To the great successful one, hail!
To the one who has attained mastery in the discipline,
   hail!
To the blue-necked one, hail!
To the boar-faced one, hail!
To the one with a lion's head and face, hail!
To the one who holds a weapon in his hand, hail!
To the one who holds a wheel in his hand, hail!
To the one who holds a lotus in his hand, hail!
To the blue-necked far-causing one, hail!
To the beneficient one referred to in this Dharani
   beginning with "Namah," hail!
Adoration to the Triple Treasure!
Adoration to Avalokitesvara!
Hail!
May these [prayers] be successful!
To this magical formula, hail!

III

Dharani of the Victorious
Buddha-Crown

Adoration to the Blessed One who is the most excellent
one in the triple world!
   Adoration to the Enlightened One, to the Blessed One!
Namely:
   Om! Cleanse [us], cleanse [us]! O one who is always

impartial! One who, being in possession of all-pervading, all-illuminating light, is pure in his self-nature, cleansed of the darkness of the five paths of existence!

Baptize us, O Sugata, with an immortal baptism which consists of the best words, of the great true phrases!

Remove disasters, remove disasters, O one who holds an eternal life!

Cleanse us, cleanse us, O one who is as pure as the sky!

O one who is as pure as the victorious Buddha-crown!

O one who is inflamed with a thousand rays of light!

O all the Tathagatas who look over [the entire world]!

O one who is perfect in the Six Paramitas!

O one who holds the great seal empowered with the spiritual power which emanates from the heart of every Tathagata!

O one whose body is as hard and pure as Vajra!

O one who is thoroughly pure, cleansed of all impediments, all fears, and all the evil paths!

Turn us away [from evils] O one who enjoys a purified life!

O one who empowers us with [the power of] the original covenant! O jewel, jewel, the great jewel! O Suchness which is reality-limit and absolute purity!

O one who is pure in his evolved enlightenment!

Be victorious, be victorious, be ever victorious, be ever victorious!

Bear in mind, bear in mind!

O one who is pure being empowered by all Buddhas!

O Vajragarbha who holds the Vajra! Let my body be like Vajra! Let those of all beings too be like Vajra!

O one who is in possession of an absolutely pure body! O one who is absolutely pure from all the paths of existence! And let me be consoled by all the Tathagatas!

O one who is empowered with the consoling power of all the Tathagatas!

Be enlightened, be enlightened, be ever enlightened, be ever enlightened!

Have them enlightened, have them enlightened, have them ever enlightened, have them ever enlightened!

O one who is most pure in a most thoroughgoing way!

O one who holds a great seal empowered with the spiritual power which emanates from the heart of every Tathagata!

Hail!

III. THE SUTRAS

The sutras most read in Zen are the *Shingyo* (*Prajnapara-mitahridaya*), the *Kwannongyo* (*Samantamukha-parivarta*), and the *Kongokyo* (*Vajracchedika*). The *Shingyo* being the shortest is read on almost all occasions. The *Ryoga* (*Lankavatara*) is historically significant, but being difficult to understand is very little studied nowadays by followers of Zen. For further information see the author's works on the sutra. The *Ryogon* (*Suramgama*) is not so neglected as the *Ryoga*. It is full of deep thoughts, and was studied very much more in China than in Japan. There are some more sutras of the Mahayana school with which Zen students will do well to become better acquainted, for example, the *Kongo-sammaikyo* (*Vajrasamadhi*), the *Yengakukyo* (Sutra of Perfect Enlightenment), the *Yuimakyo* (*Vimalakirti-sutra*), and *the Han-nyakyo* (*Prajnaparamita*). None of them have been translated into English, except the *Yuima* which is difficult to obtain now.

THE SUTRAS

I

ENGLISH TRANSLATION OF THE SHINGYO

When[1] the Bodhisattva Avalokitesvara was engaged in the practice of the deep Prajnaparamita, he perceived that there are the five Skandhas;[2] and these he saw in their self-nature to be empty.[3]

"O Sariputra, form is here emptiness,[4] emptiness is form; form is no other than emptiness, emptiness is no other than form; that which is form is emptiness, that which is emptiness is form. The same can be said of sensation, thought, confection, and consciousness.

"O Sariputra, all things here are characterized with emptiness: they are not born, they are not annihilated; they are not tainted, they are not immaculate; they do not increase, they do not decrease. Therefore, O Sariputra,

in emptiness there is no form, no sensation, no thought,
no confection, no consciousness; no eye,[5] ear, nose, tongue,
body, mind; no form,[6] sound, colour, taste, touch, objects;
no Dhatu of vision,[7] till we come to[8] no Dhatu of consciousness; there is no knowledge, no ignorance,[9] till we
come to there is no old age and death, no extinction of
old age and death; there is no suffering,[10] no accumulation,
no annihilation, no path; there is no knowledge, no attainment, [and] no realization,* because there is no attainment.
In the mind of the Bodhisattva who dwells depending on
the Prajnaparamita there are no obstacles;† and, going
beyond the perverted views, he reaches final Nirvana. All
the Buddhas of the past, present, and future, depending
on the Prajnaparamita, attain to the highest perfect enlightenment.

"Therefore, one ought to know that the Prajnaparamita
is the great Mantram, the Mantram of great wisdom, the
highest Mantram, the peerless Mantram, which is capable
of allaying all pain; it is truth because it is not falsehood:
this is the Mantram proclaimed in the *Prajnaparamita*. It
runs: '*Gate, gate, paragate, parasamgate, bodhi, svaha!*' (O Bodhi,
gone, gone, gone to the other shore, landed at the other
shore, Svaha!)"

NOTES

1. There are two texts with the title of *The Hridaya*: the one
is known as the Shorter and the other the Larger. The one
printed above is the shorter sutra in general use in Japan and
China.

The opening passage in the larger text in Sanskrit and
Tibetan, which is missing in the shorter one, is as follows: [The
Tibetan has this additional passage: "Adoration to the Prajna-
paramita, which is beyond words, thought, and praise, whose

---

* *Nabhisamayah* is missing in the Chinese translations as well as in the
Horyuji MS.
† For *varana* all the Chinese have "obstacle", and this is in full accord
with the teaching of the *Prajnaparamita*. Max Muller's rendering, "envelop",
is not good.

self-nature is, like unto space, neither created nor destroyed, which is a state of wisdom and morality evident to our inner consciousness, and which is the mother of all Excellent Ones of the past, present, and future".] "Thus I heard. At one time the World-honoured One dwelt at Rajagriha, on the Mount of Vulture, together with a large number of Bhikshus and a large number of Bodhisattvas. At that time the World-honoured One was absorbed in a Samadhi (Meditation) known as Deep Enlightenment. And at the same moment the Great Bodhisattva Aryavalokitesvara was practising himself in the deep Prajnaparamita."

The concluding passage, which is also missing in the shorter text, runs as follows:

"O Sariputra, thus should the Bodhisattva practise himself in the deep Prajnaparamita. At that moment, the World-honoured One rose from the Samadhi and gave approval to the Great Bodhisattva Aryavalokitesvara, saying: Well done, well done, noble son! so it is! so should the practice of the deep Prajnaparamita be carried on. As it has been preached by you, it is applauded by Tathagatas and Arhats. Thus spoke the World-honoured One with joyful heart. The venerable Sariputra and the Great Bodhisattva Aryavalokitesvara together with the whole assemblage, and the world of Gods, Men, Asuras, and Gandharvas, all praised the speech of the World-honoured One."

2. From the modern scientific point of view, the conception of Skandha seems to be too vague and indefinite. But we must remember that the Buddhist principle of analysis is not derived from mere scientific interest; it aims at saving us from the idea of an ultimate individual reality which is imagined to exist as such for all the time to come. For when this idea is adhered to as final, the error of attachment is committed, and it is this attachment that forever enslaves us to the tyranny of external things. The five Skandhas ("aggregates" or "elements") are form (*rupam*), sensation or sense-perception (*vedana*), thought (*samjna*), confection or conformation (*samskara*), and consciousness (*vijnana*). The first Skandha is the material world or the materiality of things, while the remaining four Skandhas belong to the mind. *Vedana* is what we get through our senses; *samjna* corresponds to thought in its broadest sense, or that which mind elaborates; *samskara* is a very difficult term and there is no exact English equivalent; it means something that gives form, formative principle; *vijnana* is consciousness or mentation.

There are six forms of mentation, distinguishable as seeing, hearing, smelling, tasting, touching, and thinking.

3. Hsuan-chuang's translation has this added: "He was delivered from all suffering and misery."

4. "Empty" (*sunya*) or "emptiness" (*sunyata*) is one of the most important notions in Mahayana philosophy and at the same time the most puzzling for non-Buddhist readers to comprehend. Emptiness does not mean "relativity", or "phenomenality", or "nothingness", but rather means the Absolute, or something of transcendental nature, although this rendering is also misleading as we shall see later. When Buddhists declare all things to be empty, they are not advocating a nihilistic view; on the contrary an ultimate reality is hinted at, which cannot be subsumed under the categories of logic. With them, to proclaim the conditionality of things is to point to the existence of something altogether unconditioned and transcendent of all determination. Sunyata may thus often be most appropriately rendered by the Absolute. When the sutra says that the five Skandhas have the character of emptiness, or that in emptiness there is neither creation nor destruction, neither defilement nor immaculacy, etc., the sense is: no limiting qualities are to be attributed to the Absolute; while it is immanent in all concrete and particular objects, it is not in itself definable. Universal negation, therefore, in the philosophy of Prajna is an inevitable outcome.

5. No eye, no ear, etc., refer to the six senses. In Buddhist philosophy, mind (*manovijnana*) is the special sense-organ for the apprehension of *dharma*, or objects of thought.

6. No form, no sound, etc., are the six qualities of the external world, which become objects of the six senses.

7. "Dhatu of vision, etc." refer to the eighteen Dhatus or elements of existence, which include the six senses (*indriya*), the six qualities (*vishaya*), and the six consciousnesses (*vijnana*).

8. "Till we come to" (*yavat* in Sanskrit, and *nai chih* in Chinese) is quite frequently met with in Buddhist literature to avoid repetition of well-known subjects. These classifications may seem somewhat confusing and overlapping.

9. "There is no knowledge, no ignorance, etc." is the wholesale denial of the Twelvefold Chain of Causation (*pratityasamutpada*), which are ignorance (*avidya*), deed (*samskara*), consciousness (*vijnana*), name and form (*namarupa*), six sense-organs (*sadayatana*), contact (*sparsa*), sense-perception (*vedana*), desire (*trishna*), attachment (*upadana*), being (*bhava*), birth (*jati*), and old

age and death (*jaramarana*). This Chain of Twelve has been a subject of much discussion among Buddhist scholars.

10. The allusion is of course to the Fourfold Noble Truth (*satya*): 1. Life is suffering (*duhkha*); 2. Because of the accumulation (*samudaya*) of evil karma; 3. The cause of suffering can be annihilated (*nirodha*); 4. And for this there is the path (*marga*).

II

THE KWANNON SUTRA[1]

At that time Mujinni[2] Bosatsu rose from his seat, and, baring his right shoulder, turned, with his hands folded, towards the Buddha, and said this: World-honoured One, for what reason is Kwanzeon Bosatsu so named?

The Buddha said to Mujinni Bosatsu: Good man, when those innumerable numbers of beings—hundred-thousands of myriads of kotis of them—who are suffering all kinds of annoyances, hearing of this Kwanzeon Bosatsu, will utter his name with singleness of mind, they will instantly hear his voice and be released.

Even when people fall into a great fire, if they hold the name of Kwanzeon Bosatsu, the fire will not scorch them because of the spiritual power of this Bosatsu. When they are

---

[1] Generally known as *Kwannon-gyo* in Japanese and *Kuan-yin Ching* in Chinese. It forms the Twenty-fifth Chapter in Kumarajiva's translation of the *Saddharma-pundarika*, "the Lotus of the Good Law". Its Sanskrit title is *Samantamukha Parivarta*. It is one of the most popular sutras in Japan, especially among followers of the Holy Path, including Zen, Tendai, Shingon, Nichiren, etc.

The Sanskrit for *Kwannon* seems, according to some Japanese authorities, originally to have been *Avalokitasvara*, and not *Avalokitesvara*. If so, *Kwannon* is a more literal rendering than *Kwanzeon* (*Kuan-shih-yin*) or *Kwanjizai* (*Kuan-tzu-tsai*). The Bodhisattva Avalokitasvara is "the owner of *voice which is viewed or heard*". From him issues a voice which is variously heard and interpreted by all beings, and it is by this hearing that the latter are emancipated from whatever troubles they are in.

The present translation is from Kumarajiva's Chinese. In the reading of the proper names, the Japanese way of pronunciation has been retained.

[2] Bodhisattva Akshayamati in Sanskrit, that is, Bodhisattva of Inexhaustible Intelligence.

tossed up and down in the surging waves, if they pronounce his name they will get into a shallower place.

When hundred-thousands of myriads of kotis of people go out into the great ocean in order to seek such treasures as gold, silver, lapis lazuli, conch shells, cornelian, coral, amber, pearls, and other precious stones, their boats may be wrecked by black storms, and they may find themselves thrown up into the island of the Rakshasas; if among them there is even a single person who will utter the name of Kwanzeon Bosatsu all the people will be released from the disaster [which is likely to befall them at the hand] of the Rakshasas. For this reason the Bosatsu is called Kwanzeon.

When, again, a man is about to suffer an injury, if he will utter the name of Kwanzeon Bosatsu, the sword or the stick that is held [by the executioner] will be at once broken to pieces and the man be released.

When all the Yakshas and Rakshasas filling the three thousand chiliocosms come and annoy a man, they may hear him utter the name of Kwanzeon Bosatsu, and no wicked spirits will dare look at him with their evil eyes, much less inflict injuries on him.

When again a man, whether guilty or innocent, finds himself bound in chains or held with manacles, he uttering the name of Kwanzeon Bosatsu will see all these broken to pieces and be released.

When all the lands in the three thousand chiliocosms are filled with enemies, a merchant and his caravan loaded with precious treasures may travel through the dangerous passes. One of the company will say to the others: "O good men, have no fear; only with singleness of thought utter the name of Kwanzeon Bosatsu. As this Bosatsu gives us fearlessness, utter his name and you will be delivered from your enemies." Hearing this, all the company join in the recitation, saying, "Kwanzeon Bosatsu be adored!" Because of this uttering the name of the Bosatsu they will be released. O Mujinni, such is the awe-inspiring spiritual power of Kwanzeon Bosatsu Makasatsu.

When people are possessed of excessive lust, let them

always reverentially think of Kwanzeon Bosatsu and they will be freed from it. If they are possessed of excessive anger, let them always reverentially think of Kwanzeon Bosatsu, and they will be freed from it. When they are possessed of excessive folly let them always reverentially think of Kwanzeon Bosatsu, and they will be freed from it. O Mujinni, of such magnitude is his spiritual power which is full of blessings. Therefore, let all beings always think of him.

If a woman desire a male child, let her worship and make offerings to Kwanzeon Bosatsu, and she will have a male child fully endowed with bliss and wisdom. If she desire a female child, she will have one graceful in features and in possession of all the characteristics [of noble womanhood], and because of her having planted the root of merit the child will be loved and respected by all beings. O Mujinni, such is the power of Kwanzeon Bosatsu.

If all beings worship and make offerings to Kwanzeon Bosatsu, they will derive benefits unfailingly from this. Therefore, let all beings hold the name of Kwanzeon Bosatsu. O Mujinni, if there is a man who holds the names of all the Bodhisattvas equal in number to sixty-two billion times as many as the sands of the Ganga, and till the end of his life makes them offerings of food and drink, clothing and bedding and medicine, what do you think? Is not the merit accumulated by such a man very great?

Mujinni said: Very great, indeed, World-honoured One!

The Buddha said: Here is another man; if he should hold the name of Kwanzeon Bosatsu even for a while and make offerings to the Bosatsu, the merit so attained by this one is fully equal to that [of the previous one], and will not be exhausted even to the end of hundred-thousands of myriads of kotis of kalpas. Those who hold the name of Kwanzeon Bosatsu gain such immeasurable and innumerable masses of blissful merit.

Mujinni Bosatsu said to the Buddha: "World-honoured One, how does Kwanzeon Bosatsu visit this Saha world?[1]

---

[1] That is, *sahaloka*, world of patience.

KWANNON
By Seisetsu Seki,
Abbot of the Tenryuji Monastery, Kyoto
(*See page 30*)

Plate I

Bodhidharma (Ta-mo, Daruma)
(*See page 73*)

How does he preach the Dharma to all beings? What is the extent of his skilful means?

The Buddha said to Mujinni Bosatsu: O good man, if there are beings in any country who are to be saved by his assuming a Buddha-form, Kwanzeon Bosatsu will manifest himself in the form of a Buddha and preach them the Dharma.

If beings are to be saved by his assuming a Pratyeka-buddha-form, the Bosatsu will manifest himself in the form of a Pratyekabuddha and preach them the Dharma.

If beings are to be saved by his assuming a Sravaka-form, the Bosatsu will manifest himself in the form of a Sravaka and preach them the Dharma.

If beings are to be saved by his assuming a Brahma-form, the Bosatsu will manifest himself in the form of a Brahma and preach them the Dharma.

If beings are to be saved by his assuming a Sakrendra-form, the Bosatsu will manifest himself in the form of a Sakrendra and preach them the Dharma.

If beings are to be saved by his assuming an Isvara-form, the Bosatsu will manifest himself in the form of an Isvara and preach them the Dharma.

If beings are to be saved by his assuming a Mahesvara-form, he will manifest himself in the form of a Mahesvara and preach them the Dharma.

If beings are to be saved by his assuming a Chakra-vartin-form, the Bosatsu will manifest himself in the form of a Chakravartin and preach them the Dharma.

If beings are to be saved by his assuming a Vaisravana-form, the Bosatsu will manifest himself in the form of a Vaisravana and preach them the Dharma.

If beings are to be saved by his assuming the form of a provincial chief, the Bosatsu will manifest himself in the form of a provincial chief and preach them the Dharma.

If beings are to be saved by his assuming a householder's form, the Bosatsu will manifest himself in the form of a householder and preach them the Dharma.

If beings are to be saved by his assuming a lay-disciple's

form, the Bosatsu will manifest himself in the form of a lay-disciple and preach them the Dharma.

If beings are to be saved by his assuming a state-officer's form, the Bosatsu will manifest himself in the form of a state-officer and preach them the Dharma.

If beings are to be saved by his assuming a Brahman-form, the Bosatsu will manifest himself to them in the form of a Brahman and preach them the Dharma.

If beings are to be saved by his assuming a Bhikshu-form, or a Bhikshuni-, or an Upasaka-, or an Upasika-form, the Bosatsu will manifest himself in the form of a Bhikshu, or a Bhikshuni, or an Upasaka, or an Upasika, and preach them the Dharma.

If beings are to be saved by his assuming a female form of the family of a householder, or a lay-disciple, or a state-officer, or a Brahman, the Bosatsu will manifest himself in the form of such a female and preach them the Dharma.

If beings are to be saved by his assuming a youth- or a maiden-form, the Bosatsu will manifest himself in the form of a youth or a maiden and preach them the Dharma.

If beings are to be saved by his assuming a Deva-, Naga-, Yaksha-, Gandharva-, Asura-, Garuda-, Kinnara-, Maho-raga-, Manushya-, or Amanushya-form, the Bosatsu will manifest himself in any of these forms and preach them the Dharma.

If beings are to be saved by his assuming a Vajrapani-form, the Bosatsu will manifest himself in the form of Vajrapani and preach them the Dharma.

O Mujinni, this Kwanzeon Bosatsu performs such meritorious deeds by assuming varieties of forms, and by visiting different lands saves and releases beings. Therefore, you will make offerings with singleness of thought to Kwan-zeon Bosatsu. In the midst of fears, perils, and disasters, it is he who gives us fearlessness,[1] and for this reason he is called in this Saha world the one who gives fearlessness.

Mujinni Bosatsu said to the Buddha: I wish now to make

[1] "Safety", or better "faith".

an offering to Kwanzeon Bosatsu. So saying, he took off his necklace strung with all kinds of precious gems worth hundreds of thousands of gold pieces, and presented it to Kwanzeon Bosatsu with this word : Venerable Sir, accept this necklace of precious gems as a Dharma offering.

Kwanzeon Bosatsu refused to accept it, whereupon Mujinni said to him : Venerable Sir, Pray accept this out of compassion for us all.

Then the Buddha said to Kwanzeon Bosatsu : Out of compassion for Mujinni Bosatsu and all the four classes of beings, and also for the Devas, Nagas, Yakshas, Gandharvas, Asuras, Garudas, Kinnaras, Mahoragas, Manushyas, Amanushyas and others, accept, O Kwanzeon Bosatsu, this necklace of his.

Then because of his compassion for all the four classes of beings and for Devas, Nagas, Manushyas, Amanushyas and others, Kwanzeon Bosatsu accepted the necklace, and dividing it into two parts he presented the one to Shakamunibutsu (Sakyamuni Buddha) and the other to the shrine of Tahobutsu (Prabhutaratna Buddha).

O Mujinni, Kwanzeon Bosatsu who is the possessor of such a miraculous spiritual power, visits in this wise this Saha world.

At that time Mujinni Bosatsu asked in verse, saying :

O World-honoured One who is in possession of exquisite features, I now again ask him : For what reason is the son of the Buddha called Kwanzeon?

The Honoured One in possession of exquisite features answered Mujinni in verse : Just listen to the life of Kwanzeon ! He is always ready to respond to calls from all quarters. His universal vows are as deep as the ocean. For ages beyond conception, he has served myriads of Buddhas and made great vows of purity.

I will briefly tell you about them. When people hear his name and see his body and think of him in their minds not vainly, they will see every form of ill effaced in all the worlds.

If an enemy wishing to harm a man pushes him down

to a pit of great fire, let his thought dwell on the power of Kwannon and the fiery pit will be transformed into a pond.

Or if drifting in the vast ocean a man is about to be swallowed up by the Nagas, fishes, or evil beings, let his thought dwell on the power of Kwannon, and the waves will not drown him.

Or if from the top of Mount Sumeru a man is hurled down by an enemy, let his thought dwell on the power of Kwannon, and he will stay in the air like the sun.

Or if pursued by wicked persons a man falls on the Vajra mountain, let his thought dwell on the power of Kwannon, and not a hair on him will be injured.

Or if surrounded by an army of enemies a man is threatened by them, each of whom with a sword in hand is about to injure him, let his thought dwell on the power of Kwannon, and the enemies will cherish a compassionate heart.

Or if persecuted by a tyrant a man is about to end his life at the place of execution, let his thought dwell on the power of Kwannon, and the executioner's sword will at once be broken to pieces.

Or if a man should find himself imprisoned and enchained with his hands and feet manacled and fettered, let his thought dwell on the power of Kwannon, and he will be released from the shackles.

If harm is going to be done to a man by means of magic or poisonous herbs, let his thought dwell on the power of Kwannon, and the curse will revert to the people from whom it started.

Or if a man should encounter a party of Rakshasas, or Nagas exhaling poison, or evil spirits, let his thought dwell on the power of Kwannon, and no harm will ever be done to him.

If a man is surrounded by wild beasts whose sharp teeth and claws are to be dreaded, let his thought dwell on the power of Kwannon, and they will quickly run away in all directions.

If a man is attacked by venomous snakes and scorpions

breathing poisonous gas ready to scorch him, let his thought dwell on the power of Kwannon, and they will all turn away from him shrieking.

When thunder-clouds burst with flashes of lightning, causing a storm of hailstones or pouring rain in torrents, let your thought dwell on the power of Kwannon and the storm will in no time clear away.

If a calamity falls on beings and they are tortured with interminable pain, [let them resort to] Kwannon who, being endowed with the mysterious power of wisdom, will save them from all troubles in the world.

Kwannon is the possessor of miraculous powers, widely disciplined in knowledge and skilful means, and in all the lands of the ten quarters there is not a place where he does not manifest himself.

The various evil paths of existence such as hells, evil spirits, beastly creatures, etc., and the pains arising from birth, old age, disease, and death—they will all by degrees be annihilated.

[Kwannon is] the one who views the world in truth, free from defilement, with knowledge extending far, and full of love and compassion; he is to be always prayed to and always adored.

He is a pure, spotless light and, like the sun, dispels all darkness with wisdom, and also subverts the disastrous effects of wind and fire; his all-illuminating light fills the world.

His body of love he keeps under control like thunder that shakes the world; his thought of compassion resembles a great mass of cloud from which a rain of the Dharma comes down like nectar, destroying the flames of evil passions.

If a man is held at court with a case against him, or if he is intimidated at a military camp, let his thought dwell on the power of Kwannon, and all his enemies will beat retreat.

[His is] a most exquisite voice, a voice that surveys the world, the voice of Brahma, the voice of the ocean—one that excels all the voices of the world. For this reason let our thought always dwell on him.

Let us never cherish thoughts of doubt about Kwanzeon

who is thoroughly pure and holy and is really a refuge and
protector in trouble, grief, death, and disaster.

He is in possession of all merits, regards all things with
an eye of compassion, and like the ocean holds in himself an
inestimable mass of virtues. For this reason he is to be
adored.

At that time Jiji Bosatsu[1] rose from his seat, and standing
before the Buddha said: World-honoured One, they are
truly furnished with no small amount of merit who listen
to his Chapter on Kwanzeon Bosatsu, in which his life of
perfect activities is described—the life of one who, endowed
with miraculous powers, manifests himself in all directions.

When the Buddha finished preaching this Chapter on
the All-sided One all the people in the assembly, amounting
to 84,000 in number, cherished the desire for the supreme
enlightenment with which there is nothing to compare.

III

THE KONGOKYO OR DIAMOND SUTRA[2]

1. Thus I have heard.

At one time the Buddha stayed at Anathapindaka's
Garden in the grove of Jeta in the kingdom of Sravasti; he
was together with 1,250 great Bhikshus. When the meal
time came the World-honoured One put on his cloak and,
holding his bowl, entered the great city of Sravasti, where he
begged for food. Having finished his begging from door to
door, he came back to his own place, and took his meal.

---

[1] Dharanindhara in Sanskrit, "the supporter of the earth".

[2] *Kongokyo* in Japanese. The full title in Sanskrit is *Vajracchedika-prajna-paramita-sutra*. It belongs to the Prajna class of Mahayana literature. Those
who are not accustomed to this kind of reasoning may wonder what is the
ultimate signification of all these negations. The Prajna dialectic means to lead
us to a higher affirmation by contradicting a simple direct statement. It
differs from the Hegelian in its directness and intuitiveness.

The present English translation is from Kumarajiva's Chinese version
made between 402-412 C.E.

When this was done, he put away his cloak and bowl, washed his feet, spread his seat, and sat down.

2. Then the Venerable Subhuti, who was among the assembly, rose from his seat, bared his right shoulder, set his right knee on the ground, and, respectfully folding his hands, addressed the Buddha thus:

"It is wonderful, World-honoured One, that the Tathagata thinks so much of all the Bodhisattvas and instructs them so well. World-honoured One, in case good men and good women ever raise the desire for the Supreme Enlightenment, how would they abide in it? how would they keep their thoughts under control?"

The Buddha said: "Well said, indeed, O Subhuti! As you say, the Tathagata thinks very much of all the Bodhisattvas, and so instructs them well. But now listen attentively and I will tell you. In case good men and good women raise the desire for the Supreme Enlightenment, they should thus abide in it, they should thus keep their thoughts under control."

"So be it, World-honoured One, I wish to listen to you."

3. The Buddha said to Subhuti: "All the Bodhisattva-Mahasattvas should thus keep their thoughts under control. All kinds of beings such as the egg-born, the womb-born, the moisture-born, the miraculously-born, those with form, those without form, those with consciousness, those without consciousness, those with no-consciousness, and those without no-consciousness—they are all led by me to enter Nirvana that leaves nothing behind and to attain final emancipation. Though thus beings immeasurable, innumerable, and unlimited are emancipated, there are in reality no beings that are ever emancipated. Why, Subhuti? If a Bodhisattva retains the thought of an ego, a person, a being, or a soul, he is no more a Bodhisattva.

4. "Again, Subhuti, when a Bodhisattva practises charity he should not be cherishing any idea, that is to say, he is not to cherish the idea of a form when practising charity, nor is he to cherish the idea of a sound, an odour,

a touch, or a quality.[1] Subhuti, a Bodhisattva should thus practise charity without cherishing any idea of form. Why? When a Bodhisattva practises charity without cherishing any idea of form, his merit will be beyond conception. Subhuti, what do you think? Can you have the conception of space extending eastward?"

"No, World-honoured One, I cannot."

"Subhuti, can you have the conception of space extending towards the south, or west, or north, or above, or below?"

"No, World-honoured One, I cannot."

"Subhuti, so it is with the merit of a Bodhisattva who practises charity without cherishing any idea of form; it is beyond conception. Subhuti, a Bodhisattva should cherish only that which is taught to him.

5.   "Subhuti, what do you think? Is the Tathagata to be recognized after a body-form?"

"No, World-honoured One, he is not to be recognized after a body-form. Why? According to the Tathagata, a body-form is not a body-form."

The Buddha said to Subhuti, "All that has a form is an illusive existence. When it is perceived that all form is no-form, the Tathagata is recognized."

6.   Subhuti said to the Buddha: "World-honoured One, if beings hear such words and statements, would they have a true faith in them?"

The Buddha said to Subhuti: "Do not talk that way. In the last five hundred years after the passing of the Tathagata, there may be beings who, having practised rules of morality and, being thus possessed of merit, happen to hear of these statements and rouse a true faith in them. Such beings, you must know, are those who have planted their root of merit not only under one, two, three, four, or five Buddhas, but already under thousands of myriads of asamkhyeyas of Buddhas have they planted their root of merit of all kinds. Those who hearing these statements rouse even one thought

---

[1] *Dharma*, that is, the object of *manovijnana*, thought, as form (*rupa*) is the object of the visual sense, sound that of the auditory sense, odour that of the olfactory sense, and so forth.

of pure faith, Subhuti, are all known to the Tathagata, and recognized by him as having acquired such an immeasurable amount of merit. Why? Because all these beings are free from the idea of an ego, a person, a being, or a soul; they are free from the idea of a dharma as well as from that of a no-dharma. Why? Because if they cherish in their minds the idea of a form, they are attached to an ego, a person, a being, or a soul. If they cherish the idea of a dharma, they are attached to an ego, a person, a being, or a soul. Why? If they cherish the idea of a no-dharma, they are attached to an ego, a person, a being, or a soul. Therefore, do not cherish the idea of a dharma, nor that of a no-dharma. For this reason, the Tathagata always preaches thus: 'O you Bhikshus, know that my teaching is to be likened unto a raft. Even a dharma is cast aside, much more a no-dharma.'

7. "Subhuti, what do you think? Has the Tathagata attained the supreme enlightenment? Has he something about which he would preach?"

Subhuti said: "World-honoured One, as I understand the teaching of the Buddha, there is no fixed doctrine about which the Tathagata would preach. Why? Because the doctrine he preaches is not to be adhered to, nor is it to be preached about; it is neither a dharma nor a no-dharma. How is it so? Because all wise men belong to the category known as non-doing (*asamskara*), and yet they are distinct from one another.

8. "Subhuti, what do you think? If a man should fill the three thousand chiliocosms with the seven precious treasures and give them all away for charity, would not the merit he thus obtains be great?"

Subhuti said: "Very great, indeed, World-honoured One."

"Why? Because their merit is characterized with the quality of not being a merit. Therefore, the Tathagata speaks of the merit as being great. If again there is a man who, holding even the four lines in this sutra, preaches about it to others, his merit will be superior to the one just mentioned. Because, Subhuti, all the Buddhas and their supreme enlightenment issue from this sutra. Subhuti, what is known as the teaching of the Buddha is not the teaching of the Buddha.

9. "Subhuti, what do you think? Does a Srotapanna think in this wise: 'I have obtained the fruit of Srotapatti'?"

Subhuti said: "No, World-honoured One, he does not. Why? Because while Srotapanna means 'entering the stream' there is no entering here. He is called a Srotapanna who does not enter [a world of] form, sound, odour, taste, touch, and quality.

"Subhuti, what do you think? Does a Sakridagamin think in this wise, 'I have obtained the fruit of a Sakrida-gamin'?"

Subhuti said: "No, World-honoured One, he does not. Why? Because while Sakridagamin means 'going-and-coming for once', there is really no going-and-coming here, and he is then called a Sakridagamin."

"Subhuti, what do you think? Does an Anagamin think in this wise: 'I have obtained the fruit of an Anagamin'?"

Subhuti said: "No, World-honoured One, he does not. Why? Because while Anagamin means 'not-coming' there is really no not-coming and therefore he is called an Anagamin."

"Subhuti, what do you think? Does an Arhat think in this wise: 'I have obtained Arhatship'?"

Subhuti said: "No, World-honoured One, he does not. Why? Because there is no dharma to be called Arhat. If, World-honoured One, an Arhat thinks in this wise: 'I have obtained Arhatship,' this means that he is attached to an ego, a person, a being, or a soul. Although the Buddha says that I am the foremost of those who have attained Arana-samadhi,[1] that I am the foremost of those Arhats who are liberated from evil desires, World-honoured One, I cherish no such thought that I have attained Arhatship. World-honoured One, [if I did,] you would not tell me: 'O Subhuti,

---

[1] That is, Samadhi of non-resistance. *Arana* also means a forest where the Yogin retires to practise his meditation.

you are one who enjoys the life of non-resistance.' Just be-cause Subhuti is not at all attached to this life, he is said to be the one who enjoys the life of non-resistance."

10. The Buddha said to Subhuti: "What do you think? When the Tathagata was anciently with Dipankara Buddha did he have an attainment in the Dharma?"

"No, World-honoured One, he did not. The Tathagata while with Dipankara Buddha had no attainment whatever in the Dharma."

"Subhuti, what do you think? Does a Bodhisattva set any Buddha-land in array?"

"No, World-honoured One, he does not."

"Why? Because to set a Buddha-land in array is not to set it in array, and therefore it is known as setting it in array. Therefore, Subhuti, all the Bodhisattva-Mahasattvas should thus rouse a pure thought. They should not cherish any thought dwelling on form; they should not cherish any thought dwelling on sound, odour, taste, touch, and quality; they should cherish thoughts dwelling on nothing whatever. Subhuti, it is like unto a human body equal in size to Mount Sumeru; what do you think? Is not this body large?"

Subhuti said: "Very large indeed, World-honoured One. Why? Because the Buddha teaches that that which is no-body is known as a large body."

11. "Subhuti, regarding the sands of the Ganga, suppose there are as many Ganga rivers as those sands, what do you think? Are not the sands of all those Ganga rivers many?"

Subhuti said: "Very many, indeed, World-honoured One."

"Considering such Gangas alone, they must be said to be numberless; how much more the sands of all those Ganga rivers! Subhuti, I will truly ask you now. If there is a good man or a good woman who, filling all the worlds in the three thousand chiliocosms—all the worlds as many as the sands of these Ganga rivers—with the seven precious treasures, uses them all for charity, would not this merit be very large?"

Subhuti said: "Very large indeed, World-honoured One."

Buddha said to Subhuti: "If a good man or a good woman holding even four lines from this sutra preach it to others, this merit is much larger than the preceding one.

12. "Again, Subhuti, wherever this sutra or even four lines of it are preached, this place will be respected by all beings including Devas, Asuras, etc., as if it were the Buddha's own shrine or chaitya; how much more a person who can hold and recite this sutra! Subhuti, you should know that such a person achieves the highest, foremost, and most wonderful deed. Wherever this sutra is kept, the place is to be regarded as if the Buddha or a venerable disciple of his were present."

13. At that time, Subhuti said to the Buddha: "World-honoured One, what will this sutra be called? How should we hold it?"

The Buddha said to Subhuti: "This sutra will be called the *Vajra-prajna-paramita*, and by this title you will hold it. The reason is, Subhuti, that, according to the teaching of the Buddha, Prajnaparamita is not Prajnaparamita and therefore it is called Prajnaparamita. Subhuti, what do you think? Is there anything about which the Tathagata preaches?"

Subhuti said to the Buddha: "World-honoured One, there is nothing about which the Tathagata preaches."

"Subhuti, what do you think? Are there many particles of dust in the three thousand chiliocosms?"

Subhuti said: "Indeed, there are many, World-honoured One."

"Subhuti, the Tathagata teaches that all these many particles of dust are no-particles of dust and therefore that they are called particles of dust; he teaches that the world is no-world and therefore that the world is called the world.

"Subhuti, what do you think? Is the Tathagata to be recognized by the thirty-two marks [of a great man]?"

"No, World-honoured One, he is not."

"The Tathagata is not to be recognized by the thirty-two marks, because what are said to be the thirty-two marks are told by the Tathagata to be no-marks and therefore to be the thirty-two marks. Subhuti, if there be a good man or a good woman who gives away his or her lives as many as the sands of the Ganga, his or her merit thus gained does not exceed that of one who, holding even one gatha of four lines from this sutra, preaches them for others."

14. At that time Subhuti, listening to this sutra, had a deep understanding of its signification, and, filled with tears of gratitude, said this to the Buddha: "Wonderful, indeed, World-honoured One, that the Buddha teaches us this sutra full of deep sense. Such a sutra has never been heard by me even with an eye of wisdom acquired in my past lives. World-honoured One, if there be a man who listening to this sutra acquires a pure believing heart he will then have a true idea of things. This one is to be known as having achieved a most wonderful virtue. World-honoured One, what is known as a true idea is no-idea, and for this reason it is called a true idea.

"World-honoured One, it is not difficult for me to believe, to understand, and to hold this sutra to which I have now listened; but in the ages to come, in the next five hundred years, if there are beings who listening to this sutra are able to believe, to understand, and to hold it, they will indeed be most wonderful beings. Why? Because they will have no idea of an ego, of a person, of a being, or of a soul. For what reason? The idea of an ego is no-idea [of ego], the idea of a person, a being, or a soul is no-idea [of a person, a being, or a soul]. For what reason? They are Buddhas who are free from all kinds of ideas."

The Buddha said to Subhuti, "It is just as you say. If there be a man who, listening to this sutra, is neither frightened nor alarmed nor disturbed, you should know him as a wonderful person. Why? Subhuti, it is taught by the Tathagata that the first Paramita is no-first-Paramita and therefore it is called the first Paramita. Subhuti, the Paramita of humility (patience) is said by the Tathagata to be no-Paramita of humility, and therefore it is the Paramita of humility. Why? Subhuti, anciently, when my body was cut to pieces by the King of Kalinga, I had neither the idea of an ego, nor the idea of a person, nor the idea of a being, nor the idea of a soul. Why? When at that time my body was dismembered, limb after limb, joint after joint, if I had the idea either of an ego, or of a person, or of a being, or a soul, the feeling of anger and ill-will would have been awakened in me. Subhuti, I remember, in my past five hundred births, I was a rishi called Kshanti, and during those times I had neither the idea of an ego, nor that of a person, nor that of a being, nor that of a soul.

"Therefore, Subhuti, you should, detaching yourself from all ideas, rouse the desire for the supreme enlightenment. You should cherish thoughts without dwelling on form, you should cherish thoughts without dwelling on sound, odour, taste, touch, or quality. Whatever thoughts you may have, they are not to dwell on anything. If a thought dwells on anything, this is said to be no-dwelling. Therefore, the Buddha teaches that a Bodhisattva is not to practise charity by dwelling on form. Subhuti, the reason he practises charity is to benefit all beings.

"The Tathagata teaches that all ideas are no-ideas, and again that all beings are no-beings. Subhuti, the Tathagata is the one who speaks what is true, the one who speaks what is real, the one whose words are as they are, the one who does not speak falsehood, the one who does not speak equivocally.

"Subhuti, in the Dharma attained by the Tathagata there is neither truth nor falsehood. Subhuti, if a Bodhisattva should practise charity, cherishing a thought which dwells on the Dharma, he is like unto a person who enters the darkness, he sees nothing. If he should practise charity without cherishing a thought that dwells on the Dharma, he is like unto a person with eyes, he sees all kinds of forms illumined by the sunlight.

"Subhuti, if there are good men and good women in the time to come who hold and recite this sutra, they will be seen and recognized by the Tathagata with his Buddha-knowledge, and they will all mature immeasurable and innumerable merit.

15. "Subhuti, if there is a good man or a good woman who would in the first part of the day sacrifice as many bodies of his or hers as the sands of the Ganga, and again in the middle part of the day sacrifice as many bodies of his or hers as the sands of the Ganga, and again in the latter part of the day sacrifice as many bodies of his or hers as the sands of the Ganga, and keep up these sacrifices through hundred-thousands of myriads of kotis of kalpas; and if there were another who listening to this sutra would accept it with a believing heart, the merit the latter would acquire would far exceed that of the former. How much more the merit of one who would copy, hold, learn, and recite and expound it for others!

"Subhuti, to sum up, there is in this sutra a mass of merit, immeasurable, innumerable, and incomprehensible. The Tathagata has preached this for those who were awakened in the Mahayana (great vehicle), he has preached it for those who were awakened in the Sreshthayana (highest vehicle). If there were beings who would hold and learn and expound it for others, they would all be known to the Tathagata and recognized by him, and acquire merit which is unmeasured, immeasurable, innumerable, and incomprehensible. Such beings are known to be carrying the supreme enlightenment attained by the Tathagata. Why? Subhuti, those who desire inferior doctrines are attached to the idea of an ego, a person, a being, and a soul. They are unable to hear, hold, learn, recite, and for others expound this sutra. Subhuti, wherever this sutra is preserved, there all beings, including Devas and Asuras, will come and worship it. This place will have to be known as a chaitya, the object of worship and obeisance, where the devotees gather around, scatter flowers, and burn incense.

16. "Again, Subhuti, there are some good men and good women who will be despised for their holding and reciting this sutra. This is due to their previous evil karma

for the reason of which they were to fall into the evil paths
of existence; but because of their being despised in the
present life, whatever evil karma they produced in their
previous lives will be thereby destroyed, and they will be
able to attain the supreme enlightenment.

"Subhuti, as I remember, in my past lives innumerable
asamkhyeya kalpas ago I was with Dipankara Buddha, and
at that time I saw Buddhas as many as eighty-four hundred-
thousands of myriads of nayutas and made offerings to them
and respectfully served them all, and not one of them was
passed by me.

"If again in the last [five hundred] years, there have
been people who hold and recite and learn this sutra, the
merit they thus attain [would be beyond calculation], for
when this is compared with the merit I have attained by
serving all the Buddhas, the latter will not exceed one
hundredth part of the former, no, not one hundred thousand
ten millionth part. No, it is indeed beyond calculation,
beyond analogy.

"Subhuti, if there have been good men and good women
in the last five hundred years who hold, recite, and learn
this sutra, the merit they attain thereby I cannot begin to
enumerate in detail. If I did, those who listen to it would lose
their minds, cherish grave doubts, and not believe at all
how beyond comprehension is the significance of this sutra
and how also beyond comprehension the rewards are."[1]

18.   The Buddha said to Subhuti: "Of all beings in
those innumerable lands, the Tathagata knows well all their
mental traits. Why? Because the Tathagata teaches that all
those mental traits are no-traits and therefore they are

---

[1] This finishes the first part of the *Diamond Sutra* as it is usually divided
here and passes on to the second part. The text goes on in a similar strain
through its remaining section. Indeed, there are some scholars who think that
the second part is really a repetition of the first, or that they are merely different
copies of one and the same original text, and that whatever variations there
are in these two copies are the result of the glosses mixed into the text itself.
While I cannot wholly subscribe to this view, the fact is that passages containing similar thoughts recur throughout the whole Prajnaparamita literature. In view of this I quote in the following only such ideas as have not
fully been expressed in the first part.

known to be mental traits. Subhuti, thoughts[1] of the past are beyond grasp, thoughts of the present are beyond grasp, and thoughts of the future are beyond grasp."

23. "Again, Subhuti, this Dharma is even and has neither elevation nor depression; and it is called supreme enlightenment. Because a man practises everything that is good, without cherishing the thought of an ego, a person, a being, and a soul, he attains the supreme enlightenment. Subhuti, what is called good is no-good, and therefore it is known as good."

26. "Subhuti, what do you think? Can a man see the Tathagata by the thirty-two marks [of a great man]?"

Subhuti said: "So it is, so it is. The Tathagata is seen by his thirty-two marks."

The Buddha said to Subhuti, "If the Tathagata is to be seen by his thirty-two marks, can the Cakravartin be a Tathagata?"

Subhuti said to the Buddha: "World-honoured One, as I understand the teaching of the Buddha, the Tathagata is not to be seen by the thirty-two marks."

Then the World-honoured One uttered this gatha:
> "If any one by form sees me,
> By voice seeks me,
> This one walks the false path,
> And cannot see the Tathagata."

29. "Subhuti, if a man should declare that the Tathagata is the one who comes, or goes, or sits, or lies, he does not understand the meaning of my teaching. Why? The Tathagata does not come from anywhere, and does not depart to anywhere; therefore he is called the Tathagata.

---

[1] *Citta* stands for both mind and thought. The idea expressed here is that there is no particularly determined entity in us which is psychologically designated as mind or thought. The moment we think we have taken hold of a thought, it is no more with us. So with the idea of a soul, or an ego, or a being, or a person, there is no such particular entity objectively to be so distinguished, and which remains as such eternally separated from the subject who so thinks. This ungraspability of a mind or thought, which is tantamount to saying that there is no soul-substance as a solitary unrelated "thing" in the recesses of consciousness, is one of the basic doctrines of Buddhism, Mahayana and Hinayana.

32. "How does a man expound it for others? When
one is not attached to form, it is of Suchness remaining
unmoved. Why?
"All composite things (*samskrita*)
  Are like a dream, a phantasm, a bubble, and a shadow,
  Are like a dew-drop and a flash of lightning;
  They are thus to be regarded."

IV

THE LANKAVATARA SUTRA

This sutra is said to have been given by Bodhidharma
to his chief disciple Hui-k'e as containing the essential
teaching of Zen. Since then it has been studied chiefly by
Zen philosophers. But being full of difficult technical terms
in combination with a rugged style of writing, the text has
not been so popular for study as other Mahayana sutras, or
instance, the *Pundarika*, the *Vimalakirti*, or the *Vajracchedika*.

The chief interlocutor is a Bodhisattva called Mahamati,
and varied subjects of philosophical speculation are discussed
against a background of deep religious concern. The topic
most interesting for the reader of this book is that of *svapra-
tyatmagati*, i.e. self-realization of the highest truth.

Some of the terms may be explained here: "Birth and
death" (*samsara* in Sanskrit) always stands contrasted to
"Nirvana". Nirvana is the highest truth and the norm of
existence while birth and death is a world of particulars
governed by karma and causation. As long as we are subject
to karma we go from one birth to another, and suffer all the
ills necessarily attached to this kind of life, though it is a form
of immortality. What Buddhists want is not this.

"Mind only" (*cittamatra*) is an uncouth term. It means
absolute mind, to be distinguished from an empirical mind
which is the subject of psychological study. When it begins
with a capital letter, it is the ultimate reality on which

the entire world of individual objects depends for its value. To realize this truth is the aim of the Buddhist life.

By "what is seen of the Mind-only" is meant this visible world including that which is generally known as mind. Our ordinary experience takes this world for something that has its "self-nature", i.e. existing by itself. But a higher intuition tells us that this is not so, that it is an illusion, and that what really exists is Mind, which being absolute knows no second. All that we see and hear and think of as objects of the vijnanas are what rise and disappear in and of the Mind-only.

This absolute Mind is also called in the *Lankavatara* the Dharma of Solitude (*vivikta-dharma*), because it stands by itself. It also signifies the Dharma's being absolutely quiescent.

There is no "discrimination" in this Dharma of Solitude, which means that discrimination belongs to this side of existence where multiplicities obtain and causation rules. Indeed, without this discrimination no world is possible.

Discrimination is born of "habit-energy" or "memory", which lies latently preserved in the "alayavijnana" or all-conserving consciousness. This consciousness alone has no power to act by itself. It is altogether passive, and remains inactive until a particularizing agency touches it. The appearance of this agency is a great mystery which is not to be solved by the intellect; it is something to be accepted simply as such. It is awakened "all of a sudden", according to Asvaghosha.

To understand what this suddenness means is the function of "noble wisdom" (*aryajnana*). But as a matter of experience, the sudden awakening of discrimination has no meaning behind it. The fact is simply that it is awakened, and no more; it is not an expression pointing to something else.

When the Alayavijnana or the all-conserving conscious-ness is considered a store-house, or better, a creative matrix from which all the Tathagatas issue, it is called "Tathagata-garbha". The Garbha is the womb.

Ordinarily, all our cognitive apparatus is made to

work outwardly in a world of relativity, and for this reason we become deeply involved in it so that we fail to realize the freedom we all intrinsically possess, and as a result we are annoyed on all sides. To turn away from all this, what may psychologically be called a "revulsion" or "revolution" must take place in our inmost consciousness. This is not however a mere empirical psychological fact to be explained in terms of consciousness. It takes place in the deepest recesses of our being. The original Sanskrit is *paravrittasraya*.

The following extracts are from my English translation (1932) of the original Sanskrit text edited by Bunyu Nanjo, 1923.

XVIII

Further, Mahamati, those who, afraid of sufferings arising from the discrimination of birth and death, seek for Nirvana, do not know that birth and death and Nirvana are not to be separated the one from the other; and, seeing that all things subject to discrimination have no reality, imagine that Nirvana consists in the further annihilation of the senses and their fields. They are not aware, Mahamati, of the fact that Nirvana is the Alayavijnana where a revulsion takes place by self-realization. Therefore, Mahamati, those who are stupid talk of the trinity of vehicles and not of the state of Mind-only where there are no shadows. Therefore, Mahamati, those who do not understand the teachings of the Tathagatas of the past, present, and future, concerning the external world, which is of Mind itself, cling to the notion that there is a world outside what is seen of the Mind and, Mahamati, go on rolling themselves along the wheel of birth and death.

XIX

Further, Mahamati, according to the teaching of the
Tathagatas of the past, present, and future, all things are
unborn. Why? Because they have no reality, being manifestations of Mind itself; and, Mahamati, as they are not
born of being and non-being, they are unborn. Mahamati,
all things are like the horns of the hare, horse, donkey, or
camel, but the ignorant and simple-minded, who are given
up to their false and erroneous imaginations, discriminate
things where they are not; therefore, all things are unborn.
That all things are in their self-nature unborn, Mahamati,
belongs to the realm of self-realization attained by noble
wisdom, and does not belong essentially to the realm of
dualistic discrimination cherished by the ignorant and
simple-minded.

The self-nature and the characteristic marks of body,
property, and abode evolve when the Alayavijnana is con-
ceived of by the ignorant as grasping and grasped; and then
they fall into a dualistic view of existence where they
recognize its rise, abiding, and disappearance, cherishing
the idea that all things are born and subject to discrimination as to being and non-being. Therefore, Mahamati, you
should discipline yourself therein [i.e. in self-realization].

XXIV

Further again, Mahamati, let the Bodhisattva-Mahasattva have a thorough understanding as to the nature of
the twofold egolessness. Mahamati, what is this twofold
egolessness? [It is the egolessness of persons and the egolessness of things. What is meant by egolessness of persons? It
means that] in the collection of the Skandhas, Dhatus, and
Ayatanas there is no ego-substance, nor anything belonging
to it; the Vijnana is originated by ignorance, deed, and
desire, and keeps up its function by grasping objects by

means of the sense-organs, such as the eye, etc., and by clinging to them as real; while a world of objects and bodies is manifested owing to the discrimination that takes place in the world which is of Mind itself, that is, in the Alaya-vijnana.

By reason of the habit-energy stored up by false imagination since beginningless time, this world (*vishaya*) is subject to change and destruction from moment to moment; it is like a river, a seed, a lamp, wind, a cloud; [while the Vijnana itself is] like a monkey who is always restless, like a fly who is ever in search of unclean things and defiled places, like a fire which is never satisfied. Again, it is like a water-drawing wheel or a machine, it [i.e. the Vijnana] goes on rolling the wheel of transmigration, carrying varieties of bodies and forms, resuscitating the dead like the demon Vetala, causing the wooden figures to move about as a magician moves them. Mahamati, a thorough understanding concerning these phenomena is called comprehending the egolessness of persons.

Now, Mahamati, what is meant by the egolessness of things? It is to realize that the Skandhas, Dhatus, and Ayatanas are characterized with the nature of false discrimination. Mahamati, since the Skandhas, Dhatus, and Ayatanas are destitute of an ego-substance, being no more than an aggregation of the Skandhas, and subject to the conditions of mutual origination which are causally bound up with the string of desire and deed; and since thus there is no creating agent in them, Mahamati, the Skandhas are even destitute of the marks of individuality and generality; and the ignorant, owing to their erroneous discrimination, imagine here the multiplicity of phenomena; the wise, however, do not. Recognizing, Mahamati, that all things are devoid of the Citta, Manas, Manovijnana, the five Dharmas, and the [three] Svabhavas, the Bodhisattva-Mahasattva will well understand what is meant by the egolessness of things.

Again, Mahamati, when the Bodhisattva-Mahasattva has a good understanding as regards the egolessness of things, before long he will attain the first stage [of the Bodhisattvahood], when he gets a definite cognition of the imageless. When a definite acquisition is obtained regarding the aspect of the stages [of Bodhisattvahood], the Bodhisattva will experience joy, and, gradually and successively going up the scale, will reach the ninth stage where his insight is perfected, and [finally the tenth stage known as] Great Dharma-megha.

Establishing himself here, he will be seated in the great jewel palace known as "Great Lotus Throne" which is in the shape of a lotus and is adorned with various sorts of jewels and pearls; he will then acquire and complete a world of Maya-nature; surrounded by Bodhisattvas of the same character and anointed like the son of the Cakravarti by the hands of the Buddhas coming from all the Buddha-lands, he will go beyond the last stage of Bodhisattvahood, attain the noble truth of self-realization, and become a Tathagata endowed with the perfect freedom of the Dharma-kaya, because of his insight into the egolessness of things. This, Mahamati, is what is meant by the egolessness of all things, and in this you and other Bodhisattva-Mahasattvas should well exercise yourselves.

XXVIII

At that time, Mahamati the Bodhisattva-Mahasattva said this to the Blessed One: Now the Blessed One makes mention of the Tathagata-garbha in the sutras, and verily it is described by you as by nature bright and pure, as primarily unspotted, endowed with the thirty-two marks of excellence, hidden in the body of every being like a gem of great value, which is enwrapped in a dirty garment, enveloped in the garment of the Skandhas, Dhatus, and Ayatanas, and soiled with the dirt of greed, anger, folly, and false imagination, while it is described by the Blessed One to be eternal, permanent, auspicious, and unchangeable. Is not this Tathagata-garbha taught by the Blessed One the same as the ego-substance taught by the philosophers? The ego as taught in the systems of the philosophers is an eternal creator, unqualified, omnipresent, and imperishable.

The Blessed One replied : No, Mahamati, my Tathagata-garbha is not the same as the ego taught by the philosophers; for what the Tathagatas teach is the Tathagata-garbha in the sense, Mahamati, that it is emptiness, reality-limit, Nirvana, being unborn, unqualified, and devoid of will-effort; the reason why the Tathagatas, who are Arhats and Fully-Enlightened Ones, teach the doctrine pointing to the Tathagata-garbha is to make the ignorant cast aside their fear when they listen to the teaching of egolessness and to have them realize the state of non-discrimination and imagelessness.

I also wish, Mahamati, that the Bodhisattva-Mahasattvas of the present and future would not attach themselves to the idea of an ego [imagining it to be a soul]. Mahamati, it is like a potter who manufactures various vessels out of a mass of clay of one sort by his own manual skill and labour combined with a rod, water, and thread, Mahamati, that the Tathagatas preach the egolessness of things which removes all the traces of discrimination by various skilful means issuing from their transcendental wisdom; that is, sometimes by the doctrine of the Tathagata-garbha, some-times by that of egolessness, and like a potter, by means of various terms, expressions, and synonyms. For this reason, Mahamati, the philosophers' doctrine of an ego-substance is not the same as the teaching of the Tathagata-garbha.

Thus, Mahamati, the doctrine of the Tathagata-garbha is disclosed in order to awaken the philosophers from their clinging to the idea of the ego, so that those minds that have fallen into the views imagining the non-existent ego as real, and also into the notion that the triple emancipation is final, may rapidly be awakened to the state of supreme enlighten-ment. Accordingly, Mahamati, the Tathagatas who are Arhats and Fully-Enlightened Ones disclose the doctrine of the Tathagata-garbha, which is thus not to be known as identical with the philosopher's notion of an ego-substance.

Therefore, Mahamati, in order to abandon the misconception cherished by the philosophers, you must strive after the teaching of egolessness and the Tathagata-garbha.

XXXV

At that time, Mahamati the Bodhisattva-Mahasattva again said this to the Blessed One:

Pray tell me, Blessed One, about the attainment of self-realization by noble wisdom, which does not belong to the path and the usage of the philosophers;

Which is devoid of [all such predicates as] being and non-being, oneness and otherness, bothness and not-bothness, existence and non-existence, eternity and non-eternity;

Which has nothing to do with the false imagination, nor with individuality and generality; which manifests itself as the truth of highest reality;

Which, going up continuously by degrees the stages of purification, enters upon the stage of Tathagatahood;

Which, because of the original vows unattended by any striving, will perform its works in infinite worlds like a gem reflecting a variety of colours;

And which is manifested [when one perceives how] signs of individuation rise in all things as one realizes the course and realm of what is seen of Mind itself, and thereby I and other Bodhisattva-Mahasattvas are enabled to survey things from the point of view which is not hampered by marks of individuality and generality nor by anything of the false imagination, and may quickly attain supreme enlightenment and enable all beings to achieve the perfection of all their virtues.

Replied the Blessed One: Well done, well done, Mahamati! and again, well done, indeed, Mahamati! Because of your compassion for the world, for the benefit of many people, for the happiness of many people, for the welfare, benefit, happiness of many people, both of celestial beings and humankind, Mahamati, you present yourself before me and make this request. Therefore, Mahamati, listen well and truly, and reflect, for I will tell you.

Assuredly, said Mahamati the Bodhisattva-Mahasattva, and gave ear to the Blessed One.

The Blessed One said this to him: Mahamati, since the ignorant and the simple-minded, not knowing that the world is what is seen of Mind itself, cling to the multitudinousness of external objects, cling to the notions of being and non-being, oneness and otherness, bothness and not-bothness, existence and non-existence, eternity and non-eternity, as having the character of self-substance (*svabhava*), which idea rises from discrimination based on habit-energy, they are addicted to false imaginings.

Mahamati, it is like a mirage in which the springs are seen as if they were real. They are imagined so by the animals who, thirsty from the heat of the season, would run after them. Not knowing that the springs are their own mental illusions, the animals do not realize that there are no such springs. In the same way, Mahamati, the ignorant and simple-minded with their minds impressed by various erroneous speculations and discriminations since beginningless time; with their minds burning with the fire of greed, anger, and folly; delighted in a world of multitudinous forms; with their thoughts saturated with the ideas of birth, destruction, and subsistence; not understanding well what is meant by existent and non-existent, by inner and outer, these ignorant and simple-minded fall into the way of grasping at oneness and otherness, being and non-being [as realities].

Mahamati, it is like the city of the Gandharvas which the unwitted take for a real city, though it is not so in fact. This city appears in essence owing to their attachment to the memory of a city preserved in seed from beginningless time. This city is thus neither existent nor non-existent. In the same way, Mahamati, clinging to the memory (*vasana*) of erroneous speculations and doctrines since beginningless time, they hold fast to ideas such as oneness and otherness, being and non-being, and their thoughts are not at all clear about what is seen of Mind-only.

Mahamati, it is like a man, who, dreaming in his sleep of a country variously filled with women, men, elephants, horses, cars, pedestrians, villages, towns, hamlets, cows, buffalos, mansions, woods, mountains, rivers, and lakes, enters into its inner appartments and is awakened. While awakened thus, he recollects the city and its inner apartments. What do you think, Mahamati? Is this person to be regarded as wise, who is recollecting the various unrealities he has seen in his dream?

Said Mahamati: Indeed, he is not, Blessed One.

The Blessed One continued: In the same way the ignorant and simple-minded who are bitten by erroneous views and inclined towards the philosophers, do not recognize that things seen of the Mind itself are like a dream, and are held fast by the notions of oneness and otherness, of being and non-being.

Mahamati, it is like the painter's canvas on which there is neither depression nor elevation as imagined by the ignorant. In the same way, Mahamati, there may be in the future some people brought up in the habit-energy, mentality, and imagination based on the philosophers' erroneous views; clinging to the ideas of oneness and otherness, or bothness and not-bothness, they may bring themselves and others to ruin; they may declare those people nihilists who hold the doctrine of no-birth apart from the category of being and non-being. They [argue against] cause and effect, they are followers of the wicked views whereby they uproot meritorious causes of unstained purity. They are to be kept away by those whose desires are for things excellent. They are those whose thoughts are entangled in the error of self, other, and both, entangled in the error of imagining being and non-being, assertion and refutation; and hell will be their final resort.

Mahamati, it is like the dim-eyed ones who, seeing a hair-net, would exclaim to one another, saying: "It is wonderful! it is wonderful! Look, O honourable sirs!" And the said hair-net has never been brought into existence. It is in fact neither an entity nor a non-entity, because it is seen and not seen. In the same manner, Mahamati, those whose minds are addicted to discrimination of the erroneous views as cherished by the philosophers, and who are also given up to the realistic ideas of being and non-being, oneness and otherness, bothness and not-bothness, will contradict the good Dharma, ending in the destruction of themselves and others.

Mahamati, it is like a firebrand-wheel which is no real wheel but which is imagined to be of such character by the ignorant, but not by the wise. In the same manner, Maha-mati, those whose minds have fallen into the erroneous views of the philosophers will falsely imagine in the rise of all beings [the reality of] oneness and otherness, bothness and not-bothness.

Mahamati, it is like those water-bubbles in a rainfall which have the appearance of crystal gems, and the ignorant taking them for real crystal gems run after them. Mahamati, they are no more than water-bubbles, they are not gems, nor are they not-gems, because of their being so comprehended [by one party] and being not so comprehended [by another]. In the same manner, Mahamati, those whose minds are impressed by the habit-energy of the philosophical views and discriminations will regard things born as non-existent and those destroyed by causation as existent.

XXXVII

Further, Mahamati, there are four kinds of Dhyanas. What are the four? They are: (1) The Dhyana practised by the ignorant, (2) the Dhyana devoted to the examination of meaning, (3) the Dhyana with Suchness for its object, and (4) the Dhyana of the Tathagatas.

What is meant by the Dhyana practised by the ignorant? It is the one resorted to by the Yogins exercising themselves in the discipline of the Sravakas and Pratyekabuddhas, who perceiving that there is no ego-substance, that things are characterized with individuality and generality, that the body is a shadow and a skeleton which is transient, full of suffering, and is impure, persistently cling to these notions which are regarded as just so and not otherwise, and who starting from them successively advance until they reach the cessation where there are no thoughts. This is called the Dhyana practised by the ignorant.

Mahamati, what then is the Dhyana devoted to the examination of meaning? It is the one [practised by those who,] having gone beyond the egolessness of things, individuality and generality, the untenability of such ideas as self, other, and both, which are held by the philosophers, proceed to examine and follow up the meaning of the [various] aspects of the egolessness of things and the stages of Bodhisattvahood. This is the Dhyana devoted to the examination of meaning.

What, Mahamati, is the Dhyana with Tathata for its object? When [the Yogin recognizes that] the discrimination of the two forms of egolessness is mere imagination, and that where he establishes himself in the reality of suchness (*yathabhuta*) there is no rising of discrimination, I call it the Dhyana with Tathata for its object.

What, Mahamati, is the Dhyana of the Tathagata? When [the Yogin], entering upon the stage of Tathagatahood and abiding in the triple bliss which characterizes self-realization attained by noble wisdom, devotes himself for the sake of all beings to the [accomplishment of] incomprehensible works, I call it the Dhyana of the Tathagatas. Therefore, it is said:

There are the Dhyana for the examination of meaning, the Dhyana practised by the ignorant, the Dhyana with Tathata for its object, and the pure Dhyana of the Tathagata.

The Yogin, while in the exercise, sees the form of the sun or the moon, or something looking like a lotus, or the underworld, or various forms like sky, fire, etc.

All these appearances lead him to the way of the philosophers; they throw him down into the state of Sravakahood, into the realm of the Pratyekabuddhas.

When all these are tossed aside and there is a state of imagelessness, then a condition in conformity with Tathata presents itself; and the Buddhas will come together from all their countries and with their shining hands will stroke the head of this benefactor.

LXVIII

At the time, Mahamati the Bodhisattva-Mahasattva asked the Blessed One to explain concerning the deep-seated attachment to the existence of all things and the way of emancipation, saying: Pray tell me, Blessed One, pray tell me Tathagata, Arhat, Fully-Enlightened One, concerning the characteristics of our deep attachment to existence and of our detachment from it.

When I and other Bodhisattva-Mahasattvas understand well the distinction between attachment and detachment, we shall know what is the skilful means concerning them, and shall no more become attached to words according to which we grasp meaning.

When we understand well what is meant by attachment to the existence of all things and the detachment from them we shall destroy our discrimination of words and letters; and, by means of our wisdom (*buddhi*), enter into all the Buddha-lands and assemblies; be well stamped with the stamp of the powers, the self-control, the psychic faculties, and the Dharanis; and, well furnished with the wisdom (*buddhi*) in the ten inexhaustible vows, and shining with varieties of rays pertaining to the Transformation Body, behave ourselves with effortlessness like the moon, the sun, the jewel, and the elements; and hold such views at every stage as are free from all the signs of self-discrimination; and, seeing that all things are like a dream, like Maya, etc., [shall be able to] enter the stage and abode of Buddhahood, and deliver discourses on the Dharma in the world of all beings and in accordance with their needs, and free them from the dualistic notion of being and non-being in the contemplation of all things which are like a dream and Maya, and free them also from the false discrimination of birth and destruction; and, finally, [shall be able to] establish ourselves where there is a revulsion at the deepest recesses [of our consciousness], which is more than words [can express].

Said the Blessed One: Well said, well said, Mahamati! Listen well to me then, Mahamati, and reflect well within yourself; I will tell you.

Mahamati the Bodhisattva-Mahasattva said: Certainly, I will, Blessed One; and gave ear to the Blessed One.

The Blessed One said to him thus: Mahamati, immeasurable is our deep-seated attachment to the existence of all things the significance of which we try to understand with words. For instance, there are the deep-seated attachments to signs of individuality, to causation, to the notion of being and non-being, to the discrimination of birth and no-birth, to the discrimination of cessation and no-cessation, to the discrimination of vehicle and no-vehicle, of Samskrita and Asamskrita, of the characteristics of the stages and no-stages. There is the attachment to discrimination itself, and to that arising from enlightenment the attachment to the discrimination of being and non-being on which the philosophers are so dependent, and the attachment to the triple vehicle and the one vehicle, which they discriminate.

These and others, Mahamati, are the deep-seated attachments to their discriminations cherished by the ignorant and simple-minded. Tenaciously attaching themselves to these, the ignorant and simple-minded go on ever discriminating like the silkworms, which, with their own thread of discrimination and attachment, enwrap not only themselves but others and are charmed with the thread; and thus they are ever tenaciously attached to the notions of existence and non-existence. [But really] Mahamati, there are no signs here of deep-seated attachment or detachment. All things are to be seen as abiding in Solitude where there is no evolving of discrimination. Mahamati, the Bodhisattva-Mahasattva should have his abode where he can see all things from the viewpoint of Solitude.

Further, Mahamati, when the existence and non-existence of the external world are understood to be due to the seeing of the Mind itself in these signs, [the Bodhisattva] can enter upon the state of imagelessness where Mind-only is, and [there] see into the Solitude which underlies the discrimination of all things as being and non-being, and the deep-seated attachments resulting therefrom. This being so, there are in all things no signs of a deep-rooted attachment or of detachment. Here Mahamati, is nobody in bondage, nobody in emancipation, except those who by reason of their perverted wisdom recognize bondage and emancipation. Why? Because in all things neither being nor non-being is to be taken hold of.

Further, Mahamati, there are three attachments deep-seated in the minds of the ignorant and simple-minded. They are greed, anger, and folly; and thus there is desire which is procreative and is accompanied by joy and greed; closely attached to this there takes place a succession of births in the [five] paths. Thus there are the five paths of existence for all beings who are found closely attached [to greed, anger, and folly]. When one is cut off from this attachment, no signs will be seen indicative of attachment or of non-attachment.

v

THE RYOGONKYO, OR SURANGAMA SUTRA[1]

There are in the Chinese Tripitaka two sutras bearing the title, "Surangama", but they are entirely different in contents. The first one was translated into Chinese by

[1] "Sutra of Heroic Deed".

Kumarajiva between 402–412 and consists of two fascicles. The second one in ten fascicles was translated by Paramiti in 705, and this is the one used by the Zen and also by the Shingon. The reason why it is used by the Shingon is because it contains the description of a mandala and a mantram called "Sitatarapatala" (white umbrella), the recitation of which, while practising the Samadhi, is supposed to help the Yogin, as the Buddhas and gods will guard him from the intrusion of the evil spirits. But the general trend of thought as followed in this sutra is Zen rather than Shingon. It was quite natural that all the commentaries of it belong to the Zen school. The terms used here are somewhat unusual— especially those describing the Mind. The sutra is perhaps one of the later Mahayana works developed in India. It treats of highly abstruse subjects. Below is a synopsis of it.

1. The sutra opens with Ananda's adventure with an enchantress called Matanga who, by her magic charm, entices him to her abode. The Buddha, seeing this with his supernatural sight, sends Manjusri to save him and bring him back to the Buddha. Ananda is thoroughly penitent and wishes to be further instructed in the art of controlling the mind. The Buddha tells him that all spiritual discipline must grow out of a sincere heart and that much learning has no practical value in life, especially when one's religious experience is concerned. Ananda had enough learning, but no Samadhi to stand against the influence of a sorceress.

2. The reason why we go through the eternal cycle of birth and death and suffer ills incident to it is our ignorance as to the source of birth and death, that is, because Mind-essence is forgotten in the midst of causal nexus which governs this world of particular objects.

This Mind-essence is variously characterized as something original, mysterious, mysteriously bright, illumining, true, perfect, clear as a jewel, etc. It is not to be confused with our empirical mind, for it is not an object of intellectual discrimination.

Ananda is asked to locate this Mind-essence. But, as his mind moves along the line of our relative experience, he fails to give a satisfactory answer. He pursues objective events which are subject to birth and death; he never reflects within himself to try to find the Mind bright and, illumining which makes all his experiences possible.

3.   Even the Bodhisattva cannot pick up this mysteriously transparent Essence out of a world of individual things. He cannot demonstrate its reality by means of his discerning intelligence. It is not there. But that the Essence is there is evident from the fact that the eye sees, the ear hears, and the mind thinks. Only it is not discoverable as an individual object or idea, objective or subjective; for it has no existence in the way we talk of a tree or a sun, of a virtue or a thought. On the other hand, all these objects and thoughts are in the Mind-essence, true and original and mysteriously bright. Our body and mind is possible only when thought of in connection with it.

4.   Because since the beginningless past we are running after objects, not knowing where our Self is, we lose track of the Original Mind and are tormented all the time by the threatening objective world, regarding it as good or bad, true or false, agreeable or disagreeable. We are thus slaves of things and circumstances. The Buddha advises that our real position ought to be exactly the other way. Let things follow us and wait our commands. Let the true Self give directions in all our dealings with the world. Then we shall all be Tathagatas. Our body and mind will retain its original virtue bright and shining. While not moving away from this seat of enlightenment, we shall make all the worlds in the ten quarters reveal themselves even at the tip of a hair.

5.   Manjusri is Manjusri; he is absolute as he is; he is neither to be asserted nor to be negated. All assertions and negations start from the truth of this absolute identity, and this is no other than the originally illuminating Mind-essence. Based on this Essence, all the conditions that make up this world of the senses are fulfilled: we see, we hear, we feel, we learn, and we think.

6.   Causation belongs to a world of opposites. It cannot

be applied to the originally bright and illumining Essence. Nor can one ascribe to it "spontaneous activity", for this also presupposes the existence of an individual concrete substance of which it is an attribute. If the Essence is anything of which we can make any statements either affirmative or negative, it is no more the Essence. It is independent of all forms and ideas, and yet we cannot speak of it as not dependent on them. It is absolute Emptiness, *sunyata*, and for this very reason all things are possible in it.

7. The world including the mind is divisible into five Skandha (aggregates), six Pravesha (entrances), twelve Ayatana (seats), and eighteen Dhatu (kingdoms). They all come into existence when conditions are matured, and disappear when they cease. All these existences and conditions take place illusively in the Tathagata-garbha which is another name for the Mind-essence. It is the latter alone that eternally abides as Suchness bright, illumining, all-pervading, and immovable. In this Essence of eternal truth there is indeed neither going nor coming, neither becoming confused nor being enlightened, neither dying nor being born; it is absolutely unattainable and unexplainable by the intellect, for it lies beyond all the categories of thought.

8. The Tathagata-garbha is in itself thoroughly pure and all-pervading, and in it this formula holds: form is emptiness and emptiness is form. *Rupam sunyata, sunyateva rupam.* This being so, the Essence which is the Tathagata-garbha reveals itself in accordance with thoughts and dispositions of all beings, in response to their infinitely-varied degrees of knowledge, and also to their karma. In spite of its being involved in the evolution of a world of multiplicities, the Essence in itself never loses its original purity, brilliance or emptiness, all of which terms are synonymous.

9. The knowledge of an objective world does not come from objects, nor from the senses; nor is it mere accident; nor is it an illusion. A combination of the several conditions or factors is necessary to produce the knowledge. But mere combination is not enough. This combination must take

place in the originally pure, bright, illuminating Essence, which is the source of knowledge.

When this is realized, all the worlds in the ten quarters including one's own existence are perceived as so many particles of dust, floating, rising, and disappearing like foam, in the vast emptiness of space which the one illuminative Mind-essence eternally pervades.

10. The question: When the Tathagata-garbha is in itself so pure and undefiled, how is it possible that we have this world of mountains, rivers, and all other composite forms which are subject to constant changes and transformations?

This doubt comes from not understanding the absolute nature of the purity of the Essence. For by purity is not meant relative purity, which is only possible by establishing a dualistic conception of reality. The Essence is neither in the world nor of the world, nor is it outside the world. Therefore the question, which is based on a dualistic interpretation of reality, is altogether irrelevant when applied to the nature of the Essence and its relation to the world.

Hence this remarkable statement: The Tathagata-garbha, which is mysteriously bright and illuminating as the Mind-Essence, is neither to be identified nor not to be identified [with the world]; it is at once this and not-this.

11. Yajnadatta, a citizen of Sravasti, one morning looked into the mirror and found there a face with the most charming features. He thought his own head disappeared and thereby went crazy. This story is used to illustrate the stupidity of clinging to relative knowledge which rises from the opposition of subject and object. As we cling to it as having absolute value, a world of topsyturviness comes to extend before us. The original bright and charming face is possessed by every one of us only when we realize the fact by reflecting within ourselves, instead of running after unrealities.

12. Now Ananda wants to know how to get into the palatial mansion, which he is told to be his own. He is not in

possession of the key wherewith he can open the entrance door. The Buddha teaches him in this way. There are two methods to effect the entrance, both of which being complementary must be practised conjointly. The one is Samatha and the other Vipasyana. *Samatha* means "tranquillization" and *vipasyana* "contemplation".

By Samatha the world of forms is shut out of one's consciousness so that an approach is prepared for the realization of the final stage of enlightenment. When one's mind is full of confusion and distraction, it is no fit organ for contemplation. By Vipasyana is meant that the Yogin is first to awaken the desire for enlightenment, to be firmly determined in living the life of Bodhisattvahood, and to have an illuminating idea as regards the source of the evil passions which are always ready to assert themselves in the Tathagata-garbha.

13. When this source is penetrated by means of Prajna, the entrance is effected to the inner sanctuary, where all the six senses are merged in one. Let the Prajna penetration enter through the auditory sense as was the case with Kwannon Bosatsu, and the distinctions of the six senses will thereby be effaced; that is to say, there will then take place an experience called "perfect interfusion". The ear not only hears but sees, smells, and feels. All the barriers between the sensory functions are removed, and there is a perfect interfusion running between them; each Vijnana then functions for the others.

The Buddha tells Rahula to strike the bell and asks the assembly what they hear. They all say that they hear the bell. The bell is struck again, and they again say that there is a sound which they hear; and that when the bell ceases to ring there is no sound. This questioning and answering is repeated for a few times, and finally the Buddha declares that they are all wrong, for they are just pursuing what does not properly belong to them, forgetting altogether their inner Essence which functions through those objective mediums or conditions. The Essence is to be grasped and not the hearing, nor the sound. To take the latter for reality

is the result of confused mentality. By the practice of Vipasyana this is to be wiped off so that the Mind-essence is
always recognized in all the functions of an empirical mind
as well as in all the phenomena of the so-called objective
world. By thus taking hold of the Mind-essence, there is a
"perfect interfusion" of all the six Vijnanas, which constitutes
enlightenment.

14.   The root of birth and death is in the six Vijnanas
and what makes one come to the realization of perfect
interfusion is also in the six Vijnanas. To seek enlightenment
or emancipation or Nirvana is not to make it something
separate from or independent of those particularizing agents
called senses. If it is sought outside them, it nowhere exists,
or rather it becomes one of particular objects and ceases to
be what in itself it is. This is why the unattainability of
Sunyata is so much talked about in all the Mahayana sutras.

In the true Essence there is neither *samskrita* (created)
nor *asamskrita* (uncreated); they are like Maya or flowers
born of hallucination. When you attempt to manifest what
is true by means of what is erroneous, you make both untrue.
When you endeavour to explain object by subject and
subject by object, you create a world of an endless series of
opposites, and nothing real is grasped. To experience perfect
interfusion, let all the opposites, or knots as they are called,
be dissolved and a release takes place. But when there is
anywhere any clinging of any sort, and an ego-mind is
asserted, the Essence is no more there, the mysterious Lotus
fades.

15.   The Buddha then makes some of the principal
persons in the assembly relate their experience of perfect
interfusion. That of Kwannon among them is regarded as
most remarkable. His comes from the auditory sense as his
name implies. It leads him up to the enlightened state of
consciousness attained by all the Buddhas, and he is now
Love incarnate. But at the same time he identifies himself
with all beings in the six paths of existence whereby he knows
all their inner feelings and aspirations reaching up towards
the love of the Buddha. Kwannon is thus able to reveal

himself anywhere his help is needed, or to any being who hears him. The whole content of the Kwannon sutra is here fully confirmed.

16. Learning is not of much avail in the study of Buddhism as is proved by the case of Ananda, who being enticed by the magical charm of a courtesan was about to commit one of the gravest offences. In the practice of Samadhi the control of mind is most needed, which is Sila (moral precept). Sila consists in doing away with the sexual impulse, the impulse to kill living beings, the impulse to take things not belonging to oneself, and the desire to eat meat. When these impulses are kept successfully under restraint, one can really practise meditation from which Prajna grows; and it is Prajna that leads one to the Essence when the perfect interfusion of all the six Vijnanas is experienced.

17. We here come to the esoteric part of the *Surangama Sutra* where the establishment of the mandala is described, together with the mantram. In this mandala the Samadhi is practised for three weeks or for one hundred days, at the end of which those richly endowed may be able to realize Srotapannahood.

18. Next follows the description of more than fifty stages of attainment leading to final enlightenment and Nirvana; then effects of various karma by which beings undergo several forms of torture in hell are explained; then the causes are given by which beings are transformed into varieties of evil spirits and of beast forms. They, however, come back to the human world when all their sins are expiated. There are beings who turn into ascetics or heavenly beings.

19. While disciplining himself in meditation the Yogin is liable to be visited by all kinds of evil beings whereby he is constantly assailed by hallucinations of various natures. These are all due to highly-accentuated nervous derangements, and the Yogin is advised to guard himself against them.

When the Yogin has all these mental disturbances well under control, his mind acquires a state of tranquillity in which his consciousness retains its identity through his waking and sleeping hours. The modern psychologist would say that he is no more troubled with ideas which are buried, deeply repressed, in his unconsciousness; in other words, he has no dreams. His mental life is thoroughly clear and calm like the blue sky where there are no threatening clouds. The world with its expansion of earth, its towering mountains, its surging waves, its meandering rivers, and with its infinitely variegated colours and forms is serenely reflected in the mind-mirror of the Yogin. The mirror accepts them all and yet there are no traces or stains left in it—just one Essence bright and illuminating. The source of birth and death is plainly revealed here. The Yogin knows where he is; he is emancipated.

20.   But this is not yet all. The Yogin must be philosophically trained with all his experiences and intuitions to have a clear, logical, penetrating understanding of the Essence. When this is properly directed, he will have no more confused ideas introduced by misguided philosophers. Along with the training in Samatha, the cultivation of Vipasyana is to be greatly encouraged.

IV. FROM THE CHINESE ZEN MASTERS

There is a large mass of literature to be called especially Zen because of its style and terminology. Until the time of Hui-neng (Yeno in Japanese) and his immediate disciples, there was not much, as far as literary expressions were concerned, to distinguish treatises specifically on Zen from the rest of Buddhist literature. But as time went on there grew up what is now known as the *Yu-lu* (*goroku* in Japanese), containing the sayings and sermons, "gatha" poems, and other literary works of a Zen master. Strictly speaking, the Yu-lu or Goroku is not limited to Zen. One of the chief characteristics of the Zen Goroku is the free use of colloquial expressions which are not found in the classical literature of China. As long as Zen appeals to one's direct experience, abstraction is too inane for the mind of a master.

FROM THE CHINESE ZEN MASTERS

I

BODHIDHARMA ON THE TWOFOLD ENTRANCE TO THE TAO[1]

There are many ways to enter the Path, but briefly speaking they are of two sorts only. The one is "Entrance by Reason" and the other "Entrance by Conduct".[2] By "Entrance by Reason" we mean the realization of the spirit of Buddhism by the aid of the scriptural teaching. We then come to have a deep faith in the True Nature which is the same in all sentient beings. The reason why it does not manifest itself is due to the overwrapping of external objects and false thoughts. When a man, abandoning the false and embracing the true, in singleness of thought practises the

---

[1] From *The Transmission of the Lamp*, XXX.
[2] "Entrance by Reason" may also be rendered "Entrance by Higher Intuition", and "Entrance by Conduct", "Entrance by Practical Living".

Pi-kuan[1] he finds that there is neither self nor other, that the masses and the worthies are of one essence, and he firmly holds on to this belief and never moves away therefrom. He will not then be a slave to words, for he is in silent communion with the Reason itself, free from conceptual discrimination; he is serene and not-acting. This is called "Entrance by Reason".

By "Entrance by Conduct" is meant the four acts in which all other acts are included. What are the four? 1. To know how to requite hatred; 2. To be obedient to karma; 3. Not to crave anything; and 4. To be in accord with the Dharma.

1. What is meant by "How to requite hatred"? He who disciplines himself in the Path should think thus when he has to struggle with adverse conditions: "During the innumerable past ages I have wandered through a multiplicity of existences, all the while giving myself to unimportant details of life at the expense of essentials, and thus creating infinite occasions for hate, ill-will, and wrongdoing. While no violations have been committed in this life, the fruits of evil deeds in the past are to be gathered now. Neither gods nor men can foretell what is coming upon me. I will submit myself willingly and patiently to all the ills that befall me, and I will never bemoan or complain. The Sutra teaches me not to worry over ills that may happen to me. Why? Because when things are surveyed by a higher intelligence, the foundation of causation is reached." When this thought is awakened in a man, he will be in accord with the Reason because he makes the best use of hatred and turns it into the service in his advance towards the Path. This is called the "way to requite hatred".

2. By "being obedient to karma" is meant this: There is no self (*atman*) in whatever beings are produced by the interplay of karmaic conditions; the pleasure and pain I suffer are also the results of my previous action. If I am rewarded with fortune, honour, etc., this is the outcome of my past deeds which by reason of causation affect my present

---

[1] "Wall-gazing".

life. When the force of karma is exhausted, the result I am enjoying now will disappear; what is then the use of being joyful over it? Gain or loss, let me accept the karma as it brings to me the one or the other; the Mind itself knows neither increase nor decrease. The wind of pleasure [and pain] will not stir me, for I am silently in harmony with the Path. Therefore this is called "being obedient to karma".

3. By "not craving (*ch'iu*) anything" is meant this: Men of the world, in eternal confusion, are attached everywhere to one thing or another, which is called craving. The wise however understand the truth and are not like the ignorant. Their minds abide serenely in the uncreated while the body moves about in accordance with the laws of causation. All things are empty and there is nothing desirable to seek after. Where there is the merit of brightness there surely lurks the demerit of darkness. This triple world where we stay altogether too long is like a house on fire; all that has a body suffers, and nobody really knows what peace is. Because the wise are thoroughly acquainted with this truth, they are never attached to things that change; their thoughts are quieted, they never crave anything. Says the Sutra: "Wherever there is a craving, there is pain; cease from craving and you are blessed." Thus we know that not to crave anything is indeed the way to the Truth. Therefore, it is taught not "to crave anything".

4. By "being in accord with the Dharma" is meant that the Reason which we call the Dharma in its essence is pure, and that this Reason is the principle of emptiness (*sunyata*) in all that is manifested; it is above defilements and attachments, and there is no "self", no "other" in it. Says the Sutra: "In the Dharma there are no sentient beings, because it is free from the stain of being; in the Dharma there is no 'self' because it is free from the stain of selfhood." When the wise understand this truth and believe in it, their lives will be "in accordance with the Dharma".

As there is in the essence of the Dharma no desire to possess, the wise are ever ready to practise charity with their body, life, and property, and they never begrudge, they never know what an ill grace means. As they have a perfect understanding of the threefold nature of emptiness, they are above partiality and attachment. Only because of their will to cleanse all beings of their stains, they come among them as of them, but they are not attached to form. This is the self-benefiting phase of their lives. They, however, know also how to benefit others, and again how to glorify the truth of enlightenment. As with the virtue of charity, so with the other five virtues [of the Prajnaparamita]. The wise practise the six virtues of perfection to get rid of confused thoughts, and yet there is no specific consciousness on their part that they are engaged in any meritorious deeds. This is called "being in accord with the Dharma".[1]

II

ON BELIEVING IN MIND (SHINJIN-NO-MEI)[2]

1.   The Perfect Way knows no difficulties
      Except that it refuses to make preferences;
      Only when freed from hate and love,
      It reveals itself fully and without disguise;

[1] Since this translation from the *Transmission of the Lamp*, two Tun-huang MSS. containing the text have come to light. The one is in the *Masters and Disciples of the Lanka* (*Leng-chia Shihtzu Chi*), already published, and the other still in MS., which however the present author intends to have reproduced in facsimile before long. They differ in minor points with the translation here given.

[2] By Seng-t'san (Sosan in Japanese). Died 606 C.E. Mind=*hsin*. *Hsin* is one of those Chinese words which defy translation. When the Indian scholars were trying to translate the Buddhist Sanskrit works into Chinese, they discovered that there were five classes of Sanskrit terms which could not be satisfactorily rendered into Chinese. We thus find in the Chinese Tripitaka such words as *prajna, bodhi, buddha, nirvana, dhyana, bodhisattva*, etc., almost always untranslated; and they now appear in their original Sanskrit form among the technical Buddhist terminology. If we could leave *hsin* with all its nuance of meaning in this translation, it would save us from the many difficulties that face us in its English rendering. For *hsin* means "mind", "heart", "soul", "spirit"—each singly as well as all inclusively. In the present composition by the third patriarch of Zen, it has sometimes an intellectual connotation but at other times it can properly be given as "heart". But as the predominant note of Zen Buddhism is more intellectual than anything else, though not in the sense of being logical or philosophical, I decided here to translate *hsin* by "mind" rather than by "heart", and by this mind I do not mean our psychological mind, but what may be called absolute mind, or Mind.

A tenth of an inch's difference,
And heaven and earth are set apart;
If you wish to see it before your own eyes,
Have no fixed thoughts either for or against it.

2. To set up what you like against what you dislike—
This is the disease of the mind:
When the deep meaning [of the Way] is not understood
Peace of mind is disturbed to no purpose.

3. [The Way is] perfect like unto vast space,
With nothing wanting, nothing superfluous:
It is indeed due to making choice
That its suchness is lost sight of.

4. Pursue not the outer entanglements,
Dwell not in the inner void;
Be serene in the oneness of things,
And [dualism] vanishes by itself.

5. When you strive to gain quiescence by stopping
   motion,
The quiescence thus gained is ever in motion;
As long as you tarry in the dualism,
How can you realize oneness?

6. And when oneness is not thoroughly understood,
In two ways loss is sustained:
The denying of reality is the asserting of it,
And the asserting of emptiness is the denying of it.[1]

7. Wordiness and intellection—

[1] This means: When the absolute oneness of things is not properly understood, negation as well as affirmation tends to be a one-sided view of reality.
When Buddhists deny the reality of an objective world, they do not mean that
they believe in the unconditioned emptiness of things; they know that there is
something real which cannot be done away with. When they uphold the
doctrine of emptiness this does not mean that all is nothing but an empty
hollow, which leads to a self-contradiction. The philosophy of Zen avoids
the error of one-sidedness involved in realism as well as in nihilism.

The more with them the further astray we go;
Away therefore with wordiness and intellection,
And there is no place where we cannot pass freely.

8. When we return to the root, we gain the meaning;
When we pursue external objects, we lose the reason.
The moment we are enlightened within,
We go beyond the voidness of a world confronting us.

9. Transformations going on in an empty world which
confronts us
Appear real all because of Ignorance:
Try not to seek after the true,
Only cease to cherish opinions.

10. Abide not with dualism,
Carefully avoid pursuing it;
As soon as you have right and wrong,
Confusion ensues, and Mind[1] is lost.

11. The two exist because of the One,
But hold not even to this One;
When a mind is not disturbed,
The ten thousand things offer no offence.

12. No offence offered, and no ten thousand things;
No disturbance going, and no mind set up to work:
The subject is quieted when the object ceases,
The object ceases when the subject is quieted.

13. The object is an object for the subject,
The subject is a subject for the object:
Know that the relativity of the two
Rests ultimately on one Emptiness.

14. In one Emptiness the two are not distinguished,
And each contains in itself all the ten thousand things;

[1] The Mind=the Way=the One=Emptiness.

When no discrimination is made between this and that.
How can a one-sided and prejudiced view arise?

15. The Great Way is calm and large-hearted,
For it nothing is easy, nothing is hard;
Small views are irresolute,
The more in haste the tardier they go.

16. Clinging is never kept within bounds,
It is sure to go the wrong way;
Quit it, and things follow their own courses,
While the Essence neither departs nor abides.

17. Obey the nature of things, and you are in concord
   with the Way,
Calm and easy and free from annoyance;
But when your thoughts are tied, you turn away from
   the truth,
They grow heavier and duller and are not at all sound.

18. When they are not sound, the spirit is troubled;
What is the use of being partial and one-sided then?
If you want to walk the course of the One Vehicle,
Be not prejudiced against the six sense-objects.

19. When you are not prejudiced against the six sense-
   objects,
You are then one with the Enlightenment;
The wise are non-active,
While the ignorant bind themselves up;
While in the Dharma itself there is no individuation,
They ignorantly attach themselves to particular objects.
It is their own mind that creates illusions—
Is this not the greatest of all self-contradictions?

20. The ignorant cherish the idea of rest and unrest,
The enlightened have no likes and dislikes:
All forms of dualism

Are contrived by the ignorant themselves.
They are like unto visions and flowers in the air;
Why should we trouble ourselves to take hold of them?
Gain and loss, right and wrong—
Away with them once for all!

21. If an eye never falls asleep,
All dreams will by themselves cease:
If the Mind retains its absoluteness,
The ten thousand things are of one Suchness.[1]

22. When the deep mystery of one Suchness is fathomed,
All of a sudden we forget the external entanglements;
When the ten thousand things are viewed in their
oneness,
We return to the origin and remain where we ever
have been.

23. Forget the wherefore of things,
And we attain to a state beyond analogy;
Movement stopped and there is no movement,
Rest set in motion and there is no rest;
When dualism does no more obtain,
Oneness itself abides not.

24. The ultimate end of things where they cannot go any
further

---

[1] *The Masters and Disciples of the Lanka* also quotes a poetical composition of So-san on "The Mysterious" in which we find the following echoing the idea given expression here:

"One Reality only—
How deep and far-reaching!
The ten thousand things—
How confusingly multifarious!
The true and the conventional are indeed intermingling,
But essentially of the same substance they are.
The wise and the unenlightened are indeed distinguishable,
But in the Way they are united as one.
Desirest thou to find its limits?
How broadly expanding! It is limitless!
How vaguely it vanishes away! Its ends are never reached!
It originates in beginningless time, it terminates in endless time."

Is not bound by rules and measures:
In the Mind harmonious [with the Way] we have the
  principle of identity,
In which we find all strivings quieted;
Doubts and irresolutions are completely done away
  with,
And the right faith is straightened;
There is nothing left behind,
There is nothing retained,
All is void, lucid, and self-illuminating;
There is no exertion, no waste of energy—
This is where thinking never attains,
This is where the imagination fails to measure.

25. In the higher realm of true Suchness
     There is neither "self" nor "other":
     When direct identification is sought,
     We can only say, "Not two".[1]

26. In being "not two" all is the same,
     All that is is comprehended in it;
     The wise in the ten quarters,
     They all enter into this Absolute Reason.

27. This Absolute Reason is beyond quickening [time] and
       extending [space],
     For it one instant is ten thousand years;
     Whether we see it or not,
     It is manifest everywhere in all the ten quarters.

28. Infinitely small things are as large as large things can
       be,
     For here no external conditions obtain;
     Infinitely large things are as small as small things can
       be,
     For objective limits are here of no consideration.
29. What is is the same as what is not,

  [1] I.e. Tat tvam asi.

What is not is the same as what is:
Where this state of things fails to obtain,
Indeed, no tarrying there.

30.   One in All,
      All in One—
      If only this is realized,
      No more worry about your not being perfect!

31.   Where Mind and each believing mind are not divided,
      And undivided are each believing mind and Mind,
      This is where words fail;
      For it is not of the past, present, and future.

III

FROM HUI-NENG'S TAN-CHING[1]

24. *Mahaprajnaparamita* is a Sanskrit term of the
Western country; in T'ang it means "great-wisdom (*chih-
hui*), other-shore reached". This Truth (*dharma*=*fa*) is to
be lived, it is not to be [merely] pronounced with the mouth.
When it is not lived, it is like a phantom, like an apparition.
The Dharmakaya of the Yogin is the same as the Buddha.

What is *maha*? *Maha* means "great". The capacity of
Mind is wide and great, it is like emptiness of space. To sit
with a mind emptied makes one fall into emptiness of
indifference. Space contains the sun, the moon, stars,
constellations, great earth, mountains, and rivers. All grasses
and plants, good men and bad men, bad things and good
things, Heaven and hell—they are all in empty space. The
emptiness of [Self-] nature as it is in all people is just like this.

25. [Self-] nature contains in it all objects; hence it is
great. All objects without exception are of Self-nature.
Seeing all human beings and non-human beings as they are,

---

[1] The Tun-huang copy, edited by D. T. Suzuki, 1934. Hui-neng=Yeno,
637–712.

evil and good, evil things and good things, it abandons them
not, nor is it contaminated with them; it is like the emptiness
of space. So it is called great, that is, *maha*. The confused
pronounce it with their mouths, the wise live it with their
minds. Again, there are people confused [in mind]; they
conceive this to be great when they have their minds emptied
of thoughts—which is not right. The capacity of Mind is
great; when there is no life accompanying it it is small. Do
not merely pronounce it with the mouth. Those who fail to
discipline themselves to live this life, are not my disciples.

26.   What is *prajna*? *Prajna* is *chih-hui* (wisdom). When
every thought of yours is not benighted at all times, when
you always live *chih-hui* (=*prajna*, wisdom), this is called the
life of Prajna. When a single thought of yours is benighted,
then Prajna ceases to work. When a single thought of yours
is of *chih*, i.e. enlightened, then Prajna is born. Being always
benighted in their minds, people yet declare themselves to be
living Prajna. Prajna has no shape, no form, it is no other
than the essence (*hsing*) of *chih-hui* (wisdom).

What is *Paramita*? This is a Sanskrit term of the Western
country. In T'ang it means "the other shore reached". When
the meaning (*artha* in Sanskrit) is understood, one is detached
from birth and death. When the objective world (*visaya*) is
clung to, there is the rise of birth and death; it is like the
waves rising from the water; this is called "this shore".
When you are detached from the objective world, there is
no birth and death for you; it is like the water constantly
running its course: this is "reaching the other shore". Hence
Paramita.

The confused pronounce [Prajna] with their mouths;
the wise live it in their minds. When it is merely pronounced,
there is at that very moment a falsehood; when there is a
falsehood, it is not a reality. When Prajna is lived in every
thought of yours, this is known as reality. Those who understand this truth, understand the truth of Prajna and practise
the life of Prajna. Those who do not practise it are ordinary
people. When you practise and live it in one thought of yours,
you are equal to the Buddha.

Good friends, the passions are no other than enlightenment (*bodhi*). When your antecedent thought is confused yours is an ordinary mind; as soon as your succeeding thought is enlightened, you are a Buddha.

Good friends, Prajnaparamita is the most honoured, the highest, the foremost; it is nowhere abiding, nowhere departing, nowhere coming; all the Buddhas of the past, present, and future issue out of it. By means of Great Wisdom (*ta-chih-hui=mahaprajna*) that leads to the other shore (*paramita*), the five skandhas, the passions, and the innumerable follies are destroyed. When thus disciplined, one is a Buddha, and the three passions [i.e. greed, anger, and folly] will turn into Morality (*sila*), Meditation (*dhyana*), and Wisdom (*prajna*).

27. Good friends, according to my way of understanding this truth, 84,000 wisdoms (*chih-hui*) are produced from one Prajna. Why? Because there are 84,000 follies. If there were no such innumerable follies, Prajna is eternally abiding, not severed from Self-nature. He who has an insight into this truth is free from thoughts, from recollections, from attachments; in him there is no deceit and falsehood. This is where the essence of Suchness is by itself. When all things are viewed in the light of wisdom (*chih-hui=prajna*), there is neither attachment nor detachment. This is seeing into one's Nature and attaining the truth of Buddhahood.

28. Good friends, if you wish to enter into the deepest realm of Truth (*dharmadhatu*), and attain the Prajnasamadhi, you should at once begin to exercise yourselves in the life of Prajnaparamita; you just devote yourselves to the one volume of the *Vajracchedika-prajnaparamita Sutra*, and you will, seeing into the nature of your being, enter upon the Prajnasamadhi. It should be known that the merit of such a person is immeasurable, as is distinctly praised in the sutras, of which I need not speak in detail.

This Truth of the highest order is taught to people of great intelligence and superior endowments. If people of small intelligence and inferior endowments happen to hear it, no faith would ever be awakened in their minds. Why?

It is like a great dragon pouring rains down in torrents over the Jambudipa: cities, towns, villages are all deluged and carried away in the flood, as if they were grass-leaves. But when the rain, however much, falls on the great ocean, there is in it neither an increase nor a decrease.

When people of the Great Vehicle listen to a discourse on the *Vajracchedika* their minds are opened and there is an intuitive understanding. They know thereby that their own Nature is originally endowed with Prajna-wisdom and that all things are to be viewed in the light of this wisdom (*chih-hui*) of theirs, and they need not depend upon letters. It is like rain-waters not being reserved in the sky; but the water is drawn up by the dragon-king out of the rivers and oceans, whereby all beings and all plants, sentient and non-sentient, universally share the wet. All the waters flowing together once more are poured into the great ocean, and the ocean accepting all the waters fuses them into one single body of water. It is the same with Prajna-wisdom which is the original Nature of all beings.

29. When people of inferior endowments hear this "abrupt" doctrine here discoursed on, they are like those plants naturally growing small on earth, which, being once soaked by a heavy rain, are all unable to raise themselves up and continue their growth. It is the same with people of inferior endowments. They are endowed with Prajna-wisdom as much as people of great intelligence; there is no distinction. Why is it then that they have no insight even when listening to the Truth? It is due to the heaviness of hindrance caused by false views and to the deep-rootedness of the passions. It is like an overcasting cloud screening the sun; unless it blows hard no rays of light are visible.

There is no greatness or smallness in Prajna-wisdom, but since all beings cherish in themselves confused thoughts, they seek the Buddha by means of external exercises, and are unable to see into their Self-nature. That is why they are known to be people of inferior endowments.

Those beings who, listening to the "Abrupt" doctrine, do not take themselves to external exercises, but reflecting within themselves raise this original Nature all the time to the proper viewing [of the Truth], remain [always undefiled by] the passions and the innumerable follies; and at that moment they all have an insight [into the Truth]. It is like the great ocean taking in all the rivers, large and small, and merging them into one body of water—this is seeing into one's own Nature. [He who thus sees into his own Nature] does not abide anywhere inside or outside; he freely comes and departs; he knows how to get rid of attaching thoughts; his passage has no obstructions. When one is able to practise this life, he realizes that there is from the first no difference between [his Self-Nature] and Prajna-paramita.[1]

30. All the sutras and writings, all the letters, the two vehicles Major and Minor, the twelve divisions [of Buddhist literature]—these are all set forth because of the people of the world. Because there is wisdom-nature (*chih-hui-hsing*), therefore there is the establishment of all these works. If there were no people of the world, no multitudinous objects would ever be in existence. Therefore, we know that all objects rise originally because of the people of the world. All the sutras and writings are said to have their existence because of the people of the world.

The distinction of stupidity and intelligence is only possible among the people of the world. Those who are stupid are inferior people and those who are intelligent are superior people. The confused ask the wise, and the wise discourse for them on the Truth in order to make the stupid enlightened and have an intuitive understanding of it. When the confused are enlightened and have their minds opened, they are not to be distinguished from the people of great intelligence.

Therefore, we know that Buddhas when not enlightened are no other than ordinary beings; when there is one thought of enlightenment, ordinary beings at once turn into Buddhas. Therefore, we know that all multitudinous objects are every

[1] The text has "the Prajnaparamita Sutra" here. But I take it to mean Prajna itself instead of the sutra.

one of them in one's own mind.[1] Why not, from within one's own mind, at once reveal the original essence of Suchness? Says the *Bodhisattvasila Sutra*: "My original Self-nature is primarily pure; when my Mind is known and my Nature is seen into I naturally attain the path of Buddhahood." Says the *Vimalakirti Sutra*: "When you have an instant opening of view you return to your original Mind."

48. The Great Master died on the third day of the eighth month of the second year of Hsien-t'ien (713 C.E.). On the eighth day of the seventh month of this year he had a farewell gathering of his followers as he felt that he was to leave them forever in the following month, and told them to have all the doubts they might have about his teaching once for all settled on this occasion. As he found them weeping in tears he said: "You are all weeping, but for whom are you so sorry? If you are sorry for my not knowing where I am departing to, you are mistaken; for I know where I am going. Indeed, if I did not, I would not part with you. The reason why you are in tears is probably that you do not yourselves know whither I am going. If you did, you would not be weeping so. The Essence of the Dharma knows no birth-and-death, no coming-and-going. Sit down, all of you, and let me give you a gatha with the title, "On the Absolute":[2]

There is nothing true anywhere,
The true is nowhere to be seen;
If you say you see the true,
This seeing is not the true one.[3]

---

[1] The text has the "body", while the Koshoji edition and the current one have "mind".

[2] The title literally reads: "the true-false moving-quiet". "True" stands against "false" and "moving" against "quiet" and as long as there is an opposition of any kind, no true spiritual insight is possible. And this insight does not grow from a quietistic exercise of meditation.

[3] That is, the Absolute refuses to divide itself into two: that which sees and that which is seen.

Where the true is left to itself,
There is nothing false in it, which is Mind itself.
When Mind in itself is not liberated from the false,
There is nothing true, nowhere is the true to be found.

A conscious being alone understands what is meant by
    "moving";[1]
To those not endowed with consciousness, the
    moving is unintelligible;
If you exercise yourself in the practice of keeping
    your mind unmoved, [i.e. in a quietistic medi-
    tation],
The immovable you gain is that of one who has no
    consciousness.

If you are desirous for the truly immovable,
The immovable is in the moving itself,
And this immovable is the [truly] immovable one;
There is no seed of Buddhahood where there is no
    consciousness.

Mark well how varied are aspects [of the immovable
    one],
And know that the first reality is immovable;
Only when this insight is attained,
The true working of Suchness is understood.

I advise you, O students of the Truth,
To exert yourselves in the proper direction;
Do not in the teaching of the Mahayana
Commit the fault of clinging to the relative knowledge[2]
    of birth and death.

Where there is an all-sided concordance of views

---

[1] "Moving" means "dividing" or "limiting". When the absolute moves,
a dualistic interpretation of it takes place, which is consciousness.

[2] *Chih, jnana* in Sanskrit, is used in contradistinction to *Prajna* which is the
highest form of knowledge, directly seeing into the Immovable or the Absolute.

You may talk together regarding the Buddha's
    teaching;
Where there is really no such concordance,
Keep your hands folded and your joy within yourself.

There is really nothing to argue about in this teaching;
Any arguing is sure to go against the intent of it;
Doctrines given up to confusion and argumentation
Lead by themselves to birth and death.

IV

YOKA DAISHI'S "SONG OF ENLIGHTENMENT"[1]

1. Knowest thou that leisurely philosopher who has gone
     beyond learning and is not exerting himself in
     anything?
    He neither endeavours to avoid idle thoughts nor seeks
     after the Truth;
    [For he knows that] ignorance in reality is the Buddha-
     nature,
    [And that] this empty visionary body is no less than
     the Dharma-body.

2. When one knows what the Dharma-body is, there is
     not an object [to be known as such],
    The source of all things, as far as its self-nature goes,
     is the Buddha in his absolute aspect;
    The five aggregates (*skandha*) are like a cloud floating
     hither and thither with no fixed purpose,
    The three poisons (*klesa*) are like foams appearing and
     disappearing as it so happens to them.

---

[1] Yoka Daishi (died 713, Yung-chia Ta-shih, in Chinese), otherwise
known as Gengaku (Hsuan-chiao), was one of the chief disciples of Hui-neng,
the sixth patriarch of Zen Buddhism. Before he was converted to Zen he was
a student of the T'ien-tai. His interview with Hui-neng is recorded in the
Tan-ching. He died in 713 leaving a number of short works on Zen philosophy,
and of them the present composition in verse is the most popular one. The
original title reads: *Cheng-tao Ke,* "realization-way-song".

3. When Reality is attained, it is seen to be without an
   ego-substance and devoid of all forms of objectivity,
   And thereby all the karma which leads us to the lowest
   hell is instantly wiped out;
   Those, however, who cheat beings with their false
   knowledge,
   Will surely see their tongues pulled out for innumerable
   ages to come.

4. In one whose mind is at once awakened to [the intent
   of] the Tathagata-dhyana
   The six paramitas and all the other merits are fully
   matured;
   While in a world of dreams the six paths of existence
   are vividly traced,
   But after the awakening there is vast Emptiness only
   and not even a great chiliocosm exists.

5. Here one sees neither sin nor bliss, neither loss nor
   gain;
   In the midst of the Eternally Serene no idle questionings
   are invited;
   The dust [of ignorance] has been since of old accumu-
   lating on the mirror never polished,
   Now is the time once for all to see the clearing positively
   done.

6. Who is said to have no-thought? and who not-born?
   If really not-born, there is no no-birth either;
   Ask a machine-man and find out if this is not so;
   As long as you seek Buddhahood, specifically exercising
   yourself for it, there is no attainment for you.

7. Let the four elements go off your hold,
   And in the midst of the Eternally Serene allow yourself
   to quaff or to peck, as you like;
   Where all things of relativity are transient and ultimately empty,

There is seen the great perfect enlightenment of the
Tathagata realized.

8. True monkhood consists in having a firm conviction;
If, however, you fail to have it, ask me according to
your ideas, [and you will be enlightened].
To have a direct understanding in regard to the root
of all things, this is what the Buddha affirms;
If you go on gathering leaves and branches, there is
no help for you.

9. The whereabouts of the precious *mani*-jewel is not
known to people generally,
Which lies deeply buried in the recesses of the Tathagata-garbha;
The sixfold function miraculously performed by it is
an illusion and yet not an illusion,
The rays of light emanating from one perfect sun belong
to the realm of form and yet not to it.

10. The fivefold eye-sight[1] is purified and the fivefold
power[2] is gained,
When one has a realization, which is beyond [intel-
lectual] measurement;
There is no difficulty in recognizing images in the
mirror,
But who can take hold of the moon reflected in water?

11. [The enlightened one] walks always by himself, goes
about always by himself;
Every perfect one saunters along one and the same
passage of Nirvana;
His tone is classical, his spirit is transparent, his airs
are naturally elevated,

[1] The fivefold eye-sight (*cakshus*): (1) Physical, (2) Heavenly, (3) Prajna-,
(4) Dharma-, and (5) Buddha-eye.
[2] The fivefold power (*bala*): (1) Faith, (2) Energy, (3) Memory, (4) Meditation, and (5) Prajna.

His features are rather gaunt, his bones are firm, he
pays no attention to others.

12. Sons of the Sakya are known to be poor;
But their poverty is of the body, their spiritual life
knows no poverty;
The poverty-stricken body is wrapped in rags,
But their spirit holds within itself a rare invaluable
gem.

13. The rare invaluable gem is never impaired however
much one uses it,
And beings are thereby benefited ungrudgingly as
required by occasions;
The triple body[1] and the fourfold jnana[2] are perfected
within it,
The eightfold emancipation[3] and the sixfold miraculous
power[4] are impressed on it.

14. The superior one has it settled once for all and for ever,
The middling one learns much and holds much in
doubt;
The point is to cast aside your soiled clothes you so
dearly keep with you;
What is the use of showing off your work before others?

15. Let others speak ill of me, let others spite me;
Those who try to burn the sky with a torch end in
tiring themselves out;
I listen to them and taste [their evil-speaking] as
nectar;

[1] (1) The Dharma-body, (2) the Body of Enjoyment, and (3) the Body
of Transformation.
[2] (1) Mirror-intuition, (2) intuition of identity, (3) knowledge of doing
works, and (4) clear perception of relations.
[3] *The Abhidharmakosa*, VIII, gives an explanation of the eight Vimoksha.
See La Vallee Poussin's French translation, Chap. VIII, pp. 203–221.
[4] For the six Riddhi, which are the supernatural products of the medita-
tions, see op. cit., VII, 122 *ff*.

All melts away and I find myself suddenly within the
Unthinkable itself.

16. Seeing others talk ill of me, I acquire the chance of
gaining merit,
For they are really my good friends;
When I cherish, being vituperated, neither enmity nor
favouritism,
There grows within me the power of love and humility
which is born of the Unborn.

17. Let us be thoroughgoing not only in inner experience
but in its interpretation,
And our discipline will be perfect in Dhyana as well
as in Prajna, not one-sidedly abiding in Sunyata
(emptiness);
This is not where we alone have finally come to,
But all the Buddhas, as numerous as the Ganga sands,
are of the same essence.

18. The lion-roaring of the doctrine of fearlessness—
Hearing this, the timid animals' brains are torn in
pieces,
Even the scented elephant runs wild forgetting its
native dignity;
It is the heavenly dragon alone that feels elated with
joy, calmly listening [to the lion-roaring of the
Buddha].

19. I crossed seas and rivers, climbed mountains, and
forded freshets,
In order to interview the masters, to inquire after
Truth, to delve into the secrets of Zen;
And ever since I was enabled to recognize the path of
Sokei,[1]
I know that birth-and-death is not the thing I have
to be concerned with.

[1] T'sao-ch'i is the name of the locality where Hui-neng had his monastery,
means the master himself.

20. For walking is Zen, sitting is Zen,
     Whether talking or remaining silent, whether moving
        or standing quiet, the Essence itself is ever at ease;
     Even when greeted with swords and spears it never
        loses its quiet way,
     So with poisonous drugs, they fail to perturb its
        serenity.

21. Our Master, [Sakyamuni], anciently served Dipankara
        the Buddha,
     And again for many kalpas disciplined himself as an
        ascetic called Kshanti.
     [I have also] gone through many a birth and many a
        death;
     Births and deaths—how endlessly they recur!

22. But ever since my realization of No-birth, which quite
        abruptly came on me,
     Vicissitudes of fate, good and bad, have lost their
        power over me.
     Far away in the mountains I live in an humble hut;
     High are the mountains, thick the arboreous shades,
        and under an old pine-tree
     I sit quietly and contentedly in my monkish home;
     Perfect tranquillity and rustic simplicity rules here.

23. When you are awakened [to the Dharma], all is under-
        stood, no strivings are required;
     Things of the *samskrita*[1] are not of this nature;
     Charity practised with the idea of form (*rupa*) may
        result in a heavenly birth,
     But it is like shooting an arrow against the sky,
     When the force is exhausted the arrow falls on the
        ground.

---

[1] According to Buddhist philosophy, existence is divided into two groups,
samskrita and *asamskrita*. The samskrita applies to anything that does any kind
of work in any possible manner, while the asamskrita accomplishes nothing.
Of this class are space regarded as a mode of reality, Nirvana, and non-
existence owing to lack of necessary conditions.

Similarly, [when the heavenly reward comes to an end], the life that follows is sure to be one of fortune.

Is it not far better then to be with Reality which is *asamskrita* and above all strivings,

And whereby one instantly enters the stage of Tathagatahood?

24. Only let us take hold of the root and not worry about the branches;

It is like a crystal basin reflecting the moon,

And I know now what this *mani*-gem is,

Whereby not only oneself is benefited but others, inexhaustibly;

The moon is serenely reflected on the stream, the breeze passes softly through the pines,

Perfect silence reigning unruffled—what is it for?

25. The morality-jewel inherent in the Buddha-nature stamps itself on the mind-ground [of the enlightened one];

Whose robe is cut out of mists, clouds, and dews,

Whose bowl anciently pacified the fiery dragons, and whose staff once separated the fighting tigers;

Listen now to the golden rings of his staff giving out mellifluous tunes.

These are not, however, mere symbolic expressions, devoid of historical contents;

Wherever the holy staff of Tathagatahood moves, the traces are distinctly marked.

26. He neither seeks the true nor severs himself from the defiled,

He clearly perceives that dualities are empty and have no reality,

That to have no reality means not to be one-sided, neither empty nor not-empty,

For this is the genuine form of Tathagatahood.

27. The Mind like a mirror is brightly illuminating and
knows no obstructions,
It penetrates the vast universe to its minutest crevices;
All its contents, multitudinous in form, are reflected
in the Mind,
Which, shining like a perfect gem, has no surface,
nor the inside.

28. Emptiness negatively defined denies a world of
causality,
All is then in utter confusion, with no orderliness in it,
which surely invites evils all around;
The same holds true when beings are clung to at the
expense of Emptiness,
For it is like throwing oneself into a flame, in order
to avoid being drowned in the water.

29. When one attempts to take hold of the true by abandoning the false,
This is discrimination and there are artificialities and
falsehoods;
When the Yogin, not understanding [what the Mind
is], is given up to mere discipline,
He is apt, indeed, to take an enemy for his own child.

30. That the Dharma-materials are destroyed and merit is
lost,
Comes in every case from the relative discriminatory
mind;
For this reason Zen teaches to have a thorough insight
into the nature of Mind,
When the Yogin abruptly by means of his intuitive
power realizes the truth of No-birth.

31. A man of great will carries with him a sword of Prajna,
Whose flaming Vajra-blade cuts all the entanglements
of knowledge and ignorance;

It not only smashes in pieces the intellect of the
    philosophers
But disheartens the spirit of the evil ones.

32. He causes the Dharma-thunder to roar, he beats the
    Dharma-drum,
He raises mercy-clouds, he pours nectar-showers,
He conducts himself like the lordly elephant or dragon
    and beings innumerable are thereby blessed,
The three Vehicles and the five Families are all equally
    brought to enlightenment.

Hini the herb grows on the Himalaya where no other
    grasses are found,
And the crows feeding on it give the purest of milk,
    and this I always enjoy.
One Nature, perfect and pervading, circulates in all
    natures;
One Reality, all comprehensive, contains within itself
    all realities;
The one moon reflects itself wherever there is a sheet
    of water,
And all the moons in the waters are embraced within
    the one moon;
The Dharma-body of all the Buddhas enters into my
    own being,
And my own being is found in union with theirs.

33. In one stage are stored up all the stages;
[Reality] is neither form, nor mind, nor work;
Even before fingers are snapped, more than eighty
    thousand holy teachings are fulfilled;
Even in the space of a second the evil karma of three
    asamkhyeya kalpas is destroyed;
Whatever propositions are made by logic are no [true]
    propositions,
For they stand in no intrinsic relation to my inner
    Light.

34. [This inner Light] is beyond both praise and abuse,
    Like unto space it knows no boundaries;
    Yet it is right here with us ever retaining its serenity
    and fulness;
    It is only when you seek it that you lose it.
    You cannot take hold of it, nor can you get rid of it;
    While you can do neither, it goes on its own way;
    You remain silent and it speaks; you speak and it is
    silent;
    The great gate of charity is wide open with no ob-
    structions whatever before it.

35. Should someone ask me what teaching I understand,
    I tell him that mine is the power of Mahaprajna:
    Affirm it or negate it as you like—it is beyond your
    human intelligence;
    Walk against it or along with it, and Heaven knows
    not its whereabouts.

36. I have been disciplined in it for ever so many kalpas
    of my life;
    This is no idle talk of mine, nor am I deceiving you;
    I erect the Dharma-banner to maintain this teaching,
    Which I have gained at Sokei and which is no other
    than the one proclaimed by the Buddha.

37. Mahakashyapa was the first, leading the line of trans-
    mission;
    Twenty-eight Fathers followed him in the West;
    The Lamp was then brought over the sea to this
    country;
    And Bodhidharma became the First Father here:
    His mantle, as we all know, passed over six Fathers,
    And by them many minds came to see the Light.

38. Even the true need not be [specifically] established,
    as to the false none such have ever been in existence;

When both being and non-being are put aside, even
  non-emptiness loses its sense;
The twenty forms of Emptiness are not from the first
  to be adhered to;
The eternal oneness of Tathagatahood remains absolutely the same.

39. The mind functions through the sense-organs, and
    thereby an objective world is comprehended—
This dualism marks darkly on the mirror;
When the dirt is wiped off, the light shines out;
So when both the mind and the objective world are
  forgotten, the Essence asserts its truth.

40. Alas! this age of degeneration is full of evils;
Beings are most poorly endowed and difficult to
  control;
Being further removed from the ancient Sage, they
  deeply cherish false views;
The Evil One is gathering up his forces while the
  Dharma is weakened, and hatred is growing rampant;
Even when they learn of the "abrupt" school of the
  Buddhist teaching,
What a pity that they fail to embrace it and thereby
  to crush evils like a piece of brick!

41. The mind is the author of all works and the body the
    sufferer of all ills;
Do not blame others plaintively for what properly
  belongs to you;
If you desire not to incur upon yourself the karma for
  a hell,
Cease from blaspheming the Tathagata-wheel of the
  good Dharma.

42. There are no inferior trees in the grove of sandal-
    woods,

Among its thickly-growing primeval forest lions alone
find their abode;
Where no disturbances reach, where peace only reigns,
there is the place for lions to roam;
All the other beasts are kept away, and birds do not fly
in the vicinity.

43. It is only their own cubs that follow their steps in the
woods,
When the young ones are only three years old, they
roar.
How can jackals pursue the king of the Dharma?
With all their magical arts the elves gape to no purpose.

44. The perfect "abrupt" teaching has nothing to do with
human imagination;
Where a shadow of doubt is still left, there lies the cause
for argumentation;
My saying this is not the outcome of my egotism,
My only fear is lest your discipline lead you astray
either to nihilism or positivism.

45. "No" is not necessarily "No", nor is "Yes" "Yes";
But when you miss even a tenth of an inch, the difference widens up to one thousand miles;
When it is "Yes", a young Naga girl in an instant
attains Buddhahood,
When it is "No", the most learned Zensho[1] while alive
falls into hell.

46. Since early years I have been eagerly after scholarly
attainment,
I have studied the sutras and sastras and commentaries,
I have been given up to the analysis of names and
forms, and never known what fatigue meant;
But diving into the ocean to count up its sands is surely
an exhausting task and a vain one;

[1] Shang-hsing, lit. "good star", was a great scholar of his age.

The Buddha has never spared such, his scoldings are
   just to the point,
For what is the use of reckoning the treasures that are
   not mine?
All my past achievements have been efforts vainly and
   wrongly applied—I realize it fully now,
I have been a vagrant monk for many years to no end
   whatever.

47. When the notion of the original family is not properly
      understood,
    You never attain to the understanding of the Buddha's
      perfect "abrupt" system;
    The two Vehicles exert themselves enough, but lack
      the aspirations [of the Bodhisattva];
    The philosophers are intelligent enough but wanting
      in Prajna;
    [As to the rest of us,] they are either ignorant or puerile;
    They take an empty fist as containing something real,
      and the pointing finger for the object pointed;
    When the finger is adhered to as the moon itself, all
      their efforts are lost;
    They are indeed idle dreamers lost in a world of senses
      and objects.

48. The Tathagata is interviewed when one enters upon
      a realm of no-forms,
    Such is to be really called a Kwanjizai (Avalokites-
      vara):
    When this is understood, the karma-hindrances are by
      nature empty;
    When not understood, we all pay for the past debts
      contracted.

49. A royal table is set before the hungry, but they refuse
      to eat;
    If the sick turn away from a good physician, how are
      they cured?

Practise Zen while in a world of desires, and the
genuine power of intuition is manifested;
When the lotus blooms in the midst of a fire, it is never
destroyed.
Yuse (Yung-shih) the Bhikshu[1] was an offender in
one of the gravest crimes, but when he had an
enlightened insight into No-birth
He instantly attained to Buddhahood and is still living
in another world.

50. The doctrine of fearlessness is taught as loudly as a
lion roars:
What a pity that confused minds inflexibly hardened
like leather
Understand only that grave offences are obstructions
to Enlightenment,
And are unable to see into the secrets of the Tathagata's
teaching.

51. Anciently, there were two Bhikshus, the one committing murder and the other a carnal offence:
Upali's insight was like that of the glowworm, and
ended only in tightening the knots of offence;
But when they were instantly enlightened by the
wisdom of Vimalakirti,
Their griefs and doubts melted away like the frost and
snow before the blazing sun.

52. The power of incomprehensible emancipation
Works wonders as innumerable as the sands of the
Ganga and knows no limits;
[To him] the four kinds of offerings are most willingly
made,
By him thousands of pieces of gold are disbursed
without involving anybody in debts;
The bones may be crushed to powders, the body cut

---

[1] The story of this Bhikshu is told in the *Sutra on Cleansing the Karma-
hindrances* (*Ching Yeh-chang Ching*).

up to pieces, and yet we cannot repay him enough
for what he does for us;
Even a phrase [issuing from him] holds true for
hundreds of thousands of kotis of kalpas.

53. He is the Dharma-king deserving the highest respect;
The Tathagatas, as many in number as the Ganga-
sands, all testify to the truth of his attainment;
I now understand what this *mani*-jewel is,
And know that all those who accept it in faith are in
correspondence [with it].

54. As to seeing it, the seeing is clear enough, but no objects
are here to be seen,
Not a person here, nor the Buddha;
Chiliocosms numberless are mere bubbles in the ocean,
All the sages and worthies are flashes of lightning.

55. However rapidly revolves the iron-wheel over my
head,
The perfect brightness of Dhyana and Prajna in me
is never effaced;
The sun may turn cold and the moon hot;
With all the power of the evil ones the true doctrine
remains forever indestructible.
The elephant-carriage steadily climbs up the steepest
hill,
Before whose wheels how can the beetle stand?

56. The great elephant does not walk on the hare's lane,
Supreme Enlightenment goes beyond the narrow range
of intellection;
Cease from measuring heaven with a tiny piece of
reed;
If you have no insight yet, I will have the matter
settled for you.

V

Baso (Ma-tsu) and Sekito (Shih-t'ou), Two Great Masters of the T'ang Dynasty

Ma-tsu (Baso) whose posthumous title was the Zen Master of Great Quietude (*ta-chi*) was to be properly called Tao-i (Doichi). His family name was Ma, from the district of Han-chou. His teaching which was originally propagated in the province of Chiang-hsi proved of great influence in the Buddhist world of the time, and he came to be generally known as Ma the Father, that, Ma-tsu.

Historically, Zen Buddhism was introduced to China by an Indian monk called Bodhidharma during the South- and North Dynasties, probably late in the fifth century. But it was not until the time of Hui-neng and Shen-hsiu that Bodhidharma was recognized as the first patriarch of Zen Buddhism in China; for this was the time when Zen to be properly so called came to establish itself as one of the strong Buddhist movements created by Chinese religious genius. The movement firmly took root with Ma-tsu (–788) and Shih-t'ou (700–790). The latter had his monastery in the province of Hu-nan, and thus Hu-nan and Chiang-hsi became the hot-bed of the Zen movement. All the followers of Zen in China as well as in Japan at present trace back their lineage to these two masters of the T'ang.

Shih-t'ou (Sekito) whose family name was Chen came from the district of Tuan-chou. His other name was Hsi-ch'ien. While still young, his religious feeling was strongly stirred against a barbarous custom which was practised among the Liao race. The custom consisted in sacrificing bulls in order to appease the wrath of the evil spirits which were worshipped by the people. Shih-t'ou destroyed many such shrines dedicated to the spirits and saved the victims. He probably acted quite decisively and convincingly so that even the elders of his village failed to prevent him from so rashly working against popular superstitions. He later embraced Buddhism, becoming a disciple of Hui-neng. The latter however died before this young man had been formally ordained as a Buddhist monk. He then went to Hsing-ssu (–740), of Chi-chou and studied Zen Buddhism. Hsing-ssu like Nan-yueh Huai-jang who was the teacher of Ma-tsu, was also a disciple of Hui-neng.

Before quoting Ma-tsu, let me acquaint you with some of Shih-t'ou's questions-and-answers (*mondo*=*wen-to*) as recorded in the *Transmission of the Lamp*.

Hsing-ssu one day asked: "Some say that an intelligence comes from the south of the Ling."

T'ou: "There is no such intelligence from anybody."

Ssu: "If not, whence are all those sutras of the Tripi-taka?"

T'ou: "They all come out of here, and there is nothing wanting."

Shih-t'ou, "Stone-head", gains his name because of his having a hut over the flat surface of a rock in his monastery grounds in Heng-chou. He once gave the following sermon: "My teaching which has come down from the ancient Buddhas is not dependent on meditation (*dhyana*) or on diligent application of any kind. When you attain the insight as attained by the Buddha, you realize that Mind is Buddha and Buddha is Mind, that Mind, Buddha, sentient beings, Bodhi (enlightenment), and Klesa (passions) are of one and the same substance while they vary in names. You should know that your own mind-essence is neither subject to annihilation nor eternally subsisting, is neither pure nor defiled, that it remains perfectly undisturbed and self-sufficient and the same with the wise and the ignorant, that it is not limited in its working, and that it is not included in the category of mind (*citta*), consciousness (*manas*), or thought (*vijnana*). The three worlds of desire, form, and no-form, and the six paths of existence are no more than manifestations of your mind itself. They are all like the moon reflected in water or images in the mirror. How can we speak of them as being born or as passing away? When you come to this understanding, you will be furnished with all the things you are in need of."

Tao-wu, one of Shih-t'ou's disciples, then asked: "Who has attained to the understanding of Hui-neng's teaching?"

T'ou: "The one who understands Buddhism."

Wu: "Have you then attained it?"

T'ou: "No, I do not understand Buddhism."

A monk asked: "How does one get emancipated?"

The master said: "Who has ever put you in bondage?"

Monk: "What is the Pure Land?"

Master: "Who has ever defiled you?"

Monk: "What is Nirvana?"

Master: "Who has ever subjected you to birth-and-death?"

Shih-t'ou asked a monk newly arrived: "Where do you come from?"

"From Chiang-hsi."

"Did you see Ma the great teacher?"

"Yes, master."

Shih-t'ou then pointed at a bundle of kindlings and said: "How does Ma the teacher resemble this?"

The monk made no answer. Returning to Ma the teacher, he reported the interview with Shih-t'ou. Ma asked: "Did you notice how large the bundle was?"

"An immensely large one it was."

"You are a very strong man indeed."

"How?" asked the monk.

"Because you have carried that huge bundle from Nan-yueh even up to this monastery. Only a strong man can accomplish such a feat."

A monk asked: "What is the meaning of the First Patriarch's coming from the West?"

Master: "Ask the post over there."

Monk: "I do not understand you."
Master: "I do not either, any more than you."

Ta-tien asked: "According to an ancient sage it is a dualism to take the Tao either as existing or as not-existing. Please tell me how to remove this obstruction."

"Not a thing here, and what do you wish to remove?"

Shih-t'ou turned about and demanded: "Do away with your throat and lips, and let me see what you can say."

Said Ta-tien, "No such things have I."

"If so, you may enter the gate."

Tao-wu asked: "What is the ultimate teaching of Buddhism?"

"You won't understand it until you have it."

"Is there anything over and above it whereby one may have a new turn?"

"Boundlessly expands the sky and nothing obstructs the white clouds from freely flying about."

"What is Zen?" asked a monk.

"Brick and stone."

"What is the Tao?"

"A block of wood."

[1]Someone asked Ma-tsu: "How does a man discipline himself in the Tao?"

The master replied: "In the Tao there is nothing to discipline oneself in. If there is any discipline in it, the completion of such discipline means the destruction of the Tao. One then will be like the Sravaka. But if there is no discipline whatever in the Tao, one remains an ignoramus."

"By what kind of understanding does a man attain the Tao?"

On this, the master gave the following sermon:

"The Tao in its nature is from the first perfect and

[1] The following *mondo* are all taken from a book known as *Sayings of the Ancient Worthies*, fas. I (*Ku tsun-hsiu yu-lu*).

self-sufficient. When a man finds himself unhalting in his management of the affairs of life good or bad, he is known as one who is disciplined in the Tao. To shun evils and to become attached to things good, to meditate on Emptiness and to enter into a state of samadhi—this is doing something. If those who run after an outward object, they are the farthest away [from the Tao].

Only let a man exhaust all his thinking and imagining he can possibly have in the triple world. When even an iota of imagination is left with him, this is his triple world and the source of birth and death in it. When there is not a trace of imagination, he has removed all the source of birth and death, he then holds the unparalleled treasure belonging to the Dharmaraja. All the imagination harboured since the beginningless past by an ignorant being, together with his falsehood, flattery, self-conceit, arrogance, and other evil passions, are united in the body of One Essence, and all melt away.

"It is said in the sutra that many elements combine themselves to make this body of ours, and that the rising of the body merely means the rising together of all these elements and the disappearance of the body means also merely that of the elements. When the latter rise, they do not declare that they are now to rise; when they disappear they do not declare that they are now to disappear.

So with thoughts, one thought follows another without interruption, the preceding one does not wait for the succeeding, each one is self-contained and quiescent. This is called the Sagaramudra-samadhi, "Meditation of the Ocean-stamp", in which are included all things, like the ocean where all the rivers however different in size, etc., empty themselves. In this great ocean of one salt-water, all the waters in it partake of one and the same taste. A man living in it diffuses himself in all the streams pouring into it. A man bathing in the great ocean uses all the waters emptied into it.

"The Sravaka is enlightened and yet going astray; the ordinary man is out of the right path and yet in a way enlightened. The Sravaka fails to perceive that Mind as it is in itself knows no stages, no causation, no imaginations. Disciplining himself in the cause he has attained the result and abides in the Samadhi of Emptiness itself for ever so many kalpas. However enlightened in his way, the Sravaka is not at all on the right track. From the point of view of the Bodhisattva, this is like suffering the torture of hell. The Sravaka has buried himself in emptiness and does not know how to get out of his quiet contemplation, for he has no insight into the Buddha-nature itself.

"If a man is of superior character and intelligence he will, under the instruction of a wise director, at once see into the essence of the thing and understand that this is not a matter of stages and processes. He has an instant insight into his own Original Nature. So we read in the sutra that ordinary beings change in their thoughts but the Sravaka knows no such changes [which means that he never comes out of his meditation of absolute quietude].

" 'Going astray' stands against 'being enlightened'; but when there is primarily no going astray there is no being enlightened either. All beings since the beginningless past have never been outside the Dharma-essence itself; abiding for ever in the midst of the Dharma-essence, they eat, they are clothed, they talk, they respond; all the functioning of the six senses, all their doings are of the Dharma-essence itself. When they fail to understand to go back to the Source they follow names, pursue forms, allow confusing imaginations to rise, and cultivate all kinds of karma. Let them once in one thought return to the Source and their entire being will be of Buddha-mind.

"O monks, let each of you see into his own Mind. Do not memorize what I tell you. However eloquently I may talk about all kinds of things as innumerable as the sands of the Ganges, the Mind shows no increase; even when no talk is possible, the Mind shows no decrease. You may talk ever so much about it, and it is still your own Mind; you may not at all talk about it, and it is just the same your own Mind. You may divide your body into so many forms, and emitting rays of supernatural light perform the eighteen miracles, and yet what you have gained is after all no more than your own dead ashes.

"The dead ashes thoroughly wet have no vitality and are likened to the Sravaka's disciplining himself in the cause in order to attain its result. The dead ashes not yet wet are full of vitality and are likened to the Bodhisattva, whose life in the Tao is pure and not at all dyed in evils. If I begin to talk about the various teachings given out by the Tathagata, there will be no end however long through ages I may go on. They are like an endless series of chains. But once you have an insight into the Buddha-mind, nothing more is left to you to attain.

"I have kept you standing long enough, fare you well!"

P'ang the lay-disciple[1] asked one day when Ma-tsu appeared in the pulpit: "Here is the Original Body altogether unbedimmed! Raise your eyes to it!" Ma-tsu looked straight downward. Said P'ang, "How beautifully the master plays on the first-class stringless lute!" The master looked straight up. P'ang made a bow, and the master returned to his own room. P'ang followed him and said, "A while ago you made a fool of yourself, did you not?"

Someone asked: "What is the Buddha?"
"Mind is the Buddha, and there's no other."

A monk asked: "Without resorting to the four statements and an endless series of negations, can you tell me straightway what is the idea of our Patriarch's coming from the West?"

The master said: "I don't feel like answering it today. You go to the Western Hall and ask Shih-tsang about it."

The monk went to the Western Hall and saw the priest, who pointing at his head with a finger said, "My head aches today and I am unable to explain it to you today. I advise you to go to Brother Hai."

---

[1] Ho-koji in Japanese. He was one of the greatest disciples of Ma, and for further quotations see my *Essays on Zen*, I, II, and III.

The monk now called on Hai, and Hai said: "As to that I do not understand."

The monk finally returned to the master and told him about his adventure. Said the master: "Tsang's head is black while Hai's is white."

A monk asked: "Why do you teach that Mind is no other than Buddha?"

"In order to make a child stop its crying."

"When the crying is stopped, what would you say?"

"Neither Mind nor Buddha."

"What teaching would you give to him who is not in these two groups?"

"I will say, 'It is not a something.' "

"If you unexpectedly interview a person who is in it what would you do?" finally, asked the monk.

"I will let him realize the great Tao."

The master asked Pai-chang, one of his chief disciples: "How would you teach others?"

Pai-chang raised his *hossu*.

The master remarked, "Is that all? No other way?"

Pai-chang threw the *hossu* down.

A monk asked: "How does a man set himself in harmony with the Tao?"

"I am already out of harmony."

Tan-yuan, one of Ma-tsu's personal disciples, came back from his pilgrimage. When he saw the master, he drew a circle on the floor and after making bows stood on it facing the master. Said Ma-tsu: "So you wish to become a Buddha?"

The monk said: "I do not know the art of putting my own eyes out of focus."

"I am not your equal."

The monk had no answer.

·   ·   ·   ·   ·

One day in the first month of the fourth year of Chen-yuan (788), while walking in the woods at Shih-men Shan, Ma-tsu noticed a cave with a flat floor. He said to his attendant monk, "My body subject to decomposition will return to earth here in the month to come." On the fourth of the second month, he was indisposed as he predicted, and after a bath he sat cross-legged and passed away.

VI

HUANG-PO'S SERMON, FROM "TREATISE ON THE ESSENTIALS OF THE TRANSMISSION OF MIND" (DENSHIN HOYO)

The master[1] said to Pai-hsiu:

Buddhas and sentient beings[2] both grow out of One Mind, and there is no other reality than this Mind. It has been in existence since the beginningless past; it knows neither birth nor death; it is neither blue nor yellow; it has neither shape nor form; it is beyond the category of being and non-being; it is not to be measured by age, old or new; it is neither long nor short; it is neither large nor small; for it transcends all limits, words, traces, and opposites. It must be taken just as it is in itself; when an attempt is made on our part to grasp it in our thoughts, it eludes. It is like space whose boundaries are altogether beyond measurement; no concepts are applicable here.

[1] Wobaku Ki-un in Japanese, died 850.

[2] One of the first lessons in the understanding of Buddhism is to know what is meant by the Buddha and by sentient beings. This distinction goes on throughout all branches of the Buddhist teaching. The Buddha is an enlightened one who has seen into the reason of existence, while sentient beings are ignorant multitudes confused in mind and full of defilements. The object of Buddhism is to have all sentient beings attain enlightenment like the Buddha. The question is whether they are of the same nature as the latter; for if not they can never be enlightened as he is. The spiritual cleavage between the two being seemingly too wide for passage, it is often doubted whether there is anything in sentient beings that will transform them into Buddhahood. The position of Zen Buddhism is that One Mind pervades all and therefore there is no distinction to be made between the Buddha and sentient beings and that as far as Mind is concerned the two are of one nature. What then is this Mind? Huang-po attempts to solve this question for his disciple Pai-hsiu in these sermons.

This One Mind only is the Buddha, who is not to be segregated from sentient beings. But because we seek it outwardly in a world of form, the more we seek the further it moves away from us. To make Buddha seek after himself, or to make Mind take hold of itself—this is an impossibility to the end of eternity. We do not realize that as soon as our thoughts cease and all attempts at forming ideas are forgotten the Buddha reveals himself before us.

This Mind is no other than the Buddha, and Buddha is no other than sentient being. When Mind assumes the form of a sentient being, it has suffered no decrease; when it becomes a Buddha, it has not added anything to itself. Even when we speak of the six virtues of perfection (*paramitas*) and other ten thousand meritorious deeds equal in number to the sands of the Ganges, they are all in the being of Mind itself; they are not something that can be added to it by means of discipline. When conditions[1] are at work, it is set up; when conditions cease to operate, it remains quiet. Those who have no definite faith in this, that Mind is Buddha and attempt an achievement by means of a discipline attached to form, are giving themselves up to wrong imagination; they deviate from the right path.

This Mind is no other than Buddha; there is no Buddha outside Mind, nor is there any Mind outside Buddha. This Mind is pure and like space has no specific forms [whereby it can be distinguished from other objects]. As soon as you raise a thought and begin to form an idea of it, you ruin the reality itself, because you then attach yourself to form. Since the beginningless past, there is no Buddha who has ever had an attachment to form. If you seek Buddhahood by practising the six virtues of perfection and other ten thousand deeds of merit, this is grading [the attainment of Buddhahood]; but since the beginningless past there is no Buddha whose attainment was so graded. When you get an insight into the One Mind you find there that is no particular reality

---

[1] *Yuan* in Chinese and *pratyaya* in Sanskrit. One of the most significant technical terms in the philosophy of Buddhism.

[which you can call Mind]. This unattainability is no other than the true Buddha himself.

Buddhas and sentient beings grow out of the One Mind and there are no differences between them. It is like space where there are no complexities, nor is it subject to destruction. It is like the great sun which illumines the four worlds: when it rises, its light pervades all over the world, but space itself gains thereby no illumination. When the sun sets, darkness reigns everywhere, but space itself does not share this darkness. Light and darkness drive each other out and alternately prevail, but space itself is vast emptiness and suffers no vicissitudes.

The same may be said of the Mind that constitutes the essence of Buddha as well as that of sentient being. When you take Buddha for a form of purity, light, and emancipation and sentient beings for a form of defilement, darkness, and transmigration, you will never have the occasion however long [your striving may go on] for attaining enlightenment; for so long as you adhere to this way of understanding, you are attached to form. And in this One Mind there is not a form of particularity to lay your hand on.

That Mind is no other than Buddha is not understood by Buddhists of the present day; and because of their inability of seeing into the Mind as it is, they imagine a mind beside Mind itself and seek Buddha outwardly after a form. This way of disciplining is an error, is not the way of enlightenment.

It is better to make offerings to a spiritual man who is free from mind-attachment[1] than to make offerings to all

---

[1] *Wu-hsin,* or *mu-shin* in Japanese. The term literally means "no-mind" or "no-thought". It is very difficult to find an English word corresponding to it. "Unconsciousness" approaches it, but the connotation is too psychological. *Mushin* is decidedly an Oriental idea. "To be free from mind-attachment" is somewhat circumlocutionary, but the idea is briefly to denote that state of consciousness in which there is no hankering, conscious or unconscious, after an ego-substance, or a soul-entity, or a mind as forming the structural unit of our mental life. Buddhism considers this hankering the source of all evils moral and intellectual. It is the disturbing agency not only of an individual life but of social life at large. A special article in one of my *Zen Essays* will be devoted to the subject.

the Buddhas in the ten quarters. Why? Because to be free from mind-attachment means to be free from all forms of imagination.

Suchness as it expresses itself inwardly may be likened to wood or rock, it remains there unmoved, unshaken; while outwardly it is like space, nothing is obstructed or checked. Suchness, as it is free both from activity and passivity, knows no orientation, it has no form, there is in it neither gain nor loss. Those who are running [wildly] do not dare enter this path, for they are afraid of falling into an emptiness where there is no foothold to keep them supported. They beat a retreat as they face it. They are as a rule seekers of learning and intellectual understanding. Many are indeed such seekers, like hair, while those who see into the truth are as few as horns.

Manjusri corresponds to *li* (reason or principle) and Samantabhadra to *hsing* (life or action). *Li* is the principle of true emptiness and non-obstruction, *hsing* is a life of detachment from form, and inexhaustible. Avalokitesvara corresponds to perfect love and Sthamaprapta to perfect wisdom. Vimalakirti means "undefiled name"; undefiled is Essence and name is form. Essence and form are not two different things, hence the name Vimala-kirti ("pure-name"). All that is represented by each one of the great Bodhisattvas is present in each of us, for it is the contents of One Mind. All will be well when we are awakened to the truth.

Buddhists of the present day look outward, instead of inwardly into their own minds. They get themselves attached to forms and to the world—which is the violation of the truth.

To the sands of the Ganges the Buddha refers in this way: these sands are trodden and passed over by all the Buddhas, Bodhisattvas, Sakrendra, and other devas, but the sands are not thereby gladdened; they are again trodden by cattle, sheep, insects, and ants, but they are not thereby incensed; they may hide within themselves all kinds of treasures and scented substances, but they are not covetous;

they may be soiled with all kinds of filth and ill-smelling material, but they do not loathe them. A mental attitude of this nature is that of one who has realized the state of *mushin* ("being free from mind-attachment").

When a mind is free from all form, it sees into [the fact] that there is no distinction between Buddhas and sentient beings; when once this state of *mushin* is attained it completes the Buddhist life. If Buddhists are unable to see into the truth of *mushin* without anything mediating, all their discipline of aeons would not enable them to attain enlightenment. They would ever be in bondage with the notion of discipline and merit as cherished by followers of the Triple Vehicle, they would never achieve emancipation.

In the attainment of this state of mind (*mushin*), some are quicker than others. There are some who attain to a state of *mushin* all at once by just listening to a discourse on the Dharma, while there are others who attain to it only after going through all the grades of Bodhisattvaship such as the ten stages of faith, the ten stages of abiding, the ten stages of discipline, and the ten stages of turning-over. More or less time may be required in the attainment of *mushin*, but once attained it puts an end to all discipline, to all realization and yet there is really nothing attained. It is truth and not falsehood. Whether this *mushin* is attained in one thought or attained after going through the ten stages its practical working is the same and there is no question of the one being deeper or shallower than the other. Only the one has passed through long ages of hard discipline.

Committing evils or practising goodness—both are the outcome of attachment to form. When evils are committed on account of attachment to form, one has to suffer transmigration; when goodness is practised on account of attachment to form, one has to go through a life of hardships. It is better therefore to see all at once into the essence of the Dharma as you listen to it discoursed.

By the Dharma is meant Mind, for there is no Dharma apart from Mind. Mind is no other than the Dharma, for there is no Mind apart from the Dharma. This Mind in

itself is no-mind (*mushin*), and there is no no-mind either.
When no-mind is sought after by a mind, this is making it
a particular object of thought. There is only testimony of
silence, it goes beyond thinking. Therefore it is said that
[the Dharma] cuts off the passage to words and puts an end
to all form of mentation.

This Mind is the Source, the Buddha absolutely pure
in its nature, and is present in every one of us. All sentient
beings however mean and degraded are not in this particular
respect different from Buddhas and Bodhisattvas—they are
all of one substance. Only because of their imaginations and
false discriminations, sentient beings work out their karma
and reap its result, while, in their Buddha-essence itself,
there is nothing corresponding to it; the Essence is empty and
allows everything to pass through, it is quiet and at rest, it is
illuminating, it is peaceful and productive of bliss.

When you have within yourself a deep insight into this
you immediately realize that all that you need is there in
perfection, and in abundance, and nothing is at all wanting
in you. You may have most earnestly and diligently disciplined yourself for the past three asamkhyeya kalpas and
passed through all the stages of Bodhisattvahood; but when
you come to have a realization in one thought, it is no other
than this that you are from the first the Buddha himself and
no other. The realization has not added anything to you
over this truth. When you look back and survey all the
disciplinary measures you have gone through, you only find
that they have been no more than so many idle doings in a
dream. Therefore, it is told by the Tathagata that he had
nothing attained when he had enlightenment, and that if he
had really something attained, Buddha Dipankara would
never have testified to it.

It is told again by the Tathagata that this Dharma is
perfectly even and free from irregularities. By Dharma is
meant Bodhi. That is, this pure Mind forming the source of
all things is perfectly even in all sentient beings, in all the
Buddha-lands, and also in all the other worlds together with
mountains, oceans, etc., things with form and things without

form. They are all even, and there are no marks of distinction between this object and that. This pure Mind, the Source of all things, is always perfect and illuminating and all-pervading. People are ignorant of this and take what they see or hear or think of or know for Mind itself; and their insight is then veiled and unable to penetrate into the substance itself which is clear and illuminating. When you realize *mushin* without anything intervening [that is, intuitively], the substance itself is revealed to you. It is like the sun revealing itself in the sky, its illumination penetrates the ten quarters and there is nothing that will interfere with its passage.

For this reason, when followers of Zen fail to go beyond a world of their senses and thoughts, all their doings and movements are of no significance. But when the senses and thoughts are annihilated, all the passages to the Mind are blocked and no entrance then becomes possible. The original Mind is to be recognized along with the working of the senses and thoughts, only it does not belong to them, nor is it independent of them. Do not build up your views on your senses and thoughts, do not carry on your understanding based on the senses and thoughts; but at the same time do not seek the Mind away from your senses and thoughts, do not grasp the Dharma by rejecting your senses and thoughts. When you are neither attached to nor detached from them, when you are neither abiding with nor clinging to them, then you enjoy your perfect unobstructed freedom, then you have your seat of enlightenment.

When people learn that what is transmitted from one Buddha to another is Mind itself, they imagine that there is a particular object known as a mind which they attempt to grasp or to realize; but this is seeking something outside Mind itself, or creating something which does not exist. In reality, Mind alone is. You cannot pursue it by setting up another mind; however long, through hundreds of thousands of kalpas, you are after it, no time will ever come to you when you can say that you have it. Only when you have an immediate awakening to the state of *mushin* you have your own Mind. It is like the strong man's seeking for his own gem hidden within his forehead : as long as he seeks it outside himself in the ten quarters, he will not come across it; but let the wise once point at it where it lies hidden, and the man instantly perceives his own gem as having been there from the very first.

That followers of Zen fail to recognize the Buddha is due to their not rightly recognizing where their own Mind is. They seek it outwardly, set up all kinds of exercises which they hope to master by degrees, and themselves work out diligently throughout ages. Yet they fail to reach enlightenment. No works compare with an immediate awakening to a state of *mushin* itself.

When you come to a most decided understanding to the effect that all things in their nature are without possessions, without attainments, without dependence, without an abiding place, without mutual conditioning, you will become free from cherishing imagination, which is to realize Bodhi. When Bodhi is realized, your own Mind which is Buddha is realized. All the doings of long ages are then found to have been anything but real disciplining. When the strong man recovered his own gem in his own forehead the recovery had nothing to do with all his efforts wasted in his outside research. So says the Buddha, "I have not had anything attained in my attainment of Enlightenment." Being anxious about our not believing this, he refers to the five eyes[1] and the five statements.[2] But it is truth, not falsehood, for it is the first true statement.

---

[1] The five eyes are: (1) the physical eye, (2) the heavenly eye, (3) the eye of wisdom, (4) the eye of the Dharma, and (5) the eye of the Buddha.

[2] In the *Diamond Sutra* (*Vajracchedika*), the Buddha makes five statements as regards the truth of his teaching.

VII

GENSHA ON THE THREE INVALIDS[1]

Preliminary Remark

When gates and courts are established, then there are
twos, there are threes, there is a realm of multiplicities;
when a deep discourse is carried on on the highest subjects
of intuition a world of sevens and eights is thoroughly broken
through. In whatever ways views and opinions may be
presented, they are crushed to pieces so that the barricades
even when they are of golden chains are successfully brushed
aside. When orders are given from the highest quarters, all
traces are wiped off, leaving nothing whereby trailing is
made possible. When do we come across such a *koan*? Let
one who has an eye on the forehead see to it.[2]

Illustrative Case

Gensha gave the following sermon:
"It is asserted by all the worthy masters of the present
time that they are working for the benefit of all beings.
[—Each keeps a shop according to his means.—Some are
rich and others are poor.]

"This being the case, what will you do if there suddenly
appear before you three kinds of invalids? [—By beating
up the weeds, we mean to frighten snakes out.—As for me,
it makes my eyes open wide and my mouth close.—We all
have to beat a retreat even for three thousand *li*.]

"Those who are blind fail to see you even when you

---

[1] Hsuan-sha, 835–908. The following is a literal translation of Case
LXXXVIII of the *Pi-yen Chi*, which is one of the most important and at the
same time the most popular of Zen texts. The words in brackets in the "Illus-
trative Case" and in Seccho's verse are those of Yengo. As to the nature and
composition of the *Pi-yen Chi*, see my *Zen Essays*, Series II, p. 237 et seq.

[2] The Remark purposes to make the reader abandon his usual relative point
of view so that he can reach the absolute ground of all things.

hold up a mallet or a *hossu*. [—Blind to the very core.—
This is no other than 'benefiting all beings'.—Not necessarily failing to see.]

"Those who are deaf fail to hear you even when
you talk volubly enough. [—Deaf to the very core!—This
is no other than 'benefiting all beings'.—Not necessarily
altogether deaf.—That something is still unheard.]

"Those who are dumb fail to speak out, whatever understanding they may have inwardly. [—Dumb to the very
core!—This is no other than 'benefiting all beings'.—Not
necessarily altogether dumb.—That something is still left
untold of.]

"What treatment are you going to accord to such
people? If you do not know how to go on with them,
Buddhism must be said to be lacking in miraculous works."
[—Quite true, this world—I am ready to give myself up
with my hands folded.—"Benefiting" already accom-
plished!—"He then struck."]

A monk asked Ummon (Yun-men) to be enlightened.
[—It is also important to go about and inquire.—Hit!]

Said Ummon, "You make bows." [—As the wind blows,
the grass bends.—Ch'ua!]

When the monk rose from making bows, [—This monk's
staff is broken!]

Ummon poked him with a staff, and the monk drew
back. Said Ummon, "You are not blind then?" [—Blind
to the very core!—Do not say that this monk has a failing
eye-sight.]

Ummon now told him to approach, and the monk
approached. [—Washed with a second dipperful of dirty
water.—Kwan-non is come! To give a "*Kwatz*!" was better.]

Said Ummon, "You are not deaf then?" [—Deaf to
the very core!—Do not say that this monk is deaf in his ears.]

Ummon further continued, "Do you understand?"
[—Why does he not feed him with the right forage?—Pity
that he then uttered a word at all.]

"No, master, I do not," was the reply. [—A double
koan!—What a pity!]

Ummon said, "You are not dumb then?" [—Dumb to the very core!—What eloquence!—Do not say that this monk is dumb.]

The monk now grasped the point. [—Stretching the bow when the burglar is off.—What old bowl is he after?]

Commentary Notes

Gensha gives this sermon from his standpoint where he is now able to sit, after years of his study of Zen, in absolute nakedness with no trumpery trimmings about him, altogether shorn of imaginations and free from conceptualism. In those days there were many Zen monasteries each of which rivalled the others. Gensha used to give this sermon to his monks:

"It is asserted by all the worthy masters of the present time that they are working for the benefit of all beings. This being the case, what will you do if three kinds of invalids suddenly appear before you here? Those who are blind fail to see you even when you hold up a mallet or a *hossu*. Those who are deaf fail to hear you even when you may talk volubly enough. Those who are dumb fail to speak out whatever understanding they may have inwardly. What treatment are you going to accord to such people? If you do not know how to go on with them, Buddhism must be said to be lacking in miraculous works."

If people understand him here as merely making reference to the blind, to the deaf, to the dumb, they are vainly groping in the dark. Therefore, it is said that you are not to search for the meaning in the words which kill; you are requested to enter directly into the spirit itself of Gensha, when you will grasp the meaning.

As Gensha ordinarily tested his monks with this statement, a monk who was staying for some time with him one day accosted him when he came up to the Dharma-hall, and asked: "Will you allow me to present my way of reasoning about your sermon on the three invalids?" Gensha said, "Yes, you may go on." Whereupon the monk remarked,

"Fare thee well, O master!" and left the room. Gensha said, "Not that, not that." We can see that this monk has fully grasped Gensha.

Later on, Hogen (Fa-yen, died 958) made this statement: "When I listened to Master Jizo (Ti-tsang) making reference to this monk's remark, I was enabled to understand Gensha's sermon on the three invalids."

I ask you now. "[Here is a puzzle for you, O monks!] If that monk did not understand Gensha, how was it that Hogen made this statement of his? If that monk understood Gensha, why did the latter declare, 'Not that, not that'?"

One day Jizo said to Gensha, "I am told that you have given a sermon on the three invalids, is that so?" Gensha answered, "Yes." Jizo then said, "I have my eyes, ears, nose, and tongue; what treatment would you give me?" Gensha was quite satisfied with this request on the part of Jizo.

When Gensha is understood, you will realize that his spirit is not to be sought in words. You will also see that those who understand make themselves naturally distinguishable from the rest.

Later when a monk came to Ummon (Yun-men, died 949) and asked him about Gensha's sermon, Ummon was ready to demonstrate it in the following way, for he thoroughly understood Gensha. Said Ummon to the monk, "You make bows." When the monk rose from making bows, Ummon poked him with a staff, and the monk drew back. Said Ummon, "You are not blind then?" Ummon now told him to approach, and the monk approached. Said Ummon, "You are not deaf then?" Finally, he said, "Do you understand?" "No, master," being the reply, Ummon remarked, "You are not dumb then?" This made the monk grasp the point.

If this monk of Ummon's had any sort of understanding about Gensha, he would have kicked up the master's chair when he was told to make bows, and no more fussing would have been necessary. In the meantime let me ask you whether Ummon and Gensha both understood the problem in the same way, or not. I tell you that their understanding is directed to one point. That the ancient masters come out among us and make all kinds of contrivance is because they wish to see somebody bite their hook and be caught up. They thus make bitter remarks in order to have us see into the great event of this life.

My own master Goso (Wu-tsu, died 1104) had this to say: "Here is one who can talk well but has no understanding; here is another who understands but is unable to talk about it. When these two present themselves before you, how will you distinguish the one from the other? If you cannot make this discrimination, you cannot expect to free people from their bondage and attachment. But when you can, I will see to it that, as soon as you enter my gate, I put on a pair of sandals and run through the inside of your body several times even before you realize. In case, however, you fail to have an insight in this matter, what is the use of hunting around for an old bowl? Better be gone!"

Do you wish to know what is the ultimate meaning of these complications in regard to the blind, deaf, and dumb? Let us see what Seccho says about it.

Seccho's Remarks in Verse

Blind, deaf, dumb! [—Even before any word is uttered. —The three sense-organs are perfectly sound.— Already finished is one paragraph!]
Infinitely beyond the reach of imaginative contrivances! [—Where do you wish to hunt for it?—Is there anything here which permits your calculations?— What relationship have they after all?]
Above the heavens and below the heavens! [—Perfectly free is the working of Truth.—Thou hast said!]
How ludicrous! How disheartening! [—What is it that is so ludicrous, so disheartening?—Partly bright and partly dark.]
Li-lou does not know how to discriminate the right colour. [—Blind fellow!—A good craftsman leaves no trace.—Blind to the very core!]

How can Shih-k'uang recognize the mysterious tune?
[—Deaf in his ears!—There is no way to appreciate
the greatest merit.—Deaf to the very core!]
What life can compare with this?—Sitting alone quietly
by the window, [—This is the way to go on.—Do not
try to get your livelihood in a cave of ghosts.—Break
up all at once this cask of coal tar!]
I observe the leaves fall and the flowers bloom as the
seasons come and go. [—What season do you think
it is now?—Do not regard this as doing-nothing-
ness.—Today, morning is followed by evening; tomorrow, morning is followed by evening.]
Seccho now remarked: "Do you understand, or not?"
[—"Repeated in the gatha."]
An iron bar without a hole! [—Coming up with your
own confession!—Too bad that he was released too
easily,—"Then he struck."]

Yengo's Comment on Seccho

"Blind, deaf, dumb!
Infinitely beyond the reach of imaginative contrivances!"

In this, Seccho has swept everything away for you—
what you see together with what you do not see, what you
hear together with what you do not hear, and what you talk
about together with what you cannot talk about. All these
are completely brushed off, and you attain the life of the
blind, deaf, and dumb. Here all your imaginations, contrivances, and calculations are once for all put an end to, they
are no more made use of, this is where lies the highest point of
Zen, this is where we have true blindness, true deafness, and
true dumbness, each in its artless and effectless aspect.

"Above the heavens and below the heavens!
How ludicrous! how disheartening!"

Here Seccho lifts up with one hand and with the other
puts down. Tell me what he finds to be ludicrous, what he

finds to be disheartening. It is ludicrous that this dumb person is not after all dumb, that this deaf one is not after all deaf; it is disheartening that the one who is not at all blind is blind for all that, and that the one who is not at all deaf is deaf for all that.

"Li-lou does not know how to discriminate the right colour."

When he is unable to discriminate between blue and yellow, red and white, he is certainly a blind man. He lived in the reign of the Emperor Huang. He is said to have been able to discern the point of a soft hair at a distance of one hundred steps. His eye-sight was extraordinary. When the Emperor Huang had a pleasure-trip to the River Ch'ih, he dropped his precious jewel in the water and made Li fetch it up. But he failed. The Emperor made Ch'ih-kou search for it, but he also failed to locate it. Later Hsiang-wang was ordered to get it, and he got it. Hence:

"When Hsiang-wang goes down, the precious gem shines most brilliantly;
But where Li-lou walks about, the waves rise even to the sky."

When we come up to these higher spheres, even the eyes of Li-lou are incapacitated to distinguish which is the right colour.

"How can Shih-kuang recognize the mysterious tune?"

Shih-kuang was son of Ching-kuang of Chin in the province of Chiang in the Chou dynasty. His other name was Tzu-yeh. He could thoroughly distinguish the five sounds and the six notes, he could even hear the ants fight on the other side of a hill. When Chin and Ch'u were at war, Shih-kuang could tell, by merely quietly playing on the strings of his lute, that the engagement would surely be unfavourable for Ch'u. In spite of his extraordinary sensitiveness, Seccho (Hsueh-t'ou) declares that he is unable to recognize the mysterious tune. After all, one who is not at all deaf is really deaf in his ears. The most exquisite note in the higher spheres is indeed beyond the ear of Shih-kuang. Says Seccho: "I am not going to be a Li-lou, nor to be a Shih-kuang, but

"What life can compare with this?—Sitting alone
    quietly by the window,
  I observe the leaves fall, the flowers bloom as the
    seasons come and go."

When one attains this stage of realization, seeing is no-seeing, hearing is no-hearing, preaching is no-preaching. When hungry one eats, when tired one sleeps. Let the leaves fall, let the flowers bloom as they like. When the leaves fall, I know it is the autumn; when the flowers bloom, I know it is the spring. Each season has its own features.

Having swept everything clean before you, Seccho now opens a passageway, saying: "Do you understand, or not?" He has done all he could for you, he is exhausted, only able to turn about and present to you this iron-bar without a hole. It is a most significant expression. Look and see with your own eyes! If you hesitate, you miss the mark for ever.

Yengo (Yuan-wu, the author of this commentary note) now raised his *hossu* and said, "Do you see?" He then struck his chair and said, "Do you hear?" Coming down from the chair, he said, "Was anything talked about?"

VIII

The Ten Oxherding Pictures

Preliminary

The author of these "Ten Oxherding Pictures" is said to be a Zen master of the Sung Dynasty known as Kaku-an Shi-en (Kuo-an Shih-yuan) belonging to the Rinzai school. He is also the author of the poems and introductory words attached to the pictures. He was not however the first who attempted to illustrate by means of pictures stages of Zen discipline, for in his general preface to the pictures he refers to another Zen master called Seikyo (Ching-chu), probably a contemporary of his, who made use of the ox to explain his Zen teaching. But in Seikyo's case the gradual development of the Zen life was indicated by a progressive whitening of the animal, ending in the disappearance of the whole being. There were in this only five pictures, instead of ten as by Kaku-an. Kaku-an thought this was somewhat misleading because of an empty circle being made the goal of Zen discipline. Some might take mere emptiness as all important and final. Hence his improvement resulting in the "Ten Oxherding Pictures" as we have them now.

According to a commentator of Kaku-an's Pictures, there is another series of the Oxherding Pictures by a Zen master called Jitoku Ki (Tzu-te Hui), who apparently knew of the existence of the Five Pictures by Seikyo, for Jitoku's are six in number. The last one, No. 6, goes beyond the stage of absolute emptiness where Seikyo's end: the poem reads:

"Even beyond the ultimate limits there extends a
        passageway,
    Whereby he comes back among the six realms of
        existence;
    Every worldly affair is a Buddhist work,
    And wherever he goes he finds his home air;
    Like a gem he stands out even in the mud,
    Like pure gold he shines even in the furnace;
    Along the endless road [of birth and death] he
        walks sufficient unto himself,
    In whatever associations he is found he moves
        leisurely unattached."

Jitoku's ox grows whiter as Seikyo's, and in this particular respect both differ from Kaku-an's conception. In the latter there is no whitening process. In Japan Kaku-an's Ten Pictures gained a wide circulation, and at present all the oxherding books reproduce them. The earliest one belongs I think to the fifteenth century. In China however a different edition seems to have been in vogue, one belonging to the

I

Searching for the Ox

Plate II

II

Seeing the Traces

Plate III

III

Seeing the Ox

Plate IV

IV

Catching the Ox

Plate V

V

Herding the Ox

Plate VI

VI

Coming Home on the Ox's Back

Plate VII

VII

The Ox Forgotten, Leaving the Man Alone

Plate VIII

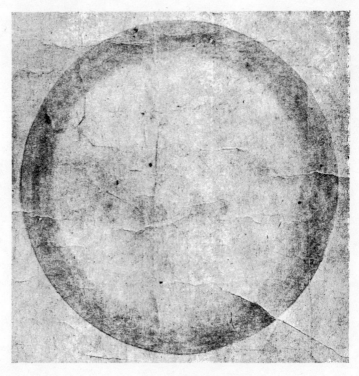

VIII

The Ox and the Man Both Gone out of Sight

Plate IX

IX

Returning to the Origin, Back to the Source

Plate X

X

Entering the City with Bliss-bestowing Hands

Plate XI

Seikyo and Jitoku series of pictures. The author is not known. The edition containing the preface by Chu-hung, 1585, has ten pictures, each of which is preceded by Pu-ming's poem. As to who this Pu-ming was, Chu-hung himself professes ignorance. In these pictures the ox's colouring changes together with the oxherd's management of him. The quaint original Chinese prints are reproduced below, and also Pu-ming's verses translated into English.

Thus as far as I can identify there are four varieties of the Oxherding Pictures: (1) by Kaku-an, (2) by Seikyo, (3) by Jitoku, and (4) by an unknown author.

Kaku-an's "Pictures" here reproduced are by Shubun, a Zen priest of the fifteenth century. The original pictures are preserved at Shokokuji, Kyoto. He was one of the greatest painters in black and white in the Ashikaga period.

The Ten Oxherding Pictures, I.
by Kaku-an

I

Searching for the Ox. The beast has never gone astray, and what is the use of searching for him? The reason why the oxherd is not on intimate terms with him is because the oxherd himself has violated his own inmost nature. The beast is lost, for the oxherd has himself been led out of the way through his deluding senses. His home is receding farther away from him, and byways and crossways are ever confused. Desire for gain and fear of loss burn like fire; ideas of right and wrong shoot up like a phalanx.

Alone in the wilderness, lost in the jungle, the boy is
  searching, searching!
The swelling waters, the far-away mountains, and
  the unending path;
Exhausted and in despair, he knows not where to go,
He only hears the evening cicadas singing in the
  maple-woods.

II

Seeing the Traces. By the aid of the sutras and by inquiring into the doctrines, he has come to understand something, he has found the traces. He now knows that vessels, however varied, are all of gold, and that the objective world is a reflection of the Self. Yet, he is unable to distinguish what is good from what is not, his mind is still confused as to truth and falsehood. As he has not yet entered the gate, he is provisionally said to have noticed the traces.

By the stream and under the trees, scattered are the
     traces of the lost;
The sweet-scented grasses are growing thick—did he
     find the way?
However remote over the hills and far away the beast
     may wander,
His nose reaches the heavens and none can conceal it.

III

Seeing the Ox. The boy finds the way by the sound he hears; he sees thereby into the origin of things, and all his senses are in harmonious order. In all his activities, it is manifestly present. It is like the salt in water and the glue in colour. [It is there though not distinguishable as an individual entity.] When the eye is properly directed, he will find that it is no other than himself.

On a yonder branch perches a nightingale cheerfully
     singing;
The sun is warm, and a soothing breeze blows, on the
     bank the willows are green;
The ox is there all by himself, nowhere is he to hide
     himself;
The splendid head decorated with stately horns—
     what painter can reproduce him?

IV

Catching the Ox. Long lost in the wilderness, the boy has at last found the ox and his hands are on him. But, owing to the overwhelming pressure of the outside world, the ox is hard to keep under control. He constantly longs for the old sweet-scented field. The wild nature is still unruly, and altogether refuses to be broken. If the oxherd wishes to see the ox completely in harmony with himself, he has surely to use the whip freely.

With the energy of his whole being, the boy has at
   last taken hold of the ox:
But how wild his will, how ungovernable his power!
At times he struts up a plateau,
When lo! he is lost again in a misty unpenetrable
   mountain-pass.

V

Herding the Ox. When a thought moves, another follows, and then another—an endless train of thoughts is thus awakened. Through enlightenment all this turns into truth; but falsehood asserts itself when confusion prevails. Things oppress us not because of an objective world, but because of a self-deceiving mind. Do not let the nose-string loose, hold it tight, and allow no vacillation.

The boy is not to separate himself with his whip and
   tether,
Lest the animal should wander away into a world of
   defilements;
When the ox is properly tended to, he will grow pure
   and docile;
Without a chain, nothing binding, he will by himself
   follow the oxherd.

VI

Coming Home on the Ox's Back. The struggle is over; the man is no more concerned with gain and loss. He hums a rustic tune of the woodman, he sings simple songs of the village-boy. Saddling himself on the ox's back, his eyes are fixed on things not of the earth, earthy. Even if he is called, he will not turn his head; however enticed he will no more be kept back.

> Riding on the animal, he leisurely wends his way home:
> Enveloped in the evening mist, how tunefully the flute vanishes away!
> Singing a ditty, beating time, his heart is filled with a joy indescribable!
> That he is now one of those who know, need it be told?

VII

The Ox Forgotten, Leaving the Man Alone. The dharmas are one and the ox is symbolic. When you know that what you need is not the snare or set-net but the hare or fish, it is like gold separated from the dross, it is like the moon rising out of the clouds. The one ray of light serene and penetrating shines even before days of creation.

> Riding on the animal, he is at last back in his home,
> Where lo! the ox is no more; the man alone sits serenely.
> Though the red sun is high up in the sky, he is still quietly dreaming,
> Under a straw-thatched roof are his whip and rope idly lying.

VIII

The Ox and the Man Both Gone out of Sight.[1] All confusion is set aside, and serenity alone prevails; even the idea of holiness does not obtain. He does not linger about where the Buddha is, and as to where there is no Buddha he speedily passes by. When there exists no form of dualism, even a thousand-eyed one fails to detect a loop-hole. A holiness before which birds offer flowers is but a farce.

> All is empty—the whip, the rope, the man, and the
>   ox:
> Who can ever survey the vastness of heaven?
> Over the furnace burning ablaze, not a flake of snow
>   can fall:
> When this state of things obtains, manifest is the spirit
>   of the ancient master.

IX

Returning to the Origin, Back to the Source. From the very beginning, pure and immaculate, the man has never been affected by defilement. He watches the growth of things, while himself abiding in the immovable serenity of non-assertion. He does not identify himself with the maya-like transformations [that are going on about him], nor has he any use of himself [which is artificiality]. The waters are blue, the mountains are green; sitting alone, he observes things undergoing changes.

---

[1] It will be interesting to note what a mystic philosopher has to say about this: "A man shall become truly poor and as free from his creature will as he was when he was born. And I say to you, by the eternal truth, that as long as ye desire to fulfil the will of God, and have any desire after eternity and God; so long are ye not truly poor. He alone hath true spiritual poverty who wills nothing, knows nothing, desires nothing."—(From Eckhart as quoted by Inge in *Light, Life, and Love.*)

To return to the Origin, to be back at the Source—
    already a false step this!
Far better it is to stay at home, blind and deaf, and
    without much ado;
Sitting in the hut, he takes no cognisance of things
    outside,
Behold the streams flowing—whither nobody knows;
    and the flowers vividly red—for whom are they?

x

Entering the City with Bliss-bestowing Hands. His thatched
cottage gate is closed, and even the wisest know him not.
No glimpses of his inner life are to be caught; for he goes on
his own way without following the steps of the ancient sages.
Carrying a gourd[1] he goes out into the market, leaning
against a staff[2] he comes home. He is found in company with
wine-bibbers and butchers, he and they are all converted
into Buddhas.

Bare-chested and bare-footed, he comes out into the
    market-place;
Daubed with mud and ashes, how broadly he smiles!
There is no need for the miraculous power of the gods,
For he touches, and lo! the dead trees are in full
    bloom.

[1] Symbol of emptiness (*sunyata*).
[2] No extra property he has, for he knows that the desire to possess is the
curse of human life.

The Ten Oxherding Pictures, II.

1. *Undisciplined*

With his horns fiercely projected in the air the beast
    snorts,
Madly running over the mountain paths, farther and
    farther he goes astray!
A dark cloud is spread across the entrance of the
    valley,
And who knows how much of the fine fresh herb is
    trampled under his wild hoofs!

2. *Discipline Begun*

I am in possession of a straw rope, and I pass it
   through his nose,
For once he makes a frantic attempt to run away, but
   he is severely whipped and whipped;
The beast resists the training with all the power there
   is in a nature wild and ungoverned,
But the rustic oxherd never relaxes his pulling tether
   and ever-ready whip.

3. *In Harness*

Gradually getting into harness the beast is now
    content to be led by the nose,
Crossing the stream, walking along the mountain
    path, he follows every step of the leader;
The leader holds the rope tightly in his hand never
    letting it go,
All day long he is on the alert almost unconscious of
    what fatigue is.

4.   *Faced Round*

After long days of training the result begins to tell
    and the beast is faced round,
A nature so wild and ungoverned is finally broken,
    he has become gentler;
But the tender has not yet given him his full con-
    fidence,
He still keeps his straw rope with which the ox is now
    tied to a tree.

5. *Tamed*

Under the green willow tree and by the ancient
   mountain stream,
The ox is set at liberty to pursue his own pleasures;
At the eventide when a grey mist descends on the
   pasture,
The boy wends his homeward way with the animal
   quietly following.

6.   *Unimpeded*

On the verdant field the beast contentedly lies idling
     his time away,
No whip is needed now, nor any kind of restraint;
The boy too sits leisurely under the pine tree,
Playing a tune of peace, overflowing with joy.

7. *Laissez Faire*

The spring stream in the evening sun flows languidly
  along the willow-lined bank,
In the hazy atmosphere the meadow grass is seen
  growing thick;
When hungry he grazes, when thirsty he quaffs, as
  time sweetly slides,
While the boy on the rock dozes for hours not
  noticing anything that goes on about him.

8. *All Forgotten*

The beast all in white now is surrounded by the
    white clouds,
The man is perfectly at his ease and care-free, so is his
    companion;
The white clouds penetrated by the moon-light cast
    their white shadows below,
The white clouds and the bright moon-light—each
    following its course of movement.

9. *The Solitary Moon*

Nowhere is the beast, and the oxherd is master of his
   time,
He is a solitary cloud wafting lightly along the
   mountain peaks;
Clapping his hands he sings joyfully in the moon-light,
But remember a last wall is still left barring his
   homeward walk.

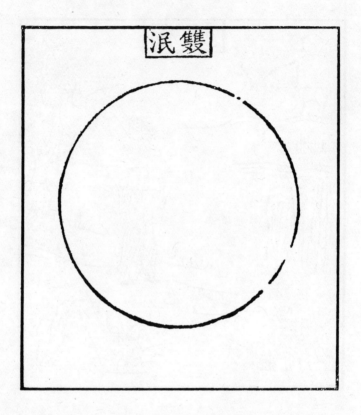

10. *Both Vanished*

Both the man and the animal have disappeared, no
    traces are left,
The bright moon-light is empty and shadowless with
    all the ten-thousand objects in it;
If anyone should ask the meaning of this,
Behold the lilies of the field and its fresh sweet-
    scented verdure.

HAKUIN ZENJI
Said to have been carved by himself
(See page 151)

Plate XIII

DAITO KOKUSHI
By Hakuin Zenji
(See page 145)

Plate XII

KANZAN (HAN-SHAN) AND JITTOKU (SHI-TE)
By Kaihoku Yusho
(One of the National Treasures of Myoshinji, Kyoto)
(See page 182)   Plate XV

BHADRAPALA
By Soyen
(One of the National Treasures of
Engakuji, Kamakura)
(See page 168)   Plate XIV

V. FROM THE JAPANESE ZEN MASTERS

Dai-o (1235–1308), Daito (1282–1336), and Kwanzan (1277–1360) are the three outstanding luminaries in the history of the Japanese Rinzai school of Zen. All the masters of this school now in Japan are their descendants. Dai-o went to China and studied Zen under Kido (Hsu-t'ang) in southern China, whose high expectations of the foreign disciple were fully justified as we can testify in the Japanese history of Zen. Daito is the founder of Daitokuji monastery and Kwanzan that of the Myoshinji, both of Kyoto. Muso (1273–1351) who followed another lineage of the Zen masters was versatile in artistic accomplishments. There are many noted gardens designed by him which are still well preserved. He was the founder of many Zen temples throughout Japan, among which the most notable one is Tenryuji at Saga, near Kyoto. Hakuin (1685–1768) is the father of modern Rinzai Zen. Without him it would be hard to tell the fate of Zen in Japan. He was no founder of a temple of any ecclesiastical importance; he lived his unpretentious life in a small temple in Suruga province, devoting himself to the bringing up of Zen monks and to the propagation of his teaching among laymen.

FROM THE JAPANESE ZEN MASTERS

I

DAI-O KOKUSHI "ON ZEN"

There is a reality even prior to heaven and earth;
Indeed, it has no form, much less a name;
Eyes fail to see it;
It has no voice for ears to detect;
To call it Mind or Buddha violates its nature,
For it then becomes like a visionary flower in the air;
It is not Mind, nor Buddha;
Absolutely quiet, and yet illuminating in a mysterious way,
It allows itself to be perceived only by the clear-eyed.
It is Dharma truly beyond form and sound;
It is Tao having nothing to do with words.

Wishing to entice the blind,
The Buddha has playfully let words escape his golden
  mouth;
Heaven and earth are ever since filled with entangling
  briars.

O my good worthy friends gathered here,
If you desire to listen to the thunderous voice of the
  Dharma,
Exhaust your words, empty your thoughts,
For then you may come to recognize this One Essence.
Says Hui the Brother, "The Buddha's Dharma
Is not to be given up to mere human sentiments."

2

Dai-o Kokushi's Admonition[1]

Those who enter the gate of Buddhism should first of
all cherish a firm faith in the dignity and respectability of
monkhood, for it is the path leading them away from poverty
and humbleness. Its dignity is that of the sonship of the
Dharmaraja of the triple world; no princely dignity which
extends only over a limited area of the earth compares
with it. Its respectability is that of the fatherhood of all
sentient beings; no parental respectability belonging only
to the head of a little family group equals it. When the monk
finds himself in this position of dignity and respectability,
living in the rock-cave of the Dharma where he enjoys the
greatest happiness of a spiritual life, under the blissful
protection of all the guardian gods of the Triple Treasure,
is there any form of happiness that can surpass his?

The shaven head and the dyed garment are the noble
symbols of Bodhisattvahood; the temple-buildings with all
their ornamental fixtures are the honorific emblems of
Buddhist virtue. They have nothing to do with mere
decorative effects.

[1] Left to his disciples as his last words when he was about to pass away.

That the monk, now taking on himself these forms of dignity and respectability, is the recipient of all kinds of offerings from his followers; that he is quietly allowed to pursue his study of the Truth, not troubling himself with worldly labours and occupations—this is indeed due to the loving thoughts of Buddhas and Fathers. If the monk fails in this life to cross the stream of birth-and-death, when does he expect to requite all the kindly feelings bestowed upon him by his predecessors? We are ever liable as time goes on to miss opportunities; let the monk, therefore, be always on the watch not to pass his days idly.

The one path leading up to the highest peak is the mysterious orthodox line of transmission established by Buddhas and Fathers, and to walk along this road is the essence of appreciating what they have done for us. When the monk fails to discipline himself along this road, he thereby departs from the dignity and respectability of monkhood, laying himself down in the slums of poverty and misery. As I grow older I feel this to be my greatest regret, and, O monks, I have never been tired day and night of giving you strong admonitions on this point. Now, on the eve of my departure, my heart lingers with you, and my sincerest prayer is that you are never found lacking in the virtue of the monkish dignity and respectability, and that you ever be mindful of what properly belongs to monkhood. Pray, pray, be mindful of this, O monks!

This is the motherly advice of Nampo;[1] old monk-mendicant of Kencho Monastery.

3

DAITO KOKUSHI'S ADMONITION

O you, monks, who are in this mountain monastery, remember that you are gathered here for the sake of religion and not for the sake of clothes and food. As long as you have

[1] This is Dai-o Kokushi's own name, Dai-o being his posthumous honorary title.

shoulders [that is, the body], you will have clothes to wear, and as long as you have a mouth, you will have food to eat. Be ever mindful, throughout the twelve hours of the day, to apply yourselves to the study of the Unthinkable. Time passes like an arrow, never let your minds be disturbed by worldly cares. Ever, ever be on the look-out. After my departure, some of you may preside over five temples in prosperous conditions, with towers and halls and holy books all decorated in gold and silver, and devotees may noisily crowd into the grounds; some may pass hours in reading the sutras and re-citing the dharanis, and sitting long in contemplation may not give themselves up to sleep; they may, eating once a day and observing the fastdays, and, throughout the six periods of the day, practise all the religious deeds. Even when they are thus devoted to the cause, if their thoughts are not really dwelling on the mysterious and untransmissible Way of the Buddhas and Fathers, they may yet come to ignore the law of moral causation, ending in a complete downfall of the true religion. All such belong to the family of evil spirits; however long my departure from the world may be, they are not to be called my descendants. Let, however, there be just one individual, who may be living in the wilderness in a hut thatched with one bundle of straw and passing his days by eating the roots of wild herbs cooked in a pot with broken legs; but if he single-mindedly applies himself to the study of his own [spiritual] affairs, he is the very one who has a daily interview with me and knows how to be grateful for his life. Who should ever despise such a one? O monks, be diligent, be diligent.[1]

DAITO KOKUSHI'S LAST POEM

Buddhas and Fathers cut to pieces—
The sword is ever kept sharpened!
Where the wheel turns,
The void gnashes its teeth.

[1] In those monasteries which are connected in some way with the author of this admonition, it is read or rather chanted before a lecture or *Teisho* begins.

IV

KWANZAN KOKUSHI'S ADMONITION[1]

It was in the Shogen period (1259) that our forefather the venerable Dai-o crossed the stormy waves of the great ocean in order to study Zen in Sung. He interviewed Hsu-t'ang (Kido) the great Zen master at Ching-tz'u (Jinzu) and under him Dai-o whole-heartedly devoted himself to the realization of Zen experience. Finally at Ching-shan (Kinzan) he was able to master all the secrets belonging to it. For this reason he was praised by his master as "having once more gone over the path", and the prophecy was also given him that his "descendants would ever be increasing". That the rightful lineage of the Yang-ch'i (Yogi) school was transported to this country of ours is to be ascribed to the merit of our venerable forefather.

Daito, my old venerable teacher, followed the steps of Dai-o who stayed in the western part of the capital; personally attending on him, he was in close contact with the master during his residence at Manju in Kyoto and at Kencho in Kamakura. Throughout the many years of attendance Daito never laid himself on a bed for sleep. He reminds us in many respects of the ancient worthies. When finally he mastered Zen, the venerable Dai-o gave him his testimony but ordered him to mature his experience for twenty years in quiet retirement. Surely enough, he proved to be a great successor truly worthy of his illustrious master, Dai-o. He resuscitated Zen which had been in a state of decline; he left an admonition for his followers to be ever mindful of keeping vigorously alive the true spirit of Zen discipline; all this is his merit.

[1] Muso Daishi is the honorific title posthumously given by an Emperor to Kwanzan Kokushi, the founder of Myoshinji, Kyoto, which is one of the most important Zen headquarters in Japan. All the Zen masters of the present day in Japan are his descendants. Some doubt is cherished about the genuineness of this Admonition as penned by Kwanzan himself, on the ground that the content is too "grandmotherly".

That in obedience to the august order of his Holiness the Ex-Emperor Hanazono I have come to establish this monastery, is due to the motherly love of my late master who chewed food for his helpless baby. O my followers, you may some day forget me, but if you should forget the loving thoughts of Dai-o and Daito, you are not my descendants. I pray you to strive to grasp the origin of things. Po-yun (Hakuun) was impressed with the great merit of Pai-chang (Hyakjo), and Hu-ch'iu (Kokyu) was touched with the words of warning given by Po-yun (Hakuun). Such are our precedents. You will do well not to commit the fault of picking leaves or of searching for branches, [instead of taking hold of the root itself].

v

MUSO KOKUSHI'S ADMONITION

I have three kinds of disciples: those who, vigorously shaking off all entangling circumstances, and with singleness of thought apply themselves to the study of their own [spiritual] affairs, are of the first class. Those who are not so single-minded in the study, but scattering their attention are fond of book-learning, are of the second. Those who, covering their own spiritual brightness, are only occupied with the dribblings of the Buddhas and Fathers are called the lowest. As to those minds that are intoxicated by secular literature and engaged in establishing themselves as men of letters and are simply laymen with shaven heads, they do not belong even to the lowest. As regards those who think only of indulging in food and sleep and give themselves up to indolence—could such be called members of the Black Robe? They are truly, as were designated by an old master, clothes-racks and rice-bags. Inasmuch as they are not monks, they ought not to be permitted to call themselves my disciples and enter the monastery and sub-temples as well; even a temporary sojourn is to be prohibited, not to speak of their application as student-monks. When an old man like myself speaks thus, you may think he is lacking in all-embracing love, but the main thing is to let them know of their own faults, and, reforming themselves, to become growing plants in the patriarchal gardens.

VI

HAKUIN'S "SONG OF MEDITATION"

Sentient beings are primarily all Buddhas:
It is like ice and water,
Apart from water no ice can exist;
Outside sentient beings, where do we find the
    Buddhas?
Not knowing how near the Truth is,
People seek it far away,—what a pity!
They are like him who, in the midst of water,
Cries in thirst so imploringly;
They are like the son of a rich man
Who wandered away among the poor.
The reason why we transmigrate through the six
    worlds
Is because we are lost in the darkness of ignorance;
Going astray further and further in the darkness,
When are we able to get away from birth-and-
    death?

As regards the Meditation practised in the Maha-
    yana,
We have no words to praise it fully:
The virtues of perfection such as charity, morality,
    etc.,
And the invocation of the Buddha's name, confession,
    and ascetic discipline,
And many other good deeds of merit,—
All these issue from the practice of Meditation;

Even those who have practised it just for one sitting
Will see all their evil karma wiped clean;
Nowhere will they find the evil paths,
But the Pure Land will be near at hand.
With a reverential heart, let them to this Truth
Listen even for once,
And let them praise it, and gladly embrace it,
And they will surely be blessed most infinitely.

For such as, reflecting within themselves,
Testify to the truth of Self-nature,
To the truth that Self-nature is no-nature,
They have really gone beyond the ken of sophistry.
For them opens the gate of the oneness of cause and
    effect,
And straight runs the path of non-duality and
    non-trinity.
Abiding with the not-particular which is in parti-
    culars,
Whether going or returning, they remain for ever
    unmoved;
Taking hold of the not-thought which lies in thoughts,
In every act of theirs they hear the voice of the truth.
How boundless the sky of Samadhi unfettered!
How transparent the perfect moon-light of the
    fourfold Wisdom!
At that moment what do they lack?
As the Truth eternally calm reveals itself to them,
This very earth is the Lotus Land of Purity,
And this body is the body of the Buddha.

VI. THE BUDDHIST STATUES AND PICTURES IN A ZEN MONASTERY

Visitors to a Zen monastery in Japan will be greeted by various Buddhist figures enshrined in the different parts of the institution. This section is devoted to the description of such figures.

I

THE BUDDHA

Each Buddhist sect in Japan has its own *Honzon*, i.e. "the chief honoured one" as its main object of worship: for instance, the Jodo and the Shin have Amida Nyorai; the Shingon, Dainichi Nyorai (Mahavairocana); the Nichiren and the Zen, Shaka Nyorai (Sakyamuni). But this tradition is not uniformly observed by the Zen sect and much latitude has been allowed to the founder of each temple or monastery.

The Buddha Sakyamuni is the proper one no doubt for all Zen institutions, for Zen claims to transmit the Buddha-heart—the first transmission taking place between Sakya-muni and Mahakashyapa. Sakyamuni thus occupies the main seat of honour on the Zen altar. But frequently we find there a statue of Kwannon (Avalokitesvara), or Yakushi (Bhaishajyaguru), or Jizo (Kshitigarbha), or Miroku (Maitreya), or even a trinity of Amida, Shaka, and Miroku. In this latter case Amida is the Buddha of the past, Shaka of the present, and Miroku of the future.

When the Honzon is Sakyamuni he is sometimes attended by a pair of Bodhisattvas and another of Arhats. The Bodhisattvas are Monju (Manjusri) and Fugen (Samantabhadra), and the Arhats are Kasho (Mahakashyapa) and Anan (Ananda). Sakyamuni is here both historical and "metaphysical", so to speak. Seeing him attended by his two chief disciples, he is a historical figure, but with Monju and Fugen who represent or symbolize wisdom and love, the two ruling attributes of the highest Reality, Sakyamuni is Vairocana standing above the world of transmigrations. Here we see the philosophy of the *Avatamsaka* or *Gandavyuha* incorporated into Zen. In fact, our religious life has two aspects—the experience itself and its philosophy.

This is represented in Buddhism by the historical trinity of Sakyamuni, Kashyapa, and Ananda, and by the metaphysical one of Vairocana, Manjusri, and Samantabhadra. Ananda stands for learning, intellection, and philosophizing; Kashyapa for life, experience, and realization; and Sakyamuni naturally for the unifying body in which experience and intellection find their field of harmonious co-operation. That religion needs philosophy is sometimes forgotten, and one of the great merits achieved by Buddhism is that it has never ignored this truth, and wherever it is propagated it helps the native genius of that land to develop its philosophy or to supply an intellectual background to its already-existing beliefs.

Perhaps it is only in the Zen monastery that the birth of the Buddha, his Enlightenment, and his Nirvana are commemorated. Mahayana Buddhism is much given up to the idealistic or metaphysical or transcendental interpretation of the historical facts so called in the life of the Buddha, and the evolution of the Bodhisattva-ideal has pushed the historical personages to the background. Vairocana or Amitabha has thus come to take the place of Sakyamuni Buddha, and a host of Bodhisattvas has completely displaced the Arhats.

But Zen has not forgotten the historical side of the Buddha's life. While Zen is not apparently concerned with earthly affairs, the fact that it has been nurtured in China, where history plays an important rôle in the cultural life of the people, points to its connection again with the earth. So the three most significant events in the development of Buddhism are properly remembered and elaborate rituals are annually performed at all the main Zen monasteries in Japan for the Buddha's birth-day, his attainment of Enlightenment, and his entrance into Nirvana.[1]

[1] Respectively: April 8, December 8, and February 15.

The Buddha's birth as represented by Zen followers places him in the most remarkable contrast to that of Christ. The baby Buddha is made to stand straight up with his right hand pointing at heaven and with his left at the earth, and he exclaims: "Above the heavens and below the heavens, I alone am the honoured one!" The voice reaches the furthest ends of the chiliocosm, and all the living beings— even matter is not dead in Buddhism—share in the joy of the Buddha's birth, realizing that they too are destined to be Buddhas.

On April 8 this baby Buddha standing in a bronze basin is taken out of the shrine, and the ceremony of baptizing the baby with sweet tea made of some vegetable leaves is performed; the tea thus used is afterwards given away to children. Recently, the celebration of this day takes place on a grand scale in all the larger cities of Japan, not only by Zen followers but by all Buddhists including monks, priests, laymen, laywomen, and children.

Sakyamuni as the Enlightened One sits on the lotus throne enshrined in the main hall of the Zen monastery. He is generally in the meditation posture.

The Nirvana scene is generally represented pictorially, except perhaps the one at the Nirvana Hall of Myoshinji, Kyoto, which is a bronze-slab. The most noted Nirvana picture is by Chodensu, of Tofukuji, the whole length of which is about sixteen yards.

Sakyamuni the Buddha in Meditation Posture

Buddha Attended by Two Bodhisattvas and Two Arhats

The Buddha's Birth

Buddha's Entrance into Nirvana

Bhaishajyaguru (*Yakushi Nyorai*)

II

THE BODHISATTVAS

When Sakyamuni is not found in the Main Buddha Hall, one of the following Bodhisattvas is enshrined in his place: Monju (Manjusri), Fugen (Samantabhadra), Kwannon (Avalokitesvara), Yakushi (Bhaishajyaguru), Miroku (Maitreya), Jizo (Kshitigarbha), or sometimes Kokuzo (Akasagarbha).

Monju and Fugen generally go in pairs and are the chief Bodhisattvas in the Avatamsaka (Kegon) conception of the world. Monju stands for Prajna. Sitting on a lion he holds a sword which is meant to cut all the intellectual and affectional entanglements in order to reveal the light of transcendental Prajna. Fugen is found on an elephant and represents love, Karuna. Karuna is contrasted with Prajna in that Prajna points to annihilation and to identity whereas Karuna points to construction and to multiplicity. The one is intellectual and the other emotional; the one unifies and the other diversifies. Fugen's ten vows are well known to students of the Kegon.

Kwannon is exclusively the Bodhisattva of compassion. In this respect he resembles Fugen. A special chapter is devoted to him in the *Hokkekyo* (*Saddharma-pundarika*) and also in the *Ryogonkyo* (*Suramgama*). He is one of the most popular Bosatsus or Bodhisattvas of Mahayana Buddhism. For an English translation of the *Kwannongyo* as rendered into Chinese by Kumarajiva see p. 30 of the present *Manual*.

Yakushi is the Bodhisattva-doctor. He holds a medicine jar in his hands and is attended by twelve gods each of whom represents one of his twelve vows. The main object of his appearance among us is to cure us of ignorance, which is the most fundamental of all the ills the flesh is heir to.

Jizo is principally or popularly the protector of children nowadays, but his original vows are to save us from wandering in the six paths of existence. He thus divides himself into six forms each of which stands as guardian in each one of the six paths. Hence the six Jizo we often find by the country roadside. He is generally represented in priestly robe, with a shaven head, and carries a long walking staff in his hand. In the Kamakura and the Ashikaga period he was quite a popular object of worship, and we find many fine artistic sculptures of this Bodhisattva in Kamakura.

Miroku is the future Buddha and at present has his abode in the Tushita Heaven waiting for his time to appear among us. He is also essentially compassionate as his name implies. He is sometimes called a Buddha and sometimes a Bodhisattva. Although he is supposed to be in one of the heavens, he is frequently encountered on earth.

Manjusri (Monju Bosatsu)

Samantabhadra (Fugen Bosatsu)

Avalokitesvara (Kwannon Bosatsu)

Maitreya (Miroku Bosatsu)

166

Kshitigarbha (Jizo Bosatsu)

III

THE ARHATS

The Arhats, generally sixteen in number, are enshrined in the second storey of the tower gate. They are all registered as dwellers in some remote mountains, and each is the leader of a large following. Their superficially grotesque and irregular appearances contrast in a strange way with those of the Bodhisattvas. They are miracle workers and tamers of the wild beasts. This characteristic seems to have excited the interest of the Zen monk-artist who has turned them into one of the favourite objects of his artistic imagination.

In a large Zen monastery the five hundred Arhats are given a special shelter in the premises.

Bhadrapala is one of the sixteen Arhats and had his *satori* while bathing. He is now enshrined in a niche in the bath-room attached to the Meditation Hall. When the monks take their bath, they pay respect to his figure.[1] The picture shown below belongs to Engakuji, Kamakura, and is one of the national treasures of Japan.

---

[1] *The Training of the Zen Monk*, p. 40.

Five of the Sixteen Arhats

Six of the Sixteen Arhats

Five of the Sixteen Arhats

IV

THE PROTECTING GODS

Of the many protecting gods of Buddhism the following
may be counted as belonging more or less exclusively to Zen,
and they have each his or her own special quarter where they
perform their several official duties for Buddhism.

The Niwo or "two guardian kings" are found enclosed
at either side of the entrance gate. They represent the
Vajra god in two forms; the one is masculine with the mouth
tightly closed, and the other is feminine with an opened
mouth. They guard the holy place from intruders.

The Shitenno or the four guardian gods are enshrined
in the Buddha-hall at the four corners of the altar. Of these
gods the most popular one is Tamonten (Vaisravana), the
guardian of the North. This fact comes perhaps from his
being the god of learning and also of wealth.

It is difficult to trace historically how Benzaiten (Sarasvati), who is the goddess of the River, finds her shrine in a
Zen monastery. Some say that Benzaiten is not Sarasvati
but Sridevi. Whoever she may be, a female form is often
found among the audience of a saintly priest, and later she
appears in his dream telling him how she who was formerly
an enemy of Buddhism is now enlightened and will be one
of its protectors, and so on. In any event there is room even
in the Zen monastery, where the severest kind of asceticism
is supposed to prevail, for a goddess to enter.

Idaten is a god of the kitchen looking after the provisions
of the Brotherhood. The original Sanskrit term for it seems
to be Skanda and not Veda as may be suggested from *i-da*
or *wei-t'o*. He is one of the eight generals belonging to Viru-
dhaka, the guardian god of the Southern quarter. He is a
great runner and wherever there is a trouble he is instantly
found there. In the Chinese monastery he occupies an
important seat in the hall of the four guardian gods, but in

the Japanese he is in the little shrine attached to the monks' dining-room.[1]

Ususama Myowo is a god of the lavatory. Ucchushma in Sanskrit means "to dry", "to parch", that is, to clean up filth by burning, by fire, for fire is a great purifying agency. Myowo is Vidyaraja, a special class of the gods who assume a form of wrath.[2]

Sambo Kojin seems to be a Japanese mountain god in the form of an Indian god. He is found outside the temple buildings. As the monasteries are generally located in the mountains this god who is supposed to preside over such districts, is invited to have his residence in the grounds so that he would be a good protector of the Brotherhood against the inimical influence of evil spirits.

Daikokuten whose Indian prototype is sometimes regarded as Mahakala is at present a purely Japanese god. He carries a large bag over his shoulder and stands on rice bales. Though his phallic origin is suspected, he has nothing, as he is, to do with it. He is a god of material wealth and like Idaten looks after the physical welfare of the Brotherhood. He is not such a universal object of respect in the Zen monastery.

Wherever the Prajnaparamita is preached or copied or recited, the sixteen "good gods" stand about the place and guard the devoted spirits against their being lured away by the enemy. As Zen is connected with the philosophy of Prajna they are also the gods of Zen. The picture below shows more than sixteen figures. Of the extra four personages standing in the foreground the two on the left are the Jotai Bosatsu (Sadaprarudita) and Jinsha Daio while the two on the right are Hsuan-Chuang with a kind of carrying-case on his back and Hoyu Bosatsu (Dharmodgata). Jotai and Hoyu are the principal characters in the *Prajnaparamita* as told in the second series of my *Essays in Zen Buddhism*. Hsuan-chuang is the translator of the *Mahaprajnaparamita Sutra* in six hundred fascicles and also that of Nagarjuna's commentary

[1] See also my *Training of the Zen Monk*, p. 106.
[2] Ibid., p. 44.

on the sutra in one hundred fascicles. While he was travelling through the desert, he was accosted by Jinsha, the god of the wilderness, who was responsible for the unsuccessful trips repeatedly attempted by the devoted Chinese pilgrims to India prior to Hsuan-chuang. The god was carrying six of the skulls of such victims about his neck. Listening to the *Prajnaparamita* as recited by Hsuan-chuang, he was converted and became a most devoted protector of the holy text. Hence his presence here.

The Two Door-Keeping Gods (Niwo)

The Four Guardian Gods

Benzaiten

Sambokojin

178

Skandadeva (Idaten)

Ucchushma (Ususamaten)

Mahakala (Daikokuten)

V

SOME OF THE HISTORICAL FIGURES

Besides these mythical personages the Zen monastery gives shelter to some other historical characters deeply connected not only with Zen but with Buddhism as a whole. Bodhidharma as founder of Zen Buddhism naturally occupies a chief seat of honour beside the Buddha Sakyamuni. With Japanese Zen followers, however, the founder of a given temple is more highly honoured, and in each of the principal Zen institutions in Japan there is a special hall dedicated to the founder of that particular monastery, where an oil-lamp is kept burning all day and night. Bodhidharma is a unique figure and may be identified wherever he is. He is one of the favourite subjects for the Zen masters to try their amateurish brush. Kwannon is perhaps another such subject.

Fudaishi (Fu Ta-shih), also known as Zenne Daishi (Shan-hui), 493–564, was a contemporary of Bodhidharma. Although he does not belong to the orthodox lineage of Zen transmission, his life and sermons as recorded in the *Transmission of the Lamp (Ch'uan-teng Lu)*[1] are full of Zen flavour, so to speak. His famous gatha is well known to all Zen students.[2] Tradition makes him the inventor of what is known as Rinzo (*luntsang*), which is a system of revolving shelves for keeping the Chinese Tripitaka. For this reason he, together with his two sons, is set up in the Buddhist library as a kind of god of literature.

The Zen monastery harbours many old eccentric characters of whom the most noted of a Chinese origin are Kanzan (Han-shan) and Jittoku (Shih-te).[3] They are vagabond poet-ascetics. Another belonging to this group of

---

[1] Fas. XXVII.
[2] *Introduction to Zen Buddhism*, p. 58.
[3] *Zen Essays*, III, Plates XIV and XV, with their accompanying explanations.

characters is Hotei (Pu-tai).[1] That Hotei plays quite a different rôle in Japanese Buddhism from what he does in China I have explained in my article in the *Eastern Buddhist*, VI, 4, "Impressions of Chinese Buddhism".

Shotoku Taishi (574–622) was really one of the most remarkable figures in the cultural history of Japan, and it is no wonder that all the Japanese Buddhists pay special tribute to his memory by enshrining his statue in one of the monastery buildings. One of the legendary stories circulating in Japan with regard to Bodhidharma is that he came to Japan after he had finished his work in China and was found in the form of a miserable beggar at Kataoka Yama, near Nara. Shotoku Taishi met him there and it is said that they exchanged poems.

---

[1] *Ibid.* Plates X and XVI, and also Second Series.

Daruma (Ta-mo, Bodhidharma)

Shotoku Taishi

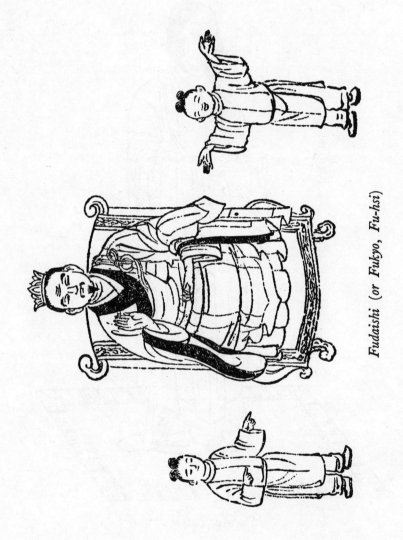

Fudaishi (or Fukyo, Fu-hsi)

INDEX

A SEASON
IN HELL

A SEASON
IN HELL

JACK HIGGINS

OPEN ROAD

INTEGRATED MEDIA

NEW YORK

For Shirley Cooper

'Revenge is a season in Hell'
—Sicilian proverb

1983

ONE

JUST AFTER FOUR, AS first light started to seep through the bamboo slats above his head, it rained again, slowly at first, developing into a solid drenching downpour from which there was no escape.

Sean Egan crouched in a corner, arms folded, hands tucked into his armpits to conserve as much body heat as possible, not that there was much left after four days. The pit was four feet square so that it was impossible to lie down even if he'd wanted to. He remembered reading somewhere that gorillas were the only animals who lay in their own ordure and didn't mind. He hadn't reached that stage yet although he'd long since got used to the stench.

His feet were bare, but they'd left him with his camouflage jump jacket and pants. A khaki-green sweatband was wound around his head like a turban, desert style. Beneath it the face was gaunt, skin stretched tightly over prominent cheekbones. The eyes were china blue and without expression as he waited, rain drifting down through the bamboo slats twelve feet above. The clay walls were wet with it and occasionally clods of earth broke free from the sides and fell into the bottom water, already three or four inches deep.

He waited, indifferent to all this, and finally heard the sound of footsteps, someone whistling flatly through the rain. The man above wore a camouflage uniform similar to his own, but slightly different, the Afghanistan pattern developed by the Russian Army for use during the occupation of that country. A sergeant, according to the rank badges on his collar tabs. Above the peak of his cap was the red star of the Soviet Army and the insignia of the 81st Regiment of Assault Paratroops.

Egan recognized all these things because it was his business. He looked up and waited in silence. The sergeant carried an AK assault rifle in one hand, an army-ration can in the other, a length of twine tied to the can.

"Still with us?" he called cheerfully in English, resting the AK beside him. "It must be wet down there?" Egan said nothing. He simply sat, waiting. "And still not talking? Ah, well, you will, my friend. They always do in the end." The sergeant lowered the ration can through the slats. "Breakfast. Only coffee this morning, but then we don't want to build up your strength."

Egan took the can and opened it. It *was* coffee, steaming in the damp air, surprisingly hot. He fought the wave of nausea—even the smell of coffee made him feel sick. To drink it was an impossibility, as his captors well knew.

The sergeant laughed. "But of course, you only drink tea. What a pity." He unbuttoned his pants and urinated down through the slats. "What about a change?"

There was no way to avoid it. Egan stayed there, squatting in the corner, staring up, still not speaking.

The sergeant picked up the AK. "Five minutes and I'll be back, and I'll expect a nice clean can. Be a good boy and drink it up or I might have to punish you."

He walked away and still Egan waited, an intent expression on his face. When the sound of the sergeant's footsteps had faded, he stood up. Five minutes. His only chance. He ripped the khaki sweatband from his head and it was immediately obvious that only the section visible to the eye was still whole; the rest had been torn into strips during the night, each one carefully plaited, the whole joined together in a crude rope.

He quickly fastened it under his arms and passed a loop around his neck, placing the loose end in his teeth. He braced his back against one wall of the pit and his feet against the other, working his way up until he could reach out and touch the bamboo slats. He took the tail of the rope from between his teeth and passed it around two of the slats, tying it securely.

Silence, only the rain falling. He was aware of the sergeant's approach from a long way off. He waited, letting the seconds pass, then kicked his feet away from the wall and dropped, at the same time crying out.

The bamboo dipped above his head, his body bounced and swung. He turned his head to one side so that the line of the rope was visible across his neck and half-closed his eyes, the rope cutting under his arms as it supported his weight.

He knew the sergeant was above him now, heard the man's cry of dismay as he knelt, pulling a combat knife from his boot, reaching through the slats to sever the rope. Egan let himself fall hard, bouncing against the wall and collapsing in a heap in the water and filth below. He lay there, waiting, aware of the slats being pulled back above, the bamboo ladder being lowered.

The sergeant came down quickly and crouched. "You stupid bastard!" he said turning him over.

Egan's two hands came in from each side, perfectly pointed in a phoenix fist, center knuckles extended, targeting the neck below each ear. The sergeant never had time to cry out. A slight groan, his eyes rolled, and he was immediately unconscious.

Egan had the man's jump boots off in moments, pulled them on and fastened them quickly. Then he crammed the camouflage cap with the red star down low over his eyes and went up the ladder cautiously.

The clearing was deserted. There was a drift of smoke above the trees which would be the house, he knew that from his first interrogation. Down through the woods was the river, perhaps a quarter of a mile. Once across and he was safe, clear through to the mountains beyond. He picked up the AK and looked out across the wood at their snow-capped peaks, then started down through the trees.

There was a trip wire within fifty yards which he carefully negotiated, another a few feet farther on, so close that they'd calculated it would not be expected. Egan stepped over it and moved through the waist-high bracken soaked with rain.

Getting out wasn't enough. Staying out was the hard part—an old SAS maxim that rang in his head as the trees on his right exploded. Not a land mine. If it had been he'd be lying in pieces. More likely an alarm charge triggered by an electronic eye beam at ground level. All this was amply confirmed when a hooter echoed mournfully through the trees from the direction of the farmhouse.

He tightened his grip on the AK, holding it across his chest, and raced through the bracken.

He sensed movement on his left, and a figure in camouflage battle dress came out of the trees, head down, to meet him. As they converged, Egan swerved, dropping to one knee, the other leg stretched out. The man tripped and Egan came up, kicked him in the side of the head and ran.

There was pain in his left knee, but, if anything, it sharpened him, and he kept on going, faster as the hillside steepened, the bracken almost jungle high here. He burst out into a small clearing as three more soldiers came out of the trees on the other side.

He went in on the run, never hesitating, loosing off a burst from the AK; swinging the butt in one man's face, shouldering another man aside, he carried on through the trees, very fast, too fast, losing his balance.

He picked himself up and started forward. The sound of a helicopter was somewhere close at hand, but the weather was on his side and the bird wouldn't dare to come too low. Through a break in the trees he could see the river, half-obscured by mist and rain.

There was a tightness in his chest and the pain in his left knee was like fire, but he kept on going, sliding farther down the steep bank that brought him at last to the river. As he picked himself up, someone leaped from the bracken and drove the butt of a rifle into his kidneys.

Egan arched backward in pain, and the rifle came around in a second, braced against his throat. He dropped his AK and ran the heel of his right boot down the man's shin. There was a cry, and as the pressure of the rifle was released, Egan jerked his head back, hard into the face behind, following this with a short, savage blow with his left elbow.

As he turned, the knee let him down finally, the leg collapsing under him as the soldier, his face a mask of blood from the broken nose, raised his own knee into Egan's face, throwing him on his back. He moved in, foot raised to stamp. Egan got his hands on it and twisted, hurling the man to one side. As he tried to rise, Egan, already up on his good knee, delivered a devastating blow under the ribs. The soldier groaned and fell back.

The helicopter was not far away now; closer still was the sound of men's voices and the barking of dogs. Egan picked up the AK and limped to the river's edge. The mist was heavy here so that it was impossible to see the other side. Water rushed by, brown and flecked with foam, swollen by the rain. The current was fast, too fast for even the strongest swimmer, so cold that survival time would be minimal.

He moved farther along the bank. Here the flood waters had risen several feet, and a tree floated, its branches caught in a bush. Recognizing his one chance for survival, he jumped into the water, the voices very close now, and flailed toward the tree. He pushed hard. For a moment, it refused to move, and then quite suddenly it was free, torn out by the current. The AK went as he grabbed for the security of the branches. Men on the bank now, dogs barking. A burst of firing, and then he was out in mid-channel, cloaked by a curtain of mist and rain.

It was cold, colder than anything he had known in his life before, numbing the senses. The cold had even taken care of the pain in his knee. The current seemed slacker now, and he drifted more slowly, cocooned in the mist. The helicopter made a couple of passes overhead, but not low enough to cause him any trouble. After a while, it moved away.

It was very quiet, only the ripple of the water, the hiss of the falling rain. His final chance, and not long to take it, with the cold eating into his bones like acid. He started to kick hard, still hanging on to the tree, pushing for the other side.

It was exhausting work, but he kept at it, aware of his own heavy breathing and then something else. A dull, muted rumbling behind him. As he turned to glance over his shoulder, a motorboat nosed out of the mist and nudged into the branches of the tree.

Half a dozen soldiers were aboard but only one stood out—the officer who leaned over the rail to look down at him. He was in his early thirties, young to be a lieutenant colonel, of medium height, with dark, watchful eyes and black hair that was far too long by any kind of army's standards. At some time his nose had been broken. Just now he wore a camouflage jump jacket and a beige beret with the officer's version of the SAS cap badge, silver wire wings with the regimental motto, "Who dares, wins," all outlined in red on a blue background. He reached strong arms into the water to haul Egan out.

"Colonel Villiers," Egan said weakly. "Didn't expect to see you here."

"I'm your control officer on this one, Sean," Villiers told him.

"Seems like I've cocked it up," Egan said.

Villiers smiled with considerable charm. "Actually, I think you were bloody marvelous. Now, let's get you out of here."

The 22nd Regiment Special Air Service is probably the most elite unit of any army in the world, its members all volunteers. Its selection procedure is so rigorous that it is not uncommon for only 10 percent of applicants to succeed. The ultimate test is the endurance march of forty-five miles in twenty hours, carrying eighty pounds of equipment over the Brecon Beacons in Wales, some of the roughest terrain in Britain—a course which has quite literally killed men attempting it.

Standing at the window of the farmhouse looking out across the trees as rain swept in across the river Wye, Tony Villiers thought of the man who had just come within inches of destruction. "My God, it really is a bloody awful place in weather like this."

The young officer sitting at the desk behind him smiled. The name on his desk said Captain Daniel Warden and he was in charge of the proving-ground courses in the Brecons. He and Villiers shared another distinction besides being serving officers in the SAS. Both were also Grenadier Guardsmen.

He opened the file in front of him. "I've got Egan's record here from the computer, sir. Really is quite outstanding. Military Medal for gallantry in the field in Ireland, reasons unspecified."

"I know about that," Villiers told him. "He was working with me at the time. Undercover. South Armagh."

"Distinguished Conduct Medal in the Falklands. Badly wounded. Eight months' hospitalization. Left knee plastic and stainless steel or what have you. Speaks French, Italian and Irish. That's a new one."

"His father was Irish," Villiers said.

"Another interesting point. He went to quite a reasonable public school," Warden added. "Dulwich College."

Like Villiers, he was an Old Etonian, and the colonel said, "Don't be a snob, Daniel. A very good school. Good enough for Raymond Chandler."

"Really, sir? I never knew that. Thought he was an American."

"He was, you idiot." Villiers crossed to the desk, helped himself to tea from a china pot and sat in the window seat. "Let me give it to you, chapter and verse, on Sean Egan, all Group Four information, and most of it very definitely not on your computer. A lot of remarkable things about our Sean. To start with, he has a rather unusual uncle. Maybe you've heard of him? One Jack Shelley?"

Warden frowned. "The gangster?"

"A long time ago. In the good, bad old days he was as important as the Kray brothers and the Richardson gang. Very well liked in the East End of London. The people's hero. Robin Hood in a Jaguar. Made his money from gambling and protection, night clubs and so on. Nothing nasty like drugs or prostitution. And he was clever. Too clever to end up serving life like the Krays. When he discovered he could make just as much money legitimately he moved into a different world. Television, computers, high tech. He must be worth twenty million at least."

"And Egan?"

"Shelley's sister married a London Irishman called Patrick Egan. He was an ex-boxer who ran a pub somewhere on the river. Shelley didn't approve. He himself never married." Villiers lit another cigarette. "And there's one thing you should get straight about him. He may be a multimillionaire who owns half of Wapping, but he's still Jack Shelley to every crook in London and a name to be reckoned with. He took a fancy to young Sean. He was the one who paid for him to go to Dulwich College, and Sean was good. Got a scholarship to Trinity College, Cambridge. Intended to read Moral Philosophy. Can you beat that, Jack Shelley's nephew reading Moral Philosophy?"

Warden was well hooked by now. "What went wrong?"

"In the spring of seventy-six, Pat Egan and his wife went across to Ulster to visit relatives in Portadown. Unfortunately they parked next to the wrong truck."

"A bomb?" Warden asked.

"Big one. Took out half the street. They were only two of the people killed. Egan was seventeen and a half. Turned his back on Cambridge and joined the Paratroopers. His uncle was furious, but there wasn't much he could do."

"Is Egan Shelley's only relative?"

"No, there's some woman in her sixties, Sean's cousin, I think. He told me once. She runs his father's old pub." Villiers frowned, thinking. "Ida, that was it. Aunt Ida. Girl called Sally, too, adopted by Pat Egan and his wife. I think her parents died when she was a baby. Shelley didn't count her—not family. He's like that. She went to live with his Aunt Ida when Sean joined up.

"Sean, sir?" Warden said. "Isn't that a little familiar between a half-colonel and a sergeant?"

"Sean Egan and I have worked together a dozen times undercover in Ireland. That alters things." Villiers's clipped public school tones changed to the accents of Belfast. "You can't work on a building site on the Falls Road with a man, risk your life every waking minute, and expect him to call you sir."

Warden leaned back in his chair. "Am I right in thinking that Egan joined the army looking for some sort of revenge on the people who'd killed his parents?"

"Of course he did. The Provisional IRA claimed responsibility for that bomb. It was the kind of reaction you'd expect from a boy of seventeen."

"But wouldn't that make him suspect, sir? I mean, his psychological assessment would throw it all up. Must have."

"Or perfect for our requirements, Daniel, it depends on your point of view. When he was a year old his parents moved to South Armagh from London, then to Belfast. When he was twelve they came back to London because they'd had enough of the situation over there. So, a boy with an Ulster background, a Catholic, for what it's worth, who even spoke reasonable Irish because his father had taught him. The kind of brain which earned a scholarship to Cambridge. Come on, Daniel, he was pulled out of the crowd within six months of joining the army. And then, he does possess one other very special attribute."

"What's that, sir?"

Villiers walked to the window and peered out into the rain. "He's a killer by instinct, Daniel. No hesitation. I've never seen anyone quite like him. As an undercover agent in Ireland he's assassinated eighteen terrorists to my certain knowledge. IRA, INLA ..."

"His own people, sir?"

"Just because he's a Catholic?" Villiers demanded. "Come off it, Daniel. Nairac was a Catholic. He was also an officer in the Grenadier Guards and that's all that concerned the IRA when they killed him. Anyway, Sean Egan has never played favorites. He's also taken care of several leading gunmen on the Protestant side. UVF and Red Hand of Ulster."

Warden looked down at the file. "Quite a man. And now you've got to tell him he's finished at twenty-five years of age."

"Exactly," Villiers said. "So let's have him in and get it over with."

When Sean Egan entered the room he was in shirtsleeve order, creases razor sharp, the beige beret tilted at the exact regulation angle. He wore shoulderstrap rank slides with sergeant's chevrons. On his right sleeve were the usual SAS wings. Above his left shirt pocket he also wore the wings of an Army Air Corps pilot. Below them were the ribbons for the Distinguished Conduct Medal, the Military Medal for Bravery in the Field and campaign ribbons for Ireland and the Falklands. He stood rigidly at attention in front of Warden, who sat behind his desk. Villiers remained in the window seat smoking a cigarette.

Warden said, "At ease, Sergeant. This is completely informal." He indicated a chair. "Sit down."

Egan did as he was told. Villiers got up and took a tin of cigarettes from his pocket. "Smoke?"

"Given it up, sir. When I got my packet in the Falklands, one bullet chose the left lung."

"Some good in everything, I suppose," Villiers said. "Filthy habit."

He was filling time and they all knew it. Warden said awkwardly, "Colonel Villiers is your control officer on this one, Egan."

"So I understand, sir."

There was a pause while Warden fiddled with the papers as if uncertain what to say. Villiers broke in. "Daniel," he said to Warden, "I wonder if you'd mind if Sergeant Egan and I had a word in private?"

Warden's relief was plain. "Of course, sir."

The door closed behind him. Villiers said, "It's been a long time, Sean."

"I didn't think you were still with the regiment, sir."

"On and off. A lot of my time's taken up with Group Four. You did a job for us in Sicily, as I recall. Just before the Falklands."

"That's right, sir. Still part of DI5?"

"On paper only. Antiterrorism is still the name of the game though. My boss is responsible only to the Prime Minister."

"Would that still be Brigadier Ferguson, sir?"

"That's it. You're well informed—as usual."

"You used to tell me that's all that kept you alive in Belfast and Derry, undercover. Being well informed."

Villiers laughed. "A damned Shinner, right to the end, aren't you, Sean, just like your Dad? Only a dyed-in-the-wool Ulster Catholic would call Londonderry Derry."

"I don't like the way they use bombs. That doesn't mean I think they haven't got a point of view."

Villiers nodded. "Seen your uncle lately?"

"He visited me in Maudsley Military Hospital a few months ago."

"Was it as difficult as usual?"

Egan nodded. "He never was much of a patriot. To him the army is just a big waste of time." There was another pause and he continued, "Look, sir, let's make this easy for you. I wasn't up to scratch, was I?"

Villiers turned. "You did fine. First time anyone has actually got out of the pit. Very ingenious, that. But the knee, Sean." He came round the desk and opened the file. "It's all here in the medical report. I mean, they've done a clever job in putting it together again."

Egan said, "Stainless steel and plastic. The original bionic man, only not quite as good as new."

"It will never be a hundred percent. Your own personal evaluation report on the exercise." Villiers picked it up. "When did you write this? An hour ago? You say here yourself that the knee let you down."

"That's right," Egan agreed calmly.

"Could have been the death of you in action. All right ninety percent of the time, but it's the ten percent that matters."

Egan said, "So, I'm out?"

"Of the regiment, yes. However, it's not as black as it looks. You're entitled to a discharge and pension, but there's no need for that. The army still needs you."

"No thanks." Egan shook his head. "If it isn't SAS, then I'm not interested."

Villiers said, "Are you sure about that?"

"Absolutely, sir."

Villiers sat back, watching him, a slight frown on his face. "There's more to this, isn't there?"

Egan shrugged. "Maybe. All those months in hospital gave me time to think. When I joined up seven years ago I had my reasons and you know what they were. I was just a kid and full of all sorts of wild ideas. I wanted to pay them back for my parents."

"And?"

"You don't pay anyone back. The bill will always be outstanding. Never paid in full. So much Irish time." He got up and walked to the window. "How many have I knocked off over there and for what? It just goes on and on, and it didn't bring my folks back."

"Perhaps you need a rest," Villiers suggested.

Sean Egan adjusted his beret. "Sir, with the greatest respect to the colonel, what I need is out."

Villiers stared at him, then stood up.

"Fine. If that's what you want, you've earned it. There is another alternative, of course."

"What's that, sir?"

"You could come and work with me for Brigadier Ferguson at Group Four."

"Out of the frying pan into the fire? I don't think so."

"What will you do, go back to your uncle?"

Egan laughed harshly. "God save us, I'd rather work for the Devil himself."

"Cambridge then? Not too late."

"I don't really see myself fitting into that kind of cloistered calm. I'd feel uncomfortable, and those poor old dons certainly would."

"Oh, I don't know," Villiers said. "I used to know an Oxford professor who was an SOE agent during the Second World War. Still ..."

"Something will turn up, sir."

"I expect so." Villiers looked at his watch. "The helicopter is leaving for regimental headquarters at Hereford in ten minutes. Grab your kit and be on it. I'll arrange for your discharge to be expedited."

"Thank you, sir."

Egan moved to the door and Villiers said, "By the way, I was just remembering your foster sister, Sally. How is she?"

Egan turned, a hand on the doorknob. "Sally died, Colonel, about four months ago."

Villiers was genuinely horrified. "My God, how? She couldn't have been more than eighteen."

"She was drowned. They found her in the Thames near Wapping. I was in the middle of major surgery at the time so there was nothing I could do. My uncle took care of the funeral for me. She's in Highgate Cemetery, quite close to Karl Marx. She liked it up there." His face was blank, his voice calm. "Can I go now, sir?"

"Of course."

The door closed. Villiers lit another cigarette, shocked and disturbed. The door opened again and Captain Warden came in. "He told me you wanted him on the helicopter, back to regiment."

"That's right."

"He's taking his discharge?" Warden frowned. "But there's no need for that, sir. He can't continue to serve in SAS, yes, but there are plenty of units who'd give their eyeteeth to get their hands on him."

"No way. He's quite adamant about that. He's changed. Maybe the Falklands did it, and all those months in hospital. He's going and that's it."

"A hell of a pity, sir."

"Yes, well, there may be ways and means of handling him yet. I offered him a job with Group Four. He turned it down flat."

"Do you think he might change his mind?"

"We'll have to see what a few months on the outside does to him. I can't see him sitting in the corner of an insurance office, not that he would need to. That pub of his father's—he owns it. He also happens to be Jack Shelley's sole heir. But never mind that now. He just gave me a shock. Told me that foster sister of his was drowned in the Thames a few months ago." He nodded to the computer in the corner. "We can pull in stuff from Central Records Office at Scotland Yard with that thing, can't we?"

"No problem, sir. Matter of seconds."

"See what they've got on Sally Baines Egan. No, make that Sarah."

Warden sat down at the computer. Villiers stood at the window looking out at the rain. Beyond the trees he heard the roaring of the helicopter engine starting up.

"Here we are, sir. Sarah Baines Egan, age eighteen. Next of kin, Ida Shelley, Jordan Lane, Wapping. It's a pub called The Bargee."

"Anything interesting?"

"Found on a mudbank. Been dead around four days. Drug addict. Four convictions for prostitution."

"What in the hell are you talking about?" Villiers turned to the computer. "You must have the wrong girl."

"I don't think so, sir."

Villiers stared at the screen intently, then straightened. The helicopter passed overhead and he glanced up. "My God!" he whispered. "I wonder if he knows?"

TWO

PARIS, ON THE RIGHT occasion, can seem the most desirable city on earth, but not at one o'clock on a November morning by the Seine with rain drifting across the river in a solid curtain.

Eric Talbot turned the corner from rue de la Croix and found himself on a small quay. He wore jeans and a parka, the hood pulled up over his head and a backpack hanging from his left shoulder. A typical student, or so he appeared, and yet there was something else. An impression of frailness, unusual in a boy of nineteen, eyes sunken into dark holes, the skin stretched too tightly over the cheekbones.

He paused under a streetlamp and looked across at the café which was his destination. La Belle Aurore. He managed a smile in spite of the fact that his hands wouldn't stop shaking. La Belle Aurore. That had been the name of the café in the Paris sequence in *Casablanca*—not that there seemed anything romantic in the establishment across the quay.

He started forward and suddenly became aware of the glow of a cigarette in the darkness of a doorway to his right. The man who stepped out was a gendarme, a heavy, old-fashioned cape protecting his shoulders against the rain.

"And where do you think you're going?"

The boy answered him in reasonable French, nodding across the quay. "The café, monsieur."

"Ah, English." The gendarme snapped his fingers. "Papers."

The boy unzipped his parka, took out his wallet and produced a British passport. The gendarme examined it. "Walker—George Walker. Student." He handed the passport back and the boy's hand trembled violently. "Are you ill?"

The boy managed a smile. "Just a touch of flu."

The gendarme shrugged. "Well, you won't find a cure for it over there. Take my advice and find yourself a bed for the night."

He flicked what was left of his cigarette into the water, turned and walked away, his heavy boots ringing on the cobbles. The boy waited until he had turned the corner, then crossed the quay quickly, opened the door of La Belle Aurore and went inside.

It was a poor sort of place, of a type common on that part of the waterfront, frequented by sailors and stevedores during the day and prostitutes by night. There was the usual zinc-topped counter, rows of bottles on the shelves behind, a cracked mirror advertising Gitanes.

The woman who sat behind the bar reading an ancient copy of *Paris Match* wore a black bombazine dress and was incredibly fat, with stringy peroxided hair. She glanced up and looked at the boy.

"Monsieur?"

There was a row of booths down one side of the café, a small fire opposite. The room was empty aside from one man seated beside the fire at a marble-topped table. He was of medium height with a pale, rather aristocratic face. The thin white line of a scar bisected his left cheek, running from his eye to the corner of his mouth. He wore a dark-blue Burberry trench coat.

Eric Talbot's head ached painfully, mainly at the sides behind the ears, and his nose wouldn't stop running. He wiped it quickly with the back of his hand and managed a painful smile. "Agnés, madame. I'm looking for Agnés."

"No Agnés here, young man." She frowned. "You don't look so good." She reached for a bottle of cognac and poured a little into a glass. "Drink that like a good boy, then you'd better be on your way."

His hand trembled as he raised the glass, a dazed look on his face. "But Mr. Smith sent me. I was told she'd be expecting me."

"And so she is, *chéri*."

The young woman who leaned out of the booth at the far end of the room stood up and came toward him. She had dark hair held back under a scarlet beret, a heart-shaped face, the lips full and insolent. She wore a black plastic raincoat, scarlet sweater to match the beret, black mini-skirt and high-heeled ankle boots. She was very small, almost childlike, which increased the impression of a kind of overall corruption.

"You don't look too good, *chéri*. Come and sit down and tell me all about it." She nodded to the fat woman. "I'll take care of it, Marie."

She took his arm and led him toward the booth past the man by the fire, who ignored them. "All right, let's see your passport."

Eric Talbot passed it across and she examined it quickly. "George Walker, Cambridge. Good—very good." She passed it back. "We'll talk English if you like. I talk good English. You don't look too well. What are you on, heroin?" The boy nodded. "Well, I can't help you there, not right now, but how about a little coke to keep you going? Just the thing to get you through a rainy night by the Seine."

"Oh, my God, that would be wonderful."

She rummaged in her handbag, took out a small white package and a straw and pushed them across. In the mirror above the fire, the man in the blue trench coat was looking at her inquiringly. She nodded, he emptied his glass, got up and went out.

Talbot had the packet open and inhaled the cocaine through the straw. His eyes closed and Agnés poured a little cognac in her glass from the bottle on the table. The boy leaned back, eyes still closed as she took a small vial from her handbag. She added a few drops of the colorless liquid to the cognac and replaced the vial in her handbag. The boy opened his eyes and managed a smile.

"Better?" she asked.

"Oh, yes." He nodded.

She pushed the glass across. "Drink that and let's get down to business."

He did as he was told, taking one tentative sip, then swallowing it all. He placed the glass on the table and she offered him a Gauloise.

The smoke caught the back of his throat harshly and he coughed. "All right, what happens now?"

"Back to my place. You catch the British Airways flight to London that leaves at noon. Carry the goods through in a body belt, only not dressed like that, *chéri*. Jeans and parka always get you stopped at customs."

"So what do I do?" Eric Talbot had never felt so light-headed, so remote, and his voice seemed to come from somewhere outside himself.

"Oh, I've got a nice blue suit for you, umbrella and briefcase. You'll look quite the businessman."

She took his arm and helped him up. As they reached Marie at the bar, the boy started to laugh. She glanced up. "You find me amusing, young man?"

"Oh, no, madame, not you. It's this place. La Belle Aurore. That's the name of the café in *Casablanca* where Humphrey Bogart and Ingrid Bergman have their last glass of champagne before the Nazis come."

"I'm sorry, monsieur, but I do not see films," she replied gravely.

"Oh, come, madame, but everyone knows *Casablanca*." He lectured her with the careful, slow graveness of the drunk. "My mother died when I was born, and when I was twelve I got a new one. My wonderful, wonderful stepmother, lovely Sarah. My father was away a lot in the army, but Sarah made up for everything, and in the holidays she let me sit up to watch the Midnight Movie on television whenever it was *Casablanca*." He leaned closer. "Sarah said *Casablanca* should be a compulsory part of everyone's education because she didn't think there was enough romance in the world."

"Now on that, I agree with her." She patted his face. "Go to bed."

It was the last conscious thing Eric Talbot remembered, for by the time he reached the door he was in a state of total, chemically induced hypnosis. He crossed the quay, moving with the certainty of a sleepwalker, Agnés's hand on his arm. They turned onto a small wharf by some warehouses, a cobbled slipway running down into the river.

They paused and Agnés called softly, "Valentin?"

The man who stepped out of the shadows was hard and dangerous-looking. His shoulders enhanced a generally large physical frame, but there was already a touch of dissolution about him, a little too much flesh, and the long black hair and thick sideburns gave him a strangely old-fashioned appearance.

"How many drops did you give him?"

"Five." She shrugged.

"Maybe six or seven."

"Amazing stuff, scopolamine," Valentin said. "If we left him now, he'd wake up in three days without the ability to remember anything he'd done, even murder."

"But you won't let him wake up in three days?"

"Of course not. That's why we're here, isn't it?"

She shivered. "You frighten me, you truly do."

"Good," he said, and took Talbot's arm. "Now let's get on with it."

"I can't watch," she said. "I can't."

"Suit yourself," he told her calmly.

She turned away and he took the boy by the arm and led him down the slipway. The boy followed without hesitation. When they reached the end, Valentin paused, then said, "All right, in you go."

Talbot stepped off the edge and disappeared. He surfaced a moment later and gazed up at the Frenchman with unseeing eyes. Valentin went down on one knee at the edge of the slipway and leaned over, putting a hand on the boy's head. "Goodbye, my friend."

It was so shockingly easy. The boy went under as Valentin pushed, stayed under with no struggle at all, only air bubbles disturbing the surface until they, too, stopped. Valentin towed the lifeless body round the edged parapet and left it sprawled on the end of the slipway, almost entirely submerged.

He walked back to Agnés, drying his hands on a handkerchief. "You can make your phone call. I'll see you at my place later."

She waited until the sound of his footsteps had faded and then started to walk along the quay. There was a movement in the shadows of a doorway and she recoiled in panic. "Who's there?"

As he lit a cigarette, the face of the man who'd been sitting in the café was illuminated. "No need to arouse the neighborhood, old girl."

He spoke in English, the kind that had a public school edge to it, and there was a weary good humor there tinged with a kind of contempt.

"Oh, it's you, Jago," she replied in the same language. "God, how I hate you. You talk to me as if I was something from under a stone."

"My dear old thing," he drawled. "Haven't I always behaved like a perfect gentleman?"

"Oh, yes," she said. "You kill with a smile. Always very good-mannered. You remind me of the man who said to the French customs officer, 'No I'm not a foreigner, I'm English.' "

"To be perfectly accurate, Welsh, but you wouldn't appreciate the difference. I presume Valentin has been as revoltingly efficient as usual?"

"If you mean has he done your dirty work for you, yes."

"Not mine, Smith's."

"The same difference. You kill for Smith when it suits you."

"Of course." There was a kind of bewildered amusement on his face. "But with style, my sweet. Valentin, on the other hand, would kill his grandmother if he thought he could get a good price for her body at the School of Anatomy. And while we're at it, remind that pimp of yours that I expect him to keep in close touch, just in case the court processes the body sooner than usual."

"He's not my pimp, he's my boyfriend."

"A third-rate gangster, walking the streets with those friends of his, trying to imagine he's Alain Delon in *Borsalino*. If it wasn't for the girls he couldn't even pay for his cigarettes."

He turned and walked off without another word, whistling tunelessly, and Agnés left too, pausing only at the first public telephone she came to, to call the police.

"Emergency?" she demanded. "I was just walking past the slipway up from rue de la Croix when I saw what looked like a body in the water."

"Name, please," the duty officer said, but she had already replaced the receiver and was hurrying away.

The duty officer filled details of the incident on the right form and passed it to the dispatcher. "Better send a car."

"Do you think it might be a crank?"

The other shook his head. "More likely some whore doing the night beat by the river who just doesn't want to get involved."

The dispatcher nodded and passed the details on to a patrol car in the area. Not that it mattered, for at that very moment, the gendarme who had spoken to Eric Talbot earlier walked down the slipway for the purposes of nature and discovered the body for himself.

Given the circumstances, the police investigation was understandably perfunctory. The gendarme who had found the body interviewed Marie at La Belle Aurore, but she had long since learned that in her line of business it paid to see and hear nothing. Yes, the young man had visited the café. He'd asked where he might get a room. He'd seemed ill and asked for a cognac.

She'd given him a couple of addresses and he'd left. End of story.

There was the usual postmortem the following morning, and three days later an inquest at which, in view of the medical evidence, the coroner reached the only possible verdict: death by drowning while under the influence of alcohol and drugs.

The same afternoon the body of the boy known as Walker was delivered to the public mortuary in the rue St. Martin, a superior name for a very mean street, where appropriate documentation was to be prepared for the British Embassy—not that such documentation ever arrived, thanks to a cousin of Valentin, an old lady employed as a cleaner and washer of bodies, who intercepted the necessary package before it left the building.

No possible query could be raised the following morning when Jago presented himself, in the guise of a cultural attaché from the British Embassy, with all the necessary documentation. The much respected firm of undertakers, Chabert & Sons, would take charge of the body, providing it with a suitable coffin. The grief-stricken family had arranged for it to be flown by a charter aircraft the following day from a small airfield called Vigny, a few miles out of Paris. From there the flight plan would take it to Woodchurch in Kent where the remains would be received by the funeral firm of Hartley Brothers. All was in order. The documents were countersigned, the regulation black hearse appeared to bear the body away.

The premises of Chabert & Son were situated by the river and, by coincidence, not too far away from where Eric Talbot had met his death.

The building dated from the turn of the century, a splendid mausoleum of a place with twenty chapels of rest where relatives could visit the loved one to mourn in some decent privacy before the burial.

As with many such old-established firms in most European capitals, Chabert's had a night attendant, a row of bells above his head. There was a bell for each chapel of rest, a cord placed between the corpse's hands against the unlikely event of an unexpected resurrection.

But at ten o'clock that evening the attendant was snoring loudly in a drunken stupor, thanks to the bottle of cognac thoughtfully left on his desk by some grieving relative. He was long gone when Valentin carefully unlocked the rear door with a duplicate key and entered, followed by Jago. They each carried a canvas holdall.

They paused beside the glass-walled office. Jago nodded at the attendant. "He's well away."

"Bloody old drunk," Valentin said contemptuously. "One sniff of a barmaid's apron is all he needs."

They proceeded along the corridor flanked by chapels of rest on either side. There was the smell of flowers everywhere, and Jago said in French, "Enough to put you off roses for the rest of your life."

He paused at the door of one chapel and glanced in. The coffin was raised on an incline, the lid half down, a young woman visible, the face touched with unnatural color by the embalmer.

Jago lit a cigarette with one hand and paused. "Like a horror movie," he said cheerfully. "*Dracula* or something like that. Any minute now, her eyes will open and she'll reach for your throat."

"For God's sake, shut up," Valentin croaked. "You know I hate this part."

"Oh, I don't know," Jago told him as they continued along the corridor. "I think you've done very well. What is this, the seventh?"

"It doesn't get any easier," the Frenchman said.

"Intimations of mortality, old stick."

Valentin frowned. "And what in the hell is that supposed to mean?"

"You'd need an English public school education to understand." Jago paused and glanced in the last chapel on the right. "This must be it."

The coffin was the only one closed. It was constructed of dark mahogany, the handles and studwork of gilded plastic in case cremation was favored. Normally, international regulations concerning the air freight of corpses required a sealed metallic interior, but this was habitually waived in the case of small aircraft flying at under ten thousand feet.

"All right," Jago said.

Valentin unscrewed the lid and parted the linen shroud underneath to reveal the body of Eric Talbot. There were two enormous scars running from chest to the lower stomach, roughly stitched together, relics of the postmortem. Valentin had spent two years as a conscript in the French Army, had served as a medical orderly. He'd seen plenty of corpses in Chad when he was on attachment to the Foreign Legion, but this was something he could never get used to. Sometimes he cursed the day he'd met Jago, but then the money …

He opened one of the holdalls, took out an instrument case, selected a scalpel and started to work on the stitches, pausing only to wipe sweat from his forehead.

"Get on with it," Jago told him impatiently. "We haven't got all night."

The air was tainted now, the sickly-sweet smell of corrupt flesh, quite unmistakable. Valentin finally removed the last stitches, paused, then eased the body open. Normally, the internal organs were replaced after the postmortem, but in a case such as this, where the body faced a considerable delay before burial, they were usually destroyed. The chest cavity and abdomen were empty. Valentin paused, hands trembling.

"A sentimentalist at heart. I always knew it." Jago opened the other holdall and took out one plastic bag of heroin after another, passing them across. "Hurry it up. I've got a date."

Valentin inserted one bag into the chest cavity and reached for another. "Boy or girl?" he said viciously.

"My goodness, I see I'm going to have to chastise you again, you French ape." Jago smiled gently, but the look in his eyes was terrible to see.

Valentin managed a weak laugh. "Only joking. Nothing intended."

"Of course. Now get the rest of it inside and sew him up again. I want to get out of here."

Jago lit another cigarette and went out, moving along the corridor to the chapel at the end. There were a few chairs, a sanctuary lamp casting a glow over the small altar and brass crucifix. All very simple, but then, he liked that. Always had done since he was a boy in the family pew in the village church, his father's tenants sitting respectfully behind. There was a stained-glass window with the family coat of arms dating from the fourteenth century, with the family motto: I do my will. It summed up his own philosophy exactly, not that it had gotten him anywhere in particular. He tipped his chair back against the wall.

"Where did it all go wrong, old son?" he asked himself softly.

After all, he'd had every advantage. An ancient and honorable name, not the one he used now, of course, but then one had to preserve the decencies. Public school, Sandhurst, a fine regiment. Captain at twenty-four with a Military Cross for undercover work in Belfast, and then that unfortunate Sunday night in South Armagh and four very dead members of the IRA whom Jago hadn't seen any point in taking in alive. Had taken every pleasure in finishing them off himself. But then that sniveling rat of a sergeant had turned him in, and the British Army, of course, did not operate a shoot-to-kill policy.

It wasn't so much that he'd minded being quietly cashiered, although it had nearly killed his father. It was the fact that the bastards had taken the Military Cross back. Still, old history now. Long gone.

The Selous Scouts hadn't been too particular in the closing year in Rhodesia before independence. Glad to get him, as were the South Africans for work with their commandos in Angola. Later, there was the war in Chad where he'd first met Valentin; he'd been lucky to get out of that one alive.

And then Smith, the mysterious Mr. Smith, and three very lucrative years—and the most extraordinary thing was that they had never met, or at least not so far as Jago knew. He didn't even know what had put Smith on to him in the first place. Not that it mattered. All that did matter was that there was almost a million pounds in his Geneva account. He wondered what his father would say to that, then got up and returned to the chapel of rest.

Valentin had carefully restitched the body and was replacing the shroud. Jago said, "Five million pounds street value. He's richer in death than he knows."

Valentin screwed down the lid again. "Six, maybe seven if it was diluted."

Jago smiled. "Now what kind of rat would pull a stroke like that? Come on, let's get moving."

They went past the office where the attendant still slept, and stepped out into the alley. It was raining and Jago turned up his collar. "Okay, you and Agnés be at Vigny tomorrow, one o'clock sharp for the departure. When the plane lifts off, ring the usual number in Kent."

"Of course." They had reached the end of the alley. Valentin said awkwardly, "We were wondering. That is, Agnés was wondering."

"Yes?" Jago said.

"Things have been going well. We thought a little more money might be in order?"

"We'll see," Jago said. "I'll mention it to Smith. I'll be in touch."

He walked away along the waterfront thinking about Valentin. A nasty bit of work. Rubbish, of course. No style. A true wharf rat, but a rat was still a rat and needed watching. He turned into the first all-night café he came to five minutes later and changed a hundred-franc note for coins at the bar, then went into a telephone booth in the corner where he dialed a London number.

He spoke quietly into the tape recorder at the other end. "Mr. Smith. Jago here." He twice repeated the number of the telephone he was using, replaced the receiver and lit a cigarette.

They had always operated this way: Smith with his answerphone and presumably an automatic bleeper to alert him to messages so that he was always the one to phone you. Surprisingly simple and no way to trace him. Foolproof.

The phone rang and Jago picked it up. "Jago."

"Smith here." The voice, as usual, was muffled, disguised. "How are you?"

"Fine."

"Any problems?"

"None. Everything as normal. The consignment leaves Vigny at one tomorrow."

"Good. Our friends will pick it up as normal. It should be making us money within a week."

"That's good."

"Your account will be credited with the usual amount plus ten percent on the last day of the month."

"That's nice."

"The laborer is worthy of his hire...."

"And all that good old British nonsense." Jago laughed.

"Exactly. I'll be in touch."

Jago replaced the receiver and returned to the bar, where he had a quick cognac. It was still raining when he went out into the street, but he didn't mind that. It made him feel good, and he was whistling again as he walked away along the uneven pavement.

But at Vigny the following afternoon the weather was not good—low cloud and rain and a ground mist that reduced visibility to four hundred yards. It was only a small airfield with a control tower and two hangars. Valentin and Agnés stayed in her Citroën on the edge of the runway and watched as the hearse arrived and the coffin was maneuvered inside the small Cessna plane. The hearse departed. The pilot disappeared inside the control tower.

"It doesn't look good," Agnés said.

"I know. We could be here all day," Valentin told her. "I'll see what's happening."

He put a raincoat over his shoulders and strolled across to the main hangar where he found a lone mechanic in stained white overalls working on a Piper Comanche.

"Cigarette?" Valentin offered him a Gauloise. "My English cousin is expecting the body of his son this afternoon. He asked me to check things out. I saw the hearse arrive. I mean, is the flight on or not?"

"A temporary hitch," the mechanic said. "No trouble taking off here, but it's not so good at the other end. The captain tells me he's expecting clearance around four o'clock."

"Thanks." Valentin took a half bottle of whiskey from his pocket. "Help yourself. You don't mind if I use your phone?"

The mechanic drank from the bottle with enthusiasm. He wiped his mouth with the back of his hand. "I don't pay the bills; be my guest."

Valentin took out a slip of paper and dialed the number written on it. It was a Kent exchange which he knew was south of London, but other than that he knew nothing of the mysterious Hartley Brothers.

The voice at the other end simply said, "Yes?"

Valentin replied in his bad English, "Hartley Brothers? Vigny here."

The voice sharpened. "Any problem?"

"Yes, the weather, but they expect to be away at four."

"Good. Call me again to confirm."

Valentin nodded to the mechanic. "Keep the Scotch. I'll be back."

He returned to Agnés in the Citroën. "That's it. All off until four. Let's try that café down the road."

The man he had been speaking to replaced the telephone and clasped his hands together, leaning forward toward the weeping woman in front of him. He was sixty and slightly balding, wore gold pince-nez glasses, black tie and jacket, white shirt pristine, striped trousers immaculate. The gold-painted name-plate on his desk said Asa Bird.

"Mrs. Davies. I can assure you that here at Deepdene, your husband will receive only the very best attention. His ashes may be strewn in our own garden of rest if you wish."

The room was half in shadow on that dull November afternoon, but the flowers massed in the corners, the oak paneling, were reassuring as was his soothing, slightly avuncular voice that had a touch of the parson about it.

"That would be wonderful," she said.

He patted her hand. "Just a few formalities. Forms to fill in. Regulations, I'm afraid."

He pressed a bell on his desk, sat back, selected a handkerchief and proceeded to polish his glasses, standing up and peering out of the window into the immaculate garden that always filled him with conscious pleasure. Not bad for a boy born on the wrong side of the blanket in the worst slum in Liverpool that had fitted him for nothing but a life of petty crime. Eighteen offenses by the age of twenty-four. Everything from larceny to, although he preferred to forget about it now, male prostitution, which had led him to the chance of a lifetime, his relationship with the aging Henry Brown, an undertaker with his own long-established firm in Manchester.

He'd taken young Asa in, not that that was his name then, and groomed him in every way. Asa had loved the death business at once, taken to it like a duck to water, soon becoming an expert on every aspect, including embalming. And then old Mr. Henry had died, leaving only Mrs. Brown, who had never had a son of her own and doted on Asa, making perhaps only one mistake. Told him that she had made him her sole heir, an error which had led to her untimely death from pneumonia, helped on her way by Asa's unfortunately leaving the windows of her room wide open on a December night after first removing the bedclothes.

Mrs. Brown's thoughtful bequest had taken him to his own establishment, developed from an eighteenth-century country house. Deepdene Garden of Rest, with its own cremation facilities. You wouldn't find better in California, and his association with the mysterious Mr. Smith hadn't done him any harm.

The door opened and a handsome young black man entered. He was tall and muscular, and the well-cut chauffeur's uniform showed him to advantage. "You rang, Mr. Bird?"

"Yes, Albert. The package from France. It will be later than we thought."

"That's a shame, Mr. Bird."

"Oh, I expect we'll manage. Is the transport ready?"

"In the rear garage, sir."

"Good. I'll just have a look." Bird turned to Mrs. Davies. "I'll leave you for a few minutes to complete those forms and then I'll help you choose a suitable coffin."

She nodded gratefully. He patted her shoulder and went out. Albert opened a large umbrella and held it over Bird's head as they crossed the cobbled yard.

"Bloody weather," Bird said. "Always seems to be pissing down these days."

"Dreadful, Mr. Bird," Albert agreed, and got the garage door open. When he pulled a dust sheet away, a gleaming black hearse stood revealed. "There you are."

Beautifully painted on the side was the legend, "Hartley Brothers, Funeral Directors," in gold.

"Excellent," Bird said. "Where did you get it?"

"Knocked it off myself in North London, Thursday.

The logbook and tax disc are from a write-off I found in a scrap-yard in Brixton."

"You're certain you won't be remembered?"

Albert laughed. "In Brixton? You, they'd remember, but me? In Brixton, just another brother, just another black face. Do we go the usual way?"

"Yes, you take the hearse. I'll follow in the Jaguar."

Which Albert knew meant just in case anything went wrong, which really meant that he would be left carrying the can while the old bastard did a runner. Not that it mattered. His day would come, Albert was certain.

"That's fine, Mr. Bird."

Bird patted his face. "You're a good boy, Albert, a lovely boy. I must think of some way to reward you."

"Not necessary, Mr. Bird." Albert smiled as he opened the umbrella again. "Serving you is reward enough," he said and they started back across the yard.

Agnés and Valentin arrived back at Vigny at four to discover that the plane had already departed. She watched Valentin hurry across to the hangar and speak to the mechanic again. She lit a cigarette and waited. Valentin returned in a little while.

"Left fifteen minutes ago."

"Did you phone?" she asked.

"Yes," he said as he switched on the engine. "And a funny thing happened. You know how sometimes an answering tape stays on even though someone has picked up the receiver?"

"Yes."

"Well, as my usual man answered, I heard a tape playing."

"What did it say?"

"It said: This is Deepdene Garden of Rest. We regret there is no one here at the moment, but leave your number and we'll get back to you."

"Now that is interesting, *chéri*." Agnés smiled, managing to look quite vicious. "A chink in Monsieur Jago's armor that could be worth a great deal."

~

Woodchurch Airfield was not much bigger than Vigny. An aero club really, used occasionally for charter or freight flights. Situated in the depths of the Kent countryside, it had no customs facilities, which meant that the customs officer who received the Cessna with Eric Talbot's coffin had to drive all the way from Canterbury. He was not pleased by the delay, wanted only to be on his way. Formalities were of the briefest. The necessary papers were signed, and he and the pilot helped Albert load the coffin into the hearse.

As Albert drove through the gate and turned into the country road, the Cessna roared down the runway and lifted into the sky. Behind him, Bird, who had stayed discreetly out of the way, took up station in the black Jaguar. Albert reached for the half-pint of vodka in the glove compartment, then shook a couple of his special pills from a bottle, driving one-handed. He washed them down with the vodka, and within a few minutes was on a marvelous high.

He checked out the Jaguar in his rearview mirror. It was already dusk, and Bird had turned on his lights. Always a cautious one, Albert thought. Never took a chance if someone else could take it for him, and usually that someone else was Albert.

"Albert this, Albert that," the chauffeur said softly, glancing into the mirror again. "I sometimes wonder what the silly old bugger thinks I am."

He took another swig from the bottle, realized too late that he was running into a bend. He dropped the bottle and swung the wheel. His off-side front wheel mounted the grass bank, collided with a block of granite which had fallen from a low wall. The hearse careered across the road, went straight through a wire fence and plowed down a slope, uprooting young fir trees on its way, sliding to a halt in a gully below, half on its side.

Only the seat belt had saved him from going through the windshield. He got the driver's door open and pulled himself out. He stood there, slightly dazed, aware of the Jaguar pausing on the road above. Bird appeared at the top of the short slope.

"Albert?" There was genuine fear in his voice.

"I'm all right," Albert called.

At the same moment he saw that the coffin had smashed through the glass side of the hearse, the lid bursting open so that the corpse hung out still swathed in the shroud. He dropped to his knees and peered under the vehicle and saw that the bottom end of the coffin was pinned underneath.

Bird scrambled down the slope to join him. "Just get him out. We'll put him in the boot of the Jaguar, but for God's sake hurry. Someone might come."

Albert reached under the hearse. There was a slight, uneasy creaking and it swayed slightly. He jumped back. "This damn thing could topple over at any moment and he's pinned by the feet."

Bird stooped, and when he straightened he was holding the vodka bottle. "Drinking again," he said furiously. "What have I told you?" He slapped Albert across the face and threw the bottle into the trees.

Albert cowered away, a hand raised, a child again. "I'm sorry, Mr. Bird. It was an accident."

Bird took a penknife from his waistcoat pocket and opened it. "Cut his stitches. Open him up. We've got to get that heroin."

"I couldn't do that, Mr. Bird," Albert said.

"Do it!" Bird cried and hit him in the face again. "I'll get a bag from the car."

He thrust the penknife into the chauffeur's hand, turned and scrambled up the slope. Albert, terrified, dropped to his knees and pulled the shroud away. The boy's eyes were open, staring at him. He averted his own eyes as best he could and started to hack at the stitches.

On the road above, Bird got the boot of the Jaguar open and found a canvas bag he used for shopping. He went back to the top of the slope and peered down into the gathering darkness. "Have you got it?"

"Yes, Mr. Bird." Albert's voice was strained and muffled.

"Put it in this."

Bird tossed the canvas bag down and looked anxiously along the road. Thank God it had happened on a side road, and the flat farmland beyond the bend meant that he could see some considerable distance. His heart was pounding and there was sweat on his face. What would Smith say? The prospect was too awful to think about.

He slid down the slope. "Are you ready, for God's sake? Have you got it all?"

"I think so, Mr. Bird."

"Right, let's get out of here."

"But they'll still find the body, Mr. Bird. Certain to."

"Even if they do, they can't trace any of us. Not in France, not here, and there is such a thing as destroying the evidence. Go on! Get up there and get the car started!"

Albert scrambled away and Bird unscrewed the cap on the fuel tank. Petrol spilled out onto the ground. He took out his handkerchief and soaked it, then went halfway up the bank. He found his lighter, touched it to the handkerchief and tossed it down onto the hearse. For a moment, he thought it was going to go out, and then a yellow tongue of flame flickered into life. By the time he reached the top of the slope, the hearse was beginning to burn. He had a glimpse of the corpse's eyes staring at him accusingly, then turned and got into the Jaguar, and Albert drove away.

Later, at his desk at Deepdene, waiting for Smith to return his call, he sipped brandy and tried to pull himself together. It was going to be all right. It had to be. Smith would understand. The telephone rang as Albert entered the room with the tea things on a silver tray. Bird held up a hand, motioning him to silence, and picked up the phone.

"Smith here."

"It's Bird, sir." Bird's hands were shaking. "Actually we've had a bit of a problem."

Smith's voice didn't change in the slightest. "Tell me about it."

Which Bird did, omitting any reference to Albert and his drinking, blaming the entire incident on a steering defect.

When he was finished, Smith said, "Most unfortunate."

"I know, but accidents will happen, sir."

"I can't comment on that, I've never had the experience," Smith said.

"So what do we do, sir? Will Mr. Jago be picking up the stuff as usual?"

"Not necessary this time. I'll take delivery of the goods tomorrow afternoon at three o'clock precisely.

You will leave it in luggage locker forty-three at Victoria Station in London."

"But the key, sir?"

"Will be in an envelope in your morning mail. I'll have a duplicate," Smith said.

"Right, sir."

"There had better not be any more accidents, Mr. Bird, or Jago will be round to have words, and you wouldn't like that, would you?"

"No need for that, sir," Bird gabbled.

"Don't worry, Mr. Bird. The young man was a nobody. They've all been carefully selected nobodies. No way of tracing him to any of us. With any luck, this should prove to be a temporary inconvenience. Good night."

Bird replaced the phone and Albert said, "What did he say?"

The older man told him. He was brighter now, relieved and reassured at the way Smith had taken things. "He's right. The kid was a nobody. The hearse was stolen. All the paperwork phony. The scuffers won't stand a chance on this one."

"Scuffers, Mr. Bird?"

"Sorry, Albert, betraying my youth there. That's what we called coppers in Liverpool when I was a lad."

Albert nodded. "I was thinking, Mr. Bird. A locker at Victoria Station. I mean, if I hung around, maybe I could catch a glimpse of him. I did it before, remember, when that Frasconi geezer turned up."

Bird shook his head pityingly. "Albert, I don't know how you've survived this long. Do you really think someone as big as Smith would be that stupid? If you even tried it, that bastard Jago would be on you like a vulture. Miracle you got away with it before. They'd find you floating down the Thames with your dick in your hand, and that would be such a waste. Now what have we here?"

"Tea, Mr. Bird." Albert poured some from Bird's favorite silver pot into a delicate porcelain cup. "Ceylon, just the way you like it."

"Lovely." Bird took a sip, then gulped it down gratefully. "Nothing like a nice cup of tea, as my old mother used to say." He glanced up at Albert, reached and patted his cheek. "You're a good boy, Albert, but a little foolish sometimes."

"A good thing I've got you to look after me, Mr. Bird," Albert said and poured him another cup of tea.

In Paris at that precise moment, Jago was listening to Smith's version of events. "A balls up is putting it mildly," he said. "What do you want me to do?"

"Nothing for the moment," Smith told him. "With luck, we might get away with it. Let's wait and see, but if things go sour, I'll need you over here to handle the disposal work. You'd better come over to London in the morning. The usual service flat in Hyde Park. I'll be in touch."

"My pleasure, sir."

Jago replaced the telephone. He stood staring down at it, then started to laugh. It really was too funny for words. He was still laughing when he went into his bedroom to get dressed.

THREE

BRIGADIER CHARLES FERGUSON HAD commanded the Group Four since its conception in 1972. He was a large, untidy man in his early sixties with a deceptively benign face who affected crumpled suits, his only hint of anything in the slightest sense military his Guards' tie. Ferguson preferred to work at home when possible in the Georgian splendor of his Cavendish Square flat, which was where he was on the following morning, sitting in comfort beside the Adam fireplace drinking tea and working his way through a stack of papers, when his Gurkha manservant, Kim, appeared.

"Colonel Villiers is here, sir. He says it's urgent."

Ferguson nodded, and a moment later Tony Villiers entered, wearing a black polo-neck sweater, Donegal tweed jacket and faded green cord slacks. His face was white, his eyes very dark, every evidence of real distress there. He was carrying a briefcase.

"My dear Tony." Ferguson stood up. "What on earth is it?"

"This report just came in, sir. Fed into the general computer, it arrived on my desk, following the usual cross-indexing procedure for service personnel." Ferguson adjusted the half-moon reading glasses he wore, walked to the window and studied the report Villiers had handed him.

"Quite extraordinary." He turned. "But why you, Tony? I don't understand."

"Eric Talbot was my cousin Edward's boy. You remember Edward, sir? Half-colonel in the Paras? Killed in the Falklands."

"Good God, yes. So you're family?"

"Exactly, sir."

"But if the boy was passing himself off as this George Walker, how did the Kent police establish his real identity so quickly?"

"The boy was only partially burned. They were able to take his fingerprints, and they were on the national computer."

"Really?" Ferguson frowned.

"The boy was a student at Cambridge—Trinity College. Last year he got picked up in a police raid on the wrong sort of party."

"Drugs?"

"That's right. It was a user-only charge, so he didn't go to jail. I've only just found this out from Central Records Office at the Yard."

Ferguson walked to his desk and sat down. "Talbot, yes, I remember Colonel Talbot's death in the Falklands now. Tumbledown, wasn't it?"

"Yes, he was liaising with the Welsh Guards."

"And the father. Baronet as I recall. Sir Geoffrey Talbot."

"He had a stroke some time ago when his wife died," Villiers told him. "He's been in a nursing home ever since. Doesn't even know what time of day it is." He paused. "Look, do you mind if I have a drink, sir?"

"Of course not, Tony. Help yourself."

Villiers went to the sideboard and poured a brandy into a cut-glass tumbler. He walked to the window and stood there peering out. "The thing is, he's my uncle, you see, sir. My mother's brother—not that we were ever close."

"Tony, I really am sorry. A good thing the old boy's not capable of taking this in. I mean, he lost one heir to the Falklands, another in this particularly distressing way." He tapped the report. "I wonder who inherits the title."

"Actually, I do, sir," Villiers said.

Ferguson removed his glasses wearily. "In normal circumstances such a thing would be a cause for congratulation."

"Yes, well, we'll forget about that and concentrate on this." Villiers opened the briefcase and produced a plastic packet which he placed on the desk in front of the brigadier. "Heroin, and the immediate opinion at the lab on briefest of examinations is that it's very, very good stuff indeed. This is the kind of article you could cut three times over and still sell on the street."

"All right, go on," Ferguson said, his face grave.

"It was found inside Eric's body when the medical examiner checked him. It also became plain to him that the boy had been dead for days and the subject of a postmortem. Apparently, he recognized the surgical technique used as French, so Kent Police tried the fingerprints on the Sûreté in Paris and came up with this."

Villiers passed another report across and Ferguson studied it. Finally he sat back. "So what have we got here? The boy goes to Paris on a false passport. Drowns in the Seine under the influence of drugs. After the postmortem, his body is claimed, using forged papers, and flown to England."

"Packed with heroin," Villiers said.

"Of which this is only a sample. Is that what you're saying?"

"It makes sense. The police have already established that the hearse was stolen. There's no such funeral firm as Hartley Brothers. The whole thing was an elaborate front."

"Which went wrong. An accident of some sort."

"Exactly. They had to retrieve the stuff quickly and get the hell out of there fast."

"So fast that this packet was overlooked." Ferguson looked grim. "You do realize what you're suggesting, don't you? The possibility that the boy was deliberately killed in the first place so that his body could be used in this way."

"That's right," Villiers agreed. "I've asked the lab for an estimate. They say, judging by the size of that packet, the body could have carried at least five million pounds' worth at street value."

Ferguson drummed his fingers on the table. "However, except for your own personal connection, I don't really see how this concerns us."

"But it does, sir, very much so. I've got a copy here of the French coroner's report." Villiers took it from the briefcase. "Notice the chemical analysis of the blood. Traces of heroin, cocaine and also scopolamine and phenothiazine."

Ferguson leaned back. "Science at school was never my strong point. Explain."

"It all started in Colombia last year. The depressive alkaloid scopolamine is produced from the fruit of shrubs in the Andes. It can be converted into an odorless serum, no color, no smell, a few drops of which can reduce any individual to a state of total chemical hypnosis for at least three days. The condition is so absolute that the victims have no recall of what they've done. Men have killed, women been totally degraded, turned into sex slaves."

"And the phenothiazine?"

"It neutralizes certain side effects. Makes the victims more docile."

Ferguson shook his head. "God help us if it ever takes root over here."

"But it has, sir," Villiers said urgently. "During the past twelve months in Ulster there have been four cases of members of the Provisional IRA executed by Protestant paramilitary forces where the postmortem has revealed the same things. Scopolamine and phenothiazine."

"And you think there could be a link with this business?"

"There could be other cases. We'll have to run a computer check, but if there is a link and if it concerns the UVF or the Red Hand of Ulster or any other Protestant extremist groups, then it *is* our business."

Ferguson sat there frowning. Finally he nodded. "Right, Tony, drop everything else or get someone in the department to handle it. I'll leave you to sort this one out. Top priority. Keep me informed."

It was a dismissal. He placed his glasses back on and Villiers took the reports and the heroin and put them in his briefcase. "There is just one more thing, sir, on the personal side."

Ferguson looked up in surprise. "Well?"

"Eric had a stepmother, sir, Sarah Talbot. She's an American."

"You know her?"

"Oh, yes. She's a very unusual woman. Eric adored her. His own mother died when he was born, and Sarah meant a great deal to him, as he did to her."

"And now you've got to tell her about this tragic business. How will she take it?"

"I'm not sure." Villiers shrugged. "She was a Cabot from Boston. Very Blue Book. Her father was a millionaire several times over. Steel, I think. She'd had no mother from an early age so they were close. She was a typical spoiled rich bitch, as she once told me, who still managed to graduate from Radcliffe with honors."

"And then?"

"She underwent a sea change at twenty-one. Hated what was happening in Vietnam. Lost a boyfriend there. Two or three years later, she ran for Congress. Almost won, too. But the voters grew progressively disenchanted with her politics, she lost the election, gave up politics entirely, got her MBA from Harvard and joined a Wall Street firm of investment brokers."

"Helped by Big Daddy's money?"

Villiers shook his head. "Started from scratch on her own and now has a considerable reputation. She met Edward on a visit to London in the National Gallery one Sunday morning. She told me once that she forgave him for being a soldier because he was the most beautiful thing she'd ever seen in a uniform and red beret."

"And there was the boy."

"As I said, it was love at first sight for both of them. I don't mean this in the wrong way, sir." Villiers sounded awkward. "But I sometimes felt she loved Eric more than his father."

"Women go with the heart, Tony," Ferguson said gently. "Where is she at the moment?"

"New York, sir."

"Then you'd better get it over with."

"Yes, I'm not looking forward to that."

"Of course this Irish connection making it a security matter does mean you could legitimately make the whole affair the subject of a D notice. That would keep it out of the newspapers, television and so on." Ferguson shrugged. "I mean, no need to make things any more unpleasant for the family than they already are."

"That's good of you, sir." Villiers walked to the door, paused, then turned. "There *is* one more thing I should mention, sir."

"More, Tony?" Ferguson said wearily. "All right, tell me the worst."

"Sarah, sir. She's a very good friend of the President."

"Oh, my God!" Ferguson said. "That's all we needed."

Victoria Station was crowded with people, queues for some of the express trains. Albert wore a brown suede jacket and jeans as he pushed his way through the throng, carrying the bulging holdall filled with heroin. Locker number forty-three was locked, of course. He took the key from his pocket and opened the locker. All very simple. He put the bag inside, locked the door and walked away.

He hesitated just by the main entrance, intrigued. He had to know, it was as simple as that, and none of Bird's overprotective hysteria could put him off. He turned around and walked back, going into one of the cafés, ordering a coffee and finding a seat by the window, from which he had a clear view of the lockers.

The café was already busy, and two women came and sat at the table, crowding him in, and then the whole thing was over in an instant. He'd been looking for a man, of course, not the gray-haired, stout old woman in a man's raincoat and beret, already at the locker, key in hand.

She got the bag out as Albert struggled to get past the women at his table, and she had disappeared into the crowd by the entrance to the underground before he could do anything. He stood outside the café, angry for a moment, then shrugged and walked away.

Smith, from his vantage point beside the newsagent's where he had witnessed everything, shook his head and said softly, "Oh, dear, I'm really going to have to do something about you, aren't I?"

Manhattan was, as Manhattan always is on a wet November evening, busy, the traffic quite impossible, the sidewalks crowded with people hurrying through the rain. Sarah Talbot eased down the window of the Cadillac and looked out with conscious pleasure.

"A hell of a night, Charles."

Her chauffeur, a tough-looking young man in a smart black suit, his cap on the seat beside him, grinned. "You want to get out and walk, Mrs. Talbot?"

"No, thanks. My shoes are by Manolo Blahnik. I got them in London on my last trip and he definitely wouldn't like me to go out in the rain in them."

She was a month away from her fortieth birthday and looked thirty, even on a bad morning. Her dark hair was held back by a simple velvet bow leaving the face clear, her gray-green eyes sparkling above rather prominent cheekbones. It was not that she was beautiful in any conventional sense, but people always looked twice. Just now she was particularly elegant in a black velvet suit by Dior. She was on her way to her favorite restaurant, The Four Seasons, on Fifty-second Street, to dine alone, strictly from choice. A personal celebration, for that afternoon she'd pulled off the deal of her career, the takeover of a chain of department stores in the midwest, and against tough male opposition. Oh, yes, my girl, she thought, Daddy would have been proud of you tonight—which didn't give her any particular satisfaction.

She said, "I need a vacation, Charles."

"That sounds fair, Mrs. Talbot. The Virgins are nice this time of the year. We could open the house, get the boat out."

"You'd be down there every other week if I let you, you rogue," she said. "No, I was thinking I might fly over to England. Visit Eric at Cambridge."

"That's nice. How's he doing over there?"

"Fine. Just fine." She hesitated. "To be honest, I haven't heard much from him lately."

"I wouldn't worry about that at all. He's a young guy and you know what students are like. Girls on their mind all the time."

He swore softly, swinging the wheel as the car in front braked, and Sarah sat back, thinking of Eric. It had been two months since she'd had a letter, and when she'd tried to get him on the phone he'd simply not been available. Still, as Charles said, students were students.

The chauffeur passed a newspaper over. "Good story in there you maybe missed. That big Mafia trial, the members of that Frasconi Mob. The judge handed them down two hundred and ten years between them."

"So?" Sarah said as she took the paper.

"Look who they got a picture of coming out of court. The guy who was responsible for putting them all away."

The man in the photo on the courtroom steps was at least seventy, heavily built, with the fleshy, arrogant face of an ancient emperor. An overcoat was draped over his shoulders and he leaned on a cane. The caption read: "Ex-Mafia Boss Rafael Barbera Outside the Court."

"He's smiling," Sarah commented.

"He should be. He owed those guys from way back. The Frasconis killed his brother in the Mafia wars twenty years ago."

"Twenty years seems a long time to wait."

"Not for those guys. They believe in paying you off if it takes a lifetime."

She read the rest of the report. "It says here he's retired."

Charles laughed. "That's good. Listen, Mrs. Talbot, I'm from Tenth Street. That's Gambino territory. Let me tell you about Don Rafael. His parents brought him over from Sicily when he was ten. He was Mafia by family tradition. Went through the ranks so fast he was Don at thirty and the smartest of them all. Never served a day of his life in prison. Not one."

"A lucky man."

"No, not lucky, smart. He retired back to the old country a few years ago, but the word is he's number one man over there. Capo Mafia in all Sicily."

At that moment, a hand appeared at her partially opened window and she turned to see Henry Kissinger reaching across from the car next to hers. She opened the window completely and leaned out. "Henry, how are you? It's been ages."

He kissed her hand. "Get back in, Sarah, you'll get wet. Where are you going?"

"The Four Seasons."

"So am I. I'll catch up with you later."

His car moved away and she sat back and closed the window. "Jesus, Mrs. Talbot, is there anyone you don't know?" Charles asked.

"Don't exaggerate, Charles." She laughed. "Just concentrate on getting us there."

She sat back and looked at the photo of Don Rafael Barbera and suddenly realized, with a certain surprise, that she rather liked the look of him.

~

The Four Seasons was very definitely her favorite restaurant, not only because of the superb food, but also the decor. The whole place had such style, from the shimmering gold curtains and dark wood to the quiet elegance of the waiters and captains.

She was seated instantly, as a favored customer, at her usual table in the Pool Room, from where she could survey the whole room. The place was crowded and she could see Tom Gayitfai and Paul Kori, the owners, hovering in the background, looking even more anxious than usual, which was hardly surprising in view of the guests. Henry Kissinger was sitting at a table to her right and the Vice-President himself was at a table at the far end of the pool, which explained the large young men in dark suits she'd noticed in the vestibule on the way in, their air of efficient, quiet violence filling her with distaste.

Her waiter appeared. "The usual, Mrs. Talbot?"

"Yes, Martin."

He snapped his fingers and the Dom Perignon 1980 was at her table in an instant.

"Looks like a fun evening," she commented.

"Actually the Vice-President is getting ready to leave, but they've all been waiting to see whether he or Kissinger would be the first to go over to the other to say hello," he told her. "Can I take your order now?"

He offered the menu, but she shook her head. "I know what I want, Martin. Crisped shrimp with mustard fruit, then the roast duckling with cherries, and since it's a big evening, I'll finish with ..."

"The bitter chocolate sherbet." They both laughed, and he started to turn away, then paused. "Heh, he's on the move."

"It seems Kissinger wins on points," Sarah said.

"Like hell it does." Martin was in a panic. "He's coming right this way, Mrs. Talbot."

He moved to one side fast and the Vice-President arrived, wearing his inimitable smile. "Sarah, you're looking as remarkable as usual. No, don't get up. I can't stop. Due at the U.N." He took her hand and kissed it. "Talking about you at the White House last night."

"Good things, I hope?" she said.

"Always good where you're concerned, Sarah," and he was gone.

People were staring at her curiously, and Henry Kissinger gave her a little nod, a slight smile on his face. Martin refilled her glass and he was smiling too. She savored the Dom Perignon, thinking about it. They'd be talking about this at the bar of "21" within an hour; the gossip columns would have it in the early editions.

"Woman of the Year next, Sarah," she said softly, and raised her glass. "To the woman who has everything." She paused. "Or nothing." She frowned. "Now why in the hell did I say that?"

And then Martin was there, leaning over the table. "Your chauffeur's in the vestibule, Mrs. Talbot. He says it's urgent."

"Really?" She got up at once, no unease in her at all, bewildered, if anything.

Charles's face should have told her, the hunted look, the way he glanced to one side as he talked. "I've got Mr. Morgan in the car, Mrs. Talbot."

"Dan?" she said. "Here?" Dan Morgan was president of the brokerage firm of which she was now a senior partner.

"Like I said, he's in the car." Charles was obviously upset. "If you don't mind, Mrs. Talbot."

The doorman held up an umbrella for her as she crossed the pavement to the car, and Dan Morgan, graying, distinguished in black tie and evening dress, glanced up at her, his face grave.

"Dan, what is this?" she demanded.

"Just get in, Sarah." He opened the door and pulled her to him. "Get Mrs. Talbot's coat, Charles. I think she'll be leaving."

Charles moved away and Sarah said, "Dan, what's going on?"

He had a large envelope on the seat beside him, she noticed as he took her hands. "Sarah, Eric is dead."

"Dead? Eric?" She was underwater now, in slow motion. "That's ridiculous. Who says so?"

"Tony Villiers tried to get hold of you earlier. When he couldn't, he phoned me." Charles returned with her coat and got behind the wheel. "Just drive," Morgan told him.

"Where to, Mr. Morgan?"

"Anywhere, for God's sake," Morgan said violently.

The car pulled away. Sarah said, "It can't be true. It can't be."

"It's all in here, Sarah." Morgan picked up the envelope. "Villiers wired it all over to the office. I went and picked it up."

She stared at the envelope and said dully, "What's in there?"

"Doctor's reports, police coroner, that sort of thing. It's not good, Sarah. In fact it's about as bad as it could be. Better you leave them till later, when you're calmer."

"No," she said, her voice dangerously low. "Now, I want them now."

She took the envelope from him, had opened it and turned on the interior light before he could stop her. Her face was wild, her eyes staring. When she had finished, she sat there, unnaturally calm.

"Stop the car, Charles," she ordered.

"Mrs. Talbot?"

"Stop the car, damn you!"

He swung the car into the curb; she had the door open before they could stop her and was running through the rain to the nearest alley. When they reached her, she was leaning against the wall beside overflowing trash cans being violently sick. Finally she stopped and turned to face them.

Morgan held out his handkerchief. "We'll take you home now, Sarah."

"Yes," she said calmly. "I'll need my passport."

"Passport?" he said incredulously. "The only things you need are the right pills and bed."

"No, Dan," she said. "I need a plane. British Airways, Pan Am, TWA, it doesn't matter which, as long as it's going to London and it's going tonight."

"Sarah!" he tried again.

"No, Dan, no arguments. Just get me home. I've got things to do." And she walked away from him through the rain and got into the back of the car.

FOUR

SHE COULD HAVE WAITED for the British Airways Concorde, the fastest passenger flight in the world. It would have had her in London in three hours, fifteen minutes, but that would have meant waiting until the following morning. By chance, Pan Am had a delayed flight leaving for London just after midnight, a Boeing 747, so she took that.

The truth was, she needed time to think. She'd left a still protesting Dan Morgan behind at Kennedy. He'd wanted to come with her, but she wouldn't have that. There were things he could do, of course. Alert their London associates. A car, a driver, the house in Lord North Street they all used when visiting London. A good address, Edward had once told her. Very convenient for Parliament and Number Ten Downing Street.

Edward, she thought. First Edward in that stupid little war. Such a waste of a fine man. Now this. She stared down through the window at the lights of New York below as the plane turned out to sea, and the pain was unbearable. She closed her eyes and felt a hand on her shoulder.

The blond stewardess who had greeted her on boarding smiled down. "May I get you a drink now, Mrs. Talbot?"

Sarah stared blankly up at her, unable to speak for a moment, and her own intelligence told her that this was shock and that she had to fight it or go under. She forced a smile. "Brandy and soda please." Strange, but for the first time since boarding, probably because of the subdued lighting, she noticed that all the seats around her were empty. In fact, she seemed to be the only person in the whole of the first-class cabin.

"Am I it for tonight?" she asked as the stewardess brought her brandy.

"Almost," the girl said cheerfully. "Just one more on the other side."

She glanced across and saw at first only the back of another stewardess in the far aisle, and then she moved to the galley and saw the other passenger. It was Rafael Barbera. She felt bewildered, shocked. For a moment, she closed her eyes and was in the back of the car again reading Charles's newspaper and looking at Barbera's photo. She'd been so happy, everything going so well, and now this terrible nightmare. She sipped some of the brandy and took a deep breath. It was just like that dreadful cable from the Ministry of Defence in London telling her of Edward's death. You fought or you went under.

The stewardess appeared again. "Would you like the menu now, Mrs. Talbot?"

At first Sarah was going to say no, but then remembered that she hadn't eaten since breakfast, and that wouldn't do at all. There'd been no time for lunch with the big deal breaking so she had a little smoked salmon, a salad, some cold lobster, eating with no kind of conscious pleasure, but because strength was important now. She was aware of Barbera on the other side of the cabin, also eating, saw him speak to his stewardess, who turned and came across. She leaned over Sarah.

"We have a movie for you, as usual, Mrs. Talbot, but as there are only two of you tonight, we won't show it unless you want us to. Mr. Barbera over there isn't bothered one way or the other."

"Neither am I," Sarah told her. "So let's skip it."

The stewardess returned and spoke to Barbera, who nodded and raised his champagne glass in salute and smiled. He spoke to the stewardess again and she returned. "Mr. Barbera was wondering if you might join him in a glass of champagne."

"Oh, I don't really think so—" began Sarah, already too late, for he was on his feet, moving with surprising speed for a man of his age and size.

He leaned on the cane and looked down at her. "Mrs. Talbot, you don't know me, but you come highly recommended. I believe you are an associate of Dan Morgan? He handles the occasional business matter for me from time to time."

"I didn't know that."

He reached for her hand, kissed it gracefully, and there was a slight quirk of amusement at the corner of his mouth. "You wouldn't. It's a special account." He eased into the chair beside her. "Now then, champagne. You need it. I've been watching you. At the very least it's been a bad day."

"Oh, no," she protested. "I don't think so."

"Nonsense." He took the two glasses from the stewardess and passed them to her. "A strange thing for a Sicilian to say, but when you are tired of champagne you are tired of life." He raised his glass. "As my Jewish friends would say, *lechayim*."

"*Lechayim*?"

"To life, Mrs. Talbot!"

"I'll drink to that, Mr. Barbera." She emptied the glass in one long swallow. "It's really very appropriate. I'm drinking to life and my son's dead. Isn't that the funniest thing you ever heard of?"

And then she dropped her glass and turned to the window and cried as she had not cried since she was a little girl, and he stroked her hair gently, motioning the worried stewardess away. Finally she was still, but she stayed curled up, staring into the shadows, letting him soothe her, a child again with Daddy, when it had been good. When it had worked. Finally, she pushed away, got up without a word and went to the toilet. She washed her face with cold water and combed her hair. When she came out, the stewardess was there.

"Are you all right, Mrs. Talbot?"

"It's quite simple. I just got news of my son's death. That's why I'm on my way to London. But I'll be fine. I won't break down on you, I promise."

The young woman instinctively flung her arms around her. "I'm so sorry."

Sarah kissed her on the cheek. "That's very kind. I see Mr. Barbera's ordered coffee, but actually I'm a tea person."

"I'll see to it."

She took her seat again beside Barbera. "All right now?" he asked.

"I will be."

"When we've talked," he said calmly and raised a hand as if to forestall protest. "This is necessary, believe me."

"All right." She opened her bag, took the battered old silver cigarette case they'd found on Edward's body at Mount Tumbledown and extracted a cigarette.

She lit it, blew smoke up at the ceiling in a strangely defiant gesture. "You don't mind?"

He smiled. "At my age, Mrs. Talbot, you can't afford to mind anything."

"How much do you know about me, Mr. Barbera?"

"They tell me you're one of the best brains in Wall Street. And when you were very, very young, were almost a Congresswoman."

"I was a rich little spoiled bitch. My father seemed to have all the money in the world. Because I didn't have a mother, he indulged me. Oh, I went to Radcliffe, graduated magna cum laude. No trouble. I was very bright, you see. I didn't need to work. I smoked marijuana like everyone else did in the sixties, and I screwed around like everyone else did." She turned sideways to look at him. "Does that shock you?"

"Not particularly."

"I had a boyfriend who dropped out of college and was drafted to Vietnam. They gave him a gun and sent him off to play. He only lasted three months. Pure mindless destruction." She shook her head. "I was very smart. I didn't join the protest movement until *after* I got my party's nomination to Congress."

"And your father didn't like that." It was a statement, not a question.

"Didn't speak to me for three years. Considered me some sort of traitor. The voters didn't think much of me either. I finally pulled out and decided to get my MBA and then go to work." She laughed. "Wall Street beckoned."

"Where you could show your father what you were made of?"

"In spades. And I did too." There was the defiance there again. "Mind you, I did please him in one way. In my husband."

"I didn't realize until tonight that you'd been married."

"Oh, yes, if briefly. To an English army colonel. It didn't last long. He was killed in the Falklands, but he did leave me my stepson."

"I see."

"I wonder if you do? Eric's mother died when he was born. I understood that because I'd gone through the same pain. I understood him and he understood me."

"And now he's gone. What happened?"

She sat there thinking about it for a moment, then got her briefcase from under the seat, opened it and took out the buff envelope containing the material Villiers had sent over from London. "Read that."

She lit another cigarette and lay back in her seat while Barbera worked through the various papers. He didn't say a word until he was finished. He carefully replaced the papers in the envelope and turned to her, his face like a stone.

"Drugs," she said. "How could he? Heroin—cocaine."

"You told me earlier how you smoked pot back in the sixties. It's an even worse problem for kids these days because it's all so available."

"You would know, wouldn't you?" The words were out before she could take them back.

He showed no anger. "Mrs. Talbot, I'm an old-fashioned man. Sure, I was what you would term a gangster, but those I harmed tended to be my own kind. To me, other people were civilians. My family had business with the unions, gambling, prostitution, even booze during Prohibition, and these are human failings which everyone understands. But I tell you this. The Barbera family never took a penny on the drugs market. My grandson, Vito, in London, for example. We got three casinos there. Restaurants, betting shops." He shrugged. "How much does a man need?"

"But Eric," she said. "I still don't understand."

"Look," he said, "it's a popular misconception that people on hard drugs are hooked by some pusher. The first fix is almost always offered by a friend. Probably he was at some student party the first time it happened. Had a few drinks ..."

"But afterwards," she said. "Afterwards came the pushers, the suppliers, all happy to keep the pot boiling. To destroy young people on the threshold of life and for what? For money."

"To some people, money is serious business, Mrs. Talbot. But let's leave that on one side. What do you intend to do about this? What do you want?"

"Justice, I suppose."

He laughed harshly. "A rare commodity in this wicked world. Look, the law is a joke. You go to court, it goes on and on. The rich and powerful can buy anything they require because most men are corruptible."

"Then what would *you* do?"

"It's difficult for me. Spilled blood cries out for vengeance, that is the Sicilian way. My son dies, he must be avenged. It isn't a question of choice. I have no choice. I can do no other." He shook his head. "You're from a different world. Violence has never had any place in your life, I suspect."

"That's true. I once saw a fistfight as we were driving through the Bronx, from my privileged position in the rear seat of a Cadillac."

He smiled bleakly. "That's good. You can mock yourself, but now there is something you must promise me you will do, and it is essential."

"What's that?"

"You must insist on seeing your son's body." He raised a hand to stop her from saying anything. "No matter how terrible an ordeal. Believe me, I know a great deal about death, and of this I am certain. You must see for yourself, you must mourn, or you will be haunted for the rest of your life."

She nodded. "I'll think about it."

"And there is one more thing you must face up to. Something quite terrible."

"And what would that be?"

"The French coroner's verdict was clear. Accidental death by drowning under the influence of drugs and alcohol."

"That's right."

"His body, Mrs. Talbot, was a considerable convenience to those who used it. It occurs to me that it might have been more than a convenience that it was available at all."

She said flatly, "You're actually suggesting that there was no accident in any of this?" It was difficult for her to get the word out, but she forced herself. "That he was murdered?"

"Please. It's all been very convenient, that's all I'm saying. I don't wish to make things worse for you than they already are. I've lived in a harsh world for too many years. I tend to suspect the worst."

"I didn't think it *could* be worse," she told him, her voice shaking with anger and the last vestiges of denial.

"I may be wrong, and in any case I'm sure the authorities would consider the possibility fully." He took out his wallet and extracted a card. "This is my grandson Vito's address in London. I'll speak of you to him. He'll do anything he can. I myself don't even leave the airport. I fly straight on to Palermo. I know it is unlikely, but if you are ever in Sicily, you will find me at my villa outside the village of Bellona in the Cammarata."

He took her hand and kissed it gently. "And now, my child, you need sleep."

She reached over and kissed him on the cheek. He smiled, stood up and went back to his own seat. She switched off the light and lay there in the darkness thinking about what he had said. The suggestion that Eric's death had not been accidental filled her with horror. She refused to accept it, pushed the thought away, and after a while she did sleep, head pillowed on her arm as the plane droned on through the night.

A journalist in Kent, alerted by a sympathetic friend in the local police force, sent a brief report of the affair to the *Daily Mail* in London. It reported only what he knew. That a hearse had crashed on a Kent country road and had caught fire. There was also the mention that a body was involved. Details being understandably sketchy at that stage, it merited no more than a paragraph at the bottom of page three because of the macabre implication. In any event, the issue of the D notice Ferguson had authorized meant that the story was deleted in later editions, but not before Eric Talbot's identity had been revealed to the world.

Jago had flown over on the breakfast plane from Paris and was at the service flat in Connaught Street close to Hyde Park by eleven o'clock. As he was unpacking, the phone rang.

Smith said, "There's a small item in the *Daily Mail* this morning. It seems the boy wasn't what he seemed. His real name was Eric Talbot and he was a student at Cambridge."

"So he used an alias," Jago said. "That's perfectly understandable. Why should it be a problem?"

"Because he wasn't a nobody after all," Smith told him. "I've made discreet enquiries from the porter at his college. Pretended to be a journalist. His grandfather's a baronet, for Christ's sake."

"Oh, dear me," Jago said, resisting the impulse to laugh out loud. "And who got us into this mess?"

"A bitch in Cambridge called Greta Markovsky. She was a student, too. A pusher. I've used her for a year now. I thought she was reliable."

It was the first hint of weakness Jago had ever noted in Smith. "But my experience of this wicked old world is that no one ever is. Where is Miss Markovsky to be found?"

"It seems she overdosed badly on heroin two nights ago. She's in some rehabilitation place outside Cambridge called Grantley Hall. A closed unit."

"Do you want me to do something about her?"

"I don't think it's necessary, certainly not at this stage, and in any case, she's never met me."

"Who has?" Jago said.

"Exactly."

"So what do you want me to do?"

"There's a coroner's inquest at Canterbury at two o'clock this afternoon. Be there."

"All right. And Bird and his boyfriend?"

"That can wait. I'll speak to you later."

"Yes, I'd better get moving."

Jago put down the phone and finished unpacking quickly. He decided against changing. There wasn't really time, not if he was to be certain of making the inquest by two.

Five minutes later he emerged from the lift into the basement garage. The car he habitually used in London, a silver Alfa Romeo Spyder, was in its usual place. When he got behind the wheel he paused only to reach under the dashboard for a hidden catch. A flap dropped down to reveal a Walther PPK, a Browning and a Carswell Silencer, all neatly clipped into place. He checked both weapons quickly, just to make sure. Life, as he had found, could be hideously full of surprises. Two minutes later and he was part of the traffic in Park Lane.

Ferguson looked up from his desk as Tony Villiers entered the room. "How is she?"

"I met her at Heathrow. Went to Lord North Street with her. Her company has a house there."

"Have you gone into things in any detail with her?"

"Not really. There wasn't the need. I sent copies of all the relevant material over to her in New York before she left. French coroner's report and all the medical stuff. She's here now. She wants to attend the coroner's inquest in Canterbury at two o'clock. I said I'd go with her. I've warned her that if she puts in an appearance, as next of kin she could be called."

"Did you now?" Ferguson frowned slightly. "Is she going to be difficult?"

Villiers managed to restrain his anger. "It would be perfectly understandable in the circumstances."

"For God's sake, Tony, you know what I mean. This could be a tricky one for all of us. Anyway, show her in, and I'll see for myself."

He moved to the window, thinking about how he should handle this distraught woman and turned, as she came into the room with Villiers, to get the surprise of his life. She wore a brown suede jacket belted at the waist and matching slacks. Her hair hung to her shoulders, a dark curtain on each side of her face, which was calm and determined.

"Mrs. Talbot." He came around the desk, at his most charming, and took her hand. "I can't tell you how sorry I am."

"Thank you."

"Please sit down."

She produced Edward's silver case from her handbag, her one sign of nervousness, and he gave her a light. She said, "Why am I here, Brigadier?"

He moved round the desk to his chair. "I don't understand?"

"I think you do. When Tony said he was bringing me here, I asked him why. He said you were his boss. That you would tell me."

"I see."

"Brigadier, my husband was a colonel in the British Army and I was a service wife for long enough to learn a few things."

"Such as?"

She turned and put a hand on Villiers's arm. "Well, I'm aware that my darling cousin by marriage here is not only Grenadier Guards, but SAS. I always was given the impression that his main line of business was military intelligence of some sort."

Villiers said wryly to Ferguson, "I told you. The smartest brain on Wall Street."

"Exactly, Brigadier," she said. "So if you're Tony's boss, what does that make you, and what's more to the point, why are you involved in what I would have assumed was a matter for the police?"

"Tony was right, Mrs. Talbot. You're an exceptional woman." He glanced at his watch and stood up. "We'd better get going."

"Where to?" she said.

"My dear Mrs. Talbot, you wanted to go to the inquest. Then by all means we'll go, and in my car. We can talk on the way."

She and Ferguson sat together on the rear seat of the Daimler limousine, Villiers opposite on the jump seat, the glass partition raised between them and the driver.

Ferguson said, "There are aspects of this case, one in particular, which do make this, at least in theory, a matter of national security rather than a more conventional crime that would be handled by the police."

"That's hardly the kind of statement to instill confidence," she said. "It takes me right back to Vietnam and my protest days. I mean, I've experienced the best the CIA has to offer at first hand, Brigadier."

"You'd better do the explaining, Tony."

"International terrorism needs money to keep going," Villiers said. "A great deal of money, not only for arms, which are expensive, but to fund operations. Drugs are a ready source of that kind of money, and we've known for some time that in Ulster both the IRA and various Protestant paramilitary organizations have been raising money by becoming involved in the trade."

"But how does this affect Eric?"

Villiers took an envelope from his pocket and passed it to her. "There's a more detailed postmortem report from France. They discovered not only heroin and cocaine but a mixture of scopolamine and phenothiazine in his blood. In Colombia, where it originated, it's known as *burundanga*."

"It induces a kind of chemical hypnosis, Mrs. Talbot," Ferguson put in. "Reduces the subject to being a zombie for a while."

"And that happened to Eric?" she whispered.

"Yes, and during the past year, four members of the IRA executed by Protestant factions in Ulster have had traces of the same drug revealed at their postmortems."

"And that's what makes it a Security matter, Mrs. Talbot. It's a very rare occurrence," Ferguson said. "Four members of the IRA in Ulster, and now your stepson."

"And you think there could be a connection?" she said.

"Perhaps the same people were involved," the brigadier told her. "That's what we're getting at. We've got a computer hunt on now covering all Western European countries."

"And what have you found?"

"Several cases in France over the past three years, all rather similar to your stepson's, actually. Death by drowning under the influence of drugs."

Barbera's suggestion could no longer be avoided.

"Which would seem to suggest to me," she said evenly, "that a number of people have been murdered while in this state of chemical hypnosis you mention."

"So it would appear," he said.

"Murdered for one reason only. So that their bodies could be used like some damned suitcase." She hammered a clenched fist on her knee. "They did that to Eric. Why?"

"Five million pounds a time, Mrs. Talbot, that's our conservative estimate of each consignment of heroin at street prices."

She took out the silver case. Villiers gave her a light. The smoking helped to stop her trembling. And it was anger she felt now. No, more than that—rage. They were entering the outskirts of Canterbury, threading their way through the ancient streets. She gazed up at the towering spires of the great cathedral.

"It's very beautiful."

"The birthplace of English Christianity," Ferguson told her. "Founded by Saint Augustine in Saxon times."

"And bombed by the Nazis in nineteen forty-two." Villiers shrugged. "Not exactly a military target, but we bombed some of their cathedral towns, so they bombed some of ours."

The Daimler turned into a quiet square. She said, "So the computer hasn't thrown up any more cases, then?"

"I'm afraid not," the brigadier said.

"That's not quite true," Villiers put in. "A case came up this morning. I didn't have a chance to tell you. Eighteen-year-old girl found in the Thames at Wapping a few months ago."

"You're sure?"

"I'm afraid so, sir." Villiers paused. "Actually, she was Egan's foster sister, sir."

Ferguson was astonished. "You mean Sean Egan?"

"Yes."

"Good God."

Sarah interrupted. "And who would this Sean Egan be?"

"A young sergeant who served with me in the SAS. Badly wounded in the Falklands. He's just left the Service."

"Tell me about him," she demanded, but at that moment they pulled in at the curb at the bottom of a row of steps leading up to an imposing Georgian building.

"No time for that now, my dear," Ferguson told her as the chauffeur opened the door. "We're here."

There were a dozen or so people in court, mostly of the sort who sought free entertainment. Jago sat on the back row and noticed the brigadier, Sarah Talbot and Tony Villiers as they came in—not that it meant anything to him at that precise moment, but Villiers gave him pause for thought. There is a saying in the British Army that it takes an old Academy man to know one, and Jago recognized the young colonel instantly for what he was, civilian clothes or not.

The clerk of the court got the proceedings started. "The court will rise for Her Majesty's coroner."

They all stood. The coroner, a tall scholarly-looking man in a dark suit who, to Sarah's surprise, wore no robes, entered and sat down.

"The court will come to order," the clerk said. "Normally in an inquest of this kind the presence of a jury would be mandatory. However, this is not a usual case, and the jury procedure will not be necessary."

The clerk passed the coroner a paper. He examined it, then glanced up. "Is Colonel Villiers in court?"

"Sir." Villiers stood up.

"I take heed of this D notice served by you on behalf of the Ministry of Defence and accept it. I would make the point to any members of the press present that the issue of the D notice makes it an offense punishable by imprisonment to report any details of these proceedings. Colonel Villiers, you may sit down."

"Thank you, sir."

The coroner continued. "The facts of the death of Eric Malcolm Ian Talbot have already been established by the coroner's court in Paris, where the death took place."

Sarah wanted to shout out, to stand up and dispute what was being said, and Villiers, as if sensing what she was thinking, took her hand firmly.

The coroner went on. "The lamentable turn events have taken after this unfortunate young man's death are a matter for investigation by the proper authority. Is the next of kin in court?"

It took a moment for it to sink in, and then she rose. "Here, sir."

"Take the stand, please." She went forward, stepped up and stood at the rail. The coroner glanced at the paper before him. "You are Mrs. Sarah Talbot, presently residing in the City of New York in the United States of America?"

It was all so formal—so precise. "That is correct."

"Please state your relationship to the deceased."

Sarah moistened dry lips. "I was his stepmother."

"The body of your stepson is at present in the city mortuary. Have you identified it, Mrs. Talbot?"

"No, sir."

The clerk passed another paper up. The coroner examined it. "Fingerprint evidence presented to this court makes it possible for me to waive that requirement. I will issue you with a burial order." He paused. "You have the profound sympathy of this court, Mrs. Talbot."

"Thank you."

She stepped down, stunned that it was over so quickly, and the clerk cried, "The court will rise for Her Majesty's coroner."

Everyone stood, and there was a general move to the exit. Villiers said, "It could have been worse. You did well, Sarah."

Jago, crowding in behind, heard her say, "Far worse to come, but it can't be avoided."

"What on earth could that be?" Ferguson asked.

"Eric," she said simply. "I want to see him."

Villiers put an arm around her shoulders. "No need for that, Sarah. No need to go through it. I've seen him and it isn't Eric any more. I've got everything arranged. They'll bring him up to London this afternoon, service at Greenhill Crematorium, ten o'clock in the morning. All taken care of."

"I need to see him," she said firmly. He looked at Ferguson; the brigadier nodded. Wearily Villiers said, "All right, let's get it over with."

He was right, of course. It wasn't Eric, the blackened, twisted creature revealed when the attendant pulled out the drawer and removed the white rubber sheet, and yet she stood there for a long, long moment remembering his hand in hers at the wedding, full of happiness, full of trust. Finally she nodded to the attendant and walked away, followed by the two men.

They got into the Daimler, and as it drove away Ferguson said, "Are you all right, Mrs. Talbot?"

She turned to him, eyes burning. "All my life I've been what they describe as a good person. Your average decent citizen. Three cheers for the American way and the rule of law. Well, I've got news for you, Brigadier. I don't feel quite so well disposed today. I want the bastards who did that to him. I want them to pay."

Villiers's face was white. "Sarah!"

"That's how I feel, Tony. That's exactly how I feel." And she turned away and stared out the window.

Jago made a call to the usual number from a phone box at a service station outside Canterbury, and Smith rang him back within a couple of minutes.

"He's getting worried," Jago told himself, and proceeded to fill Smith in with what had happened.

"What did you think of her?" Smith asked.

"I liked her. A real lady. Lots of style and balls of brass, that's my opinion."

"I've been doing some checking. Her old man left her a few millions when he died. On top of that she's a hotshot broker on Wall Street. She's staying at a house her company keeps for visitors on Lord North Street."

"I'm impressed," Jago said.

"But the two men with her, Villiers and Ferguson—what in the hell goes on?"

"If you want my opinion, based on my seven years serving Her Gracious Majesty, I'd say they were Intelligence."

"But why? It doesn't make sense." There was a pause. "Get back to London fast. I'll phone you at your flat at six. Be there."

They dropped Ferguson off, and Villiers went on to Lord North Street with Sarah. The house was a pleasant, tall narrow building of the Regency period. The only staff employed was a maid who came in the mornings, so they had the place to themselves.

There were two packing cases in the hall, and Sarah said, "What's this?"

"Eric's effects. I had them clear his room at Trinity College. I thought you'd like to sort through them."

"Oh, thank you so much, Tony. It was a kind thought."

She was into the first packing case instantly, and Villiers said, "I'll make some tea."

He was standing at the stove waiting for the kettle to boil when she came in carrying a large book bound in blue Moroccan leather. "Look what I've found."

"What is it?" Villiers asked.

"Some sort of diary he kept."

He glanced over her shoulder as she opened it and sat at the table. "Good heavens, it's in Latin," he said.

"Eric's favorite subject. Something else we had in common. I majored in classical languages at Radcliffe. Latin and Greek. My father thought it was a terrible waste of time."

Villiers poured the tea. "What's it say?"

She started on the first page, translating fluently and with obvious ease. " 'Today, I arrived at Trinity. So exciting. Cambridge is wonderful, Sarah came for the weekend to settle me in. We went on the river in a punt and afterwards sat under the mulberry tree that Milton planted in the Fellows Garden at Christ's College. She returns to New York tomorrow. I'll miss her like hell.' "

She stopped reading, closed the book and clasped it to her. "Tony, if you don't mind, I'd like you to go now because I think I'm going to cry, and I don't think I'll be able to stop for quite some time."

He put a hand briefly on her shoulder. "All right, Sarah, I'll see you in the morning," he said and went out, closing the door softly behind him.

Smith said, "Right, this is what happens. I've managed to get an apartment on the top floor of a house on the opposite side of the street from where the Talbot woman is staying. Had to pay a year's lease, but there it is."

"Is it directly opposite?"

"Almost. Two doors down. Sufficient for our purposes. The porter is expecting you to move in tonight. Your name is James Mackenzie. You'll have a delivery at nine o'clock."

"We're going to do a little eavesdropping, I presume?"

"Exactly. There's a directional microphone which can pick up every word spoken in that house, no trouble. It has an ultrafrequency function that picks up telephone conversations. The whole thing will be linked to a recorder. I want to know what goes on over there."

"All right, you've got it."

"There's also a new laser-orientated directional microphone for your car. I want to cover every possibility."

"Fine," Jago told him. "Taken care of, I guarantee it."

He put the phone down and went into the kitchen, whistling, realizing that he was actually beginning to enjoy himself.

At Greenhill Crematorium the following morning there were just Sarah, Villiers, Ferguson and the minister, of course. The whole thing was as bad as it could be. Background choir music played on a tape, and the minister spoke with a parsonical whine to his voice like a music-hall comedian's joke.

"I am the resurrection and the life, saith the Lord: he that believeth in me, though he were dead, yet shall he live."

She stifled an insane impulse to laugh. Why not *she* that believeth in me? Why was everything *he*?

The taped music swelled, the coffin moved out of sight on the conveyor belt through the dark opening to the oven beyond. The minister shook Sarah's hand. She was aware of his mouth opening, but didn't hear a word, and then they were outside.

Ferguson said, "I'll be on my way. You'll see Mrs. Talbot home, Tony?"

"Of course, sir."

He took her hand. "I may not see you again. I suppose you'll be going back to New York."

"No, I don't think so, Brigadier," she said.

"Oh, dear, I hope you're not going to be awkward, Mrs. Talbot," Ferguson said.

"Most American citizens having a problem in London would contact our embassy," she told him. "Not me, Brigadier. You see, my father was one of the President's oldest friends. All I have to do is pick up the phone and call the White House. Would you rather I did that, Brigadier?"

Ferguson was angry, but managed a smile. "I don't really think that will be necessary, Mrs. Talbot."

She walked to the waiting car. A moment later Villiers got in beside her.

"Would you do that, Sarah?" he said as the car drove away. "Would you really drag the President into this?"

"Tony, I'd shake hands with the Devil himself on this one if I had to." She took out Edward's silver case and selected a cigarette. "But that may not be necessary if you're sensible. Now, tell me about Sean Egan."

FIVE

THE LONDON ASSOCIATES HAD arranged a car for her, a black Mercedes sedan. The driver was a middle-aged cockney called George, who drove with incredible skill, pushing his way through the heavy afternoon traffic from Westminster along Victoria Embankment.

"You really seem to know how to handle the traffic, George."

"You've got to, Mrs. Talbot, or you'd never bleeding well get any-where these days. All right for me though. I was a cabby for twenty-six years."

"So you know the city then."

"I should do. Can't go on the road in a London cab until you've done the Knowledge."

"The Knowledge? What's that mean?"

"Knowing the city backwards, that's what it means, Mrs. Talbot. Now where did you want to go first. The Tower?"

"No," she said. "A place called Wapping. Do you know it?"

"Stone me, I should do. That's my patch. I was born in Cable Street. God, I could tell you some stories. Mind you, I live in Camden now, but it's not the same."

"So you're a cockney then?"

"Too bleeding true, Mrs. Talbot. A genuine East Ender. What was it you wanted exactly?"

She produced the envelope Villiers had reluctantly given her from her handbag and took out the contents. There was a photo of Egan in service dress, just head and shoulders, the blank face giving nothing away. A couple of sheets of paper provided all she needed to know. Then there were the things that Villiers had said about Egan, some of which had shocked her. So much violence in one so young. It was difficult to grasp.

She said, "I want to go to a place called Jordan Lane. Do you know it?"

He glanced sideways in surprise. "Jordan Lane? That's not far from the old London docks. Next to Hangman's Wharf. That's no place for you."

"Why not?"

"They're all just a little bit wicked round there." It was her first example of the cockney tendency to understatement. "I mean, it's still a bit like the old days."

"In what way?"

"The Pool of London and the Thames used to be the biggest port in the world, then things went sour. The unions got it wrong, and everybody turned to Amsterdam. A year or two back you could have walked down through Wapping and found nothing but rusting cranes, empty docks, and warehouses boarded up."

"And now?"

"There's a lot happening. New housing, warehouse developments. You see it's very convenient for the City so all these flash young kids, brokers and bankers, with a hundred grand a year and a Porsche, are moving into the area and squeezing the locals out."

"But not at Hangman's Wharf."

"No." He seemed evasive now. "Things are still pretty much the same down there."

She consulted the sheet of paper in front of her again. "Do you know a man called Jack Shelley?"

The car swerved slightly, but he regained control. "Everybody in Wapping knows Jack Shelley, Mrs. Talbot. What would you want to know about him for?"

"I understood he was a famous gangster."

"In his day, but not any more. Now he's legit. He owns Hangman's Wharf itself and the whole river frontage, and what he doesn't own, he controls."

"And do people like that?"

"The locals do. He doesn't go in for developments. Doesn't throw people out on the street. Mind you, he's got millions these days. Electronics, computers, couple of casinos."

"A respectable businessman in fact?"

"Not like the old days." George chuckled. "He was a right villain. Smash and grab, robberies. Then there was the Darley Warehouse job. A million in gold bullion and that was real money in those days."

"And he never went to jail?"

"Six months when he was a kid. That's all he ever did. He was a legend in the East End. The Kray Brothers and the Richardsons, people were scared to death of them, but not Jack Shelley. If you were in trouble you went to Jack. If you needed a couple of quid he'd probably give you a pony."

"A pony?"

"Sorry, Mrs. Talbot, the cockney in me again. Twenty-five pounds to you."

"A regular Robin Hood, it seems."

"Yes, well, all that was years ago. When they locked up people like the Krays and the Richardsons and threw away the key, Jack changed his ways. I suppose he realized you could do just as well in legitimate business if you had the brains."

They were passing Tower Bridge now and moved along St. Katharine's Way into Wapping High Street. Sarah consulted her fact sheet again. "Yes, Jordan Lane. It's a public house called 'The Bargee.' "

George swerved into the side of the road and pulled up. He turned to her. "Now look, Mrs. Talbot. The Bargee is no place for your sort, believe me."

Some yards behind them, Jago, who had also stopped in the silver Spyder, adjusted the directional microphone and turned up the volume on his car radio to which it was linked. He could hear everything perfectly. It was really very amusing. The truth was, the more he saw of Sarah Talbot, the more he liked her.

"And what exactly is my sort, George?" she inquired.

He said patiently, "Look, most jobs done in London, bank holdups, bullion, that sort of thing." He hesitated. "They're all done by sixty or seventy men and everyone in the East End knows who they are. The Old Bill knows who they are. That's the police to you. They're all solid family men who love their kids, the kind of men who consider a noncer, a child molester, to be the lowest thing on God's earth, which he bleeding well is."

"But they're also the kind of men who'd shoot you dead if you got in the way?"

"Just like the Mafia, Mrs. Talbot. Nothing personal. Just business. Five or six come together according to the job requirement. That's how it works."

"And what has all this got to do with The Bargee?"

"A lot of them hang out there."

"Good," she said. "It sounds interesting. Let's go. You can buy me a drink."

"Mrs. Talbot, what am I going to do with you?" He groaned and kept driving.

Behind them, the Spyder pulled out from the curb and followed.

The Bargee was at the end of Jordan Lane, the entrance on the corner looking out across the river, but it was no dive; that was her first surprise. The exterior was freshly painted, as was the sign above the door, and there were flowers in the window boxes. George held the door open for her and she went in.

The main bar had a low white-painted ceiling with black beams, the floor was covered with red tiles much faded with years of usage and constant cleaning. There were seats in the two bay windows, tables scattered about the room and a long mahogany bar, all very Victorian, with bottles on the shelves behind and an ornate mirror.

There were no more than a dozen customers, all men, and there was a momentary silence as Sarah and George were inspected. Ida Shelley stood behind the beer pumps pulling a pint for someone. She was sixty-five, Sarah knew that, but looked older, the hair very gray, unmistakable signs of heavy drinking in the lined face.

George said brightly, "Now, then, Ida, and how are you?"

She frowned for a moment and then recognition dawned. "George

Black. Well, I never did. Haven't seen you in years. Thought you moved to Camden."

"I did, Ida."

"Look at you, all posh in your uniform. Not in the cabs any more?"

"Chauffeuring now, Ida. This is Mrs. Talbot from New York. She wanted to see a real East End pub."

"Well, we're that all right. Nice to see you, love. Here, have a drink on me to celebrate. What's it to be?"

Sarah had a gin and tonic and George a pint of best bitter. As Ida was pulling it, he said, "How's Sean these days?"

Sarah glanced at him sharply. Ida said, "Up and around. He caught a right packet in the Falklands. They thought he was going to lose his leg."

"Is that a fact?"

"He's finally got some sense and packed it all in."

"And young Sally?"

Her face went blank, wiped clean. "Sally passed away, George, earlier this year."

He looked shocked. "I'm sorry to hear that."

"Yes, well, you'll have to excuse me. I've got customers."

She moved down the bar and Sarah and George sat in a window seat. "She seemed upset," Sarah said.

"She would be. Lovely girl, Sally."

"Ida's daughter?" She already knew the answer to that, but was probing.

"God, no. Ida is a Shelley too. Jack's cousin, but she's only been married to one thing in her life—the bottle. The young guy I asked about, Sean, he's Jack's nephew. His parents used to have this place. He owns it now. Been in the army for a few years and Ida's been running it for him. That's why she's got her name on the licensee's plate over the door. Sally was his foster sister."

At that moment a door at the back of the bar opened and Sean Egan came out. She recognized him instantly, although the peculiar vividness of the china-blue eyes was a shock. He wore a black T-shirt, black leather bomber jacket and jeans. He spoke briefly to Ida, waved to someone who called and then lifted the bar flap and moved to the door without even glancing at George and Sarah.

"Hey, there's Sean," George said.

"I know." She stood up. "Let's go."

"Leave it out. I haven't finished my beer, Mrs. Talbot."

"Now George!" she said firmly and went out.

Egan was unlocking the door of an old red Mini. As they got into the Mercedes he started to drive away. "Mini Cooper," George said. "They don't make them like that any more. Flat out they're like a bleeding racing car."

"Follow him, George."

"Look, Mrs. Talbot, what in the hell is going on?" he asked as he switched on the ignition.

"Just follow him, George, that's all for now." She lit a cigarette and added calmly, "And if you lose him, I'll have your guts for garters, isn't that what you cockneys would say?"

The journey took quite some time as they followed Egan up through Camden and into Kentish Town, finally turning into Highgate Road, with George giving her a running commentary.

"Parliament Hill over there," he told her. "God knows where he's going." And then a moment later, "Oh, yes, I do. The cemetery."

"The cemetery?" she said.

"Highgate Cemetery, just coming up."

There were iron railings now, and through the trees Sarah could see headstones and the occasional marble cross. There were a number of cars parked beside a gate. The Mini Cooper stopped and George pulled the Mercedes into the curb, staying well behind.

"This place is famous," he told her. "There's another section over there that's the really interesting bit, but they keep the gate locked these days. Catacombs from Victorian times cut into the hillside. Egyptian gates, tombs. Really weird. Used a lot in horror films over the years." He shuddered. "You could just imagine Dracula creeping around up there."

"And this side?"

"Oh, lots of famous people in there. They've got Karl Marx amongst others, but ordinary folk too."

Egan emerged from the Mini Cooper. He was carrying a bunch

of flowers. He went in through the gate. Sarah said, "Wait for me, George," and got out of the Mercedes. She could see Egan up ahead, and she followed him along a path between a jumble of graves, monuments of every kind on either side: marble angels, great crosses, sarcophagi. The place had a considerable Gothic charm although in spots everything seemed overgrown, the undergrowth rampant.

Egan had stopped at a grave which was topped by a colossal head. He stood there looking at it for quite a while, and Sarah turned away and pretended to be examining a grave herself—not that it was really necessary. There were other people about, and a woman with two children came toward her, then passed by.

Sarah turned to see that Egan was on the move. She paused briefly at the monument he had stopped at and found that the huge head was that of Karl Marx. She glanced up at it, turned and found that Egan had gone. She hurried forward in sudden panic, and when she came to the next turning she saw him through the trees, standing looking down at another grave.

He squatted on his haunches beside it, removed a clump of dead flowers from a marble urn and replaced them with the fresh ones he had brought. He stayed there without moving for at least ten minutes, and she waited in the trees, watching from behind a large marble tomb.

It started to rain a little. He glanced up, then stood, looked down at the grave again, crossed himself, then walked away. Sarah waited until he'd turned into the main path before moving forward quickly. The grave was a simple one with a black marble headstone. The inscription in gold letters said, "Sally Baines Egan aged eighteen years. Greatly loved."

She hurried back along the main path. She could see him going out through the main gate, and he was already getting into the Mini Cooper as she emerged into the road. It had started to rain quite hard now and she ran to the Mercedes and scrambled inside.

"He was visiting his sister's grave," she said.

"Did you speak to him?" George asked.

"No."

"Look, what's this all about, Mrs. Talbot? Maybe I can help."

"No, George, nobody can help me on this one. Be a good guy and just drive."

The Mini Cooper pulled away and they went after it as, farther back, Jago pulled out of the line of parked cars and followed.

"Real November weather this," George said as the rain hammered down. "Going-home time and nearly dark. I could lose him in the rush-hour traffic."

"Just do your best."

She leaned back, thinking. Why hadn't she spoken to Egan when she had the chance? And then she realized, looking back on it, that she had felt like an intruder. But there was something more. Somehow, she knew that to speak to him, to make herself known, was to take an irrevocable step from which there could be no going back, and the truth was, she was afraid. Afraid of what that might mean.

Egan drove around for an hour and a half, moving into Islington and out to Tottenham, where he finally stopped outside a small workingman's café and went inside. He sat at a table by the window and ordered.

"Egg and chips," George said. "Lucky bugger. I'm starving."

"I'll make it up to you, George."

Listening to the conversation in the Spyder at the end of the street, Jago smiled and said softly, "What about me, sweetie? I'm starving too."

Egan finally came out, got into the Mini Cooper again and set off. "Where to now?" George muttered. "It's nine o'clock, Mrs. Talbot."

They found out soon enough. Egan drove down into Hampstead and turned into the forecourt of a garage opposite the tube station. They pulled in at the side of the road and watched him speak to an attendant in the glass office. He handed the man his keys, came out and crossed the road to the entrance to the tube.

"According to the sign, that place offers a tuning service for specialist cars," George said. "He must be leaving his."

She was out of the Mercedes in a second. "I'll make my own way back."

She slammed the door before he could protest and ran across the road, dodging through the traffic.

"Oh, dear, here we go," Jago said softly, switched off the radio, got out of the Spyder and followed her.

Sarah went down the stairs after Egan and into the main hall. She saw him get a ticket from the fifty-pence machine and did the same, following him through the barrier and down the escalators until finally they came out on the platform.

A train had just come in and people were hurrying forward. She saw Egan board and tried to follow, but there were a number of people still getting off and she was pushed to one side. The doors of the next coach were opposite her and, as they started to close, she jumped in. Jago, just behind her, managed to squeeze through a second later.

Sarah moved to the end of the coach. It didn't connect with the next one, but she could see Egan through the glass door about halfway along, and she sat where she could observe him. Jago, sitting nearby, picked up a newspaper someone had left.

There were only half a dozen other passengers, two old ladies, a young black girl, a teenage couple who looked like students. Jago opened the paper and watched covertly. The train coasted into the next station, Belsize Park.

When the door opened, four youths burst in. Shaven skulls, studded denims, lace-up boots. One had a swastika tattooed between his eyes, another had his left nostril pierced and wore a gold nose ring. One of his friends was drinking from a half-pint bottle of whiskey.

"Take care, the maniacs are here!" he screamed.

The one with the swastika tattoo leaned over the black girl. "Heh, look what I've found. A black monkey." His fingers fastened in her hair.

The girl was terrified, already pleading, tears in her eyes. "Please, let me go."

He slipped his other hand up her skirt. "You should be pleased I take the time with a piece of black meat like you."

His friends started to laugh, faces like animals, completely cruel, and Sarah, rage welling up inside her, jumped up and grabbed at the boy's shoulder. "Leave her alone."

He swung round in surprise and something moved in his eyes. "Well, well, what have we here? A real lady. Wouldn't you say she was a real lady, Harold?"

The friend to whom he had appealed nodded. "I'd agree with that, Kevin."

"Too good for the likes of us, but maybe she could learn to like us, with a little persuasion."

He pushed Sarah down roughly and the one with the nose ring laughed. "Or learn to like it."

They crowded in. For a moment, Sarah knew overwhelming fear, and then Jago stood up and without a word, delivered a vicious blow to Kevin's kidneys, knuckles extended. Kevin screamed and fell to one knee. Jago pivoted, his right elbow swung back catching Harold under the chin. The boy fell to the floor, hands tearing at his throat, his eyes bulging, the swastika somehow obscene between them.

They were coasting into Chalk Farm station. Jago smiled amiably and said to her, "Dreadful, some of the people one meets on trains these days."

People were hurrying to get out, anxious not to be involved. Sarah stared at him, mutely grateful, and then, beyond him through the window, saw Egan cross the platform and make for the exit. She darted through the door and went after him. There was a silence, the doors still open, two of the youths on the floor, the others bending over them.

Jago moved forward, a smile on his face. "They didn't do too well, did they?"

He slipped out onto the platform and the boy with the nose ring shouted, "You bloody ponce, I'll show you."

He came through the door, a flick knife in one hand. As the blade jumped, Jago caught the wrist, half-turned, twisting the arm into a rigid bar until the boy dropped the knife. Jago's clenched fist descended like a hammer, there was an audible crack and the boy screamed.

"Oh, dear, I've broken his arm for him," Jago said, and pushed him back through the door to land in a heap on his friends as the train pulled away.

When he reached the bottom of the escalator, he could see Sarah at the top just behind Egan. Jago went up the escalator on the run and reached the entrance hall to see Egan pause, looking out at the pouring rain. As Sarah walked up to him, Jago moved in close, picking a newspaper from a wastebasket, opening it and leaning against the wall.

He heard her say, "Mr. Egan. I must talk to you."

"It's about time," Egan said. "You've been following me around for long enough."

"You knew?" she said blankly.

"As a good friend of mine used to say, you wouldn't last long on a wet Saturday night in Belfast. You stuck out like a sore thumb in the saloon bar of The Bargee and at regular intervals since. I must admit, you've got staying power—even if you lack subtlety. What can I do for you?"

"I'd like to talk." She hesitated, seeking the right words. "I need your help."

"Lady, I can't even help myself."

He turned up his collar and stepped out into the rain. She said desperately, "Please listen. It concerns your sister."

He turned, an extraordinary stillness to him now. "My sister?"

"Yes, Sally. Sally Baines Egan. You visited her grave today."

"And what would you have to say to me about her?"

"Not so much about Sally, but a great deal about the manner of her going, Mr. Egan."

"The manner of her going?" He nodded. "Oh, you have a way with words, Miss … ?"

"Talbot—Sarah Talbot and it's Mrs." She added by way of explanation, "I'm a widow, Mr. Egan, and I had a stepson who is now dead, just as you had a foster sister who is now dead. I think we should talk about that."

"All right," he said. "Where would you suggest?"

"I have a house in Lord North Street."

"That's on my way home anyway." He raised an arm to a passing cab, which pulled in. "We'll go back to Hampstead and get my car."

"But I thought you'd left it at that garage."

"Oh, there was nothing wrong," he said as he followed her into the cab. "I'd just got tired of trolling around. I wanted to see what you'd do."

It was five minutes before Jago managed to get a cab and follow them to retrieve his Spyder. Not that it mattered. He knew his final destination, and the equipment was all set up and functioning. He leaned back in the seat and lit a cigarette. It had really been quite an evening. Very enjoyable, and Egan in action had been very good indeed. It was going to be a pleasure doing business with him.

The lights were already on inside at Lord North Street when Jago arrived. He hurried inside the house across the street where Smith had leased the top-floor apartment.

The porter, sitting at his desk reading a newspaper, glanced up. "Nasty night, Mr. Mackenzie."

"Good for the garden, that's about all."

"Not in November it isn't," the porter told him morosely. "No messages, sir."

The place only had four floors so it was hardly worth waiting for the tiny lift. Jago went up the stairs two at a time. Three minutes later, he was pouring himself a Scotch and listening to Sean Egan and Sarah Talbot.

The sitting room of the house in Lord North Street was pleasant enough and furnished to suit the Regency period of the place. There was the correct wallpaper, the right silver, suitable carpeting and drapes. There was also a distinct impression of interior design that didn't sit comfortably on Egan.

There was a library table standing by one bay window, piled with books. Eric's Moroccan leather diary was on top where Sarah had left it. Egan opened it idly and was examining it when she entered the room with tea things on a tray.

"This is interesting," he said. "A Cambridge diary in Latin."

She put down the tray and took the book from him, closing it. "Yes, it was my stepson's. You read Latin?"

"I did it at school, if that's what you mean."

"Oh, yes, you were at Dulwich College." She poured the tea. "You intended to go to Cambridge yourself, didn't you?"

He took the cup she offered but didn't sit down. "How come you know so much about me?"

"It's simple," she said. "I told you I was a widow? Well, my husband was a colonel in the British Army, killed in the Falklands. His cousin is your old commanding officer, Tony Villiers."

Egan smiled slowly and nodded. "Tony playing games again. I might have known." He put down his cup. "Well, it won't work. I've already told him I won't join him at Group Four. Tell him I meant it."

He made for the door and she said desperately,

"Please, Mr. Egan, just hear me out." She extended a hand imploringly. "I honestly don't know the first thing about this Group Four business."

He stood looking at her searchingly for a moment, then walked to a wingback chair by the window and sat down. "All right, Mrs. Talbot. What's it all about?"

She opened the drawer in the library table, took out the envelope containing the material Villiers had sent to New York. "Read that."

She found that her hands were shaking, went to the sideboard and poured herself a brandy which she drank neat. She walked to the window and peered down into the rainy street, ignoring Egan. She felt more lonely than she had ever felt in her life and filled with a restless longing. She wanted to be able to whisper, "Where are you, my darling?" but there was no darling. No Edward, and now, no Eric.

Egan stood up behind her, his reflection plain in the dark glass. "Are you all right, Mrs. Talbot?"

"The telephone is only an echo in an empty room," she said. "Especially if there isn't anyone there any longer. Have you ever thought of that? It's a profoundly philosophical statement. You were going to read philosophy yourself at Cambridge, weren't you?"

"Sit down," he said gently.

She did as she was told, and he sat on the edge of the table. "What are you trying to say to me? Your son is dead, I understand that, and how you feel, but ..."

"Not dead, Mr. Egan, murdered, one of several similar cases reported in Paris in the last two or three years. If you read the small print in the postmortem report, you'll notice they found evidence of heroin and cocaine in Eric's body, but also traces of a rare drug from Colombia called burundanga. It totally destroys the individual's will power."

"So?" he said.

"There have also been four cases of IRA gunmen killed by Protestant paramilitaries during the past twelve months where the victims showed traces of the drug. I got that from Tony and his boss."

"That old spider Ferguson?" Egan nodded. "But what does it all mean? What do you want from me?"

"Because of the security implications, there doesn't seem to be much of a police investigation, and the French authorities are satisfied that Eric and the others all died accidentally."

"Which could be true. It's a bad habit drug addicts have."

"Not true in this instance. The burundanga indicates that, and it's a lead, don't you see? In the whole of Western Europe, so few cases. The same individuals must be behind it."

"And you want them?"

"Oh, yes, Mr. Egan, I want them very badly indeed."

"Revenge, Mrs. Talbot, is that it?" He shook his head. "There's a Sicilian proverb: 'Revenge is a season in Hell.' I know, because I've been there, and you come away with nothing."

She paced across the room, turned to face him. "I know why you joined the army. Can you deny you wanted revenge for the bomb that killed your mother and father?"

"Quite correct. I was seventeen. I needed to do it. To be honest, I think I'd have gone crazy if I hadn't done something positive at the time."

"Then can't you see that's how I feel?"

He took her hands gently. "Mrs. Talbot, I killed a lot of people over there in Ireland. On three occasions they were women. Oh, pretty violent women, I must admit, but it cuts a piece of you away each time. I killed again and again. Did I ever get the person responsible for that bomb? That's highly unlikely. It didn't bring my parents back, it didn't make me feel any better. In fact, it made me feel worse, and you know something else, Mrs. Talbot? It destroyed everything for me because when I came home, I found it didn't exist any more—I lost something back there. An ability to feel—to care about anything."

"Perhaps you should stop trying to care or looking for reasons. Maybe you should just act," she told him.

"What's this, free therapy?"

"There was some trouble on the subway tonight. Four youths, you know the sort? They were intimidating a black girl. I told them to leave her alone and they started on me."

"What happened?"

"It was incredible. There was a man sitting opposite. Very well dressed. Navy-blue Burberry, military tie."

"What happened?"

"He didn't say a word. Simply stood up and attacked. It was all very professional, elbows and things. Suddenly there were two on the floor.

And he laughed about it. Apologized." She shook her head. "He just didn't seem the sort."

"You mean he was a gentleman."

"I suppose I do, but whatever he was, he acted. He didn't enter into a dialectic. He went into action."

"There's a saying in the Koran that there's more truth in one sword than in ten thousand words. I learned that a long time ago," Egan told her.

"In Ireland?" Sarah asked.

"Good God, no. On the streets of Wapping, when I was a kid—the first time I tried to talk myself out of a fight and got beaten to a pulp instead by three other boys." Egan grinned. "I must have been all of eight years old. It was a rough neighborhood. You grew up fast or went under. You had to have bottle—lots of bottle."

"Bottle?" She frowned.

"Courage—nerve. No fear, that's the big secret. Never ever be afraid, no matter what the odds. My uncle taught me that when he found me crying on the pavement, blood on my face. He kicked me up the backside and told me to go and find them and have another go. You die, he said, if that's what it takes, but you don't give in, ever."

"That would be the famous Jack Shelley?" she said.

"You know about him?" Egan said. "Is there anything you don't know?"

"I don't think so. Tony's briefing was very thorough. The boy from the streets who went to public school, won a scholarship to Cambridge and became a soldier instead."

"An honorable profession. Somebody has to do it."

"Somebody has to be the public hangman," she said, "but I don't see why it has to be you."

He ran a hand over his face and smiled. "Look, give me one of those cigarettes of yours. I shouldn't, it's bad for my lungs these days, but what the hell. It's the shank of the night and the rain is falling."

She gave him the cigarette reluctantly and offered a light. He coughed a little almost at once, turned to the bay window, opened it and sat in the window seat, looking out at the rain. "I like cities at night, especially on this kind of night. Rain hissing down through the streets washing everything clean. It's as if anything's possible."

"Don't you normally feel like that?"

"Not for quite a while now. Something went from me a long time ago, Mrs. Talbot, and now I don't care."

"That's a terrible thing to say." She was genuinely shocked.

"No, not terrible, just different. You see, most men involved in crime or violence have one thing in common. They're desperate to win. I'm not worried whether I win or not. Live or die. It doesn't make any difference in the end."

"I don't agree," she said, surprised at the strength in her own voice. "Dying is easy. It's living that's hard. Having the strength to carry on."

"Like I said earlier, you do have a way with words." He tossed the cigarette out into the rain. "Let's get down to cases. Let's see if I've got it right. You want revenge for the death of your stepson."

"Justice," she put in. "I just want justice."

"There's no such thing any more, and you're not being honest. You want revenge. You want someone to pay the bill."

He paused, gazing at her intently, and she finally nodded and turned away. "All right. Call it what you like."

"But a nice well-brought-up lady like you who's traveled first class all her life wouldn't really know how to go about it, so what she wants is somebody like me, macho man with a gun in his hand, to hunt the bad guys down. Somebody who knows the ropes. Am I right?"

She nodded. "Yes, I suppose that just about sums it up."

"Well, I won't do it, Mrs. Talbot. I told you soldiering was an honorable profession. When I killed there was a reason. What you're looking for is some kind of assassin. I'm sorry about Eric, but it isn't a good enough reason from my point of view."

He turned as if to make for the door. She said quickly, "Maybe not, but Sally should be reason enough."

He went very still, then turned slowly. "What about Sally?"

"I'm sorry, Sean," she whispered. "Her postmortem indicated death by drowning under the influence of drugs."

"I know that."

"There were traces of the scopolamine there as well."

"That *burundanga* stuff?"

"I'm afraid so. Tony's people have been making a computer search.

Sally's case has been the only one to come up in England so far." She moved close and gripped his arms. "Don't you see, Sean? There must be a link with Paris, with Ulster...."

He shook her off, went to the bay window and opened the door to the right that gave access to the balcony. He stood there, face up to the rain, and she lit a cigarette nervously and waited.

Jago on the other side of the street moved to the window with a pair of Zeiss night glasses and focused them. Egan had his eyes closed, face still raised. "Oh, dear," Jago whispered, "Mr. Smith's not going to like this one little bit."

SIX

IN THE BATHROOM, EGAN toweled his head, damp from the rain, then carefully combed his hair. He examined his face in the mirror. It was reasonably composed, the only sign of stress a muscle twitching slightly on the left side of his mouth. But he was in control and that was all that mattered. He went back into the sitting room and found Sarah by the window.

"I'm sorry, Sean," she said. "Sorry I had to be the one to tell you."

"As they used to say in Crossmaglen when I was a wee boy, God forgive you for lying. Jesus, Mrs. Talbot, you're a nice enough lady, but you've got what you wanted, so why pretend?"

He helped himself to Scotch at the sideboard. She said, "Listen, I'm Sarah, not Mrs. Talbot. Now, what will you do?"

"Check the facts with Villiers."

"What if he won't help?"

"Oh, there are ways around that." He sipped some of the whiskey. "I've been playing rough games for some years now. It leaves one with a wide circle of entirely the wrong set of acquaintances."

"Like your uncle?" she suggested.

"One possibility. I'll probably have a word with him, but Villiers first."

"And what about me?"

He laughed harshly. "You don't give up, do you? The kind of people I'm looking for are like nothing you've ever known in your privileged life. Creatures from another planet. They'd kill you without thinking about it, and that would probably be after you'd kept them amused for the weekend. Believe me, you're well out of it."

"But I'm not out, I'm in," she said. "From the moment Eric died I was in."

He stood looking at her, frowning slightly, then swallowed the rest of his whiskey. "All right, have it your way. I want a word with my Aunt Ida first so we'll call at The Bargee. Afterwards I'll take you to meet my uncle. It should prove to be a significant stage in your education. And bring that envelope with you."

From his window, Jago watched them drive away while he waited for Smith to return his call. The phone rang. He lifted the receiver.

"What's happening?" Smith demanded.

Jago recounted the events of the evening and the substance of the conversation at the house in Lord North Street. "She's got him annoyed," Jago said. "Which could mean trouble."

"The interfering bitch," Smith said viciously.

"I know, old stick, can't women be the devil?"

"Everything's a joke to you, isn't it?" Smith said, anger in his voice.

"Only way to get by in this miserable life," Jago told him brightly. "What do you want me to do? Knock 'em off?"

"No, that's no good. Jack Shelley may be a respectable business-man these days, but underneath the Savile Row suit he's still the villain he always was, and to the London underworld he's still the governor. Knock his nephew off and he'd turn London upside down. The Talbot woman is just as bad. She's a friend of the President of the United States, for Christ's sake. Anything happened to her, there'd be hell to pay."

"They'd probably send in the Sixth Fleet," Jago observed.

"Very funny."

"So what do I do?"

"Stay close to them. In fact, make sure nothing happens to them. If any leaks appear, you plug them. Just make sure they never get close to anyone who can be helpful."

"I see. What you really mean is I make sure that if they do get close to anyone, nobody talks."

"That's it exactly," Smith said. "Now get moving. You know where they've gone."

Sean and Ida were in the kitchen; Sarah waited in the small sitting room. There were several photos on the sideboard, most featuring Egan. As a boy, stiff and awkward in a school tie and blazer, with a couple who were obviously his parents, and then in uniform, very handsome with the SAS cap badge on the beret, the pilot's wings, the medal ribbons. There was one outside the gates of Buckingham Palace, presumably after an investiture, Egan in dress uniform, Ida on one side in hat and best coat, and on the other a man who could only be Jack Shelley.

He wasn't particularly large, but his power was unmistakable. The face was amiable enough, full of an animal vitality, but there was a kind of mocking contempt in the smile. It occurred to Sarah that it was the smile of a man who didn't care for other people very much.

She opened a door and found herself in the main bar. As it was after closing time, there was only a small security light on, and she stood there breathing in the stale smell of beer and smoke and was aware of Ida's voice crying out, the sounds of muffled sobbing through the kitchen door.

Sarah went back into the sitting room and saw another photo on the mantelpiece—Egan, once again in uniform, and a pretty young girl, obviously Sally. Small, dark-haired, a good face, turned slightly profile, gazing up at Egan, all the love in the world on her face.

The kitchen door opened and Egan and Ida came in. The old woman's face was swollen with weeping. When she saw Sarah holding the photo, she took it from her.

"Sally, love," she moaned and she looked at Sarah. "I never knew what happened, what went wrong. One minute she was still at school, seventeen and life before her. She changed overnight. Became a different person. Drinks, drugs, then the police pulling her in for walking the pavement. The shame of it. Even Jack couldn't seem to control her any more."

"Don't upset yourself, Ida," Egan told her. "Make yourself a cup of tea and go to bed. We'll be off."

"Not that Jack really cared, except for appearances," Ida continued, and said to Sarah, "She wasn't family, you see."

She sat down, holding the photo to her, and Egan took Sarah by the arm. "Let's go," he said, and they left, closing the door quietly.

They got into the Mini Cooper and he drove away quickly, keeping to the river, turning into a narrow street lined with old Victorian warehouses a couple of minutes later. Egan braked to a halt at the end on a pier overlooking an old boat basin and the river.

"Hangman's Wharf. This is where he lives. He has an apartment on the top floor of the warehouse there."

"Are you sure he'll be in?"

"If he isn't, we'll try his club. 'Jack's Place,' it's called. Very low-life. Another stage in your education. Have you got the envelope?"

"Yes." She passed it across.

"Good. Saves time. You stay here. I'll need to speak to him first."

Egan got out and walked away. She locked the car doors and sat there, a little nervous, painfully aware of the quiet. A hooter sounded mournfully as a ship moved down the river. Behind her, Jago walked up the street and moved into the darkness of a doorway, watching, feeling strangely protective.

Egan went up in the old freight elevator, floor by floor, no cage, just the open platform. As it reached the top, a man in his mid-forties stood watching, arms folded. He was at least six feet tall, wore a loose-fitting suit, had a hard, raw-boned face and big hands. He was obviously ready for anything, face set, but now a look of incredulity appeared. "It's you, Sean. You're a sight for sore eyes." The lift jolted to a halt. "Hello, Tully, how's every little thing?" "Great, Sean, just great." His big arms went around Egan in a bear hug. "It's been too long. Jack goes on about you all the time. You hurt him going to the palace for the D.C.M., just you and Ida."

"I took him last time, didn't I?" Egan said. "Who else is here?"

"Gordon. You remember Gordon Varley? He's driving for Jack now, Jack sent him on the chauffeur's course at Rolls Royce."

"Nothing changes," Egan said. "Everything still top show. Where's Jack?"

"Down the other end. He'll be tickled pink."

He opened a door and led the way into a corridor. A dark mulatto man, a smaller edition of Tully, appeared in the kitchen door. He was in shirt-sleeves, drying a plate.

A look of astonishment appeared on his face. "Gawd help us, it's you, Sean!"

"Hello, Gordon. Still as ugly as ever," Egan said, and passed along the corridor.

When Tully opened the door, they entered an enormous room that had originally been the entire top floor of the warehouse. Rows of iron pillars supported the ceiling, which was painted white. The wooden floorboards had been sanded, then stained and sealed. Expensive Chinese rugs were scattered about, and on the right, a bronze Buddha six feet high stood in an alcove bathed in a white light. In fact, the predominant theme was Chinese—statues, artifacts everywhere, silk wall hangings and ivory-and-black lacquer screens at the far end where the main seating area was, several low couches in a circle around an enormous black lacquer table.

Mozart was playing softly, one of the horn concertos, and Jack Shelley sat at a black desk inlaid with gold. He was in shirt-sleeves and wore horn-rimmed reading glasses. Just now he was working through a mound of paper, and the figures on the computer screen next to him kept changing quietly.

"Look who's here, Jack," Tully said.

Shelley glanced up. He went very still, then took off the reading glasses. "Nice of you to look in after all this time." He nodded to Tully. "Wait in the kitchen, Frank."

Tully went away, his footsteps echoing. Egan helped himself to a cigarette from a box on the desk. "You know how it is, Jack."

He reached for the lighter and Shelley grabbed his wrist. "Oh, no you don't, my old son, not in my gaff. Bullet in the lung. What you trying to do, commit suicide?"

"Still trying to run my life, Jack." Egan pulled his wrist free and lit the cigarette. "Worse than my old sergeant major."

"Jock White? He's still around, that bastard," Jack said. "Got an old farm in a bleeding marsh the other side of Gravesend."

"I know," Egan said.

"You'd go and see him, but not me, your own flesh and blood? Haven't even given me a bell since you got out of hospital. That's out of order, Sean. I'm your uncle. The only family you've got in the world."

"You're forgetting Ida."

Shelley laughed. "Yes, well, she's bleeding well easy to forget, isn't she?"

Egan shook his head. "You never change, Jack. Still a king-sized bastard." He took the envelope from inside his bomber jacket. "Here, read this lot and we'll talk."

He tossed the envelope onto the desk and walked across to the windows overlooking the Thames. The view was marvelous and never failed to move him. Shelley had had the doors leading out onto the old freight platform glazed, and Egan opened them, stepped out and stood at the rail.

After a while Shelley joined him, his face grim. He held up the reports. "A right carve-up and no mistake, but what's it got to do with you?"

"The kid had a stepmother, Sarah Talbot. American woman, just in from New York. I'm helping her."

"You're helping her?" Shelley was incredulous. "What's wrong with her bleeding husband, for Christ's sake?"

"He was killed in the Falklands."

"Jesus!" Shelley stamped around. "So he was killed in the Falklands. I mean, what was a Yank doing down there?"

"He was a colonel in the British Army, and he wasn't a Yank."

"Oh, very good. It gets better. But why you?" He held up the papers. "This is for the Old Bill, not you. Never get involved in other people's troubles. How many times have I told you that?"

"The kid had traces of a drug called *burundanga* in him."

"Never heard of it," Shelley said.

"Well, it exists. It turns people into the walking dead. That means it's easy to kill them off properly and make it look kosher. Eric Talbot was one case. There have been several others in Paris and four in Ulster during the past twelve months, all IRA."

"Paris, Ulster, the bleeding IRA?" Shelley was really working himself up. "And a drug that sounds like a new brand of decaffeinated coffee. I still say, what's it got to do with you?"

"And one case in London," Egan said. "A young girl drowned in the Thames at Wapping called Sally Baines Egan."

Shelley went very still, jaws clenched together, glaring at him, then flung the papers down on the desk. After a while he carefully put the papers back in the envelope and handed it to Egan. He sat down at the desk. He seemed composed now.

"You're sure about this? I mean, how do you know?"

"My old boss, Colonel Villiers, got it out of the computer for me. It was there all the time, the fact of it. Just didn't make any sense to anyone before. It was just an item in the small print, if you follow me."

"Small print?" Shelley's face was terrible to see. "I'll get the bastards behind this, every last one of them, and I tell you what, my son. They'll be a long time dying. Nobody pulls a fast one in my backyard. Sally might not have been family to me, but she was to you, God help you. And you're all I've got." He got up, crossed to a drink cabinet and poured brandy from a cut-glass decanter into a glass. He swallowed it down and turned to Egan, holding up the decanter.

"No, thanks," Egan said.

"Well, I will." Shelley poured another.

"So what are you going to do?" Egan asked.

"I'll put the word out in every manor in London. I'll get the old firm on it. There's a lot of people owe me favors, including some very high-ranking gentlemen at Scotland Yard. I'll find out who these bastards are and I'll have their fucking hands cut off, and that's just for openers. I may have lunch with bank chairmen at L'Escargot, but I'm still Jack Shelley. I'm still the governor, and don't you forget it."

"When did I ever?" Egan said.

"Don't take the piss out of me, my old son, you're more like me than you know. Now tell me about the Talbot bird."

"Not a bird," Egan said. "A real lady, this one."

"Really?" Shelley grinned. "I like that. Bit of class, right?"

"A lot of class, Jack, also very rich. Her father left her half of Fort Knox. Also very bright. She's a Wall Street broker and she's important, Jack. Friends right up to the White House."

"Really?" Shelley took his jacket from the back of his chair and pulled it on. He adjusted his tie. "I can't wait. When can I see her?"

"She's sitting downstairs in my car now."

"Downstairs?" Shelley was aghast. "In that bleeding tin can of yours? Jesus, I sent you to public school to learn how to be a gentleman. I give up. I really do."

He walked out very rapidly, calling as he passed the kitchen, "All right, you two, move your arses."

Tully and Varley arrived on the run, Varley pulling on his jacket. They all got into the lift and it started down.

Shelley said to Egan, "I was going to the club for a bite to eat. You might as well join us, only the lady can come with me in the Roller. You can follow on."

"We'll see what she says," Egan told him.

"I know what she'll say if she's got any bleeding sense."

They got out of the lift at the bottom and Varley hurried across to the white Rolls Royce Silver Spur and got in. The others walked out onto the dock and approached the Mini Cooper. Sarah saw them coming, opened the door and got out.

"Mrs. Talbot." Shelley took her hand in both of his. "A great pleasure, believe me. I've got to apologize for my nephew, leaving you on your own like this. I thought I'd taught him some manners, but kids today ..." He shrugged.

"That's perfectly all right, Mr. Shelley."

Shelley was immediately impressed. "Yes, well, anyway, Sean's filled me in on everything and I don't want you to worry. I'll clear this up personal, just give me a few days."

"That's marvelous."

"Enough of that now, I've got a little club not far from here. I was just going along for a bite of supper." At that moment the Rolls Royce arrived. "I thought you might appreciate a ride in a decent car. My nephew can follow us in the sardine can."

"That's really not necessary," Sarah said.

"But I insist." He escorted her to the Rolls and opened the rear door.

Tully said to Sean, "He was real proud of you, Sean, being a hero and all that. The medals."

"I'm sure he was," Egan said.

"Frank, get your arse over here." Tully hurried across and got in the front. "We'll see you there," Shelley called to Sean and put the window up.

Egan stood there while the Rolls drove up the street and turned the corner. It was very quiet. He walked to his car, started to open the door and paused, some sixth sense stirring. It was as if something waited there in the shadows, but that was silly. Too much Belfast time, he told himself, got in the car and drove away. A second later, Jago slipped out of the doorway and hurried along the street.

Jack's Place was another warehouse conversion by the river, not too far away. The car park was in the old unloading yard. The Rolls Royce was already there when Egan arrived, and he parked beside it. He walked along the street toward the front entrance, the name clear above the door in an old-fashioned red neon sign. There was a queue waiting to get in—four young men at the front in designer suits.

One of them wore a gold Rolex and sported a diamond in his left ear. He was getting annoyed with the doorman, an amiable giant of twenty stone called Sammy Jones, who also wrestled on TV in his spare time.

"How much longer?" he demanded.

"You'll have to wait, man," Sammy Jones told him and then, as Egan bypassed the queue, he smiled. "Hey, Mr. Egan, great to see you. Come right in."

"What's he bleeding got that the rest of us don't?" the man with the Rolex demanded.

"I wear after-shave, not perfume," Egan said. "You should try it." And as the man snarled and moved forward, he stepped inside.

From Egan's description, Sarah expected something far worse, but the decor was excellent, with a thirties theme, the roof mirrored, a beautiful cocktail bar with crystal lights behind and high leather stools, and the waiters wore white monkey jackets like shipboard stewards.

She and Shelley were sitting in a corner booth, Tully standing against the wall behind, arms folded. On the way in, Shelley had been treated like royalty, constantly having to stop to shake hands. And it was the evidence of money that surprised her most. Everyone was expensively dressed, although some of the women were decidedly overdone.

The head waiter bustled over. Shelley said, "Henri, this is Mrs. Talbot, a very special friend. We'll have a bottle of Krug for starters, the nonvintage." He turned to her. "Best champagne in the world, Krug nonvintage. Something special they do with the grapes. What about something to eat?"

"I don't think so. I'm not very hungry."

"Nonsense, got to feed you up. Bring us a pile of smoked salmon sandwiches, Henri, and some pâté or something."

"Certainly, Mr. Shelley."

"And bring Frank a large Scotch."

A wine waiter bustled up with the Krug in an ice bucket. "You like it?" Shelley asked her. "The place, I mean?"

"It's fascinating."

"I used the same guy who did my apartment. You must see that sometime. A bit of a poof, but you know what gays are like. Nobody to beat 'em at the interior design game. I told him I wanted the place to look like a Fred and Ginger movie, and that's what he gave me. They used to have a bar like that at the Ritz before the war. He copied it, or that's what he told me."

"Maybe he was telling the tale, Jack, just to keep you happy," Tully put in.

"You drink your Scotch and keep stum." Shelley grinned. "He doesn't like gays. Always wants to believe the worst. You notice the band? I didn't want a bleeding disco. Can't hear yourself think."

She glanced across at the trio on the tiny bandstand who were playing music appropriate to the decor, and at the same moment she saw Egan enter the room. In his jeans and black bomber jacket he looked quite alien, and people turned to stare curiously as he moved through the crowd.

"Look at you, for Christ's sake," Shelley said. "Dressed as if you're going to work at Covent Garden market."

Egan reached for the champagne bottle, filled a glass and sat down. "I'm comfortable, that's all that counts."

"He's got the shares in my business I gave his mother, Mrs. Talbot.

Three million quid. Would you believe that? Never touches a penny. And when I die," he shrugged, "at least twenty, not that I've any intention of going just yet."

Henri delivered the sandwiches personally and Egan helped himself. "I see you've got the usual select crowd in tonight. Manchester Charlie Ford over their spending big. Is it true he and his boys did that security van job in Pimlico last week?"

"That's the word." Shelley shrugged. "Old-fashioned stuff, that. Blokes like Charlie never learn. Stocking masks, sawn-off shotguns and security vans always puts you in Parkhurst for fifteen years, sooner or later." He nudged Sarah and there was a certain pride in his voice when he said, "Mind you, there's some of the best-known villains in London here tonight. They all come here. Here or to Sean's bleeding pub."

There was a sudden fuss up at the bar and Egan recognized the man with the gold Rolex from the door and his three friends bellowing for service.

"Who the hell is that?" Shelley demanded.

"Kid called Tiller, Bert Tiller," Tully said. "He's a ponce. Was in Soho, but he's expanding. Those are some of his boys. The one with the red hair is called Brent. Don't know the others."

Sarah turned inquiringly to Egan. "A ponce lives off women," he told her. "What you'd call a pimp."

"If there's one thing I got no time for, it's the kind of scumbag who lives off women. Drugs and women," Shelley said. "I never made a penny out of either in my life."

"Mind you, he's cemented a few people up in the North Circular Road in his time," Egan observed.

"That's different—that was business. You don't get anywhere with a pipe in your pocket pretending it's a gun." He folded his arms and stared across at the noisy group. "Look at that ponce with his gold watch and the Armani suit, probably earned by a load of fifteen-year-old girls servicing old men. I'd really like to give him a going over."

Tiller happened to turn and noticed Shelley's glare. He stopped laughing for a minute, then said something to his friends. They all turned to look, and burst into laughter. Tully straightened and Shelley put a hand up. "Leave it, Frank. Not now."

Sarah said, "If you'll excuse me for a minute."

She got up and crossed through the dancers, went up the steps by the bar to the ladies' room. Tiller and his friends stopped talking and watched her all the way. As she went in through the door there was another outburst of laughter.

"Not good," Egan said, refilled his glass with champagne and swallowed it down in a single gulp.

"Get ready, Frank," Shelley said softly. "I think you're going to have to do a little chastising."

Sarah emerged and made for the steps. Tiller grabbed her by the arm. He leaned down and whispered something in her ear. She tried to slap his face and he held her, laughing, and then Egan was there, well ahead of Frank. He simply reached up, punched Tiller behind the right knee so that the leg buckled and he lost his balance and fell backward onto the dance floor. The crowd got out of the way fast and Tiller tried to get up, and then Shelley was there, stamping down hard, grinding his heel into the back of the hand.

"Keep still or I'll break your fucking fingers."

Sarah came down the stairs and Egan pulled her behind him. Tully stood waiting, his great arms dangling, daring the other three at the bar to make a move, and then Sammy Jones appeared from the bar with Varley, who was swinging a baseball bat.

Shelley took his foot off the hand and Tully pulled Tiller up and twisted an arm behind his back. Shelley patted his face. "Now you run off home like a good boy and don't come back because if you do—" he patted Tiller's face again—"I'll put you on sticks for six months." He nodded to his minders. "Now get this scum out of here."

The crowd parted as Tully, Jones and Varley herded the four out; then the music started and people began to dance again.

"Come and sit down, Mrs. Talbot," Shelley said. "In my own place, and to a friend. A bleeding disgrace."

When they sat, she found that her hand shook so much she nearly spilled the champagne. She put the glass down carefully. "I think I've very definitely had enough for one day. I'd like to go home."

"Of course," Sean said.

"I'll take you in my car," Shelley put in. "No, I insist." And as Tully returned, he said, "You and Varley go and get the Roller ready. We'll be along in a minute."

She was too tired to argue. She followed Shelley out, Egan trailing closely behind. It was raining again and Sammy Jones said, "You wait here. I'll go and tell them to bring the car up, Mr. Shelley."

"Not worth it," Shelley said. "Give us an umbrella."

He put it up and stepped out into the street, an arm linked with Sarah's, and Egan said, "Got a cigarette, Sammy?"

"I sure have, Mr. Egan." Sammy gave him one, and a light. "Here, keep the packet."

"I shouldn't, but I will."

Egan went down the steps. The door closed behind him. Shelley and Sarah were halfway to the car park when suddenly Tiller and one of his friends stepped out of a doorway and confronted them. At the same time, Brent and the fourth member of the gang came up some basement steps behind them.

Shelley said calmly, "Team-handed, eh? Just about your style." He raised his voice and cried, "Frank, where are you?" At the same time he closed the umbrella and lunged, using it like a sword, catching Tiller's companion under the chin. The unfortunate youth fell to the pavement, hands tearing at his collar.

Egan arrived, running silently, stamping one foot behind Brent's knee, grabbing a wrist, forcing the man's arm up behind him, then running him through the gate in the railings to fall headfirst down the basement steps. The fourth youth backed away in horror, dodging Tully and Varley as they came running, fleeing for his life.

And Tiller didn't show any fear, simply took out a cutthroat razor and opened it. "Big man," he said. "Jack Shelley, the governor. Well, let's see how good you are."

Shelley waved Tully and Varley away. "Leave him," he said.

In the same moment Tiller slashed out, the blade slicing into Shelley's sleeve. Shelley took a step back and examined it. "You little bleeder. I paid a grand for this at Gieves and Hawkes. You've ruined it."

His foot flicked forward, catching Tiller under the kneecap. Tiller started to double over and Shelley raised a knee into his face, at the same time catching the wrist and twisting the arm up so that Tiller was forced to drop the razor; then Shelley hauled him over to the railings and forced his palm down on one of the spikes.

"Now then, you ponce, how tough do you feel?"

Sarah cried out, "No, Mr. Shelley, please don't!"

He turned to look at her, eyes glazed. "Please!" she said again.

He nodded and threw Tiller at Tully and Varley. "All right, get him out of my sight. Kick his arse and send him on his way." He turned to Egan. "Take the lady home. I'm sorry about this, Mrs. Talbot. It turned out to be like a bad night in Belfast."

She walked away, Egan's arm around her shoulder. They passed Tully and Varley frogmarching Tiller down the street, got in the Mini Cooper and drove away quickly.

Tully and Varley dragged Tiller into the car park. Shelley strolled in a moment later. "You've got the bastard then?"

"I figured you'd want a word, Jack," Tully said.

"I certainly do. Put him down on his back." They threw Tiller down and Tully and Varley held him.

"For God's sake, Mr. Shelley," Tiller pleaded.

"For God's sake? I'm God here, my old son," Shelley told him, "and you've been right out of order. You need a lesson." He stamped down on the right shin very hard and a bone cracked. "I said I'd put you on sticks for six months and I just did. I always keep my promises. And one more thing." He pulled the gold watch from Tiller's wrist. "There you are, Frank. You always wanted a Rolex. Be my guest."

He walked to the Rolls Royce, got in. Tully and Varley hurried after him, Tully clutching the Rolex. They drove away leaving the unfortunate Tiller writhing in agony. There was a step in the darkness, and Jago appeared and looked down at him.

"Are you all right, old man?"

Tiller moaned and managed to croak, "Help me."

"Yes, I thought you were," Jago said cheerfully, and he got into the Spyder and drove away.

When they reached Lord North Street, Egan took the key from Sarah and opened the door. She looked exhausted and sad.

"A hard night on the town," he said.

"A nightmare."

"I warned you what you were getting into." She moved into the hall and they stood there for a moment. "Have you had your lesson?"

"No, Sean, I need to go on. More than ever now."

"You stubborn fool," he said. "You just won't learn, will you?" And then he had an idea. "You've seen the violence in action tonight. That's fine, but how would you feel about dishing it out yourself?"

"What do you mean?"

"Could you shoot someone if you had to?"

"I don't know." She was drained, unable to think straight. "I really don't know."

"All right. Tomorrow's Saturday. I'll take you downriver to see a friend of mine. Jock White, my old sergeant major. He has a farm in a marsh the other side of Gravesend. Runs survival courses. We'll see what you're made of." He shrugged. "It'll help fill in the time while Uncle Jack tries to turn something up."

"Anything you say."

"Go to bed." He smiled. "I'll see you tomorrow, and not too early." He closed the door and went down the steps to his car.

Jago listened to the tape a few minutes later and then contacted Smith. They discussed the evening's events.

"You'd think it would have finished her off," Smith said. "First plane home and so on."

"Not the sort," Jago said. "Lady of pluck and determination. About this farm at Gravesend. You want me to go?"

"Of course."

"Then it's time I changed vehicles. Sensible precaution. Arrange for a Land Rover or something like that in the morning. I can switch the equipment in a few minutes."

"I'll see to it," Smith said.

The line went dead. Jago drew the curtain slightly and looked across the street at her house. There was a light in the bedroom. It went out.

"Sleep tight, sweetie," he whispered. "You've earned it."

~

Egan drove into the yard at the side of The Bargee and killed his lights. As he got out of the Mini Cooper, he noticed a sedan at the back of the yard. Its lights were suddenly switched on and Tony Villiers got out.

"Sean." He nodded. "How are you?"

"Pretty fair. To what do I owe the honor?"

"She found you then?"

"That's right."

"Keep her happy, Sean, no more than that. I don't want her involved in anything. You understand?"

"She told me about Sally," Egan said. "About what you found on that computer."

"That was privileged information. There won't be any more, and remember one thing, Sergeant. For your first six months after release from the army you're still subject to military law. In your case, you're also on priority reserve. With your security classification, I can haul you back any time I want."

"Colonel Villiers," Egan said, "why don't you go to hell?" And he opened the door and went inside.

Villiers stood there for a moment and then smiled reluctantly. "That's my Sean," he said softly.

SEVEN

IT WAS RAINING THE following morning when they set off just before noon. Sarah felt herself again, fit and surprisingly cheerful. They never seemed to leave the city, which amazed her.

"London seems to go on forever," she observed.

"It only seems that way." Egan grinned. "Soon out of it now. Dartford coming up."

They were through Dartford and into Gravesend almost before she knew what was happening. Beyond Gravesend, they moved into a different world. A desolate landscape of flat green fields broken by marsh, all drifting toward the river.

She said, "I'm not too sure I like it. Strange to find such a place so close to London."

"Yes, you get the feeling nothing's changed much here."

There were sea creeks and mud flats and in the far distance she could see large ships moving down to the sea. Here and there reeds grew almost as high as a man. They drove along a narrow road raised like a causeway, then passed through a small village called Marton where there was a caravan site.

"Who on earth would want to come to a place like this for a holiday?" she demanded.

"Bird watchers. Nature lovers. This kind of place would be just their cup of tea," Egan said. "It isn't everybody who wants to be on the beach at Cannes."

Jago, a quarter of a mile behind, smiled softly. "I do, old man. Just give me the chance."

He was driving a green Land Rover, a fishing basket and rod case in the back, plus a canvas holdall. He wore a crumpled tweed hat and a green parka and waterproof leggings and boots. There was a pair of Zeiss glasses on the seat beside him.

Just outside Marton a wooden sign to the right said, "All Hallows Farm," and the place was clearly visible through the trees, a rambling house with stabling and barns joined to it, the whole surrounding a courtyard reached by an archway in a wall. Egan and Sarah drove in and he braked to a halt.

"Jock?" Egan called and sounded the horn.

There was no response. Sarah said, "What a marvelous place. It looks very old."

"Parts of it are sixteenth century. Jock's wife owned it. Came down through her family. She died some time ago. He took his papers after the Falklands campaign and settled here." There was no response to his knocking. "Let's see if we can find him."

They followed a path up through trees and along a small valley, a stream gurgling through. It was very quiet and undeniably scenic.

"It's lovely," Sarah said.

"Oh, sure, only don't drink the water." He nodded toward the stream.

"Why not?"

"Try it and you'll soon see. This is a salt marsh."

They moved on, following a path between tall reeds. She said, "You've known Jock White long then?"

"Ever since I transferred to the SAS. We've served together in the Oman, Cyprus, Ireland and then the Falklands."

"How old is he?"

"Supposed to be sixty, but I think he's lived forever. He was in the Korean War, for God's sake, Borneo, Aden. Oh, and Vietnam on secondment with the Australian SAS." He glanced sideways at her. "Did you know Villiers was in Vietnam?"

"No, I didn't." She was shocked.

"Yes, there are few places the SAS don't go. But getting back to Jock, he runs survival courses here for anyone willing to learn."

"He sounds like a very special kind of man."

"He's that all right. More than a legend in the regiment—an icon."

A rough voice with only a hint of a Scots burr said, "Don't listen to a word, lassie, he was always big for exaggeration."

As they turned, Jock White stepped out of the reeds. He was a giant of a man with unkempt gray hair and a white beard, wearing a camouflage jump jacket, corduroys and rubber boots. A shotgun was tucked under his arm. There was a movement in the reeds and a yellow Labrador appeared. From her appearance, she'd recently had pups. She whined, wriggled and approached Egan in delight.

He crouched to caress her. "Hello, who's a lovely girl then?" He said to Sarah, "This is Peggy, sheer delight, and this," he looked up at the older man, "is Jock White. Whenever he did a tour in South Armagh, the IRA used to shut up shop and go to Florida for the winter."

"Cheeky young devil," Jock said. "Always was. You're in bad company, lassie."

"Not now, Mr. White." She took his hand. "Sarah Talbot."

"Oh, I like this one, Sean. For once you've done something right. Let's go back to the house and we'll have a cup of tea. You're staying, of course?"

"We had hoped to."

"That's good." The big man drew her arm through his and they went back along the track.

Jago drove through Marton as far as the sign to All Hallows, then reversed and went back. He'd noticed the small caravan site behind the village garage and entered through the gate. An old man in overalls and a cloth cap was standing on a stepladder painting one of the caravans. He turned and looked at Jago.

"Something I can do for you?"

"You the proprietor?"

"Fancy word, but true enough."

"You wouldn't happen to have a caravan for rent, would you?"

The old man propped his brush across the tin of paint and descended the ladder. "How long for?"

"Tonight—maybe tomorrow as well."

The old man peered into the back of the Land Rover. "Fisherman, are you?"

"Bird watcher, really."

"Just as well, you wouldn't catch much with that gear around here." He turned, scratching his backside. "Well, take your pick. No one else here this time of the year. Ten quid a night and there's a gas cylinder included."

"Marvelous." Jago got his bag and the fishing gear out of the Land Rover.

"I own the garage as well. We keep most things in the shop there. What name?"

"Mackenzie." Jago smiled charmingly and followed him toward the nearest caravan.

The sitting room had a ceiling so low that Jock White's head almost touched it. The fireplace was large enough to stand in. There were chairs, an old sofa bed, a sideboard with a few photos from service days on it, and books everywhere, a pleasant clutter to everything.

Jock White sat on the window seat, a pair of steel-rimmed army issue spectacles on the end of his nose, working his way through the papers relevant to Eric's death. The French windows stood open, and Sarah was sitting in the garden with a basket of puppies, Peggy crouched beside her. Egan sprawled by the fire, smoking a cigarette. Every so often he coughed quite badly.

Jock said, "Are you trying to kill yourself or what, laddie?"

Egan shrugged. "Come off it, Jock, it's all one in the end. You know how much scrap metal I'm carrying around."

"How's the knee?"

"I get by."

Jock sighed, removed his spectacles and held up the papers. "A dirty business this."

"You could say that."

Jock looked out at Sarah in the garden. "A fine young woman like her shouldn't be getting herself mixed up in this sort of thing."

"She's very determined," Egan told him. "Got the bit between her teeth. Wants to take them on, face to face."

Jock White shook his head. "So why have you brought her here?"

"We've got the weekend to spare while my uncle's people see if they can come up with anything. I thought she might find it interesting. I mentioned your survival courses." He stood up and put a log on the fire. "There's another thing. She's never even pulled a trigger in her life. I'd like to think she couldn't, when it comes to the crunch."

The older man nodded. "You're still a cunning young swine, laddie. What you're really saying is you want me to put her off by putting her through it."

"Exactly."

"You always were a hard young bastard," Jock said. "I'm going to take her for a walk. You stay here and mind your business."

He picked up his jump jacket, pulled it on and went out to Sarah. "How about you and me taking a breath of air, lassie?"

"That would be nice, Jock."

They left the garden by a small gate and went up through the trees, following a stream. He said, "I'm sorry about your son."

She paused and looked at him searchingly. "You're the first person who's called him that. Most people say stepson."

"Oh, it isn't always the blood tie that's important. It's how people feel. I get a feeling he couldn't have been more important if he'd been your own flesh and blood."

She reached up and softly patted his cheek. "That's one of the nicest things anyone has ever said to me."

They continued the walk. "I knew your husband," he said. "Served with him in Aden a long time ago. There was a district called the Crater dominated by Marxist guerrillas. When they ambushed a number of our lads he took a platoon in to rescue them. All he carried was a swagger stick in his right hand. I can see him now, right out in front as if he was on a Sunday afternoon stroll, daring them to shoot."

"They got him in the end, didn't they?" she said.

He glanced at her, puzzled, then saw the point. "I suppose that's one way of looking at it."

"I've never understood soldiers. The first boy I ever loved was killed in Vietnam. It always seems so stupid."

"Sometimes necessary, lassie. The trick is to live here and now in the timeless moment. To act as if that's all there is. No beginning, no end."

Jago, on top of a dike in the far distance, watched them through his Zeiss glasses. Seeing her with White he felt almost overwhelmed by resentment that someone else should be allowed the contact he was denied. A feeling of desolation touched him for a moment.

He said softly, "Now don't start going soft on me now, old man."

"It's so lovely." Sarah shivered slightly in the cold as she looked out across the salt marshes.

"It's been a sanctuary for some since Roman times," Jock said. "Then there was Saxons here. Outlaws hunted by the Normans. Centuries later it was the smugglers, revenuers breathing down their necks. There's a bit of that still goes on, mind you."

"That's it," she said. "A place of shadows. A dead world."

"Never that, lassie. There's life here. Crab in the gulleys, fish in the creeks, curlew and redshank and brant geese fly here every winter all the way from Siberia. All a man needs to survive is here."

"And that's what you teach, survival?"

"If it pleases you. You could survive a holocaust with what I teach, but then there are those who deny life. Poor, miserable creatures who would curl up and die without a roof over their heads, a wrapped loaf and milk delivered to the doorstep in a carton."

She laughed. "You think I'm like that?"

He waved his hand. "Those reeds, woven properly, make a fine dwelling and proof against all weather. Almost every living thing on this marsh can be eaten. Insects for their protein. Crows, hedgehogs." He stooped at the side of the track, grabbed into the ooze and came up clutching a large toad. "Fine eating, Mrs. Talbot. Would you have the stomach for it? Or dried worms? There's real protein for you."

She was fascinated by the sheer ugliness of the toad. "Well, I don't suppose worms would go down very well on the menu at The Four Seasons."

"What's that?"

"My favorite Manhattan restaurant." She touched the toad gently with one finger. "Actually, he's too sweet to eat."

"I've a suspicion you're going to become a trial to me, Sarah Talbot." He replaced the toad carefully in the ooze. "Come on, we'll go back now."

She took his arm. "I think you've been talking to Sean. I think you're trying to put me off this whole business."

"You're wrong, lassie. My concern is to stop you from wasting your life up a dark alley that's going to lead nowhere."

"Look, I don't have any choice. If I did nothing, I think I'd go out of my mind."

"I understand that." He sighed heavily. "And while you're here, we might as well make use of your time, I suppose. In any case, with any luck that villain Shelley will come up with the right answers in a day or two and you can go home."

"We'll see," she told him, and at the same moment realized, to her horror, that she didn't want that at all. My God, Sarah, she thought, what's happening to you?

One of the barns had been turned into a kind of gym, the walls neatly whitewashed. There were climbing bars, weight-lifting equipment and ropes dangling from the ceiling beams. In the center of the floor were several judo mats. Sarah was wearing a track suit, Jock White an old sweatshirt and running shorts. Egan sprawled on a bench wearing his usual bomber jacket and jeans, watching them.

"Karate and judo, in fact all the martial arts, take a long, long time to learn—too long. Someone like you I can teach four or five things to do if someone attacks you, that's all."

"I was threatened by some punks last night on the subway."

"What happened?"

"A man interfered. He knocked two of them down."

"Then what?"

"I don't know. I took off."

"He must have been good," Jock said, "but you'll probably never meet anyone like him again because most of the time if you're attacked, no one will help. In fact, they'll run the other way."

"So what do I do?"

"You must be as mean or vicious as necessary. The kind of man who'll attack you might start reaching for your handbag, but he'll have rape on his mind before he's finished. So, it's fingernails, stiletto heels, a thumb in his eye—anything it takes."

"All right, where do I start?"

"Well, as we're all adults, a man's most vulnerable with what he's got between his legs. Still nothing like a good kick in the crotch. Here, try kneeing me."

"I don't think I could," she said.

"Yes, you bloody well can. As it happens, I'm wearing a protector, but a rapist would be much more likely to be ready for action when he grabs you." And grab her he did. " 'Come on, darling, be nice to me,' that's what he'd say. His weakness would be that he wouldn't expect a nice girl like you to react violently." She was gasping now, his strength enormous, crushing her. "Go on, knee him in the balls!" he cried and pulled her even closer, his breath hot on her face.

For a moment there was terror as she fought to free herself, and then something else surfaced, a kind of rage, a hatred, for the moment, of everything male. "You bastard!" she screamed, and swung her knee up between his legs with all her force, felt it connect painfully with the plastic protector.

"Marvelous." He had her by the shoulders, laughing. "Perfect. Right in the goolies. He's on his back and you're on your way."

"I didn't think I could do anything like that," she said, panting heavily as the adrenaline continued to course through her.

"Anybody can. It's survival, lassie. The instinct to keep on living and the willingness to do anything necessary. With most people it's buried deep, but it's there in us all. It just needs coaxing out. Now do that again."

For at least half an hour they worked on that one simple technique. Then Jock White took her further.

"Physically you'll never match up to a man. That's a fact of life, so for you, it's always got to be technique. You've got longer fingernails. Right, when he gets his arms round you, grab his lower lip, using both hands. Dig your nails in, then twist as if you're pulling things apart.

Believe me, the sheer agony of that will blow his mind for long enough for you to get on your bike." He smiled. "With this one, I'd appreciate your treating me gently."

She had him howling with pain within seconds. Egan applauded. "You've got a natural here, Jock."

"You shut up," Jock winced. "Gently, lassie, gently. I'm not as young as I was."

She practiced for about twenty minutes until he was satisfied. "Now as I said, you're a woman, so no point in trying to punch him in the mouth, but if you form a phoenix fist, you'll always inflict pain wherever you hit him. Squeeze your hand together, allow the middle knuckle to protrude between the fingers." She followed his example. "Excellent. It's like a nerve being touched wherever that goes in. Under the chin, in the throat, the temples. Oh, and under the nose. The septum's very vulnerable. Come over here."

He stood behind the large punching bag and held it. "All right, phoenix fists with both hands and start punching."

Sarah attacked vigorously. Egan got up and yawned. "I think I'll turn in."

"Lazy bastard!" Jock said.

"Night, Sean," Sarah called.

Egan paused, crossing the yard, and breathed in the salt air. There was a half-moon; the night was alive with stars and it was quiet, only a dog barking hollowly somewhere in the distance. For the first time in years, he felt life stirring in him. It was a strange and uncomfortable sensation. There was laughter from the barn now, and he listened for a moment. She was enjoying herself, that was certain. In fact, things were not working out as he had expected, but then, that was life. He went in and closed the door.

Jago lay in the long grass by the causeway. He wore earphones and the directional receiver from the Land Rover was at his side. He could hear the sounds of combat from the barn clearly, every grunt, every groan, Sarah's excited laugh.

"That's it, lassie, harder," Jock was saying. "Hit me harder."

And Jago found himself laughing too. "Give it to him, Sarah." He rolled on his back and looked up at the moon. "What a woman," he said softly. "What a bloody marvelous extraordinary lady."

"We stay for an hour," Sean told her. "Not a move till I tell you. He'll be the enemy and he'll come looking. You'd like to beat him, wouldn't you?"

"Oh, yes," Sarah said.

It was just before noon the following day. She wore an old para-trooper's jump smock Jock had given her, jeans and jump boots. They were in the marsh, deep in the reeds in about two feet of mud and water. She was cold, very cold, and then it started to rain, which didn't help.

"He's coming," Egan whispered.

Like her, he wore an old combat smock, the hood pulled up. He gently parted the reeds and she saw Jock White advancing toward them, a shotgun cradled in one arm. One minute he was there and then he simply disappeared.

"Where did he go?" Sarah whispered.

"He's trying to make us break cover. Just follow me and do what I do."

They crawled through the reeds, slipped over the edge of a dike down into a narrow creek that disappeared into the further reeds. "That's the way through," Egan said. "Like an underground tunnel."

She followed him, crawling through ice-cold water and slime, at times only her head above the surface. The stink was terrible, and at one moment a water rat streaked through the water in front of her. It took every ounce of control to stifle the scream. And then, after what seemed an eternity, Egan paused.

"Almost through. We should come out by the main causeway, cross over, down through the woods and home, the kettle on before he gets back. Lead the way, I'll follow."

She nosed out through the final barrier of reeds, her head coming up out of the water cautiously, and found Jock White up above her, sitting on the edge of the causeway filling his pipe. "Oh, there you are," he said. "What kept you?"

Toward evening she felt strangely restless. Egan had walked into Marston to get cigarettes. He was smoking more, she'd noticed. Probably her influence, but it was her one bad habit and her one concession to the strain of her situation. Jock slept peacefully in front of the fire, Peggy and the puppies at his feet.

Sarah looked out. Dusk was beginning to fall. Another hour and it would be dark. On impulse, she opened the door, stepped out and crossed the courtyard. She was wearing an old track suit and track shoes. She went up through the wood, starting to run when she reached the causeway.

Jago had been out for a walk on his own account; he saw the figure in the distance, raised his Zeiss glasses and realized it was Sarah the moment she sprang into focus. He kept walking, some distance away from her, watching as she turned along one narrow dike after another. He paused to focus on her again, suddenly felt water lap across his feet and, when he turned, realized that the tide was coming in fast, a bore pushing across the estuary, washing in over the marsh.

He started to run, working his way from one dike to another, most of them already a foot under water, until he reached the edge of the marsh and scrambled up onto the main causeway. He turned quickly, but there was no sign of Sarah.

At that moment she was a good two hundred yards toward the estuary, where there was some comparatively high ground. It was only on breaking out of the reeds that she found herself knee-deep in water.

She turned, saw the rapid movement of the sea in across the marsh, realized her predicament and started to run as best she could. It was Jock she thought of then, and what he'd said about trouble. No one to rely on. Only yourself. She couldn't panic; there was no time. Just keep on the move, trying to follow the lines of the dike tops just under water.

She was almost at the causeway now, and it started to rain, a great, gray sheet of it reducing visibility to almost nothing, the world closing in on her. Something seemed to move up there, a marsh ghost, a phantom, she couldn't be sure, and then she went under, was choking, fighting for her life.

Something fell across her face, the sleeve of a parka and she grabbed for it, floundering, looked up and found Jago at the other end, leaning over the edge of the dike, face pale, the scar very pronounced.

"Good girl, Sarah, hang on!"

She tried, went under again, feeling the current pull at her feet, and then she had the sleeve securely, held on tight as he hauled her in and up onto the causeway. The reeds banked away on the other side into the gathering gloom.

She turned over and looked up at him and recognition dawned. "But I know you. You're the man from the subway."

"How perceptive, old girl." Jago rolled up his parka.

And then she was on her hands and knees, being very sick indeed, the salt-marsh water turning her stomach inside out. When she finally finished, she found herself alone, only the wind in the reeds, the rain a little lighter now, the falling darkness.

She started to walk, squinting through the twilight in search of her rescuer, and heard a voice call, "Sarah?"

Peggy was the first to reach her, leaping up, snuffling excitedly. Egan and Jock arrived a few moments later.

"Are you all right?" Egan demanded. "When Jock woke up and found you gone he went crazy. The tides here are notorious. They make the marsh a death trap."

Jock got his combat jacket off and put it over her shoulders. "Dear God, lassie, you're soaked. What happened?"

"I got caught by the tide, almost drowned, and then a man appeared on the causeway like some ghost. He got me out." She choked, trembling with cold. "He saved my life. Then I was sick, and when I looked up he was gone."

Egan said, "That doesn't make sense."

"Even less sense when I tell you it was the same man who saved me on the subway the night before last."

Egan turned to Jock. "Tony Villiers. It must be."

"I'd go along with that."

"I don't understand," Sarah said.

"This man's turned up twice now. That can only be because he's been following you, and that means Villiers has put one of his Group Four operatives on the job."

"Damn him!" Sarah said.

"Come now, lassie, I know Colonel Villiers," Jock said. "Served with him for years. A fine gentleman. Anything he does will be out of concern for you."

They started back to the farm. Egan said, "In fairness, this might not be the colonel's doing at all. Probably that old bastard Ferguson. Not that it matters. I'll find out what's going on. I'll even find out who your mysterious friend is. After all, he's saved your bacon twice now."

"Yes, well, all I want right now is a nice hot bath," she said. "So please lead me to it as fast as possible."

After dinner, they went down to the old wine cellar, which Jock had converted into a shooting range. There was a trestle table with several weapons on it, earmuffs and spare ammunition clips. The targets were cardboard figures of Russian soldiers at the far end against a bank of sandbags.

Egan lit a cigarette and sat on the end of the table, one leg swinging. Jock said to Sarah, "Have you ever fired a handgun before?"

"Never, and I'm not sure that I could."

"Oh, you could fire it all right, anybody can do that.

The question is, could you shoot someone if you had to?"

He indicated the first gun, a rather large weapon, she thought. "Browning, nine-millimeter, semi-automatic. Takes thirteen plus one up the spout. Preferred handgun of the SAS." He nodded at Egan. "My laddo here prefers it to a submachine gun in a crowd. In the hands of a marksman a very deadly weapon."

She picked up the smaller handgun. "And this?"

"Walther PPK, semi-automatic. Takes seven plus one in the hold, if that's what you want. I wouldn't call it a lady's gun. James Bond uses one, but it will slip into your handbag easily and it will definitely stop any man I've ever come across dead in his tracks." Carefully, he taught her the safety procedures, then made her load and unload the gun until she thought she could do it in her sleep. "Now, what I want you to do is hold it like this, keep both eyes open, look along the barrel at the middle soldier and squeeze the trigger."

She did as she was told, holding the Walther in both hands, and the firing seemed so rapid, so easy, the sound of it dulled by the earmuffs. Still, she couldn't deny the trembling of her hands, the sweat pouring down her face, the terrible nausea.

Jock pulled the card forward. There wasn't a single hit. "Never mind," he said. "Most people can't hit a barn door with a handgun. Try again."

Again, the same overwhelming symptoms of fear and loathing, with the result no better. Egan said, "This is a waste of time, Jock. She hasn't got the stomach for it."

"Can you do any better?" she demanded angrily.

He picked up the Browning, screwed a silencer on the end, then flung his arm forward without apparently taking aim. There were three dull thuds, and a hole appeared in each of the hearts of the three targets.

"Let me show you something." He took Sarah by the arm and led her down the shooting range. "Now raise your arm and touch that target between the eyes." She did as she was told. "Now pull the trigger."

"What?" she demanded, and suddenly there was sweat on her palm as she gripped the butt of the Walther.

"I said pull the trigger."

She did as she was told. A hole appeared between the eyes.

"That's what you're going to have to do. You're going to have to be that close." Egan turned back to the table and put the Browning down. "There you are, Jock, she can blow a man's brains out with the best of us."

She was bone-tired and fell asleep almost at once when she went to bed, coming awake with a start to feel a hand over her mouth, Egan's voice in her ear. "Don't make a sound, just get up and pull your track suit on."

"What is it?" she demanded.

He put a finger to his lips. "Don't argue, just do it."

She was dressed in seconds and joined him at the door, which he had partially opened. It was then that she saw he had the Browning in his right hand, the Carswell silencer screwed to the end of the barrel.

"Sean, what is it?"

He passed her the Walther PPK. "Here, you're going to need this. Someone's killed Jock."

She couldn't take it in. "That's not possible."

"I just found him in the sitting room. It's not a pretty sight. We've got to get out of here."

He opened the door and started down the stairs, and she went after him. The sitting-room door was partially open. She heard Peggy whining. She stepped in the room to see Jock lying on his back in front of the fire, blood on his face, a great deal of blood, eyes staring, the dog snuffling anxiously at him.

Her stomach turned, and Egan pulled her away roughly. "Just do as you're told if you want to get out of here in one piece."

He opened the back door. It was raining again. He led the way across the yard into the garage and slid behind the wheel of the Mini Cooper. As she got in the passenger seat, he switched on the ignition. Nothing happened.

"No go," he whispered. "We've been got at. Let's try Jock's old station wagon."

They got out of the Mini Cooper and moved into the next barn. Sarah waited, not getting in, as Egan got behind the wheel. The red light came on although the engine wouldn't turn over, and then he tried the lights and the twin beams splayed out through the open door revealing the sinister figure of a man in black with a stocking mask over his face, a pump-action shotgun in his hands.

As he fired, Egan jumped from behind the wheel, shoving Sarah against the wall, and fired back. He pushed her toward the back of the garage and opened the door leading to the gym. "Run for it, Sarah."

She started across the gym, Egan behind her, and the lights turned on. There was another blast of the shotgun, and Egan went down, the Browning sliding across the floor.

Sarah turned. The man in black stood in the doorway for a moment, then started forward. She crouched beside Egan. There was blood on his jump jacket. He whispered, "Shoot him, Sarah. Shoot the bastard."

Her hand came up, holding the Walther, but she couldn't pull the trigger; it was as simple as that. The man stood over her and slowly raised the shotgun. She moaned, her arm fell to one side.

Egan suddenly reached, grabbed the Walther from her hand and fired three times at point-blank range, but the man in black didn't go down. Instead, he pulled off the stocking, and Jock White looked down at her.

"Now do you understand, Sarah Talbot?" he said gravely.

It was raining again the following morning when she and Egan left. Jock walked out to the Mini with them, Peggy at his heels. "I suppose you think we were very unfair?" he said.

"Not really. You taught me a lesson. You proved to me that I can't pull the trigger."

"A souvenir." He took the Walther from his pocket. "What you Americans call an ace in the hole, just in case."

She hesitated, then put the gun in her handbag and kissed him. "You're a great guy, Jock White."

"I should have been twenty years younger, lassie."

"That would have been too much to take."

She got in the car and Jock leaned down to the window.

"You said you'd find out what Villiers was up to. You know Alan Crowther left the Department last year, don't you?"

"Alan Crowther is exactly who I was thinking of." Egan grinned. "I love you, you old bastard," he said over the roar of the car's engine.

Jago was parked on the causeway in the Land Rover listening in. He let them go, gave himself three minutes, then followed. Alan Crowther? That sounded interesting. He started to whistle softly.

EIGHT

THIS MAN CROWTHER?" SARAH asked. "Where does he fit in?"

"Alan? Oh, he's quite a character," Sean replied. "A Yorkshireman who married a German. His wife was not only Jewish but Marxist, so he went home with her to Dresden in East Germany. He became a professor at the university there. His specialty was conceptual thought in computers."

"That's a tall order," she said.

"The Japanese are pretty close to achieving it and it's what everybody is after. Working toward creating a generation of computers with the ability to think for themselves. Anyway, Alan wasn't too happy under the Communists. He figured that if London had been good enough for Marx, it was good enough for him. He made approaches to the Christian Underground; they passed the happy news on to our people."

"Who were more than delighted to have him?"

"Exactly." Egan nodded. "He and his family were smuggled out in a farm wagon at a little border crossing post where the guards had been bribed. At the last moment someone machine-gunned the truck as it passed into West Germany. Alan's wife and two sons were killed."

"My God," she said. "How terrible. But he survived?"

"I suppose you could call it that. He didn't carry on with his academic work. Took over the experimental side of the computer department at DI5. He's a genius, of course, no other word for it."

"And he's still there?"

"No. He found out last year that the unfortunate business of the machine-gunning of the truck getting him out of East Germany was the work of a double agent called Kessler. He'd betrayed Crowther and his family to cover his own tracks. What Alan discovered was that our people knew all about it, but they'd kept quiet for ten years because Kessler was still useful to our side."

"That's the most disgusting thing I ever heard."

"Exactly what Alan thought. He simply walked out. Caused a hell of a stink, not only because he's the best there is, but because of what he knows."

"And he'll help us?"

"I think so. He has a house in Camden by the canal. We'll go straight there, but I want to make a couple of phone calls first."

"And I'd better check in with the office as well. They must think I've died."

He swung the car into a service station, got out and walked across to a telephone booth. Sarah stretched a couple of times, then went to join him. She opened the door of the other booth and placed her call to Dan Morgan, overhearing snatches of Egan's conversation as she waited for her own call to go through.

"Jack, is that you? Sean here. Have you come up with anything?"

Shelley was seated at his desk in a white terry-cloth robe, his hair damp from the shower. He emptied his coffee cup and pressed a button on the desk. "Not a thing, my old son, but it's only Monday morning, for Christ's sake. Scotland Yard takes the bleeding weekend off, to all intents and purposes, but somewhere, someone knows something, and we'll find them. Stay in touch."

He put down the phone and a pretty young Filipino maid entered, trim in black silk dress, stockings and high-heeled shoes. "More coffee, Maria," he said and slipped an arm around her waist as she picked up the tray.

"Certainly, señor."

He fondled her bottom. "Jesus, you've got a great arse, girl. Go on, get out of here before I change my mind. I've got work to do."

Villiers was at Ferguson's flat in Cavendish Place when Egan phoned DI5 headquarters. They patched it through and Villiers, standing at Ferguson's desk, took the call.

"Who's the character you've had tailing Sarah?" Egan demanded.

"Explain," Villiers told him.

"He came to the rescue in the tube at Chalk Farm the other night when some skinheads were bothering her. Knocked hell out of two of them. Then he pulled her out of the marsh at Jock White's place yesterday when the tide caught her."

"What's he look like, this man of mine?"

"According to Sarah, medium height, good-looking, well-spoken, hot stuff at handling himself. She said he really sorted those skinheads. Oh, one distinguishing feature. A scar from the corner of the left eye to the mouth. He must be new. I thought I knew all your people at Group Four."

"So did I, Sean. Sorry—can't help."

"You're a damned liar," Egan told him.

Villiers replaced the receiver. The brigadier looked up inquiringly. "What was all that about?"

Villiers told him. "Anything to do with you, sir?"

"My dear Tony, devious I may be, but not in a matter like this, believe me."

"Then who can it be?"

"Her guardian angel from the sound of it. Still, it would be useful to know who he is. Try a description check on the computer and see who it throws up."

"Needle-in-a-haystack stuff, sir."

"Nonsense. Amazing what those computers can come up with in two or three days. Now, phone the details through and let's get on with some work."

As they crossed the Thames at Waterloo Bridge, Sarah said, "I've been thinking about our mystery man. If he's not with Tony, what about your uncle?"

Egan shook his head. "Be logical. Jack didn't meet you until after the incident on the tube."

"You're right," she said. "How silly of me. Why didn't you mention him to your uncle when you talked?"

"I don't have to tell him everything. No need, and it always pays to hold something back. Anyway, the bloke is a Group Four man. Villiers is lying. It makes perfect sense that he'd have someone keeping an eye on you."

He turned the Mini Cooper into a side street close to Camden Lock and turned again into a street named Water Lane. It was lined with Victorian terraced houses, and there were a great many cars parked at the curb. Egan pulled into a tiny driveway at the end house, which looked over the canal.

"This is it!" He got out and went to the door and knocked. "This was a bargemaster's house in the old days," he told her.

The door opened and a man appeared, tall, gangling, about sixty, with iron-gray hair and a graying beard. He wore a blue-and-white bow tie and a navy-blue cardigan with a shawl collar. He held a dark-brown Burmese cat in the hollow of his left arm.

He smiled delightedly. "Sean, my dearest boy." He reached forward to embrace him, still clutching the cat. "Where have you been all this time?"

"Oh, getting my act together. I'd like you to meet Mrs. Sarah Talbot from New York."

"Mrs. Talbot. A great pleasure." He had a slight Yorkshire accent which was rather pleasant. "And this is Samson, so named because he is the weakest and most foolish cat in the neighborhood."

"Alan, we need your help," Egan told him.

"That's what friends are for," Crowther answered. "So come in, why don't you?"

Parked in the Land Rover farther down the street Jago had got most of this. Now he pressed the encoder button on the car phone and rang Smith. He had a reply within ten minutes.

"How did the weekend go?" Smith asked.

"All right. They spent the time trying to turn her into Wonder-woman. She almost drowned in the marsh when the tide caught her. Luckily I was around and managed to haul her out in the nick of time."

"She saw you?"

"Only briefly."

"I don't like that."

"You can't have it both ways, old boy. You're the one who told me to make sure nothing happened to her or Egan. As a matter of interest, Egan's convinced I must be one of Villiers's minions from Group Four."

"That's something, I suppose. Where are you now?"

"Water Lane, Camden. They're visiting Alan Crowther, who used to be in charge of computer research at DI5. I'll listen in for a while and phone you if anything new comes up."

He replaced the receiver, sat back and turned up the radio.

Alan Crowther's sitting room was quite small, furnished mainly with Victorian pieces; two paintings by Atkinson Grimshaw hung on the walls, both done in the 1870s. One was a scene of the Embankment at night, the other a nocturne, Tower Bridge by moonlight, a barquentine drifting downriver.

"These are really excellent," Sarah commented.

Crowther, sitting in a couch by the window, reading the contents of the envelope, didn't reply. Finally he looked up, first at Egan sitting opposite, then at Sarah, and his face was sad. "I'm sorry, Mrs. Talbot, truly sorry."

"Such pure evil is hard to understand," she said.

"Not to me, I'm afraid." He turned to Egan. "So what's been happening? Tell me everything." Egan described the events of the past few days. When he was finished, Crowther said, "What do you want from me?"

"My uncle's people are doing what they can, but you might be able to give us a few shortcuts."

"And how could I do that?"

"You've got one of the best private computer systems in London in that study next door. King of the hackers. Access Group Four's main file. Interface. Anything you have to. Just pull out everything they've got on this thing. There could be details Villiers is holding back."

"Ferguson," Crowther corrected him. "Tony is a good man, Sean, but like the rest of us he has to do as he's told."

Egan said, "You didn't. You gave them two fingers."

"There's such a thing as the Official Secrets Act. The sentence handed down for this kind of thing would be heavy, to say the least."

Sarah said, "I know computers. I work on Wall Street. I would have thought it impossible to access a high-security system such as they have. Even if you could break in, wouldn't their alarm system indicate the fact?"

"Oh, sure." He nodded. "But there are ways round that."

"He put the damn system together for them," Egan said. "Come on, Alan, after what those bastards did to you, you don't owe them a thing." His face was intense as he leaned forward. "Your family. Do I need to remind you?"

"No," Crowther said gravely. "But I said *kaddish* for them a long time ago. Life goes on, my young friend." He turned to Sarah. "My wife, and therefore my two boys, were Jewish."

Suddenly, Sarah felt rotten about the whole thing. "I'm sorry, Mr. Crowther. This is all wrong. You've suffered enough. Why should you involve yourself in my affairs?" She turned to Egan. "Let's go."

"No, wait," Crowther told her. "Edmund Burke once said that the only thing necessary for the triumph of evil was for good men to do nothing." He stood up.

"Who am I to argue with Edmund Burke? Come next door."

The study had wall-to-ceiling shelves filled with books, and there was a computer bank at one end which was as sophisticated as anything Sarah had seen. "This is amazing," she said.

"I created most of it myself." He sat down at a keyboard. "Now sit over there and shut up. This could take time."

She and Egan did as they were told. It was very quiet, only a slight hum from the equipment, the sounds of the keys barely audible. It was perhaps five minutes later that he grunted in satisfaction. "I'm in. Now let's see what they have."

Eric Talbot's name appeared, the file and then the facts surrounding the case. The link with burundanga was recorded, the names of the other victims in Paris, Sally, and then a continuation section concerning the dead IRA gunmen in Ulster.

"Any information on the Prods who did it?" Egan demanded.

Crowther shook his head. "No, it simply says that the word is they were not UVF. Possibly Red Hand of Ulster or some other extremist group."

"You're sure there's not a privileged-information section under another code?"

"Definitely not." Crowther went back to work and finally sat back. "There you are—the only piece of interesting information not mentioned in those reports Villiers sent you. Greta Markovsky. Cambridge student aged twenty-one. Heroin user. Also suspected by the police of being a pusher. Apparently a close friend of your stepson."

Egan examined the facts on the screen. "Look at that. She and Eric were busted at the same party in that drugs raid last year."

"Where is she now?" Sarah asked.

"Grantley Hall, just outside Cambridge on the road to Ely. It's a rehabilitation unit. She's in the care of a psychiatrist called Dr. Hannah Gold," Crowther said.

"Could she help?" Sarah turned to Egan.

"There's only one way of finding out." He said to Crowther, "Alan, you're a jewel. We'll get moving. Cambridge next stop." He took Sarah by the arm and pushed her to the door. "I'll be in touch."

"*Mazel Tov!*" Alan Crowther called and then they were gone.

But Jago was already on his way, had left the moment he heard Greta Markovsky's name mentioned, phoning Smith instantly. Within minutes the car phone rang.

"We're in trouble," Jago said. "They've got on to Greta Markovsky."

"How did they manage that?"

"Crowther accessed Group Four's computer. She was on it. Patient at the Grantley Hall place outside Cambridge."

"I don't want her talking," Smith said.

"She won't. I'm already on my way and I'm ahead of them."

Jago replaced the receiver, took the cut down into the motorway at the next turn and drove north very fast indeed.

As the Mini Cooper turned into the Kentish Town Road, Sarah said, "I've been thinking. What if they won't let us speak to her?"

"We'll have to deal with that as it comes," Egan told her. "You'll just have to see how far your transatlantic charm gets you with this Dr. Gold. Woman-to-woman stuff."

He concentrated on his driving. She opened her handbag to forage for the cigarette case and found the Walther. Her hand closed over the butt. It was a strange sensation. She shivered, took out a cigarette and sat back, smoking nervously.

Jago made excellent time to Cambridge, driving straight through, pausing only once at a small flower shop on the outskirts of the town where he bought a dozen red roses. He chose a greeting card that said "Get Well Soon" and wrote on the bottom "To Greta, Lots of Love." The whole transaction took no more than three minutes, and he was on his way,

He found Grantley Hall with no trouble, a country house which stood in extensive grounds and was reached by a driveway. He left the Land Rover in a car park at the side of the building. He took off his parka, rolled up his shirt-sleeves, got a pair of sunglasses from the glove compartment and put them on. Clutching the bunch of roses, he approached the porticoed entrance and went inside. There was a large, cool hall tiled in black and white, a sweeping staircase in front of him, a corridor to the left and one to the right. A porter in peaked cap and blue uniform behind a desk looked up inquiringly.

Jago approached cheerfully. "Bankhouse Flowers. You got a Miss Greta Markovsky staying here?" He deliberately assumed a cockney accent.

The porter checked a list in front of him. "Markovsky. Oh, yes, here she is. Room fifteen, second floor."

"What do I do, take 'em up?" Jago inquired.

"Do you hell, son. They're all locked up in there. Junkies mostly. So much stuff in 'em it's coming out of their ears."

"Is that a fact?" Jago said.

A nurse in a white uniform came down the stairs leading a gaunt, gray-haired woman in a dressing gown. The porter said, "Leave 'em here. I'll see she gets them."

"Fair enough." Jago put the roses on the desk, glanced along the corridor to the left and saw a door at the far end. "I'll see you then."

The porter had already returned to his magazine. Jago went outside, across the car park and around to the side of the building. The wall was festooned with iron fire-escape ladders, but he found the door he was looking for. He opened it, slipped inside and found himself at the other end of the corridor from the hall. There was a staircase on his right, probably servants' stairs from the old days. He started toward it, then noticed a door standing ajar. He peered into a linen room. Beside the sheets and the blankets and towels there was a pile of white coats, neatly folded.

"Very thoughtful," he said softly, pulled one on, left and went up the stairs quickly to the second floor.

When he opened the door at the top he entered a long corridor. It was silent except for the sound of music faintly in the distance. He walked along it confidently, pausing only at a side turning which gave access to a glass door with a Fire Escape sign above it. He opened the door quickly, stood on a steel catwalk and, leaning over the rail, looked eighty feet down to the paved courtyard below.

He went back along the corridor and came to number fifteen. There was the sound of muffled sobbing from inside. Jago took a deep breath, then eased back the security bolt and passed inside.

The girl who crouched in the corner wore a white linen smock and her feet were bare. Her head was on her knees, her long dark hair hanging loose. When he knelt beside her, she raised her head slowly. The eyes were sunken, the skin translucent, bones showing through.

"Greta?" he said gently.

She moistened dry lips. "Who are you?" she whispered hoarsely.

"I've come to take you home, love." He raised her up.

"Home?"

"Yes, this way. I'll show you." Jago put an arm around her and led her out into the corridor, closing the door behind him. They walked a few paces and he turned her into a side corridor and opened the fire door. "There you go, love."

She stepped onto the catwalk and stood there, the wind molding the smock around her. "I feel sick," she moaned.

He stood behind her, arms around her, and kissed her gently on the neck. "I know, love, you're better out of it."

He eased her forward, placed a hand between her shoulder blades and catapulted her over the rail. He was already moving back inside as she hit the courtyard eighty feet below. He was down the rear stairs two at a time, at the bottom in seconds, tearing off the white coat, draping it over a convenient peg on his way out.

There were voices shouting somewhere at the rear of the building, and an alarm bell sounded as he climbed behind the wheel of the Land Rover and drove away down the long drive increasing his speed only when he turned into the main road. He reached for a cigarette and lit it, fingers rock-steady, then dialed the contact number.

After a while, Smith replied. "How did it go?"

"Went like a charm. Couldn't be better."

"Are you sure?"

"You know the old saying? Canaries don't sing, especially dead canaries."

As he replaced the receiver he saw the Mini Cooper coming toward him on the other side of the road. He glanced down until it had passed, then watched it go on from his driving mirror.

"Too late, Sarah," he said, "entirely too late," and he drove on into Cambridge.

As Egan and Sarah Talbot walked into the main entrance at Grantley Hall, three nurses pushed a trolley along the corridor carrying a draped body. A woman doctor in a white coat, a stethoscope around her neck, followed. She was about thirty-five, with dark hair arranged in a bun. It gave her a slightly severe look that was accentuated by the gold-rimmed spectacles.

"Number one operating theater," she said. "And keep her there until the police arrive." She turned to the desk, took out a pen and made a note on the file she was holding.

The porter said to the visitors, "Yes, what can I do for you?"

"Is Dr. Gold available?" Sarah asked.

The woman at the desk turned. "I'm Hannah Gold."

"My name is Egan. And this is Mrs. Sarah Talbot. We were hoping to have a word with you about Greta Markovsky."

"You'll be lucky," the porter said grimly. "Missed her by twenty minutes, you have."

"Not funny, Alfred," Dr. Gold said. "Come this way." She walked down the corridor, opened a door into an office. She went behind the desk. "Please sit down. What can I do for you?"

"Greta Markovsky," Sarah said. "I was wondering if we could see her?"

"You already have, I'm afraid," Dr. Gold said. "She was on the trolley that passed you in the hall just now."

Sarah said in horror, "What happened?"

"It would seem someone failed to secure the bolt on the door. There will have to be an enquiry into that, of course. She fell from the fire escape on the second floor into the courtyard. The only good thing is that she died instantly."

"Was it an accident or suicide?" Egan asked.

"We'll never know that now. She was very ill. It's entirely possible that she simply lost her balance when she ventured onto the catwalk and fell over the rail. The height could have made her feel dizzy. On the other hand, suicide is common with her type of patient. She tried to slash her wrists the first night she was in here." She took off her glasses and polished them with a tissue. "May I ask what your interest was?"

Sarah glanced at Egan. He nodded and she took the envelope from her bag and handed it over. Hannah Gold took the reports out and read them quickly. Her face remained impassive as she replaced them in the envelope and pushed it across the desk.

"There was a connection between your stepson and Greta, is that what you're saying?"

"They appeared in court together on a drugs charge last year," Sarah told her.

"But surely this is a matter for the police?"

"Of course," Egan said smoothly. "It's just that things seem to be moving rather slowly, and Mrs. Talbot is understandably concerned. She was hoping that the Markovsky girl could have filled in some of the blank spaces."

"I'm sorry," Dr. Gold said. "Even if I knew anything, it would be improper for me to comment. A question of the doctor-and-patient relationship."

"Of course." Sarah stood up. "I understand perfectly."

Hannah Gold said, "I'll see you out." She accompanied them along the corridor and paused on the steps at the main entrance. "Look, Mrs. Talbot, she was a sick girl and very heavily overdosed with heroin when she came here. She rambled a great deal. Childhood, her mother, that sort of thing. She'd been abused by her father, which didn't help."

"How terrible," Sarah said.

"What I can tell you is of no help, I'm afraid. Not once in my sessions with her did she mention an Eric Talbot. I have my notes. And I'd have remembered."

Sarah shook her hand. "Thank you, you've been very kind."

"I'm sorry, Mrs. Talbot. Sorry for her and very sorry for you." She stayed there watching them all the way to the car park.

They got into the Mini Cooper. Egan said, "That's it, then?"

"Yes," Sarah said. "That is very definitely it. Another dead end. Back to London, Sean." And she leaned back in her seat and closed her eyes.

It was raining when they returned to Lord North Street, dull, cold November rain. Jago, already back in his flat, saw them arrive and go in. He settled in a chair by the window where he could watch and listen. Sarah said wearily, "I'll make some tea," and went into the kitchen.

Egan stood at the bay window. He lit a cigarette, coughed over it a little, then turned idly to the library table. Eric's blue Moroccan leather diary was on top of a pile of books. He sat in the window seat and started to leaf through the pages, all filled with Latin in careful handwriting, trying to decipher a phrase here and there. He stiffened, staring incredulously at the page before him, and stood up. Sarah came in at that moment with the tray.

"What is it?" she asked, putting the tray down.

"She's here on this page. Look for yourself." Egan handed her the diary. "Greta Markovsky."

She took it from him with a sense of wonder. She hadn't worked through it before; she'd been too upset. But now she sat down and started to read. At that moment, the front doorbell sounded and Egan looked out and saw Jack Shelley on the step, a fawn overcoat draped over his shoulders, the Rolls Royce parked at the curb.

Jago had gone into the kitchen to make coffee and he returned to the window in time to see Shelley enter the house. He put his coffee down quickly and turned up the volume of the receiver.

Shelley, in the hall, said to Sean, "I thought I'd call and see how things were. We still aren't making progress."

"Well, *we* are," Sean said. "We discovered Eric had a girlfriend, a pusher, who was in court with him on a drugs rap last year. A Greta Markovsky. We went to see her in a drugs rehabilitation clinic outside Cambridge."

"And?" Shelley demanded eagerly.

"She's topped herself. Took a dive from a fire-escape catwalk, but we've just found her name in a diary the boy left."

"A diary?"

"Yes, he kept a diary in Latin. That's what he was studying at Cambridge."

"Well, that's a lot of bleeding good, Latin," Shelley commented. "We'll need a sodding professor to translate."

"As it happens, Mrs. Talbot majored in Latin and Greek at Radcliffe."

They went into the sitting room and Sarah, at the window, looked up, pale with excitement. "It's all here," she said. "Every damn thing."

She put the diary down, hands shaking, and it was Shelley who put an arm round her. "You come and sit down. Take your time and tell us."

"Greta Markovsky recruited him to act as a drug courier, provided him with a false passport in the name of George Walker. She was acting for a man she refers to as Mr. Smith."

Shelley frowned. "Well, that name doesn't sound any bells. Go on."

"He was to go to Paris. A café by the Seine near the rue de la Croix called La Belle Aurore."

"That's the last place he was seen alive," Sean said. "It was mentioned in the French coroner's report. Run by a woman called Marie something or other. She gave him a drink and sent him on his way with a couple of possible addresses of rooms for the night."

"What isn't mentioned in the report is that he was to ask for a girl called Agnés. He was to say that Mr. Smith sent him."

For a moment there was silence, then Shelley said grimly, "That's it, then, Paris next stop."

"You mean you'll come with us?" Sarah said.

"Try and stop me." He seemed to have come alive with a kind of animal vigor. "Besides, I've got a few useful contacts over there. Spent a year in Paris a long time ago while a spot of bother was sorted out here." Egan tried to speak and Shelley said, "Don't argue. For one thing we'll need a couple of shooters when we get there. Can't take anything through customs." He glanced at his watch. "Right, I'll get back to the office. You'd better pack a bag, darling." He patted her on the shoulder. "We'll sort it, never fear."

He beckoned to Egan, who followed him out into the hall. As soon as they left, Sarah opened her purse and took out the Walther. As Shelley had said, no way of taking a thing like that through customs. She weighed it in her hand, an unlooked-for tingle of excitement in her stomach. Angry with herself, she crossed to a Sheraton bureau, opened one of its drawers and put the Walther inside. Strange, but it was as if she were trying to hide it from herself.

Shelley opened the front door and went down to the Rolls. Varley was sitting in front. Shelley said to Sean, "Get in for a minute."

"All right."

They got in the back and Shelley pressed the button to raise the glass divider, blocking Varley off. "I'm not sure she should come, but I figure she'd raise cain if we tried to say no."

"She certainly would."

Shelley picked up the car phone and dialed his number. Frank Tully answered at once. Shelley said, "Frank, I'm on my way in. Phone British Airways and book three seats on the Paris flight."

"Which one, Jack?" Tully demanded.

"How do I know which bleeding one? Give us, say, two hours to get to Heathrow and book in. Find one that fits round about then and pack me an overnight bag. Then get the black book out of the top drawer of my desk, the one with the special addresses. There's a Pierre Dupont there and a Paris number. Ring him. He speaks English. Tell him Jack Shelley will call tonight and he'll expect to get tooled up. I'll be with you in twenty minutes."

He replaced the receiver. Sean said, "You're enjoying this, aren't you?"

"Too bloody true, my old son. We're going to get these bastards. Now get moving. I'll see you and the lady at Heathrow."

When the phone rang Jago picked it up instantly. "What's happening?" Smith asked.

Jago told him, quickly and concisely: the diary and what it had revealed, Jack Shelley, everything. "It seems to me we're in what the Americans call deep shit, old man," he said.

"Not if we stay cool. Lots of planes to Paris from Heathrow. You said they were going British Airways. That's Terminal Four."

"That's right."

"You go Air France. They leave from Terminal Two, don't they? You'll be there in an hour. You can phone Valentin and Agnés from Heathrow. Warn them what to expect."

"And what they get if they step out of line," Jago said.

"They won't step out of line, there's too much in it for them," Smith said.

"You still want me to use kid gloves with the Talbot woman and Egan?"

"Definitely."

"I could knock Shelley off for you," Jago said cheerfully. "I mean, he is turning out to be rather a nuisance."

"Be your age. Shoot Jack Shelley and we'll have half the London underworld on our backs as a matter of principle. He's a national institution."

"All right, but maybe I could just shoot him a little," Jago said. "To encourage the others. Isn't that what the French say?"

"Just use your discretion and get it right. There'll be another big bonus in it for you."

"Music to my ears," Jago said. "Lucre, filthy lucre, as my old Scots nanny used to say. It'll be the death of me yet."

He put down the phone. Within three minutes he was on his way down to the basement garage. When he turned into the street in the Spyder, the Mini Cooper was still outside Sarah Talbot's house, and he grinned as he drove past it.

⌒

As Sarah came down the stairs, Egan was on the phone to Alan Crowther, bringing him up-to-date. "Is there anything you want me to do?" Crowther asked.

"Yes, access any relevant system you can think of. Not only DI5, but Central Records at Scotland Yard. See if there's anything on this Mr. Smith."

"Not much to go on. About as common a name as you can get."

"But a very uncommon man or I miss my guess. I'll have to run, Alan." He put down the phone and said to Sarah, "All right, let's get going. This time it looks as if we're really going to get somewhere."

NINE

IN PARIS, AT LA Belle Aurore, Jago sat in the back room with Agnés and Valentin. "This could be trouble," Valentin said. "Big trouble."

"Not if it's handled right," Jago said. "They only know one thing that they didn't know before. That the boy came here saying Mr. Smith sent him and asking for Agnés. They don't even know you exist, Valentin."

"So what are you suggesting?"

"Well, let's look at what we have here. Agnés, a convicted prostitute who does what her pimp tells her."

"I don't understand."

"You will." Jago opened a copy of *Paris Soir.* "Here, on page four, is the report of an inquest on one Henri Leclerc, shot dead in a gun battle with the police a week ago."

Valentin laughed harshly. "I knew that bastard well enough."

"It says here that Leclerc was a well-known gangster with convictions for armed robbery, drug pushing and organized prostitution. It even gives his address in Montmartre."

"But what has it got to do with us?" Agnés demanded.

"You were one of his girls, don't you see? He told you to wait here that night for a boy named George Walker who identified himself as being from the mysterious Mr. Smith. You were then to give the boy Leclerc's address and send him on his way." Jago shrugged. "That was your only part in the affair. End of story. You just happened to be one of Leclerc's *poules* that he picked on to perform this little favor, and as we all know, you girls always do as you're told."

Agnés gazed at him in awe. "That's good. Very good."

Jago looked at Valentin. "You agree?"

Valentin nodded slowly. "Agnés is right. It does make sense."

"Of course it does. Our friends will be off on a wild-goose chase which can only lead to a blind alley because Leclerc is dead." He finished his cognac and stood up. "Right, I'll see you later. I've got things to do." And he went out.

Agnés said, "That takes care of it then?"

"Hell it does." Valentin poured another cognac and scowled. "If anything goes wrong on this, Agnés, it's you and I who'll be left holding the baby, not our clever friend. He'll be long gone." He rubbed his unshaven chin. "No, it's better to get rid of them once and for all. No messing around."

"But how do we do that?" she whispered.

He considered the matter and smiled. "How about this? When they get here, you tell them about me. You say you sent the boy to see me that night at my place."

"The flour mill? Fournier's?"

"That's it. I'll be waiting there with a couple of the boys, suitably equipped, naturally. Our friends from London won't know what's hit them."

"Jago won't like that."

"Jago can go and screw himself. We'll deal with him too at the right moment."

"And Smith?"

"He'll still need someone in Paris, won't he? And we have a foot in the door now he and Jago aren't aware of. We know about the place in Kent. This Deepdene Garden of Rest."

She nodded slowly. "It's clever, Valentin, I'll give you that."

"Of course it is. All it needs to succeed is for you to give the acting performance of your life when they turn up, and let's face it, *chérie*, you've been doing that in bed for years." He kissed her, pleased with himself. "We'll talk to Marie later. Now be a good girl and get me another cognac."

It was just before seven when the airport taxi turned into rue de la Forge and stopped outside a large double-fronted shop. The windows were lit, revealing a selection of antiques behind security grilles. The sign above the door in gold and black simply said, "Pierre Dupont."

They got out and Shelley paid the driver off with a handful of francs. "*Bonne chance,* my old son," he said as the taxi disappeared. "Well, this is it." He looked up at the sign. "Pierre Dupont, antique dealer *extraordinaire,* amongst other things," he commented.

"He certainly knows his antiques," Sarah said, looking in the window.

"There's nothing this bloke doesn't know. Here, this way." Shelley led them into an alley at the side of the shop and pressed a bell at a door halfway along. "When he was a kid he was a gunman with the Union Corse, that's a kind of French Mafia that operates in Marseilles. Then he got smart. Realized he had a brain, know what I mean?"

There was a security voice box. Someone said, "*Qui est là?*"

"Jack Shelley, you old bastard."

The door opened. The man who stood there was quite small, with a heavily tanned face, clipped moustache, dark wavy hair. He wore a black velvet evening jacket and trousers in the same color.

"Jack. You're a sight for sore eyes. It's been too long. Far too long." His English was excellent. "You look wonderful." He embraced Shelley, kissing him on both cheeks.

"Here, none of that frog nonsense," Shelley said. "And you know what I think about garlic. This is my nephew, Sean, and Mrs. Talbot."

Dupont took her hand. "A great pleasure, madame."

"You'll have to watch him," Shelley told her. "I've never known anyone have so much trouble with his trousers round women."

They moved on through the shop's interior, an Aladdin's cave, everything from authentic Samurai swords to Louis-Quatorze furniture.

"How come you look younger than when I last saw you ten years ago?" Shelley asked as they entered an elegant sitting room which doubled as an office.

"Oh, the tanning salons play their part, and I must confess my hair now owes more to the chemical manufacturers than it does to nature. But to business. What exactly are your requirements?"

"A motor, for starters."

"There's a Citroën in the garage you may use."

"And the boy and me need tooling up. The thing is, we need to have a serious business discussion with some of your compatriots, and I don't think poking two fingers through my pocket's likely to convince them."

"No problem." Dupont pulled an oil painting back on the wall, revealing a safe. He quickly twirled the combination dial and opened it, rummaging inside. When he turned, he was holding two handguns, which he put on the desk. "All right?"

Shelley picked up the first, a Smith & Wesson .38 revolver. "Perfect. I always did like playing Cowboys and Indians. What's this piece of tin?"

Egan picked up the black metaled automatic. "Makarov. It's a standard-issue weapon in most Eastern European armies. Not much stopping power, but it does the job."

"Right." Shelley slipped the revolver in his raincoat pocket.

"This way." Dupont took them through the kitchen and down a few steps to a basement garage. It contained a Renault and a black Citroën. "Do you want me to come with you, Jack?"

"No, you stay out of it. Hold the fort. That sort of thing." He turned to Sarah. "No good asking you to stay, I suppose?"

"What do you think?"

He shrugged. "Okay, but stay back and don't interfere." He opened the rear door of the Citroën for her. "This is serious business, Mrs. Talbot. When you go in, you go in hard. You don't play patty-fingers. Understand?"

"I get the point, Mr. Shelley."

"I hope you do." He nodded to Sean. "Let's get moving."

They left the Citroën on the other side of the small quay and walked across to La Belle Aurore. Light spilled out from the windows across the damp cobbles. When they peered inside, the place was empty except for fat Marie sitting behind the bar.

Shelley said, "Right, in we go, and don't forget what I said, Mrs. Talbot. You behave yourself."

He opened the door and led the way in. "Evening." He nodded, and Sarah and Egan sat on bar stools. "You do speak English, madame?"

"But yes, monsieur."

"Yeh, well, I think that should be an essential requirement for Europeans, now we're all in the Common Market, and while you're considering that piece of wisdom you can pour us three Pernods and listen to what my friends here have got to say."

She frowned warily, but produced three glasses, a water jug and a bottle of Pernod. "I don't understand, monsieur."

Sarah said, "The other week the body of a young Englishman was found in the Seine nearby. In the coroner's report, the night patrolman said that he'd seen him coming in here."

Egan said, "When interviewed, you told the police that the boy seemed ill and that he was looking for a bed for the night. You gave him a drink and a couple of addresses and sent him on his way."

"That's true, monsieur, a great tragedy. I remember it vividly." She shrugged. "But I told the police all I knew."

"Interesting," Egan said. "I saw the police report indicating everything found in his possession. There were no addresses. I find that strange." He turned to Shelley. "Don't you find that strange?"

"No," Shelley said. "Not strange. I find it fucking unbelievable. I mean, here's this kid at midnight, on drugs and so sick you give him a free drink. He asks you to suggest where he might get a bed and you expect me to believe you wouldn't write it down?"

"Please, monsieur," she stammered.

"Added to which you failed to mention to the police the fact that the boy gave you a password," Egan told her. "He said Mr. Smith had sent him and he wanted Agnés."

"Agnés?" she whispered.

"That's it," Shelley said. "Very popular girl, Agnés. Much in demand, and now, we'd like to meet her."

"I know no one of that name."

Shelley took out the revolver and showed it to her. "I could tell you that if you don't come clean on this Agnés slag in the next five seconds,

I'll put a bullet through your left knee, but ammunition's expensive."
He put it back in his pocket. "So we'll have to seek an alternative."

He reached across, grabbed her by the hair and smashed the Pernod bottle on the edge of the bar. When he held it up, the shards of broken glass were inches from her face.

She screamed. "No, monsieur!"

Sarah Talbot tugged at his sleeve. "Mr. Shelley, for God's sake!"

"You stay out of it!" he snarled.

Marie collapsed totally. "I'll get her, monsieur. I'll get her. She's in the back room."

"See what I mean?" Shelley appealed to Sarah and Egan as he put down the broken bottle. "All you have to do is be a little bit reasonable in this life."

Valentin, behind the curtain at the rear, an arm about Agnés's waist, whispered, as Marie approached, "You know what to do, *chérie.* Make it good. I'll see you soon," and he slipped out the side door.

Marie came through the curtain and stood there inquiringly. Agnés nodded. The older woman turned and went back into the bar and the girl followed her, a hand on her hip, a provocative enough figure in a miniskirt and black plastic raincoat.

"Monsieur?" she said to Shelley. "You wanted to see me?"

"You are Agnés?" Sarah asked.

"That's right, madame."

"One night the other week a young Englishman came here using the name George Walker."

Agnés shrugged. "Perhaps—perhaps not. I can't say I remember."

"She's been walking the pavement so long it's addled her brains." Shelley grabbed her by the arm. "Don't fuck about with me, you little slag. He was told to say he was from Mr. Smith and ask for Agnés."

Marie said quickly, "Tell him, *chérie,* for your own sake. He's an animal, this one."

"All right. Just let me go." Agnés pulled away and nursed her bruised arm. "I don't know who Mr. Smith is. I work for a pimp called Valentin. He told me to be here the night the boy came in. I was to send him to Valentin and that's all I know."

"Where?" Egan demanded.

"The other side of the quay, along the river a little. There's an old flour mill. Fournier's, it's called. Valentin has an office there. Uses the place for business."

"Such as?" Shelley asked.

"I don't know. Hot cars sometimes."

"Great." He turned to Egan and Sarah. "So let's go and see this creep, Valentin, and you, darling—" he grabbed Agnés's arm—"can come along and see the fun."

Jago, watching in the shadows outside, had seen Valentin emerge from the side door of La Belle Aurore and hurry away across the quay.

"Oh, dear," he said. "That wasn't in the script." When the others emerged, Shelley clutching Agnés by the arm, and set off in the same direction, he shook his head, waited a moment, then went after them. So he was being double-crossed, but then, he'd budgeted for that.

"Poor old Valentin," he said softly, "what a stupid man you are."

A river taxi moved past, festooned with colored lights, laughter drifting across the water. The old Fournier mill was eight stories high and in an advanced state of dilapidation, windows boarded up, paint peeling. It had a vaguely menacing air.

Shelley said to Egan, "I've been thinking. All a bit easy, know what I mean?" He turned to Agnés. "It's just possible this little cow is playing naughty girls."

"No, monsieur, I swear it," Agnés told him fearfully.

"All right, I'll take it from the rear." Egan turned to Sarah. "If Jack's right, it might be better if you waited here."

"On the other hand, if I do go in," she said, "I would think it would make whoever is in there feel more secure."

"I told you she was a smart lady, my son. Now, on your bike." Shelley, pushing Agnés in front of him, crossed the street to the entrance.

There was a small Judas gate set in the larger one, the kind used by workers for easy access. It opened to Agnés's hand and he went after her, followed by Sarah.

Egan moved up the alley at the side and pulled down a counterbalanced fire ladder. He went up quickly, finding a broken window on the third level. He felt inside, sprang the catch and climbed in. Jago, from the shadows of the alley, watched him go and then followed.

Egan was in a large storeroom filled with packing cases. He crossed to the door, opened it and moved along a dusty passageway. Below, the central hall was illuminated by a single bulb. There were several motorcars down there, and a ladder climbed up to a glass office in which Valentin sat writing at a desk.

Shelley and the two women appeared in the patch of light, and at the same moment, Egan heard a whisper, a hint of a movement in the shadows of the gallery on the floor below. He turned, went down the stairs quickly and paused. Someone whispered, "Get ready, Jules."

Agnés called, "Valentin, are you there?"

There were two men on the gallery. One of them was holding an Uzi submachine gun, the other a pump-action shotgun. Egan slipped up behind the one with the Uzi and chopped him very hard across the back of the neck. The man went down with a groan.

The other said, "Jules, are you there?"

Egan made a slight noise, but said nothing and then, when the man was close enough, kicked him in the crotch and lifted a knee in his face.

Jago, in the darkness of the landing above, but on the other side of the central hall, had observed everything. "Very good, old man," he whispered. "Excellent technique."

Below, Valentin came out of his office and down the steps. "And what have we here?" he demanded, tickling Agnés under the chin. "What have you been up to?"

"What we have here, you flyblown ponce," Shelley told him, "is a number of things which I require your assistance in sorting, such as Agnés here, and a gentleman named Mr. Smith, and a young English boy calling himself George Walker who Agnés tells me she passed on to you."

Valentin patted her face. "You've been a bad girl again, *chérie.* I'll have to discuss that with you later."

"The only person you discuss anything with is me," Shelley told him. "Me and my friend here." And he took the Smith & Wesson from his pocket.

Valentin laughed. "You have it wrong, monsieur. It is I who give the orders here, not you. My friends and I, to be more exact." He looked up and whistled. "Jules? Charles?"

Egan appeared from the shadows and crossed the hall. "I think he means the two men he had up there with the Uzi and the shotgun. They're taking a nap at the moment."

Valentin turned and started up the stairs and Shelley grabbed him by the ankles and dragged him down. "Scumbag!" he snarled and put the muzzle of the Smith & Wesson to Valentin's back. "Smith, who is he? Tell me or I'll blow your spine out."

"No, monsieur!" Agnés screamed. "Please don't. He doesn't know who Smith is. Neither of us do. We deal with Jago. Only with Jago."

"Who's Jago?" Egan demanded.

"The devil, monsieur. He always acts for Smith."

And then Egan had a wild idea. "He's very English—right? Good-looking? Scar down the side of his face?"

"That's right, monsieur."

Sarah said, "The man from the subway."

"And All Hallows. It seems we've been well covered." He turned to Agnés. "What happened to the boy?"

She hesitated. Shelley rammed the barrel of his gun under her chin. "Tell him or you'll be making your excuses to Saint Peter."

Terrified, she told the truth for once in her life. "Valentin drowned him in the Seine."

"After drugging him? The special drug?"

She took a deep breath. "Yes."

Sarah turned away. Egan said, "And there were others?"

She nodded reluctantly. "Yes, several."

Shelley said, "I've got a good mind to scramble his brains right now," and he turned his gun to Valentin.

"Please, monsieur, don't harm him. If you spare him I can tell you something very interesting."

"What's that?" Egan asked.

"We used to have to ring a funeral firm in Kent called Hartley Brothers."

"It was phony," Egan said.

"I know, monsieur, but once, the answering machine was on in the

background while our man spoke to us. Valentin heard it say 'Deepdene Garden of Rest.' " She opened her handbag and took out a piece
of paper. "See, monsieur, I wrote it down and the number."

The weapon Jago balanced across the rail was a Colt Woodsman
target pistol. It was only .22-caliber, but that was quite enough in the
hands of an expert marksman. He shot Valentin in the right temple,
killing him instantly.

Egan knocked Agnes down and pushed Sarah Talbot back into the
shadows. Shelley fired wildly up into the darkness, crouching.

Jago said softly, "Just a little nick, old stick. Teach you your manners." He took careful aim and shot him in the left shoulder.

Shelley lost his balance and fell back into the shadows. He put a
hand inside his jacket and brought it out, covered with blood. "Jesus,
Sean, I've been shot!" he said in wonderment.

"Out!" Egan ordered. "We've got what we came for." He pulled
Shelley up and pushed him toward the door. "Go on, Sarah."

He turned and clutched at Agnes, and she pushed him away. "No,
leave me."

She crawled to Valentin and crouched over him, moaning. Egan
slipped through the Judas gate and followed the others to the Citroën.
Sarah had put Shelley into the back. Egan got behind the wheel and
drove away.

"Where to?" he demanded.

"Dupont's place," Shelley told him. "I need patching. Then we get
our arses up to Charles de Gaulle and back to London." He winced.
"Christ, it hurts."

"It always does," Egan told him.

Sarah said, "Do you think it was this man Jago?"

"It could be," Egan said. "I'll get Alan Crowther to do some checking when we get back. I'd really like to know who the gentleman is."

There were steps approaching across the floor and Agnés looked up to
see Jago appear, the Colt in his right hand, at his side.

"You killed him," she said.

"Never mind that. What did you tell them?"

"Nothing."

"Don't lie, sweetie. I heard Egan say, 'We've got what we came for.' "
He shook his head. "Now don't be stupid."

She said, "It wasn't me, it was Valentin. When he spoke to the man
at Hartley Brothers he heard one of those message tapes in the background. It said it was Deepdene Garden of Rest."

"And you told them?"

She nodded. "I thought he was going to kill Valentin." She looked
up at him. "Instead, you did."

"Yes, well, that's how it goes. You shouldn't have joined." He started
to walk away and paused. "I was forgetting."

"Yes, monsieur."

As she looked up, he shot her twice in the heart. She fell back
across Valentin. Jago slipped the Woodsman into his Burberry pocket.

"Poor silly little bitch," he said, turned and stepped out through the
Judas gate.

The doctor Dupont had summoned cut away Shelley's bloodstained
shirt and did what he could. Finally he shook his head. "To retrieve the
bullet would require an operating theater, monsieur."

"No way. You patch me up and give me another injection for the
pain. Surgery can wait until I get to London. I know a good doctor. An
Indian named Aziz. Has a clinic for posh alcoholics in Bell Street. He'll
handle this for me."

"Are you sure, Mr. Shelley?" Sarah asked.

"All I want to do is get back to London, girl." He grinned. "Never
liked frog doctors. They give you the pills up your backside. Now find
me a clean shirt and jacket, Pierre, and get us out of here."

An hour and a half later they caught a British Airways flight from
Charles de Gaulle. Jago was not so lucky. He missed the last Air France
plane for London by twenty minutes. Nothing for it but to wait until
the breakfast plane.

He decided to book his ticket while the going was good and
approached the Air France desk. The girl on duty said, "If you'd still
like to go tonight, sir, you can. The plane is delayed on the apron. A
minor technical problem. With any luck, no more than an hour."

Jago checked his watch. Heathrow by one o'clock. He gave her his most charming smile and said, "That's wonderful, mamselle. How well you French know how to run things."

She blushed and handed him his ticket, and he walked away. Luck indeed. There was obviously the chance that the others were still in Paris, but even if Shelley had managed to hold himself together and they'd made the last BA flight, Jago himself would have plenty of time left to deal with Bird and his black friend.

He found a telephone and dialed the Kent number. It was Bird who answered. "Yes?"

"Jago here. I'm in Paris. I'll be arriving at Heathrow at one. I need to see you. I'll come straight down."

"Certainly, Mr. Jago. Any problems?"

"Good Lord, no. Just a bit of business Mr. Smith thought you might like me to put your way. You'll wait up for me?"

"Of course."

Bird had been in the study playing checkers by the fire with Albert, and had been considering the pleasures of bed when the phone had rung. He replaced the receiver.

Albert said, "What did he want?"

"He's coming in from Paris. Wants me to stay up for him. Business, he said."

"Sod him," Albert said. "I wanted to go to bed."

"Well, you can't, duckie, so go and get me a Scotch like a good boy and we'll have another game."

As he crossed toward the departure lounge, Jago was whistling softly. Things couldn't have worked out better. As he went through the gate, he was smiling.

The clinic in Bell Street was in St. John's Wood, a discreet establishment in what had been an imposing Victorian townhouse with its own grounds. Dr. Aziz lived on the premises and had been summoned from his bed by the night porter when they arrived just before midnight. A quick examination, and he had Shelley straight into surgery. Egan and Sarah waited in the doctor's study, drinking tea. Too much had happened, and the strain showed in Sarah's face.

Egan said, "You look bushed."

"I am," she said. "You don't. You're like your uncle. You seem to thrive on it."

"I was going to study philosophy, remember. Heidegger once said that for authentic living what was necessary was the resolute confrontation of death. How does that strike you?"

"Like a great deal of philosophy. Total garbage."

The door opened and Dr. Aziz, a tall cadaverous Indian, entered. He was still wearing operating scrubs. He laid the bullet on the desk in front of Egan. "I got it out. No trouble."

Egan examined it. "Two-two. That's interesting. Probably a Woodsman. A real marksman's weapon." He looked up at Aziz. "Will he be all right?"

"A few days' rest, that's all he needs, but this comes expensive, Mr. Egan. A serious professional risk for me."

"You'll be taken care of. Can we see him?"

"I don't see why not, but he needs sleep. Make it brief."

He led the way out and along the dimly lit corridor past several doors, finally opening one at the far end. Shelley was propped up in bed against pillows, eyes closed, the room in shadows, only a night light on.

"He's asleep," Sarah whispered. "The anesthetic, I suppose."

"Actually he would only allow me to give him a local," the doctor told her.

Without opening his eyes, Shelley said, "Too bleeding true. Never know what you might say under the other kind." He was looking at them now. "I'm getting too old for this kind of gig. What are you going to do now?"

Egan glanced at Sarah. "This one looks as if she needs a year's sleep. I'll take her back to Lord North Street. Tomorrow's another day. We'll see if we can locate this Deepdene place in the morning."

"Keep me posted."

Shelley closed his eyes and Sarah took his hand. "Mr. Shelley?" He looked up at her. "Thank you," she said.

He smiled. "That's all right, girl. Get off home to bed."

He closed his eyes again. Aziz nodded and they went out quietly.

At Lord North Street, Egan unlocked the door for her and followed her in. She turned, looking very tired, and he said, "You need your bed."

"I know. I feel terrible."

"I warned you what it would be like."

She said, "Will you do something for me?"

"Anything."

"Stay the night. There are four other bedrooms to choose from."

"The couch will be fine." He smiled. "Great places to sleep on, couches, especially if they're large enough. Better than beds."

"All right." Impulsively she came forward and kissed him on the cheek. "Thanks, Sean. Thanks for everything." And she turned and went upstairs.

He made tea in the kitchen, and while he was waiting for the kettle to boil, took out the slip of paper Agnés had given him with the number for the fictitious Hartley Brothers. There was a telephone on the wall. He lifted the receiver and asked for directory enquiries.

He gave the operator the number. "It's on the Kent Exchange. Am I right?"

"That's correct, sir."

"Deepdene Garden of Rest. I wonder if you'd mind checking the address for me?"

She was back to him within seconds. "Here it is. Deepdene Garden of Rest, Maltby, near Rochester."

"Thank you."

He replaced the receiver, put a tea bag in a mug and poured boiling water over it. He stirred in a little milk and went into the sitting room, drinking tea and thinking about things. Sarah was dead to the world, would probably sleep for twelve hours, but he wasn't. He checked his watch. It was exactly one o'clock.

Maltby, near Rochester. At this time of night he could make it in an hour.

He let himself out of the house quietly, opened the boot of the Mini

Cooper and pulled down the flap that contained the tool kit. There was a Browning in there also. He hid it inside his bomber jacket, got behind the wheel and slipped away into the silent streets.

TEN

THERE WAS A FURTHER delay in Paris, not much, but it meant that it was half past one when Jago arrived at Heathrow. As he had only hand luggage with him, he walked straight through, picked up the Spyder and was on his way within ten minutes.

Egan, at that moment, was driving through Rochester. With the roads empty at that time of the morning, he'd had a clear run, pushing the Mini Cooper up to its limit. He found Maltby on his road map, five miles on the other side of Rochester, but came to his destination quite unexpectedly on the right-hand side of the road before he reached the village. The imposing sign said "Deepdene Garden of Rest and Crematorium." It also promised twenty-four-hour service, which, in the circumstances, was exactly what he was looking for. He turned the Mini Cooper in through the gate and went up the drive.

Asa Bird, bored with the long wait for Jago, had gone down to the preparation room. He had two funerals in the morning, both bodies due for the crematorium afterward, and an embalming. He always handled the latter personally, for he prided himself on his expertise, especially with difficult cases, and this was certainly one—a young man killed instantly in a car crash, with severe facial injuries.

Bird pulled out one of the cold drawers and examined the body as Albert came in with a cup of tea. "He looks bad, Mr. Bird," Albert said.

"Not by the time I've finished with him. The wax, the makeup. They can do wonders and we have to consider the relatives. I mean, his poor mother has been hurt enough. She doesn't have to see him like this."

"You're a good man, Mr. Bird," Albert assured him.

"I try to do my best, Albert," Bird said. "Now let's check the ovens. Don't want anything going wrong in the morning."

They left by a rear door and crossed to a large barn that had been converted into a crematorium. Albert opened the door, switched on the light and led the way in. There was a small landing, eight or nine steps down to the main room below. It was all very neat, the walls painted white, a bank of electronic apparatus and two black ovens with glass doors.

Bird went down, pressing a button, firing first one oven then the other. "Excellent," he said.

At that moment the bell sounded from the entrance hall. "Jago," Albert said.

Bird nodded. "You let him in. I'll see him in the study." And they went out.

Bird had just seated himself behind the desk in his study when the door opened and Albert came in. Bird frowned. "Where is he?"

"It isn't Jago," Albert said. "It's a client. A Mr. Brown. Says his mother's just died."

Bird checked his watch. It was two-fifteen. "An inconsiderate time to go, I must say."

"We do advertise a twenty-four-hour service," Albert pointed out.

"All right," Bird said impatiently. "Show him in. Let's get on with it." Albert turned to the door and hesitated. "Well, what is it?" Bird demanded.

"Something about him, I'm not sure what, but it's there."

Bird frowned and nodded his head slowly. "All right, Albert, five minutes, then ring through from the office. I'll join you there. We'll talk about it."

Albert went out. Bird sat there, drumming with his fingers on the desk. The door opened and Albert showed Egan in.

"Mr. Brown."

Albert left, and Egan came forward and shook hands. "It's very good of you to see me at such a ridiculous time, Mr. Bird."

"Not at all, Mr. Brown, please sit down." Bird indicated a chair. "What can I do for you?"

"My mother's been ill for some time. She lives on the other side of Rochester. I got a call to say she was fading fast so I came down from Scotland as quickly as I could. Got in an hour ago to find she'd just died."

"So sad." Bird nodded. "But there's a time for everything, Mr. Brown, for all of us. So, you'd like us to handle things for you?"

"The thing is, I'm an engineer in the oil game," Egan said. "Should be flying out to Iraq tomorrow. I can postpone it a day, but that's all. Luckily, a neighbor of my mother's mentioned you—the fact that you were so close by and that you offer a twenty-four-hour service."

"Death, Mr. Brown, has no sense of time," Bird told him and picked up his pen. "Now, just a few details."

"Actually," Egan told him, "I had heard of your establishment before. Businessman I met in London told me about it. What was his name now?" Egan frowned. "Oh, yes, Smith. That was it. Mr. Smith."

The pen was poised above the form Bird had drawn forward. Now he placed it down carefully and stood up. "Smith? No, that doesn't strike any chords. Actually, I wonder if you could excuse me for a moment."

He went out into the hall and opened the door into the small general office next door, where Albert was waiting. "What's going on?" Albert demanded.

Bird motioned him to silence, pulled back a painting on the wall and looked through the mirror into his study where Egan was going through the desk drawers quickly. "You were right, Albert, there is something about him."

"What are we going to do?" Albert asked.

"I'll offer him a facilities tour. When we get to the crematorium, you'll be waiting behind the door and give it to him hard, Albert, but leave enough energy in him so he can tell me who he is."

"And then?" Albert demanded.

"That depends. If necessary, you'll have to warm the oven up, won't you? Now get moving."

Bird followed him out, hesitated outside the study, rattled the door-knob and went in. Egan was sitting in the chair where he had left him.

Bird said, "You know, it occurred to me, especially as you're pressed for time, that I could show you our facilities now, Mr. Brown. You do wish for cremation, I assume?"

"I think so," Egan said.

"Very wise. As the prayer book says, ashes to ashes." Bird opened the door and led the way out. "We can choose a suitable casket afterwards."

"Thank you," Egan said.

When Bird opened the door to the courtyard, it was raining, drifting down through the lamplight in silver spray. He found an umbrella from the corner stand. "The crematorium's on the other side of the yard, I'm afraid."

He held the umbrella over both of them, their arms touching lightly, and he trembled slightly, which would have been enough to alert Egan anyway even if it had not been for the fact that he was expecting some sort of move.

Bird opened the door and put down the umbrella. "After you."

"Not at all, Mr. Bird, after you." Egan pushed Bird forward with such force that he stumbled down the steps, clawing at the banister, and ending up in an untidy heap at the bottom. At the same moment, Egan slammed the door back against the wall. Albert, standing behind it holding a club, received the door full in his face, breaking his nose instantly. Egan slammed the door in hard again. Albert howled and dropped the club.

Bird tried to get up and collapsed again. "Christ, I think I've broken my ankle."

When Egan pulled back the door, Albert was on his knees sobbing, the handsome face ruined, blood everywhere. Egan put a hand on the door as if to hit him again and Bird cried out in horror.

"Don't—please don't."

Egan went down the steps and took out the Browning. "I'll kill him if I have to. It's up to you."

"Who are you?" Bird said. "What do you want?"

"Information. Give it to me, and your boyfriend here is off the hook. If not …" Egan shrugged. "It's your choice."

Bird glanced from side to side wildly. Egan cocked the Browning. Bird cried, "All right, anything you want."

"Fine." Egan took out a cigarette and lit it. "I know all about your Hartley Brothers activities, the corpses from France packed with heroin. I also know you work for Smith. Isn't that true?"

"Yes." Bird nodded eagerly.

"Who is he?"

"I don't know."

Egan raised the Browning, went back to the steps and lifted Albert's head. He placed the muzzle of the gun against it.

Bird shrieked, "It's the truth, for God's sake. I don't know who he is."

"Then how do you manage business?"

"You call him on an answering-service number. You can never phone him direct. Sooner or later he phones back."

"And you've never seen him?"

"No, only Jago, the man who acts for him. He's been here a few times."

It occurred to Bird for a moment to tell Egan that Jago was expected at any minute. On the other hand, if he did turn up at the right moment, that would be too bad for Egan. So, best to keep quiet on that point.

"Describe Jago for me."

"Oh, a real gent. Ex-officer. Public school accent."

"And a scar from the left eye to the corner of the mouth?"

"That's it," Bird said. "You've met him then?"

"Not quite." Egan stood looking down at him, and Bird tried to smile ingratiatingly. Egan raised his voice, made himself sound threatening. "You know what I think? That you're wasting my bloody time, and I don't like that. Don't like it at all."

He grabbed the half-conscious Albert by the hair, raised the gun again, and Bird cried, "I've told you everything. I've never met Smith and I only see Jago now and then and I can only contact him through Smith."

"No one else?" Egan said. "In the entire organization? You expect me to believe that?"

"It's true," Bird gabbled, and then paused. "Just a minute. There was something I'd forgotten."

"You'd better remember."

"Smith gave us an order one day last year to leave a suitcase full of heroin in a left-luggage locker at King's Cross Station. Albert did the delivery but the silly young bugger couldn't resist hanging around afterward. He saw who picked the case up. Saw him and recognized him."

"Who was it?"

"A man called Frasconi—Danielo Frasconi. His picture was in all the papers last year. There was a big trial to do with the drugs business in London. The Mafia Connection, they called it. They implied that Frasconi was big stuff. Anyway, he got off. Witnesses disappeared or changed their stories. The usual thing."

Egan said, "So what did you do?"

"Do?" Bird demanded. "What could we bloody well do? That's what I told that silly young bugger there. Those people don't play games. With them, killing is just part of business." He took out his handkerchief and wiped his face. "I suspect it's that way with you, Mr. Brown."

"It's been said before," Egan told him.

He turned, went up the steps, stepped over Albert and walked across the courtyard in the rain, slipping the Browning into his bomber jacket as he went. He went around the side of the building to the car park and slid behind the wheel of the Mini Cooper. *Frasconi—Danielo Frasconi.* It was a lead, but to where? There was only one person who could give him a quick answer to that—Alan Crowther.

As he turned into the main road and picked up speed, the Spyder was approaching. Jago recognized the Mini Cooper at once and kept on going, watching its taillights recede in his mirror. His quick glimpse had told him there was only one person in the car, who had to be Egan. Strangely enough, Jago's main feeling was one of admiration.

"I'll say this for you, old son," he said softly. "When you move, you really move fast." He slowed and turned through the main gates.

Bird got up and leaned on the rail, looking up at Albert. "Are you all right, love?"

Albert groaned and his eyelids flickered. Bird hopped across to a sink in the corner, turned on the tap and wet a cloth. As he started to come back, Jago appeared in the doorway. He stood there, hands deep in the pockets of the navy-blue Burberry, a figure of considerable menace, and Bird groaned and sank into a chair at the small table in front of the ovens.

"You have been having yourself a time," Jago remarked, and he leaned down and examined Albert. "Poor sod, there go his good looks and, let's face it, those, plus his backside, were all he had to offer." He lit a cigarette and leaned on the rail. "So, my friend Egan's been here?"

"Brown, Mr. Jago," Bird said eagerly. "Brown was his name."

"Egan," Jago said. "Twenty-four or five, slim build, hard face, black leather jacket, jeans?"

"That's him." Bird nodded.

"So what did you tell him?"

Bird managed to look puzzled. "Tell him, Mr. Jago?"

"Don't play games," Jago said patiently. "He didn't come here to pass the time of day. He came to ask you about bodies from Paris, Eric Talbot, Mr. Smith and, very possibly, me. So what did you tell him?"

"But what could I tell him, Mr. Jago?"

Jago pulled Albert to his feet, held him up for a moment and then threw him backward down the steps. He landed awkwardly and there was a hollow crunch when his skull hit the tiles. Jago came down the steps and kicked him in the ribs.

Bird screamed. "No, don't hurt him. I'll tell you. I'll tell you everything."

He started to gabble, the words spilling out of him as he went through what he'd told Egan. When he was finished, he sat there quietly sobbing.

Jago looked down at Albert, and stirred him with his foot. "I wonder how many other times he did that, lurked around playing Peeping Tom?"

"Only the once, Mr. Jago, I swear it."

"But once was enough, because he saw Danielo Frasconi, and he's a very important man indeed. And now our friend Egan knows, and

Mr. Smith isn't going to like that. He isn't going to like that at all." He leaned down and examined Albert more closely, then straightened. "Not that it's going to mean much to him any more. He's dead."

"Albert!" Bird wailed. He stood up, lost his balance and fell over. He lay there for a moment, then started to crawl toward the chauffeur.

Jago walked across to the ovens, and pressed the automatic starting buttons. The ovens flared at once. He waited a second or two until the gas jets were peaking, then opened both glass doors. Flames swept out immediately and paint on the walls above the oven bubbled in the intense heat.

Bird cried, "No, Mr. Jago, you mustn't do that. There'll be a blowback."

Jago ignored him, picked up a can of cleaning spirit from the table on the corner, crossed the room quickly and went up the steps, unscrewing the cap on the can as he went.

There was horror on Bird's face now and he tried to get up, stumbled and fell across Albert. "For God's sake, no!"

Jago emptied the contents of the can over the wooden banisters and steps, threw the can down and struck a match. Everything fired instantly. Bird screamed as flames touched one of his trouser legs. He beat at it in vain. Behind him the entire wall and ceiling were on fire, flames roaring out of the ovens.

"See you in hell, old man," Jago called and went out, closing the door behind him. A minute later, and he was turning the Spyder out of the gate and taking the road to Rochester.

He checked the time—three o'clock—and wondered what Egan's next move would be; but he'd find that out soon enough when he got back to Lord North Street. And there would be Smith to bring up-to-date in the morning. A hell of a lot to tell him. Certainly he'd be as mad as hell about the Frasconi thing because that would jeopardize the entire Sicilian connection. Oh, yes, Smith wasn't going to like that one little bit. For some reason, that amused Jago intensely and he sat back, a slight smile on his lips, and concentrated on his driving.

Egan decided to go straight to Alan Crowther's instead of Lord North Street. Crowther was an insomniac who often worked through the night, he knew that, but when he pulled up in front of the house in

Water Lane just before four o'clock, it was in darkness. He got out and tried the bell, but there was no response. He tried a couple of times more, then went through the passage to the rear, found the spare key to the back door which Crowther always left under one of the rockery stones in the small garden.

It was warm in the kitchen. He turned on the light, then boiled a kettle and made a cup of tea. Wherever Crowther was, he'd soon be back, for he never went away, never took holidays. Egan went into the sitting room, finished his tea, then lay on the large couch, arms folded. After a while he slept.

He came awake to the sound of the front door. He swung his legs to the floor and checked his watch. It was five o'clock. Then Alan Crowther came in, but an Alan Crowther Egan had never seen before. He wore a dark woolen cap pulled down almost to eye level, heavy pullover, blue parka, jeans and lace-up boots, and carried a small backpack on his shoulders.

"Sean. My God, you gave me a scare," he said.

"Sorry. I let myself in at the back door with the spare key. I needed to see you. But what is all this? Where the hell have you been, dressed like that?"

"You've discovered my guilty secret." Crowther removed his leather gloves, took off the backpack and parka. "Come in the kitchen. I'm frozen. My need for about a gallon of hot coffee is immense."

In the kitchen, he put on the percolator, spooned in coffee and turned, rubbing his hands. "A good night. I've been to Birmingham and back. By train, of course, the only way to travel."

"By train?"

"Not the way you mean." He sat down at the table and laughed. "When you reach my age you want something different, but what? That's the problem. Too late to learn to fly or climb the Eiger."

"So?"

"I'm a freightbagger, Sean. Met a fellow in a pub in Camden a year ago who put me on to it. An architect." He smiled. "We jump freight trains, just for the hell of it. Always at night, of course."

"You must be mad," Egan said incredulously.

"I'm in good company if I am. We're not yobs, Sean. Amongst my colleagues, if I may call them that, are accountants, City financiers, two doctors and at least one professor from the University of London."

He went to get his coffee and Egan said, "People like that? But why?"

"Kicks, dear boy, that's how we get them. Danger, excitement. Hopping on a moving train in the dark as it rolls out the freight yard behind Paddington or Victoria stations isn't exactly easy. It takes nerve. That thing called bottle you're always on about."

"Crazy." Egan shook his head. "You must be."

"Tonight was a short run because I wanted to get back, but I've been as far as Glasgow sitting in a Ford Escort on a flattop all the way. Marvelous sense of freedom, especially as you roar through a brightly lit station. Mind you, you have to take care on that run. Up Liverpool way, gangs of young ruffians board, looking for car radios to pinch, and that means railway police, so you have to be on your toes."

"Crazy," Egan repeated.

"Nonsense. Best thing that ever happened to me, but what about Paris?"

Egan brought him up-to-date. When he was finished he said, "So, Smith's definitely behind everything. Have you come up with anything on him while I've been away?"

"Not a thing. Oh, lots of crooks named Smith, and of every shape and variety, but nobody who would fit your man." Crowther shrugged. "Of course, that isn't surprising, is it? After all, Smith isn't his real name, that stands to reason."

"Which leaves us with two leads. Jago and Danielo Frasconi. Can we see what you can dig up?"

They went into the study, Crowther put down his coffee and got to work. "I'll do Frasconi first. That should be simple. With his record, they'll have him on file at CRO Scotland Yard." Two minutes later, he nodded. "I'm in." The facts started to unfold before them. "My goodness, it's like a sequel to *The Godfather*."

The Frasconis were a powerful Mafia family based in Palermo, controlled by twin brothers, Danielo and Salvatore, thirty-five years of age. They obtained the bulk of the family's income from drugs. The London end of the business involved two casinos and an interest in a chain of betting shops. They also owned three hotels.

"All a front to launder their drug earnings," Egan commented.

"It would appear that Danielo ran things over here until the drug squad nailed him last year," Crowther said. "He beat every charge brought against him except one. Assaulting a police officer. Served six months at Armley Prison, Leeds, and returned to Sicily on his release."

"Give me a printout on that," Egan asked.

"Certainly."

The printer started to chatter. "Now for friend Jago," Egan said.

"I'll stay with Scotland Yard." Crowther went to work and finally sat back. "Only three—an unusual name, you see. A burglar in Cardiff, a man doing life for murder in Durham Prison and an ex-City accountant at present doing five years in Parkhurst for fraud. Not much joy there."

"All right," Egan said. "What do we know about him? Ex-Army, or I miss my guess. What most people in our class-ridden society would call a gentleman. A hell of a good man when it comes to trouble and handling himself. Scar on the left cheek."

"Sort of man who if he'd once been Army might well turn to the mercenary bit," Crowther suggested.

"That's a thought," Egan said. "You could try known mercenaries. I need a cup of tea. I'll get you another coffee while I'm at it."

As he started for the door Crowther said, "Didn't you say you mentioned him to Villiers?"

"Yes, but that was when I thought he was one of his boys at Group Four."

"You're missing the point." Crowther scratched his head. "You see, you know now that Jago doesn't work for Ferguson's lot, but Villiers knew that when you made the accusation. If I know our Tony, he wouldn't let that go. He'd want to know as much as you who the mystery man with the scar was. Set up his own search."

"That makes sense." Egan nodded. "Group Four again. See what they've got."

He made his tea and was pouring Crowther a fresh cup of coffee when he heard the other man's shout of triumph. He carried the cup through as Crowther looked up, beaming with delight.

"Here it is. It's a K insert. That means put on file within the last twelve hours. Tony must have had a battery of computers working on this one. Jago is an alias. Otherwise this gentleman fits perfectly."

There was a computer picture of Jago from army records that included the scar. "As you can see, he got that serving with his regiment as part of the U.N. peacekeeping force in Lebanon." Crowther sipped some of his coffee.

"Harry Andrew George Evans-Lloyd," Egan said. "Substantive rank, Captain. Military Cross in Ireland, reason unspecified."

"Dishonorable discharge," Crowther added. "Four at one blow. In the fairy story that was the tailor killing flies on his jam and bread. With the good Captain Evans-Lloyd it was four IRA gunmen shot in the back of the head."

"And were they what they seemed to be?" Egan pointed out.

"Exactly. Not too nice for his old man. Retired major general and still alive. Look at his son's roll of honor. Selous Scouts in Rhodesia, commando stuff for the South Africans in Angola."

"For which read death squad," Egan commented.

"That nasty business in Chad," Crowther added. "But nothing for the past three or four years."

"Nothing known, you mean," Egan added. "Give me a print of that too."

Crowther sat back. "What will you do now, go to Villiers? After all, you know more than his people at the moment."

"I don't know. It's up to Mrs. Talbot, really, or that's the way I see it." Egan took the printouts and folded them. "I'll be on my way. I can't thank you enough, Alan."

"It was nothing, but take care. I don't know what Villiers intends to do about Jago, if that's what we're still calling him, but remember, Sean, he's a thoroughly dangerous man."

"I will."

As they went to the door Crowther chuckled. "Very funny, really, the great Jack Shelley on his back with a bullet in the shoulder. Serves him right, playing games like that at his age."

"Just as daft as freightbagging at yours," Sean remarked, and went out into the cold morning street.

It was six o'clock, the streets were beginning to stir as he drove down to The Bargee. He parked in the yard, let himself in at the kitchen door and went upstairs quietly. Ida's door was partially open. He could hear her heavy breathing as she slept, closed her door and went to his own room. He showered and shaved, changed to fresh underclothes, shirt and jeans and left the room.

Ida's door opened and she came out. "Sean, it's you. I've been worried, you staying out so much. You're not in trouble, are you?"

"Trouble?" He grinned. "When was a good-looking girl trouble? Don't you worry about me." And he hurried downstairs and out the door.

She went back to bed, but couldn't sleep. After half an hour of tossing and turning, she went downstairs, put the kettle on to boil and made some toast. There was a knock at the kitchen door. When she opened it, she found Tony Villiers standing there.

"Hello, Ida, I know it's early, but I thought I might find Sean here."

"Come in, Colonel Villiers. You just missed him. Cup of tea? It's fresh made."

She poured it out for him. Villiers said, "He was here last night then?"

Alarm bells started in her head. She said, "Of course he was."

He smiled. "Good for you, Ida, only I happen to know he wasn't."

She said, "Are you trying to say he's in trouble?"

"No, but he could be." He took out his wallet and produced a card which he put on the mantelpiece. "My telephone number is on there, Ida, a special line that reaches me anywhere, day or night. If you ever need me, if you ever have anything to say, you know what to do."

He went out. She sat down at the table, stirring her tea, eyes blank, and then she started to cry.

At seven o'clock, Jago, who had slept by the window with a rug over him for a couple of hours, awakened and looked down into Lord North Street. There was still no sign of the Mini Cooper, and silence from the house. He checked his watch again and called Smith.

He was in the kitchen making coffee when the return call came. "Where are you?" Smith asked.

"Back in London at the apartment."

"What happened in Paris?"

"It's a long story," Jago told him.

"Well, get on with it. I haven't had my breakfast yet."

Jago poured coffee and drank it as he talked. When he was finished, Smith said, "Not good."

"Why not? Valentin and that silly little tart out of the way. Shelley on his back in a hospital bed. Bird and his boyfriend incinerated. All avenues blocked except for Frasconi, and I'm entirely at your service on that one."

"Danielo Frasconi's back in Palermo and he intends staying there. London got too hot for him. Mrs. Talbot and Egan wouldn't last half a day if they went over there. You know the Mafia."

"So what's the problem?"

"You and me," Smith said. "She and Egan now know we exist."

"Yes, old stick, but the joke is, that won't do them any good at all because I'm not me and you're not you. You worry too much." Jago laughed. "Have your breakfast. I'll keep you posted."

He put down the kitchen phone and got the bread out for toast. A moment later he heard sounds from the equipment in the sitting room and hurried in. Sarah was speaking to Egan. Jago looked out and saw the Mini Cooper parked outside the house. He got his coffee, came back and settled down to listen. Suddenly he stiffened and sat up.

"Evans-Lloyd, that's his real name," Egan was saying.

Sarah, in her dressing gown, sat on the window seat reading the printouts, occasionally making comments. Finally she said, "I don't understand this man. He's a killer, we know that, and yet he's saved me twice. Why?"

"Maybe you're not on his list," Egan said. "If he's the kind of professional I think he is, then everything's business. He has targets or a job to do. That's what he's paid for, no more, no less. He's not so much a murderer in the criminal sense of the word as an assassin, or that's how he sees it."

"You're seriously trying to tell me there's a difference?" Sarah said.

"The Assassins were founded in Persia during the eleventh century. They used to get high on hashish, hence the name. They believed only in the action of the moment. They would kill for anyone who paid for their services, but the true assassin was totally committed once he'd taken the blood money. No going back, whatever happened, even at the cost of his own life."

"And you think Jago is like that?"

"It's a kind of honor with a man like him. The only pride he has left," he told her.

She nodded. "Let's forget him for the moment. What about Danielo Frasconi?"

"He's in Palermo and he won't be back."

"All right, we could go there."

Egan shook his head. "It's another world. The Mafia still run everything that counts. Inconvenience people like the Frasconi brothers, and you're found in the gutter if you're found at all."

"Just a moment." She crossed the room, opened a drawer in the Sheraton bureau. Beside the Walther PPK from Jock White was the card Rafael Barbera had given her on the plane. She came back and gave it to Egan. "Read that."

"Vito Barbera, Grosvenor Apartments, South Curzon Street." He was puzzled. "I don't understand."

"I've got Mafia connections, Sean, and of the very highest quality. Have you ever heard of Don Rafael Barbera?"

"Yes," he said reluctantly. "He's Capo Mafia in all Sicily. Boss of bosses."

"How do you know that?"

"Because I've operated in Sicily. I shouldn't even hint at this, it's a security breach on my part, but the main reason I didn't want to work for Ferguson and Group Four is because I was on attachment to them from SAS, just before I went to the Falklands. Attachment in Sicily."

"What were you doing?"

"I wouldn't ask if I were you. Let's say we're back to Assassins again and leave it."

"I met Barbera on the plane coming over," she said stubbornly. "I was very upset. We talked about Eric. He was understanding and kind." She held up the card. "This is his grandson, Vito Barbera. He runs the family business in London. Casinos, betting shops, restaurants. No drugs."

"Who says so?"

"Don Rafael, and I believe him. He was on his way to Palermo, but he told me he'd speak to his grandson about me. That he'd tell him to help me in any way he could." She was very determined now. "I intend to see Vito Barbera, Sean. If you won't help, I'll go alone."

They stood there confronting each other, and then the doorbell rang and Egan looked out the window and saw Ferguson and Tony Villiers on the steps.

ELEVEN

IT WAS EGAN WHO opened the door. Villiers pushed his way past, looking angry. "I've been looking for you."

Ferguson followed. "Morning, young Sean," he said brightly.

"What's got into him?" Egan asked as he closed the door.

"He's not happy, not happy at all," Ferguson said. "Thinks you're leading the lady into what I believe the bullfighters term the circle of danger when you should really be curbing her excesses. To be perfectly frank, I agree with him."

He went into the sitting room and Egan followed. Villiers was confronting Sarah. "We have what's called a moving-search system on our computer. If we put your name on it, it picks up whatever's happening to you on computers elsewhere. Credit cards, which restaurants you're eating at, where you shop. Wonderful aid to keeping tabs on what you're up to."

"Strange," Sarah told him. "I'd always thought the Gestapo went out of business in nineteen forty-five."

"My dear Mrs. Talbot," Ferguson said, "we only have your best interests at heart, you must see that. Tony feels that this young idiot," here he glanced at Egan, "is rather allowing your enthusiasm to run away with him."

"The computer picked up that you'd both gone to Paris on a British Airways flight yesterday," Villiers said. "And with Jack Shelley."

"You came back in a rush close to midnight and booked Mr. Shelley into a rehabilitation clinic for alcoholics in St. John's Wood," Ferguson put in, smiling. "I've been familiar with Mr. Shelley's activities for years, and whatever other failings he has, and they are numerous, I can assure you he doesn't have a drinking problem."

"Which intrigued us so we made enquiries at the clinic," Villiers said. "Oh, very discreetly of course. The good Dr. Aziz doesn't suspect a thing."

"But what we found does confirm our suspicions that you've had a lively night out in Paris, Mrs. Talbot, if it cost Jack Shelley a bullet in the shoulder," Ferguson said.

Sarah said, "I've got nothing to say."

Villiers turned to Egan angrily. "Are you trying to get her killed or what?" He took a white sheet from his pocket and unfolded it. "The man with the scar on his face on the underground who you thought worked for me? Well, he didn't. We put a computer search on, explored every possibility and came up with this."

He passed the printout across. It was a facsimile of what Crowther had given Egan on Jago. Egan pretended to read it, then passed it to Sarah. "Captain Harry Evans-Lloyd," she said and turned to Egan. "Jago?"

"Jago?" Villiers said. "What are you talking about?"

"That seems to be the name he's known by," Egan told him, and glanced at Sarah, who nodded. "He's a contact man for someone we only know as Mr. Smith."

"Smith?" Ferguson frowned. "That doesn't strike any chords."

"Well, he does exist," Sarah told him. "He's behind everything."

Ferguson unbuttoned his coat and sat down. "I really think it might be an idea if you told us what's been going on."

Sarah said, "You might as well handle that, Sean. I don't see any reason to hold back any essential facts." And yet there was something in her eyes that was telling him otherwise.

Egan picked his way briefly through the affair: Jago's appearance not only on the underground, but at All Hallows; the abortive visit to see Greta Markovsky; the discovery of Eric's diary. He made no mention of Alan Crowther's part in the affair at all, but launched into an account of what had happened in Paris. Before he could reveal what Agnés had told them about Deepdene Garden of Rest, Sarah cut in.

"All right, Tony, so if it gives you any satisfaction, we went all that way for nothing."

"Yes, well as a matter of interest, after we discovered Shelley had been wounded, I phoned a friend of mine in Service Five, that's a rather important department of French Security," Villiers said. "I asked him to check police sources and see if there'd been any gunplay in Paris last night." He took out a small notebook. "Claude Valentin, thirty-eight, a real all-around bad lad, shot to death. Also his girlfriend. A known prostitute, named Agnés Nicole. I'd say our friend Jago was responsible for that."

"A very dangerous man," Ferguson commented.

Villiers said to Egan, "So, Agnés and this man Valentin didn't tell you anything at all?"

Sarah cut in quickly. "They didn't get a chance. It all happened so fast."

Egan, taking his cue from her, said, "We'll never know the truth now, but I think they must have been trying to double-cross Jago in some way, if it was Jago, that is. Then the shooting started from up above. Jack was hit. I just wanted to get Mrs. Talbot out of there."

Ferguson stood up and buttoned his coat. "I'm sure you see now, Mrs. Talbot, that it's far better to leave these things to experts."

"And Jago?" Egan put in. "What about him? Will you pick him up?"

"First we have to find him," Ferguson said. "And friend Smith. But then, as I said before, there are security aspects to the affair. That's why one wouldn't want gentlemen with hairy knuckles from the drug squad at Scotland Yard handling things." He turned to Villiers. "We'll go now, Tony."

He went out. Villiers said, "What will you do now, Sarah, go home?"

"I'll see, Tony." She reached up and kissed him on the cheek. "Try not to worry about me."

"But I do," he said, and he followed Ferguson out.

The brigadier was already in the rear of the black Daimler as Villiers joined him. Ferguson tapped on the window and the driver started the car. "What do you think, sir?" Villiers asked.

"Oh, they haven't told us everything," the brigadier said. "That was obvious. They have a further lead, that's my guess."

"So what do we do?" Villiers demanded.

"At this stage, let them get on with it. We'll monitor the situation. It could lead us to where we want to be, Tony." Villiers looked grim and the brigadier laughed. "My dear Tony, you can't hold her hand forever. Now let's get back to Curzon Street. There's a lot to be done."

Egan said, "That was pretty devious. No mention of Bird and the Deepdene place."

"Because that would have disclosed the link with the Frasconis and I don't want that, not yet. I want to deal with Vito Barbera myself. See what he has to say. Are you game, Sean?"

"Oh, what the hell, why not? We've come this far."

"I'll get dressed."

She reached the door and he said, "There is one thing."

"What's that?"

"Agnés was still alive when we left the mill, which means Jago must have killed her after we'd gone." Egan shook his head. "He's a bad bastard."

"I know," she said, "I know," and she went out and upstairs quickly.

Jago was on the line again to Smith within minutes. "Not good, I'm afraid," he said when he was finished.

"The understatement of the age," Smith told him. "First of all, Group Four know your identity."

"No problem," Jago said. "They don't intend a general search for me, my mug on the wall of every police station. This is a security affair as far as they are concerned, and that's because of the Irish link. Never pays to get involved with those people, I've told you before. Too volatile."

"But somebody will be looking for you. The Talbot woman knows your face, the rest have a photo."

"So I change, old stick." Jago laughed. "I've done it before, believe me, or which me do you want to believe? There are several locked up tight in my old black makeup box. I was a great loss to the National Theatre."

"But now Ferguson and Villiers know *I* exist," Smith said. "They'll be thinking their way to me is through you."

"And there's the joke, old man," Jago said. "Even I don't have the slightest idea who you are, unless, of course, you care to reveal all." He stiffened as he heard Sarah's voice on the speaker. "Got to go, they're getting ready to move."

Instead of the usual Burberry, he varied his image. A checked sports jacket, scarf at the neck, a pair of black Ray-Ban sunglasses and a camera over his shoulder. He hurried down to the garage and got into the Spyder. As he eased out of the entrance, Sarah and Egan emerged from the house and got into the Mini Cooper. They drove away and Jago followed.

The Flamingo in Corley Street was not the Barbera family's most important casino. For one thing, it was the smallest, had never aspired to the kind of opulence that most of the larger establishments offered, but Vito Barbera had a soft spot for it. He'd once been its manager, although that was fifteen years ago, as a very young Sicilian in London to learn the language and the business.

The main gaming room was thickly carpeted and furnished in excellent taste, murals of Garibaldi's march on Rome painted on the walls. There were the usual gaming tables available as one would expect the world over and a wonderful bar in onyx and crystal, tables scattered around it.

Vito Barbera sat at the bar in his shirt-sleeves, a dark, rather intense young man, very handsome, a hint of classical Greek in his face, which in view of Sicily's history was not surprising. He was examining last night's accounts, a glass of champagne and orange juice at his elbow. The far door opened and one of the club porters came in.

"Lady and gentleman to see you, sir, a Mrs. Talbot." He put a card on the bar top. "Asked me to give you this, sir."

Vito examined the card, frowning, then his face cleared. "Of course, show the lady in."

The man went out and came back with Sarah Talbot and Egan. Vito went around the bar to greet them. "Mr. Barbera," she said, "I'm Sarah Talbot and this is Sean Egan. I believe your grandfather may have spoken to you about me?"

"Indeed he has, Mrs. Talbot." He kissed her hand gallantly. "I've had my orders, believe me, and they are to do anything I can to assist you." He went back behind the bar. "But first, join me, please. No Sicilian likes to drink alone."

He poured fresh orange juice and champagne into two glasses. Sarah settled herself on a bar stool. "That's very kind."

He toasted her gravely. "So, how can I be of service?"

She glanced at Egan and then explained as briefly as possible.

Barbera's face hardened. "I can now see why my grandfather sent you to me. In what way can I be of service?"

Egan said, "We now know rather more than we did. The man behind all this, the Mr. Big, is called Smith. Does that ring any bells with you?" Vito shook his head. "Or Jago, does that help? He's the middleman."

"No, neither name means a thing."

"All right," Sarah said, "let's try Frasconi—Danielo Frasconi."

Something unholy glowed in Vito Barbera's eyes. "Frasconi?"

"Apparently he was heavily involved with the drug trade in London. Is that true?" Egan asked.

Vito nodded. "He should have got twenty years, but his people went to work on the witnesses. He did a short sentence for assault and went back home. But how is he involved in this?"

"Apparently there's a connection between the Frasconis and Smith," Egan said. "We know Danielo Frasconi took delivery of a suitcase packed with heroin from one of Smith's people here in London last year."

There was a short pause. Barbera poured himself another glass of champagne and drank it slowly. He said, "Let me explain. Back home my grandfather is Capo Mafia in all Sicily, number one man, but there are those who don't like this."

"The Frasconi brothers?" Egan suggested.

"Exactly. My grandfather will not, and never has, soiled his hands on drugs. He is an old-fashioned man. The Frasconis on the other hand—" Vito shrugged. "They have attempted his life three times in the past year. Oh, he'll win in the end. He's finished them off in New York, but it's a difficult situation."

He hesitated and Egan said, "There's more?"

Vito said, "I know nothing of this man Smith. I'd have to ask my grandfather about that. What does interest me in your reports are those deaths in Ulster."

"Why?" Sarah asked.

"Terrorists over there on both sides have been involved in the drug trade, that's common knowledge, but there have been rumors that the Frasconis have had an Irish connection for some time. The use of that drug burundanga, and now the link with Smith and the Frasconis here in London, speaks for itself."

"So what do you suggest we do now?" Egan asked.

"I'll phone my grandfather, speak with him, bring him up-to-date with things and then we'll talk again later this afternoon."

"Here?" Sarah asked.

"I don't see why not. I've got other business as well, but I could be back by three."

"Fine." Sarah and Egan got up, and Vito Barbera came around the bar and walked to the entrance with them.

"Don't worry, Mrs. Talbot." He took her hand. "I'm certain my grandfather will come up with something."

"What now?" Sarah asked as they drove away.

"I thought we'd see how Jack is, then something to eat perhaps. Fill the time in until we see Barbera again."

"Do you really think Don Rafael can help?"

"I wouldn't be surprised. I get the distinct impression that in helping us he'd be helping himself," Egan told her, and pulled into the curb outside the clinic in Bell Street.

As they got out, Jago parked a few yards away and waited.

Shelley was sitting up against the pillows eating grapes and watching a cartoon on television. "Cartoons in the morning, that's all you get," he complained.

"There's always the Open University on the other channel," Egan suggested.

"Very funny. Now what's been happening?"

Sarah and Egan told him, between them. When they were finished, Shelley said, "All right, nobody has the slightest bleeding idea who

Smith is, but Jago's another matter. They should be able to run him down on the information they've got, no trouble."

"I'm not so certain," Egan said. "He's clever and it's possible they don't want to pin him down just yet. The security implications."

"Yeah, well fuck 'em with their stupid bleeding games," Shelley said. "John Le Carré's got a lot to answer for. I mean, these geezers take it seriously." He shook his head. "All right, Smith doesn't mean a thing to me, but Frasconi does. They're evil bastards. This Danielo creep was lucky to get back to Sicily, and there he'll stay, but that means he's beyond your reach."

"And Barbera?" Sarah asked.

"Never met the old boy, but I've seen Vito around. We've never clashed. Like me, they've got legitimate business interests."

The door opened and Aziz came in. "Long enough, I think. He needs rest."

"Stuff that. What I need is a good-looking nurse in suspenders," Shelley replied. He called to Sarah and Egan as they left, "Keep me posted."

They ate in an Italian restaurant on Fourth Street and Jago, in the Spyder up the road, ate a sandwich from a nearby takeout and talked to Smith.

"Does Barbera have anything on you?" Jago asked.

"Not a thing as far as I know."

"But there is the Frasconi connection. What if he's heard something about that? And the Irish link?"

Smith said, "Yes, that wouldn't be good."

"All right," Jago said. "I'll take care of it."

Sarah and Egan sat in the Mini Cooper a few yards down from the Flamingo and waited. She said, "This could be it—some sort of solution."

"Perhaps," Egan said. "We'll see." And then Vito Barbera appeared.

"There he is," Sarah said and they got out.

A yellow British Telecom truck roared around the corner, bounced onto the pavement and tossed Barbera into the air. The truck reversed and Barbera tried to get up. Incredibly, the truck roared forward again and slammed him into the railings. It reversed into the road and drove away at full speed. People were running from several different directions, and a small crowd had already collected as Sarah and Egan arrived.

Someone said, "He's dead!"

Sarah took a step forward and Egan pulled her away. "No, leave it!" he said in a low voice. "We can't do anything here."

He led her along the pavement to the Mini Cooper. She slumped in her seat, covering her face with her hands.

Jago dumped the stolen Telecom truck several streets away, walked a quarter of a mile to where he'd left the Spyder and drove off. When he reached Lord North Street, the Mini Cooper was already outside the house. He parked the Spyder in the garage and hurried up to his apartment to listen.

"So that's it," Egan said.

Sarah drank her tea slowly. "No, that's not it as far as I'm concerned. We can go to Sicily. See Don Rafael. He has a villa outside the village of Bellona in a place called the Cammarata."

"That's the worst area in Sicily," Egan said. "A wilderness of sterile valleys, nothing but mountain and burning sun. The Italian Army had ten thousand men up there at one point trying to catch Salvatore Giuliano, the Robin Hood of Sicily, and they couldn't do it. Had to get his best friend to betray him in the end." He shook his head. "It's not on. I'll do many things for you, but I refuse to take you to Sicily." He stood up. "Now if I were you, I'd have an early night. Try and get some sleep. I'll see you in the morning."

"All right," she said dully.

They walked to the door. "If you've got a spare key, I'll let myself in," he said. "Just in case you're asleep."

"Of course." She gave him one. "I'll see you in the morning then."

Egan left and she went into the kitchen, made some more tea and sat at the table, her hands around the cup, thinking.

Jago watched Egan drive away. "Poor old Sarah," he said. "What a shame."

He went into the bedroom, whistling cheerfully, showered and changed. What he really needed was a decent meal. There was a French restaurant within walking distance; he'd gone there before, and now seemed a very suitable time to take two or three hours off. There was no sound from the house. He checked that the recorder was on and went downstairs.

Sarah poured a second cup of tea and felt a little calmer. She wasn't angry with Egan. She could see what he meant. It made perfect sense, all very logical, only she wasn't interested in sense and logic. She got the telephone book, found the number she needed and rang the booking clerk at Heathrow.

"Can I fly to Palermo this evening?" she inquired.

"Not direct, I'm afraid. Flights to Palermo are via Milan or Rome. There's a direct flight to Catania, but that's on the other side of the island, and it doesn't leave until tomorrow."

"No, that's no good."

There was a murmur of voices at the other end and the woman came back. "Actually, madam, my colleague's just reminded me we have a holiday charter flight flying direct to Palermo. It leaves at six from Gatwick. It doesn't give you long to get there, but there is space available. I could book you a seat."

"Please do," Sarah said. "What time do we get in?"

"Nine o'clock our time. It's a three-hour flight. You lose an hour. It will be ten there."

Sarah made the booking and rang for a taxi. She went upstairs, changed, put a few things in an overnight bag, her passport, traveler's checks, everything she needed, and hurried downstairs. She stopped in the hall long enough to write a note for Egan and left it propped up on the hall stand. As she went out, the taxi arrived. She jumped in and was on her way.

Egan had a meal in a small café near Piccadilly, but he wasn't very hungry. He parked the car and walked around the streets for a while. His knee was aching, a sure sign of stress, and he went into a pub, ordered a Scotch and sat down. He was right, he knew that. Everything he'd said to Sarah Talbot made sense, but he felt bad about it, and the thought of her sitting there alone in the house in Lord North Street was too much to bear. He finished his Scotch, got up and left.

He let himself in with the key she'd given him, aware of the silence and of the note at the same moment. He read it with horror and immediately phoned Alan Crowther.

Crowther said, "What's all this then?"

"Access British Airways computer. See if they have Sarah Talbot on a flight out to any airport in Italy, or to Palermo direct."

It took Crowther no more than a minute. "She's on a BA charter flight out of Gatwick. What's she up to?"

"Trying to commit suicide," Egan said. "Alan, I've got to get over there fast."

"How can you do that, old son? You aren't Icarus."

"I could be. Group Four have a Lear Jet on twenty-four-hour standby at Walsham, near Canterbury, operational on the instant. Ready to fly anywhere."

"Yes, but only with Ferguson's direct authorization," Crowther pointed out.

"Which you can give them," Egan told him. "Access Group Four's computer. Top secret, eyes only order, to expect Sergeant Sean Egan and expedite flight to Palermo, Sicily, most immediate."

Crowther started to laugh. "You're mad."

"Yes, but will you do it?"

"I don't see why not. Ferguson's face when he finds out will be a picture."

"Good," Egan said, "But that's not all. Direct order to Group Four's man in Palermo, that's Marco Tasca. Tell him to expect me and to have the Cessna standing by. Say it's a repeat of the Angelo Stefano affair, and to have all necessary equipment ready. Tell him this time the target is Bellona. The villa of Rafael Barbera."

"What on earth are you up to?" Crowther demanded.

"Don't have time to explain. It'll take me an hour to get to Walsham. Make sure they're ready for me when I get there." He slammed down the phone and went out on the run.

Jago said, "I only just found out. I went for a meal. I thought she was set for the night."

"It doesn't matter now," Smith said. "She's put her head on the block for the last time. I've had enough. I'll ring the Frasconis. Let them know to expect her."

"You said you didn't want her harmed," Jago reminded him.

"Yes, well, this is in another country."

"And Egan?"

"Can take his chances, and with those people, they won't be very good, believe me. You can leave it to me from now on. Mrs. Talbot's finished." The line went dead, and Jago was surprised to find how much he didn't like that. Didn't like it at all.

"Finished, is she?" he said softly, then picked up the phone and rang Heathrow. The best they could do was a late flight to Rome. He could connect to Palermo first thing in the morning.

He went into the bedroom, got his second case from the wardrobe, opened it and took out a large black tin box. Inside was a superb actor's makeup kit, a selection of hair dyes. There were also several passports:

British, American, Swedish. The photo in each one was genuinely that of Jago, but in a suitable disguise. He chose another British passport in the name of Charles Henderson, Company Director, and got to work, starting on his hair first.

Summoned from the shower when Smith phoned, Salvatore Frasconi took the call in the main sitting room of the villa, dressed in a white bathrobe, a towel around his neck. His twin brother, Danielo, listened in on the extension.

When Smith was finished, Salvatore said calmly, "Leave it to me. She won't trouble you further, or this Egan. You have my word."

He put the phone down and started to towel his head. Danielo said, "What do you think?"

Salvatore went out on the terrace of the villa, Monte Pellegrino at one side, the whole sweep of Palermo, the bay, a large ferry plowing in on the other. Danielo followed him out.

Salvatore combed his hair carefully. "To be honest, what interests me isn't so much the woman and the Englishman. It's her connection with that old spider Barbera. The situation has infinite possibilities."

There was a bottle of Zibibbo, the anise-flavored wine from the island of Pantellaria, in an ice bucket on the table. Salvatore poured two glasses and gave his brother one. "The news of the death of Vito will have reached Barbera by now," he said. "He won't feel too good, he'll be off his guard."

"You think so?" Danielo asked.

"Sure, he's an old man, but one thing is certain. From what Smith tells me, if this woman goes to see him, he'll receive her. As I say, that raises interesting possibilities."

"Such as?"

"That villa of his outside Bellona. Electronic alarms, electric fence on top of the wall."

"I know. A fortress, but we've been over this before. Impossible to get in."

"Not for the woman."

Danielo frowned in bewilderment and Salvatore said impatiently, "She needs a car and a driver to get her there. She'd never find it herself. We just make sure it's our car and our driver she chooses at the airport. That's easy enough. The other drivers will do as they're told because they want to stay in business. Our man drives her to Bellona and we have a hit squad follow close behind."

"And then?"

"He's bound to be admitted to drive her up to the house. She'll stay, he'll leave. On the way out he takes care of the gate guard and our boys move in."

"I see." Danielo nodded. "Maybe she won't want to make the visit tonight. It's a two-hour drive, remember. Almost midnight by the time she got there."

"Look, even if she decides to spend the night in a hotel and go on tomorrow, it's the same, isn't it?" Salvatore shook his head. "In any case, I don't think that will happen. If what Smith says is true, this woman is crazy. She won't be able to wait. She'll want to see the Don tonight."

Danielo said, "It's perfect, Salvatore. Brilliant."

"Sure it is, and I tell you what I'll do, Danielo. I'll make you a nice present. You can be the one to go in with the boys and finish the old bastard off." Salvatore got up and walked to the balustrade, looking down at the harbor. "A good thing you got me looking after you, little brother. Now pour me another glass of wine."

And Danielo, the younger by thirty minutes, rushed to comply, as always.

The airfield at Walsham, used by Group Four and the SAS generally for clandestine operations, had been a bomber station during the Second World War, employed mainly by Flying Fortresses of the American 8th Air Force, which explained the length of the single runway. It had been discreetly maintained ever since, and people in the local farming community had always thought it some sort of research establishment.

It was maintained by selected RAF personnel, and when Egan arrived at the gate, they told him to leave the Mini Cooper, and a sergeant took him the rest of the way by Land Rover. The Lear Jet was waiting on the apron by the control tower.

The duty officer, a squadron leader, was standing talking to a young man in flying gear. The squadron leader said, "Sergeant Egan? We were warned to expect you. Rush job, eh?"

Egan handed over his passport and SAS security card. A lucky thing that as he was legally a serving soldier for another six months, as Villiers had reminded him, the card was still in his possession.

The squadron leader handed them back. "Fine. This is Harvey Grant, the copilot."

The pilots on this service were all freelance, very specially recruited, Egan knew, although usually ex-RAF. Grant and Egan shook hands. "We'll get going then. My chum's got things warmed up nicely."

They went up the ladder and he closed the door. "How long?" Egan asked.

"In this baby, two hours if we get the sort of winds the met report indicates. This is a stopover job?"

"That's right."

"How long for?"

"Budget for twenty-four hours, but be on constant standby, ready to leave instantly as required."

"That's fine. Fasten your seat belt."

Egan did as he was told and lay back in the seat. There would be hell to pay when Ferguson and Tony found out about this, but he didn't care. He closed his eyes as the plane lifted off and considered his next move, remembering his last visit to Sicily. Only a couple of months before the Falklands had exploded. Another job for the dirty tricks department. The Stefano business.

Angelo Stefano, a Dublin-born Italian and expert gunman for the Provisional IRA whose final coup had been the killing of eight British soldiers in a roadside bombing in South Armagh. He'd fled from the wrath of the SAS to Sicily, where he'd holed up in the mountain village of Massama in the Cammarata, impossible to reach, every shepherd on every peak in the mountains a watchdog.

Marco Tasca, Group Four's man in Palermo and an expert pilot in his own right, had flown Egan into the Cammarata by night. Egan had parachuted in from eight hundred feet, surprised Stefano tending the sheep in the high meadow above his uncle's farm at dawn and killed him—not that it had bothered him. Stefano was a mad dog who deserved to die.

Of course, getting out in one piece was always going to be the problem. He'd been saved by the unexpected. Stefano had been using a motorcycle to herd the sheep, a Montessa dirt bike, the kind many shepherds used in the high meadows these days. So he'd made the airport at Punta Raisi and got out intact after all.

It would be interesting to see if he could repeat the performance, especially with his left knee the way it was these days, but that was in the lap of the gods.

Jago's hair was much lighter now, almost the color of straw. He carefully combed it back from his forehead as he blow-dried it. The special instant-tan gel he had put on his face earlier had already darkened his skin, and the line of the scar had faded completely. He selected a blond moustache, carefully gummed it into place and trimmed it a little. The blue horn-rimmed glasses he selected were slightly tinted. He adjusted them, comparing himself in the mirror with the passport photo. The effect was astonishing. More than satisfactory.

He moved quickly now, clearing everything away, then dressed, wearing the checked sports jacket and flannels. He took only an overnight bag and a light fawn raincoat. No possibility of carrying a gun, of course, airport security being the way it was these days, so he'd be a little naked when he reached Palermo. Still, he'd cross that bridge when he came to it. He hurried downstairs.

TWELVE

THE FLIGHT FROM LONDON arrived ten minutes early at Punta Raisi Airport. Sarah went straight through, ahead of the crowd of holiday makers who formed the rest of the passenger list, and presented her passport.

The uniformed immigration officer was courtesy itself. He examined her passport and stamped it. "Welcome to Sicily, Mrs. Talbot. Business or pleasure?"

"Business, I suppose," Sarah said, adding, with some truth, "I'm visiting friends. A death in the family."

"How sad. I'm so sorry, signora."

He returned her passport, and as she moved away, he nodded to a small man in a tan suit who was leaning against the wall reading a magazine. The man hurried ahead of Sarah across the concourse and out through the glass doors to where the taxis waited. The drivers were lounging in a group, smoking and talking together. The man in the tan suit made a sign, and one of them came forward, a young, muscular man in a short-sleeved white shirt, dark curling hair escaping from under a tweed cap.

"Is she here, Bernardo?" he asked.

"The first one through. She hasn't got any luggage. The good-looking one. You make your bones on this one, Nino. The Frasconis will be very grateful."

"You can depend on me, Bernardo."

As Bernardo moved off, Sarah emerged and hesitated. Nino came forward. "Can I be of service, signora?" he asked in Italian.

Sarah said, "I don't speak Italian."

"Ah, American," he said in English, and took off his cap. "I lived in New York for three years. My uncle has a restaurant in Manhattan. You know Manhattan?"

He was already reaching for her overnight bag. "Oh, yes, I think you could say I know Manhattan," she told him, hanging on to the bag.

"Where you want to go, Palermo? I take you to a good hotel."

"No," she said. "I want to go to a village called Bellona."

He feigned surprise. "Hey, that's a long way, lady. Bellona is near Monte Cammarata. Forty, maybe fifty miles."

"How long would it take?"

"The main highway is okay, but the side roads into the high country are another matter." He shrugged. "Two hours. Yes, I get you there in two hours for one hundred dollars."

"I can tell you've lived in New York," she said. "All right, let's go." And she gave him her overnight bag.

"You won't regret it," he said. "I've got a great car for you. Air-conditioning. See for yourself." They crossed the road to a line of taxis. He paused beside a black Mercedes and opened the door. "My name is Nino, signora. Nino Scacci."

"And mine is Talbot." As he slid behind the wheel, she added, "You know Bellona?"

"Sure. I've been there before."

"Then you know the house of Don Rafael Barbera?"

He turned sharply. "Is that where we're going, signora? You're a friend of Don Rafael?"

"That's right."

"You should have told me sooner. For you I'd have made it fifty dollars."

"Don't worry about it, Nino, a deal's a deal. Now let's get going."

On the other side of the road, Danielo Frasconi watched them go by from the rear seat of an Alfa Romeo sedan. He looked very dashing in a designer jacket of soft black leather, a white scarf at his throat. The man in the tan suit, Bernardo, sat up front beside the driver, a hard-looking young man in a denim jacket.

"Okay, let's go," Danielo said. He leaned forward as they pulled away and put a hand on the driver's shoulder. "And remember, Cesare, not too close." He laughed. "After all, we all know where we're going."

In spite of the bright moonlight, the main highway was just another highway the same the world over, plenty of traffic about. "It's a pity we're not making the run by day," Nino said, "so you can see something, especially when we go up into the high country."

"I hear it can be very hot."

"Hot as the Sahara sometimes. Better in the spring. You can smell the orange groves for miles. Lots of flowers in the high meadows. Poppies, iris, stuff like that, but the people are poor here—real poor. You think you've seen poverty in New York, signora? Believe me, you've seen nothing."

"And the Mafia?" she said. "That's still as strong as ever?"

"Oh, sure. You get Mafia everywhere. The police, the unions, even the aristocracy. You want to stay in business here, the Mafia gets a piece of your action." He shook his head. "Nothing changes."

Suddenly that phrase was going round and round in her head. Nothing changes. And he was right—nothing ever does. Thinking about that, she closed her eyes and slept.

The Lear Jet taxied over to the private plane area of the airport at Punta Raisi, and when the door opened, Egan saw Marco Tasca walking toward him. He was a small, dark-haired man of fifty with a smile of perpetual good humor; he had been at one time a fighter pilot in the Italian air force. He'd resigned his commission to fly for the Biafrans in the Nigerian civil war, and not for the money, but because he had believed passionately in their cause. It was after that unfortunate episode that Ferguson had recruited him. Since the work he was employed on in the fight against international terrorism was as much to his own country's benefit as England's, the Italian Secret Service tended to look discreetly the other way regarding his activities.

As Egan came down the steps, Marco flung his arms around him. "Hey, Sean Egan, it's great to see you," he said in Italian.

Egan replied in rapid and fluent Italian. "And good to see you, Marco."

Harvey Grant, the Lear Jet's copilot, appeared at the top of the ladder, and Marco said in English, "I've made arrangements for you and your friend to use the crew facilities in the main terminal. You're expected. I've also arranged for the Lear to be refueled."

"Fine," Grant said, and smiled at Egan. "Whatever it is, good luck. Don't do anything I would."

Marco led Egan across the apron to where a Cessna Conquest stood waiting. They went into the hangar and Marco unlocked an office door and switched on the light.

"I couldn't believe it when the order came through. Barbera's place at Bellona." He shook his head. "Anyway, I phoned a friend in the Mafia Squad at police headquarters. He sent me these by a police motorcyclist. Naturally, he has no idea what I wanted them for."

There were three aerial photos of the Barbera villa, taken at very low level. It looked old, very traditional, sprawled across an open hillside, nestling in palm trees and other lush semitropical vegetation. The whole was surrounded by a high wall.

"As you can see, the approach road is in the open for two hundred meters, there is an electric fence on top of the wall, electronic warning devices. Contrary to popular belief, no dogs. It seems Don Rafael hates dogs like some people hate cats. Look, what is this, Sean? What's Don Rafael to you? He can't be the target, surely?"

"You sound as if you like him," Egan said as he examined another photo, this time taken from a higher altitude, showing the villa, the ridge above it, the village of Bellona in the valley below.

"I respect him," Marco said. "Most people do."

"And the Frasconis?"

Marco spread his hands. "Rubbish compared to the old man. They've tried to knock him off a few times. Got nowhere, and it's my opinion they never will."

"His grandson, Vito, was murdered in London earlier today."

"Holy Mother of God." Marco crossed himself. "The Frasconis?"

"Indirectly. Someone they have shared business interests with."

"The Don will extract a terrible price for this," Marco said.

"I'm sure he will. How long to fly to Bellona if we leave now?"

"Fifteen minutes." Marco shrugged. "Maybe twenty. It's a good night for it, full moon, but Sean, you aren't going to try to drop into the grounds? Too difficult for me when I make my pass, because of the ridge at the back of the house."

"As long as you get me there, that's all I ask. There's a woman on her way there now, maybe there already for all I know. Lamb amongst wolves, Marco." Egan grinned. "She needs me."

"Fine, then let's get going." Marco moved to another table. There was a Browning in a shoulder holster, a Carswell silencer, an Armalite rifle, stock folded, and a British Army standard-issue parachute. "Everything's here, I think."

Egan slipped off his jacket, pulled on the shoulder holster, then put the jacket on again. Then Marco helped him into the parachute harness. Egan tightened it quickly, all the expertise of having made over a hundred drops over the years coming to his aid. He picked up the Armalite.

"Okay, let's do it, Marco." Together, they left the hangar and hurried across to the Conquest.

Sarah came awake with a start to Nino's voice calling, "We're here, signora—Bellona."

Her head was muzzy but she pulled herself together and saw that they were passing through the narrow streets of a village, the houses appearing tall by contrast. They moved into a square with a church on one side. There was a wine shop on another, lights strung through the trees, music on the night air, people dancing.

"Looks like there's been a wedding," Nino commented.

Children ran alongside the car, laughing. He increased speed, they left the village behind and started up a steep incline through pine trees. As they emerged, they saw the villa, surrounded by its walls, two hundred meters away in the moonlight.

Nino stopped the car at the iron-barred gates. There was a gate-house, a light on inside, and a man in a dark corduroy suit came out holding an Uzi submachine gun.

"What do you want?" he asked in Italian. "No visitors."

Nino got out of the car and confronted him through the bars. "I got a lady here from the airport to see the Don. An American lady. Signora Talbot." The gatekeeper stared through the bars at Sarah suspiciously and Nino said, "You better phone the Don. If you send her away, he'll have your balls cut off, she's a friend of his."

The gatekeeper went into his office, and through the window they saw him pick up the phone. He spoke briefly and put the phone down. The electronically operated gates started to open and he hurried out.

"Tell the lady I'm sorry," he said to Nino. "The Don says take her straight up to the house."

Nino eased the Mercedes up the drive through the lush vegetation. A cloud passed across the moon, and somewhere above their heads in the darkness there was the sound of an airplane. It seemed to fill the night for a moment, then dwindled away toward the north.

The Mercedes pulled up in front of the villa. Rafael Barbera stood at the top of the steps on the veranda. He wore a gray suit and leaned heavily on a cane. There was a long cigar in his left hand. A large, heavily built man in an excellent suit of black worsted stood behind him.

"Mrs. Talbot. A wonderful surprise and a great pleasure."

He put his cigar in his mouth and took her hand. She said, "Don Rafael, I had to see you. It's about your grandson, Vito."

"But I know about Vito, Mrs. Talbot. I had a phone call from a business associate in London. Victim of a street accident, he told me."

"I saw it, Don Rafael. I was there. It was no accident."

He showed no emotion, simply took her arm. "How much did this rogue charge for the cab?"

"One hundred dollars."

"A thief." He turned to the man at his shoulder. "Jacopo, give him twenty-five and send him on his way."

"An honor, Don Rafael." Nino clutched his cap in his hands. "A great honor."

The Don and Sarah walked into a large, cool hall, passed through an anteroom and out onto a terrace at the rear overlooking the garden.

Barbera said, "I've only Jacopo with me tonight. I've let the rest of my staff go to a wedding party in the village. I expect that they'll be there all night."

"Don Rafael," she said. "Your grandson was murdered. Murdered in cold blood because he was trying to help me."

He said calmly, "Tell me everything, Mrs. Talbot. Everything you know."

Nino honked his horn as he approached the exit. The gatekeeper pressed the button, the gates started to open. Nino stopped the car and looked out of the window, a cigarette in his mouth. "Heh, you got a match?"

The gatekeeper came forward, took a lighter from his waistcoat pocket and flicked it. At the same moment, Nino's hand came up holding a Beretta with a silencer on the end. He shot the gatekeeper between the eyes, the force of the bullet throwing the man back against the wall, then he inched the Mercedes forward so that the gates couldn't be closed and flashed his lights on and off.

Danielo, standing beside the Alfa in the pine trees, saw the signal and grinned excitedly. "He's done it. Let's go!"

He ran along the track across the open ground toward the villa, drawing a .45 Colt Automatic from a shoulder holster. Bernardo carried a Schmeisser machine pistol, and Cesare a sawed-off shotgun, the Lupara, the mark of a real Mafioso, a man with the balls to go in close.

They reached the gate and Nino said, "He took her in the house. I saw only one other man there. Maybe the others are at the party in the village."

"Good!" Danielo said. "You've done well. You stay here and be ready. When we leave, we leave fast."

He moved up the drive and turned into the palm trees, followed by the other two. Nino lit a cigarette nervously and got behind the wheel. He heard nothing, only the wind in the palms, and then something cold and hard touched his temple and a quiet voice said, "If you make a sound, I'll blow your brains out. Now get out of the car."

What made the Conquest particularly suitable for the task in hand was the Airstair door which made a clean exit possible. The problem was the ridge at the back of the villa. It gave Marco only a brief pass at eight hundred feet, his engine throttled back, a few seconds only before it was necessary to boost power and climb steeply.

He glanced over his shoulder into the cabin at Egan crouching beside the door and yelled, "Here we go, Sean. One chance is all you get. Count to ten!"

Egan started to count, hands braced on the door, one foot on the top step, the Armalite slung from his neck. The ground below, the villa, the mountainside were clear in the moonlight, and then a cloud passed over the moon and there was only darkness, and he dived headfirst into it. His body was buffeted by the aircraft's slipstream with such force, as the Conquest banked to starboard, that he turned over, the sling of the Armalite slipping over his head, the weapon falling into the night.

He pulled his ripcord, and a moment later there was a crack as the khaki silk blossomed above his head. At eight hundred feet, a parachutist has thirty seconds before he hits the ground, and Egan was already counting, staring down into the darkness below, no supply bag on a lead to hit the ground first and warn him to get ready.

At the last moment, fortune smiled. The cloud passed, and in the sudden bright moonlight he saw the orange grove on the hillside to one side of the villa just below him. He had time to haul in his rigging and alter direction, landing in the meadow a few yards from the edge of the grove.

He rolled expertly, came to his feet and pressed the clip to release his harness. Then he tested his knee and found, to his relief, that everything seemed in perfect working order. He started down through the orange grove and crossed to the wall at the side of the villa. The electric fence along the top was clearly visible and he worked his way along, looking up, hoping to see a reachable branch from a tree on the other side.

He paused at the corner and drew back as he saw Danielo Frasconi and his two henchmen running up to the gate, pausing to talk to Nino standing beside the Mercedes. They moved on and Nino lit a cigarette and got behind the wheel. Egan took out his Browning. He reached in the window and touched the muzzle to Nino's temple.

"If you make a sound, I'll blow your brains out. Now get out of the car."

No Sicilian this. The Italian was too pure, like they spoke in Rome, but there was enough menace in the voice to make Nino do exactly as he was told. He got out, hands raised, and Egan searched him expertly and found the Beretta. He slipped it inside his jacket and looked beyond Nino to the body of the gatekeeper.

"This is Frasconi business, right?"

"Please, signor, I'm only a driver," Nino protested.

Egan hit him across the face, then grabbed his hair and put the muzzle of his weapon under Nino's chin. "You're half a second from parting company with your brain."

"All right, signor. I work for the Frasconis, but I'm only a cabdriver. They ordered me to pick up a woman at Punta Raisi and bring her here."

"And did you?"

"Yes, signor, an American lady. She's inside with Don Rafael."

Egan nodded at the dead gatekeeper. "And you did this?"

"I had no choice, signor. They made me, Danielo and his boys. They'd have killed me if I hadn't done as I was told. It was the only way they could get in."

Egan hit him across the side of the head and Nino went down as if pole-axed. Egan reached in the Mercedes and sounded the horn, holding it down, then he ran up the drive very fast.

On the terrace, Jacopo was serving fresh coffee to the Don and Sarah when the horn sounded down by the gate. Don Rafael frowned and put down his cup. "What's that?"

A second later, Egan's voice rang out. "Sarah, it's Sean Egan. Warn Don Rafael. Danielo Frasconi and two of his men are somewhere in the garden."

Without hesitation, Don Rafael pulled Sarah to the floor and Jacopo dropped to one knee, drawing a revolver from a waist holster. A second later and Bernardo, in the bushes, opened up with the Schmeisser, raking the terrace with bullets.

Egan burst through the undergrowth, saw Bernardo crouched in the bushes, Cesare at his side. He went in on the run, shot Bernardo in the back twice, and then his knee gave, the leg buckling under him as he went down. Cesare turned, the shotgun raised, and Jacopo stood up on the terrace and shot him in the back of the head. He vaulted over the balustrade into the undergrowth and crouched beside Egan.

"Are you all right, Mr. Egan?" Don Rafael called.

Egan tested his knee gingerly, and finding that it seemed to work, stood up. "I'm fine. There's one more."

Jacopo looked down at the two bodies. "It must be Danielo, Don Rafael!"

"Then let's see if we can flush him out." Incredibly, Barbera stood up and put his cigar back in his mouth. "Where are you, Frasconi? Afraid to face an old man?"

At the far end of the terrace, some thirty paces away, Danielo Frasconi slipped out of the bushes and fired wildly, his bullet splintering woodwork beside the window. Egan's arm swung up and he fired twice. Frasconi was hurled backward, his legs twitched for a moment and he lay still.

Jacopo went forward and dropped on one knee to examine him. He looked up. "Two in the heart, not a finger's breadth between them. Some shooting," he added in admiration.

Sarah stood up, white and shaking. "Sean, how did you get here?"

"You might say I've just dropped in," he told her.

"Mr. Egan, however improbable the miracle that brought you here, the fact is that I owe you my life," Don Rafael said. "In the present circumstances, the most important thing is that we drink to that, so please come inside."

Nino Scacci, nursing a swollen head, was terrified, and yet he made his way through the bushes cautiously a minute or two after the sounds of gunfire had ceased. He found the bodies of Bernardo and Cesare first. There was laughter from inside the house. He moved forward and saw, to his horror, Danielo Frasconi's body lying below the far end of the terrace. Nino crept away fast, then ran down the drive. No point in taking the Mercedes. They'd hear him starting up, give chase. He ran the two hundred meters to the pine wood and found the Alfa parked just inside. Thank God the key was in the ignition. He started the engine.

He drove down through the village where the party was still underway and kept going, dangerously fast, considering the state of the road, until half an hour later he turned onto the main highway from Agrigento to Palermo. There was a transport café opposite, the kind of place open twenty-four hours a day. He went inside and found a telephone.

Salvatore Frasconi said, "You can't go back up to Bellona, you'd be spotted at once." He was standing by the open French windows of his bedroom, a towel around his waist. "Stay where you are. Anyone leaving Bellona doesn't have any choice. They've got to come out on the main highway right there."

"Okay, Don Salvatore. I'll do as you say."

"The first sign of the woman and this Englishman, or Don Rafael himself on the way to Palermo, phone me."

Frasconi put down the telephone and stood looking out to sea. The dark-haired young woman sitting up in bed, her breasts bare, said, "What is it, Salvatore? What's wrong?"

"They've killed Danielo." His voice was anguished.

"Mother of heaven!" She crossed herself. "Who has?"

"Don Rafael Barbera and his men."

"So, what will you do?"

Frasconi turned, and his face was terrible to see. "What do you think?"

Don Rafael stood in front of the fire and Egan and Sarah sat on a couch opposite. "I will tell you now exactly what I told Vito on the telephone. Everything I know."

"We'd be very grateful," Sarah said.

"Not at all. This is some way of paying my debt to you. As I told you at our last meeting on the plane, Mrs. Talbot, I have never engaged in the drug trade. In fact, I make it as difficult for those who do as I can."

"The Frasconis, for instance?" Egan asked.

"Exactly. I've been locked in a struggle with the Frasconi family for some years. I've destroyed them in New York, ruined their London operation. They've tried to kill me, failed every time, and thanks to you, Mr. Egan, failed again tonight. I stand on the brink of true success. Only Salvatore is between me and the total destruction of the Frasconi family." He laughed. "It's like a Greek tragedy."

"What about Smith?" Sarah asked. "Does he mean anything to you?"

"Oh, yes. There have been several members of the Frasconi family who, having seen the writing on the wall, have turned to me. There is little that I do not know of their operation. Smith's name has been mentioned many times. They do a great deal of business with him, that much is obvious, but his identity remains as much a mystery to me as to you."

"Another blind alley," Egan said.

"Not entirely. This Irish connection you mentioned? I can be of assistance there. One of my informants was used as a courier by the Frasconis to Ulster."

"Now that *is* interesting," Egan said. "Have you got details?"

"Oh, yes." Barbera went to his desk, opened it and took out a file. He skimmed through some papers. "You know Ulster, Mr. Egan?"

"You could say that."

"There is a place called Ballycubbin on the coast, a fishing village. It's south of Donaghadee."

"I know the area well," Egan said.

"There's a country house a couple of miles outside Ballycubbin called Rosemount, owned by an Irish aristocrat. Sir Leland Barry, the man's name is."

"And where does this get us?" Egan asked.

"This Sir Leland is bitterly opposed to the activities of the IRA. He controls an extremist Protestant group known as the Sons of Ulster. I think you will find they were responsible for the four deaths you mentioned. Their entry into the drug trade has been a means of sustaining their activities financially."

"And the Frasconis were involved?" Sarah said.

"As I told you, their courier visited this Sir Leland on more than one occasion. He heard Smith's name mentioned several times. They are all linked, the Frasconis, the Sons of Ulster and our mysterious Mr. Smith in London."

"Well, that's something." Egan turned to Sarah. "Real progress at last."

She stood up and said to Barbera, "I can't thank you enough."

He took her hand. "Jacopo will show you to your rooms. In the morning he can take you back to Punta Raisi for your plane. He tells me there's a perfectly good Mercedes at the gate. You can use that."

"And Salvatore Frasconi?" Egan said.

"You can leave him to me, Mr. Egan." Don Rafael smiled bleakly. "All debts will be paid, believe me."

Jago caught the breakfast flight from Rome to Punta Raisi and was driving down to Palermo in a taxi by eight-thirty. His Italian was not fluent, but acceptable, and he engaged the driver in conversation, first passing him a twenty-dollar bill.

"I find myself in a predicament, my friend."

"And what would that be, signor? Perhaps I can help?"

"I'm here on business of a kind which requires me to carry large sums of money. To be frank, I would be happier if I had a pistol in my pocket."

"For this, a permit is required, signor. From the police."

"Unfortunately my time is limited. I wondered if you might have a suggestion?"

He passed the driver another twenty-dollar bill, which he accepted with alacrity. "Actually, signor, come to think of it, I know a pawnbroker called Buscotti who might be able to help. People sometimes pawn guns as they pawn their jewelry."

"Would Signor Buscotti require a permit?"

"No, signor." The driver laughed. "But I think he might require a fifty-dollar bill in place of one."

He delivered Jago to Buscotti's establishment ten minutes later and waited while the Englishman went inside. Jago reappeared surprisingly quickly, one hundred and fifty dollars poorer, a Beretta Compact semiautomatic pistol in his holdall.

"Everything okay, signor?" the driver asked.

"Couldn't be better. You know the villa of Don Salvatore Frasconi?"

The driver turned, surprise on his face. "You're a friend of Don Salvatore's, signor?"

"We have business interests in common," Jago said. "Now take me there." And he sat back.

Salvatore was having breakfast on the terrace, still in his bathrobe, when the maid showed Jago in. Salvatore snapped his fingers and the man in the black suit who stood behind him moved forward. "Search him, Paolo."

Paolo ran his hands over Jago's body and stood back, satisfied. "I say, is this really necessary, old boy?" Jago asked, at his most English.

"You say you're from Smith?" Salvatore said. "What's your name?"

"It says Henderson on the passport, but your brother Danielo will remember me from his London days as Jago."

"Danielo is dead." Salvatore spread butter on a roll. "So what do you want?"

"First, my profound sympathies for your loss. He was a great man. Second, in the matter of the woman, Talbot," Jago said, "Mr. Smith has changed his mind. He wants her intact."

"Well, in this case he can want," Salvatore said. "She and this English friend of hers have a direct responsibility for my brother's death. They're mine now. They belong to me. They'll be returning to Palermo today, must do so if they wish to leave the island, and when they do ..."

His eyes were wild, dark shadows beneath them. Jago smiled and stood up. "Ah, well, that's an entirely different situation. I'm sure Mr. Smith will understand. I'll take up no more of your time then."

He got out fast and returned to the taxi. The driver said mournfully, "For some reason, signor, I doubt whether you're a friend to the Frasconis. Can I have my fare and go?"

"After you've taken me to the nearest car-hire firm," Jago said.

There was a suitable establishment five minutes away, another fifteen was needed for the necessary documentation, so that thirty minutes after his interview with Frasconi, he was sitting in a red Ford on the opposite side of the road from the villa.

Nino's task, waiting in the car park of the café at the Bellona road junction, was made easier by the fact that when Egan, Sarah and Jacopo appeared, they were in his own Mercedes. It turned onto the main highway and Nino ran to the phone.

At his villa, Salvatore listened and checked his watch. "Okay, they should be here in, say, an hour and fifteen minutes. You stay close behind. We'll cut them off somewhere in Palermo. You just be ready."

"Yes, Don Salvatore." Nino dropped the phone, ran out to the Alfa and went after them.

Salvatore put the phone down and turned to Paolo. "They're coming, Paolo, they're coming. Now it's my turn." And he went into the bedroom to change.

Fifteen minutes later he drove out through the main gates of the villa in a blue Maserati, Paolo at the wheel. As they turned into the road, Jago switched on the Ford's engine and followed them.

"At least you'll fly back in style," Egan said to Sarah. He was sitting up front beside Jacopo, who was driving. Sarah sat in the rear.

She said, "Don't you think it's likely that Ferguson will have discovered by now that his precious Lear Jet has flown the coop?"

"I should imagine so." Egan glanced out the window. They were well into Palermo, moving down toward the dock area.

"Which would indicate the distinct possibility of a reception committee," Sarah suggested.

"I'd say that's a reasonable deduction," he agreed.

"So what are they going to do? Arrest you?"

"We'll have to see."

"And do we tell them about Ballycubbin and the Sons of Ulster?"

"We shall have to see about that as well."

They were passing along a quiet street, warehouses on their right, the harbor beyond, when suddenly a blue Maserati hurtled by and pulled up in front so that Jacopo had to brake. "Stupid bastard!" he snarled and Salvatore leaned out of the passenger window and fired at them.

"Christ, it's Frasconi!" Jacopo swung the wheel, taking the Mercedes into a side street that ran down toward the harbor between tall warehouses.

Egan turned and saw not only the Maserati pursuing them, but a red Alfa, and at that moment, Jacopo, cursing, found a wall at the end of the street and turned into a narrow entrance that brought them out onto a deserted dock. He drove very fast to the far end of the dock, but there was nowhere to go, just a dark entrance on the left, and not having much choice, he drove inside.

It was an enormous building, dark and gloomy, a great wide channel filled with green water running up the center, obviously used for some sort of boat building in the past. The Mercedes roared toward the other end. Jacopo, realizing there was no exit, executed a stunning speed skid, turning the car in a circle so that it was traveling back the way it had come.

The Maserati and the Alfa were both halted, blocking the way, and Salvatore jumped out, a Beretta in his hand, and fired twice. A bullet drilled through the windshield of the Mercedes and struck Jacopo between the eyes. The Mercedes swerved, spun across the dock and plunged into the channel. Egan had barely time to wind up his window as the Mercedes went nose down some forty feet and settled on the bottom. Sarah was terrified as the water started to rise about her.

"Don't panic!" he said. "You wait until the water's up to the roof, then try the door. You'll find it will open easily then. Just go up slowly. I'll be right behind."

He had the Browning ready in his hand. As the water level reached her chin, a scream rose in her throat, but she fought it down and took a deep breath. The water flooded over her head, and she tried the door. It opened to her touch, and she climbed out of the car and drifted up through the green water, aware of the distorted shapes of the three men above waiting on the edge of the dock. She surfaced, looked up into Salvatore's hate-filled eyes, Paolo on one side of him with a gun, Nino on the other.

"Bitch!" Salvatore said and took careful aim.

And then Sean Egan erupted from the water beside her, the Browning extended in both hands. He fired twice, once at Nino, catching him in the throat, the second taking Paolo just above the left eye, and then the gun jammed.

Salvatore raised his Beretta, madness in his eyes, there was a squeal of brakes and a Ford Escort skidded to a halt behind him. Jago leaped out on the other side. "Frasconi!" he called.

Salvatore half-turned, and Jago shot him three times, knocking him over the edge of the dock into the water. Sarah and Egan floated there. Jago walked to the edge of the dock. She looked up into the tanned face with the blond hair and moustache, the glasses. Just a hint of something there, but she didn't know what, until he spoke.

"I don't know, Sarah, but you really have a thing about water, don't you?" He shook his head. "I'd get the hell out of there and go home if I were you."

He disappeared. They heard the Ford engine start up and move away. Sarah said, "Jago! It was Jago, Sean, but different. The man's a magician."

Egan took her arm and pulled her toward a ladder. "I don't care what he is; his advice is sound."

He helped her up the ladder. A few moments later they were in the Maserati making for Punta Raisi airport as fast as possible.

THIRTEEN

IT WAS JUST AFTER ten when the Lear Jet taxied over to the main hangar on its arrival at Walsham. When Grant opened the door and Sarah walked down the steps she found Tony Villiers standing at the bottom, Ferguson's black Daimler parked a few yards away.

"Tony, I can explain everything," she said, tensely watching for his reaction. "Is Brigadier Ferguson in the car?"

"No, he's at his flat. I'm to take you there." Villiers turned to Egan as they walked to the car. "I've been in touch with Marco in Palermo this morning."

"Let's get one thing straight, Colonel," Egan told him. "Marco's not at fault in any way. He received an operational order, coded correctly, with the right security classification, and he played it by the book."

"So it would appear." Villiers followed Sarah into the car and Egan sat opposite them on the jump seat. "Marco tells me the Frasconi brothers are no longer with us?"

"So I hear," Egan said.

"I trained you well, Sean."

Egan shook his head. "Don't let me take all the credit. Jago turned up. To be honest, he saved our hides for us. Knocked off Salvatore Frasconi just when things were looking rather bad."

"There's only one thing," Sarah put in. "His appearance was completely transformed. I didn't realize it was him until he spoke."

"If he returns to London today, there's your chance to get him," Egan said.

"I doubt it." Villiers shook his head. "Not if he's as well disguised as Sarah indicates. A very resourceful man, our friend Jago."

He seemed curiously subdued, and Sarah frowned. "Is anything wrong, Tony?"

"Well, yes, actually." He took her hand in his. "Sir Geoffrey died yesterday morning."

"Oh, no." She felt genuine pain, closed her eyes and turned away, remembering all of it. Her marriage that day at Stokeley, the reception at the hall afterward, Edward in dress uniform, Eric home from school for the occasion and Sir Geoffrey so happy.

"I'm so glad he was too ill to know about Eric," she said finally.

"I went ahead with the funeral arrangements," Villiers told her. "I hope you don't mind?"

"Why should I? After all, you're the head of the family now. No more Talbots." She was close to breaking. "When is the funeral?"

"This afternoon at three."

"At Stokeley?"

"Of course."

She said to Sean, "Stokeley Hall's in Essex on the River Crouch. Only an hour's run from London if you're lucky with the traffic. It's another world." Her voice was brittle now. "England like it used to be. The Talbots have lived there for five hundred years, only not any more, because there aren't any more left."

And at that, she turned from both of them and the dam broke.

At that moment, Jago was arriving at Leonardo da Vinci Airport in Rome. Egan and Sarah Talbot would be making a fast trip back to England in the Lear Jet, so much was obvious, which meant that he would be out of contact with them for some time. Not completely, of course, because the equipment he had left in place at his apartment would record whatever took place in the house at Lord North Street, which was something, at least.

What concerned him more was his present position. Saving Sarah Talbot's life was one thing, acting like a damned poseur was another. He'd blown his cover. True, it was unlikely that she could give a very accurate description, but Villiers and the Group Four people would be alerted, and that could be enough.

He looked up at the electronic flight board and started to smile because the situation was absurdly simple. There was a British Airways direct flight to Glasgow leaving at lunchtime and arriving in that fair city at four-thirty. And from Glasgow there was a shuttle service, planes down to London and back all the time.

He went to the desk, made a booking, then went to the bar, got a glass of white wine and went into a phone booth to call Smith. He sat there, enjoying the wine and smoking a cigarette. It was fifteen minutes before Smith called him back.

"What are you doing in Rome?"

"Waiting for a plane. I'm on my way back."

"You've been to Sicily?"

"That's right," Jago said.

"I told you to stay out of it."

"Yes, well, I considered that, and it occurred to me that taking everything into consideration it was more sensible to be around, just in case I was needed."

"And were you?"

"I'm afraid not. Salvatore Frasconi turned my services down flat. He was hell-bent on getting them all—Barbera, Egan and Sarah Talbot."

"And what happened?"

As usual when transmitting bad news to Smith, Jago found that he was enjoying himself. "Alas, the word is that the Frasconis are no more. The bodies of Danielo and two other men were found in a ditch outside Bellona. I heard that on the radio on my way to the airport. Egan killed Salvatore," Jago lied, and added cheerfully, "the ladies in Palermo will be beating their breasts in anguish tonight."

"Your sense of humor will be the death of you one of these days," Smith remarked. "Where are Egan and the Talbot woman now?"

"Winging their way back to the old country in their Lear Jet at the taxpayers' expense."

"And you?"

"Won't get in until this evening, a problem of plane connections. There is, by the way, one point I feel I should raise."

"What's that?" Smith demanded.

"The question of what, if anything, Barbera's been able to tell them."

"Not a damn thing," Smith said, "because he didn't know anything."

"Let's be frank," Jago said. "You've always handled the Irish end of things yourself, never let me in on the act. I don't know who you deal with there, but I do know the Frasconis were involved. Am I right so far?"

"So what if you are?" Smith said reluctantly.

"An old fox like Barbera would have made it a number one priority to find out as much as he could about the Frasconis' business interests. He must have had men penetrate their organization. There must also have been Frasconi men who turned to his side. In those circumstances, I don't think you can be certain he knew nothing of their dealings in Ulster."

"I suppose you could be right," Smith admitted.

"Did they have direct dealings with the people in Ulster, for example?" Jago asked. "Did anybody visit there?"

There was a heavy silence before Smith said, "Yes, as a matter of fact, they did."

"Then I'd give them a bell, old stick, just in case Egan and Sarah Talbot turn up there too." As a final twist of the screw he added, "Of course what would be even worse, the lovely couple might decide to come clean with Ferguson and Villiers for a change. Your friends would have the RUC and the army breathing down their necks then."

"I take the point," Smith said. "I'll see to it. Speak to me tonight when you get in."

Sir Leland Barry was shooting clay pigeons on the lawn at Rosemount, his splendid old Georgian house outside Ballycubbin. A retired judge of the High Court, he was a distinguished-looking man of seventy-three, immaculate in riding breeches and polished brown boots, brown Donegal tweed jacket and matching cap. His hair and neatly trimmed moustache were snow-white. "Pull!" he called.

The gamekeeper, crouched by the trap, yanked the lever and two clays soared into the sky. Sir Leland blasted the one on the left, but missed the right. "Damn!" he said softly.

Behind him the butler crossed the lawn with the trailer phone. "A call, sir, from London."

"Who is it?" Sir Leland demanded.

"A Mr. Smith, sir."

Sir Leland handed him the shotgun. "Hold that." He took the phone and walked across to the wall above the moat and leaned on it. "Barry here."

"We could have trouble," Smith said.

"Tell me."

Smith covered the situation in a few brief sentences. When he was finished Barry said, "There's no problem. If this chap Egan and the woman turn up they'll be dealt with."

"And the Security forces?" Smith asked.

"My dear chap," Sir Leland said patiently, "the Security forces pose no threat to me. Quite the reverse, in fact, so don't worry. You can safely leave things in my hands."

He went back to the butler, gave him the phone and reclaimed his shotgun. He reloaded and nodded to the gamekeeper. This time, when he fired, both clays disintegrated very satisfactorily into a cloud of dust.

Ferguson turned from the window, cup and saucer in his hand, and drank a little tea. Villiers was standing in front of the fire, Sarah and Egan sitting opposite each other.

"A remarkable man, Jago," Ferguson said. "On top of everything else, it would seem he's turned himself into the man with a thousand faces." He emptied his cup. "Of course, there is one interesting point."

"What would that be, sir?" Egan asked.

"He does seem to have an uncanny ability to follow you around." He handed his cup to Sarah. "I think I'll have a refill." He turned to Egan. "As for you, your *Boys Own Magazine* exploits don't particularly impress me. We've spent enough money over the years in training you,

God knows, but there is the much more serious matter of how you accessed our computer system."

Egan said, "You don't really expect me to answer that, do you?"

"Come off it, Sean," Villiers cut in. "There's only one person with the ability to access that system, and we all know who it is. Alan Crowther."

"A bad business." Ferguson sipped his fresh cup of tea. "Particularly for Alan. A very serious breach of the Official Secrets Act, amongst other things."

"But this is nonsense," Sarah cut in. "At their offices on Cannon Street, our associates have one of the most sophisticated computer systems in London. Naturally they've afforded me full facilities while I'm over here. I accessed your system, Brigadier."

"Really, Mrs. Talbot?" he said.

"I wouldn't last long in Wall Street financial circles these days without an expert knowledge of computers. I'd be happy to demonstrate," she added.

"I don't believe a word of it," Villiers said.

"Oh, come now, Tony," Ferguson said, "would you doubt the lady?" He turned to her. "Irrelevant now, my dear. Much more interesting to know what, if anything, you came up with in Sicily."

She glanced at Sean Egan. He said, "I think we should speak up. It's too important to hold back now, for many reasons."

She took a deep breath. "All right. What we knew before we went was that the moving force behind everything is this man Smith, identity a mystery, Jago, his right-hand man."

"And the Frasconis?" Ferguson asked. "Where do they come in?"

"Smith and the Frasconis have been heavily involved together in the drug business, but more than that, there was an Irish connection," Sarah said, "which would appear to link directly with the deaths of those four IRA gunmen by a Protestant extremist group."

Ferguson said calmly, "Are you saying you know who they are?"

"Yes." She nodded. "A man originally employed by the Frasconis as a courier to Ulster went over to the Barbera side of things. He told Don Rafael everything."

"And?"

"It was the Sons of Ulster," Egan put in.

"Really?" Ferguson turned to Villiers. "We know all about them, don't we?"

"I don't think they've been very active recently," Villiers said.

Ferguson nodded. "Anything else?"

"Oh, yes," Sarah said. "The man in charge."

Ferguson frowned. "Of the Sons of Ulster?"

"Yes." She nodded. "Sir Leland Barry. He operates from a house called Rosemount outside a village on the coast named Ballycubbin."

There was silence. Ferguson and Villiers glanced at each other, then the brigadier went to his desk and sat down. "That's very interesting."

"Then what are you going to do about it?" Sarah demanded.

Ferguson looked at Villiers. "Try and explain the intricacies of Ulster politics to her. She might listen to you."

"Sir Leland Barry represents one of the oldest families in Ulster," Villiers said. "He's the fifth baronet. During the Second World War he served with considerable distinction as an officer in the Ulster Rifles. In later years, he had an even more distinguished career as a barrister in London, as well as Ireland. At one time he was a member of Parliament at Stormont."

"As an Ulster Unionist, I presume?" Egan said.

"He could hardly be anything else," Ferguson replied. "He is, after all, a Protestant."

"So were Wolfe Tone, Charles Stewart Parnell and Erskine Childers," Egan pointed out. "They were also Irish nationalists in their day."

Villiers said, "Be that as it may, Sir Leland Barry is a considerable defender of the Protestant cause. He was a judge for many years, and as such, very much an IRA target. In March 1982, they attempted to kill him. A roadside bomb as his car was passing in Fermanagh. He escaped serious injury himself, but his wife was killed."

There was silence. Ferguson said, "He retired from the bench three years ago. Since then he has been elevated to the position of a Grand Master in the Orange Lodge. He is on excellent terms with the government, and his help to the Security Services on a number of occasions has been incalculable."

"Several years ago he headed a government inquiry into allegations of misconduct against certain officers of the Royal Ulster Constabulary," Villiers said. "His findings gave them a very clean bill of health indeed."

"Whiter than white," Ferguson added. "I need hardly say it has made him rather popular in RUC circles."

Sarah stared at them in bewilderment. "I don't think I understand what you're saying to me, or perhaps I just don't want to."

It was Egan who gave her the answer. "It's really very simple. What they're trying to get across to you is that for security reasons, he gets away with it. The fact that he's also, according to our information, a terrorist, is simply an inconvenience."

"You're out of order, Sergeant," Ferguson told him sharply.

"Why? Because he's telling the truth?" Sarah shook her head and her voice rose. "I can't believe this."

Villiers interrupted. "I'm sorry, Sarah, there's a lot more to it than you realize."

"You'll just have to trust us, Mrs. Talbot," Ferguson added.

Sarah put her cup down carefully and stood up. "You're not going to do anything, are you?"

Ferguson said bleakly, "Mrs. Talbot, it ends here. From now on this is a matter for the Security Services, not you. Under the powers vested in me I could have you deported to the United States. That is not a road I wish to follow. However, I formally warn you against any attempt to leave this country for Ulster." He turned to Villiers. "You will see that Mrs. Talbot's name is posted on the blacklist at all departure points for Ireland, both sea and air."

"Certainly, sir," Villiers said.

"And you'd better include this young fool." Ferguson turned to Egan. "As you well know, you are still subject to military discipline. I could have you court-martialed, but I'd hate to do that. You're a fine soldier, Egan, and I'm old-fashioned enough to believe that should still count for something. You've served the Crown well."

"Dear God," Sarah Talbot said in disgust. "Just let me out of here." And she walked stiffly to the door.

Villiers said, "Go with her, Sean. I'll see you at the funeral."

"You mean you really intend to put in an appearance after this?"

Egan shook his head. "You've got nerve, Colonel, I'll give you that," and he went out.

Villiers said to Ferguson, "My God, Leland Barry running the Sons of Ulster. Do you think it's true?"

"I see no reason to doubt it. I never did like the man. Of course the problem is, what can one do about it? There are rather special circumstances there, Tony."

"I know, sir."

"So." Ferguson got up and came round the desk. "Don't be too downhearted. There's always a way. First, we'll go round to Curzon Street and you can dig out everything we have on the Sons of Ulster. That should fill the time nicely until the funeral."

"You're going to go, sir?"

"Oh, yes, Tony." Ferguson nodded as he crossed to the door. "Not, I regret to say, for the usual reasons of decency and compassion, but because I'll need to speak to Mrs. Talbot again, or, to put it more neatly, I suspect she'll need to speak to me."

Egan left Sarah at Lord North Street and drove to The Bargee. Ida and the barman were just getting ready to open for the lunchtime trade. When Egan looked in, she came over to him at once.

"You all right, Sean? Where have you been?"

"I had business to attend to," he told her.

"I'll get you something to eat. We won't be busy for a while."

"No, thanks," he said. "I've got to change. I'm going to a funeral."

He went upstairs, took a dark-blue worsted suit, white shirt, dark tie from the wardrobe. He showered and changed, and when he went down she was still in the kitchen.

"You look very nice," she said and adjusted his tie. "Have you been in touch with Jack?"

"I haven't had a chance since yesterday."

"He phoned me around breakfast time from that nursing home. Didn't sound too good."

"I'll check on it." He kissed her on the forehead. "I have to go, Ida."

She stood at the door, watched him drive away, then closed it and walked slowly back into the bar.

Sarah was wearing her black velvet suit when she came downstairs. Egan was on the phone to the clinic in St. John's Wood. He put the receiver down as she came into the room.

"How are things?" she asked.

"They could be worse. Apparently he developed a temperature during the night. Aziz found there was a minor infection of the wound. He's had him in surgery, opened it up again and restitched him."

"Did you speak to your uncle?"

"No, he's back in bed under sedation." She walked to the window and looked out. Egan said, "It's time we were off."

She said, without looking around, "They're not going to do anything, are they?"

"I don't think so," he said. "I think there's more to it than they're telling us. More to Sir Leland Barry."

"Yes," she said, "that was my impression." She turned and smiled tightly. "Now, let's get going." And she crossed the room quickly and led the way out.

As they followed the coffin out of the old Norman church, it started to rain. The churchwarden produced several umbrellas, obviously kept against such a contingency. Villiers put one up and held it over Sarah.

"It always rains at funerals," Sarah said in a dull voice. "Why is that?"

Villiers had an arm about her shoulders. "Not long now."

Behind them, Ferguson and Egan shared an umbrella. The housekeeper from Stokeley Hall and three servants followed, and a handful of villagers brought up the rear.

Sarah turned to look at Villiers with another tight smile. "We'll have to start calling you Sir Anthony, won't we? Sir Tony doesn't sound quite right."

He couldn't think of a thing to say to that, and they continued through the graveyard to the Talbot family plot enclosed by railings. The grave stood open and ready, two gravediggers waiting at a respectful distance, sheltering under the trees.

There was no stone for her husband, for he was buried, according to British Army custom, in the Falklands where he had fallen. No stone for Eric, only ashes now. She stood there, every sense numbed as the coffin was lowered.

The churchwarden held an umbrella over the rector to protect his vestments from the rain, but the words that were said were a meaningless jumble, nothing sinking in. And then she was at the graveside, bending to pick up a little wet earth. As it thudded on the coffin, it was as if a mist cleared in her head.

This is real, she thought, and I can't do anything about it, just as I couldn't do anything about Edward. But not Eric. Eric is different.

She knew then that she couldn't let it go, not then or later. Mechanically, she shook hands with the rector, accepted his condolences and walked away toward the car, Villiers hurrying after her.

Ferguson said, "Oh, dear, trouble, I fear."

"What in the hell did you expect?" Egan asked as they went after them.

Villiers was trying to talk to her as they arrived. She ignored him and turned to Ferguson, face flushed, eyes glittering. "I'm going to ask you once more, Brigadier. Do you intend to do anything about Sir Leland Barry?"

"I think I've covered that business more than adequately," he said gravely.

"Fine." She turned to Egan. "Let's go."

She got into the Mini Cooper and Egan slipped behind the wheel. As he started the engine, Ferguson leaned down to the window and said to her, "Don't do anything foolish, Mrs. Talbot. You will find it impossible to leave this country for Ulster, believe me."

Egan drove away, and Villiers said softly, "Damn it, Brigadier, I hate to see that."

"Make sure you have a good man on her," Ferguson told him as he walked to the Daimler.

They got in and it moved away. Villiers said, "Isn't there anything we can do about Barry?"

"You know the position there, Tony, the difficulties. He's too entrenched." Ferguson shrugged. "No, *we* couldn't do a thing. I have every faith that she will, of course."

"How can she?" Villiers said. "Blocked at every airport, all the ferries denied to her?"

"Oh, young Sean will find a way. You know how resourceful that boy is. That's why I want him working for me."

Villiers said, "You wanted it this way. That's why you talked to her the way you did."

"Anger, that's what she needed, and now she's very angry indeed." Villiers turned away, unable to speak. "It'll be all right, Tony. With your man keeping tabs on her, we'll be in business the moment she makes a move. It's up to you to follow in close pursuit." He added impatiently, "Don't you see? This way we get at least some sort of chance at Barry, and that's better than no chance at all."

"My God!" Villiers said. "I don't believe I'm hearing this."

"Don't look at me like that, Tony, be your age. In this business you have to dirty your hands sometimes to get results. We both know that, so let's have no more nonsense." And he leaned back and closed his eyes.

"Look—" Egan began as he turned onto the main road, but she put up a hand to stop him.

"No talk, Sean, just drive."

She wound down the window, left it open in spite of the rain, and smoked one cigarette after the other all the way back to London, as Egan worked his way through the rush-hour traffic until they reached Lord North Street.

He switched off the engine. "Do you want me to come in?"

"Very much so." She went up the steps, unlocked the door, and he followed her into the sitting room. She turned to face him. "Maybe you're used to the mad ways of your Secret Service, but I'm not." She was furious. "Your uncle was a gangster for years, a villain, isn't that what you call it?"

"That's right."

"He's done more for me, given me more help, risked his life even ..."

"I know," Egan interrupted. "Now calm down."

"Calm down? Sean, they've put us on the blacklist, proscribed from traveling to Ulster, and Barry gets away with everything." She was shaking with rage. "Well, I'll get to Ireland if I have to swim."

"Let's hope it won't come to that," he said calmly.

She was stopped dead in her tracks, staring at him. "You mean you'll help me?"

"It's getting to be a habit. Too late to break it now," Egan said. "Change your clothes and then we'll go and see what Alan Crowther can come up with."

Alan Crowther sat back from the computer screen and shook his head. "No wonder they can't touch him. Over the years he's had connections up to Downing Street level, the support of the Orange Lodge and the adoration of the RUC."

"There's got to be more," Egan said.

"Yes, there's a limited-access secondary," Crowther told him. "Give me a minute." He tapped away, then nodded. "Would you look at that?"

"What is it?" Sarah asked, leaning forward.

"Well let's try and reduce it to simple terms. He's a double-crossing old swine who hasn't scrupled to nail his own people when necessary."

"But I don't understand," she said.

"The Protestants are split into factions as much as the Republican movement," Egan told her. "Ulster Defence Association, UVF, extremist groups such as the Red Hand of Ulster and Barry's own outfit, the Sons of Ulster. There's always been a power struggle."

"According to this, he's turned in other Protestant extremists whenever it's suited him," Crowther said.

"He's even betrayed his own people to the IRA," Egan added.

"On several occasions, and just look at the killings he's been involved in, the dirty tricks." Crowther shook his head. "No wonder he's protected. They wouldn't dare put him on trial in an open court."

"And Ferguson and Tony know about this?" Sarah asked.

Egan nodded. "But that doesn't mean they were involved with Barry or took part in any of his goings-on."

"He's right," Crowther told her. "Most of the secondary material is derived from other sources—the DI5 Irish section's computer and the RUC's confidential dealings file."

"And they'd work with a man like that?" Sarah said. "Collaborating with extortion, betrayal of friends, murder?"

"There are those who believe the end justifies the means," Egan told her. "It's a dirty little war over there. If you knew some of the things I've done ..." He turned away, swore softly and turned to face her. "Goddammit, no! Anything I did, there was always a reason. But this ..." He gesticulated helplessly at the screen.

"And Ferguson and Tony?"

"I've known them both for years. Tony's one of the hardest men I know, but honorable. As for Ferguson—well, I've known him to pull some strokes, but compared to Barry, he's Mother Teresa."

Crowther said, "One more thing, and it isn't on that computer. The deaths of those four IRA gunmen where burundanga was used. That should be added to Barry's list of achievements."

Egan said, "Ferguson and Tony are probably as frustrated by the situation as anyone."

Sarah took a deep breath. "Okay. Sean, how do I get to Ulster?"

"Never mind that for a moment," he said. "What do you want to go for?"

"To confront Sir Leland Barry."

"To what purpose?" Egan spread his hands. "I mean, you can't shoot him. You're incapable of pulling the trigger. Jock White proved that. Or do you want me to shoot him for you?"

"No," she said. "I don't expect you to do that any more than I expect justice any longer. But it does seem probable to me that of all the people we've been involved with, Sir Leland Barry is the one most likely to hold the secret of Smith's identity."

"That's true," he said. "I can't argue with you. The only difficulty would be in getting the bastard to open his mouth."

Sarah smiled. "I'm sure you'll find an adequate way of persuading him. You usually do. Now, how do we get to Ulster?"

"By sea," he said simply.

"Don't be ridiculous," Crowther said. "They'll have all the ferries blocked."

"I'm not talking about the ferries," Egan said. "I'm talking about a thirty-foot motor cruiser. Something with a cruising speed of, say, fifteen knots, rigged for deep-sea fishing. The kind of thing keen fishermen hire for a week."

"Go on," Sarah said.

"There's a boatyard just outside Heysham. That's on Morecambe Bay on the Lancashire coast. A nice clear run up around the northern tip of the Isle of Man to the Ulster coast. Sail straight into Ballycubbin. The man who owns the boatyard is an ex-Royal Naval Petty Officer called Webster—Sam Webster. He's about seventy now. In fact, the place is falling about his ears, but he's reliable. I've worked with him before."

"Will he help?"

"He won't believe we're going out after shark, if that's what you mean. On the other hand, he'll keep his thoughts to himself if I offer him enough money, but it would have to be in cash."

"There's at least a thousand pounds in tens and fifties in the safe in the study at the house," she said. "Even more in traveler's checks."

"He wouldn't know what they were," Egan said. "Which still leaves us with the problem of getting there. You see, we were followed here by a red Ford Escort van parked just along the street. If you tie that in with the telephone repairmen down the manhole at the other end, it all adds up to Ferguson's boys keeping a close eye on us. I wouldn't mind betting there's someone out back as well."

Crowther looked at his watch. It was just after six. "Actually, I have a rather jolly idea. How would you two like to join the freightbagger's club, fully paid-up members, for free?"

"Are you joking?" Egan said.

"Not at all. Freight schedules are my hobby these days. There's one out of Victoria at seven-thirty to Scotland. It usually stops in Lancaster freight yard at eleven-thirty. How far is Heysham from there?"

"Seven or eight miles, I think," Egan said.

"Well then. I'll come with you. Show you the ropes. The outing will do me good. There's a return freight at half-past midnight. I'll be back here by five."

"Freightbagging," Sarah said. "I don't understand."

"He'll explain while I'm away," Egan told her. "I want to call Webster at Heysham and I don't want to do it from here. I think the repairmen at that manhole at the end of the street are tapping the phone. And I'll get the cash from your house if you tell me where the safe is and the combination."

She gave him the information. "You'll take care, Sean?"

"Don't I always?"

He left the house and set off in the Mini Cooper. The Ford Escort pulled out and followed. He stopped outside Camden tube station, went inside, bought some cigarettes at a kiosk and got some change, then he went into a telephone booth and called Sam Webster in Heysham. The phone rang for a long time, and it began to look as if no one was there when suddenly the phone was picked up.

A hoarse voice said, "Who the hell is that?"

"It's Sean Egan, you old rogue, that's who the hell it is."

"Jesus, Sean." Webster roared with delight. "Where did you spring from? I heard you got hit in the Falklands."

"Yes, well, I got back from that one all right," Egan said. "Listen, have you still got the *Jenny B*?"

"I certainly have. Why?"

"I'd like to hire her. Take a lady friend of mine on a fishing trip."

"And when would you be wanting her?"

"Tonight. Should be at your place by midnight."

Webster laughed. "Fishing trip, is it? I wasn't born yesterday, boy, but I'll tell you what I'll do. Seeing it's you, I won't charge you a thousand pounds. I'll do it for seven-fifty and throw in the fuel."

"Done," Egan said. "I'll see you at midnight."

He went back to the Mini Cooper, got in and drove straight to Lord North Street. He was inside for no more than three minutes, came out with the thousand pounds and drove away, the Ford in close attendance.

At The Bargee, he parked the Mini Cooper in the courtyard, got the Browning from the tool kit in the boot and went inside. Ida was in the bar. He didn't bother her, simply phoned for a cab and went up to his room to change into denims and boots, a sweat shirt and his black leather jacket.

He found a small holdall and put the Browning in it, then he pulled back the carpet between the side of the bed and the wall, lifting a loose floorboard to reveal an assortment of weapons. He took a couple of extra clips for the Browning and a Walther in a holster especially made to fit around the ankle. He put them in the holdall with a can of Mace and went downstairs to the bar.

"I'll have a Scotch, Ida," he said, went to the window and looked out at the Ford across the road.

A couple of tough-looking eighteen-year-olds were sitting at the next table drinking beer and playing dominoes. "How's it going, Sean?" one of them asked.

"Not so good. There's a bloke across the street in a Ford Escort van been bugging me all night." Egan took out a ten-pound note and dropped it on the table. "Slit his tires, only don't let him see you, and have a drink on me."

"A pleasure."

They were out of the pub like a shot, one of them with a knife already open in his hand. They disappeared into the shadows. Ida came over with the Scotch. He swallowed it down. "I'll be away for a day or two, Ida."

"Again? Where to this time?"

"Across the water," he told her.

She grabbed his arm. "Not Belfast again, Sean, you promised." There was genuine fear on her face.

He kissed her cheek, just as the taxi arrived. "See you soon, Ida."

He ran out and got into the cab. As it left, the Ford Escort tried to follow and came to an abrupt halt. Egan sat back, content.

He had the cabdriver drop him at the end of the street and strolled past the telephone repairmen, noticing a sedan parked at the side of the house by the entrance to the back alley. When he went into the house, Sarah and Crowther were waiting in the kitchen, Crowther in the woolen hat, parka and boots he'd worn on the previous occasion. He'd supplied Sarah with a green army parka.

"I've got rid of one," Egan said. "But there's still the repairmen, so we'll try the back."

"There's one there too," Crowther said. "I checked earlier. He's sitting in a small Peugeot sedan."

"I'll go first and deal with him," Egan said. "Then straight through the back streets to Camden Road. We'll get a taxi from there to Victoria. After that, we're in your hands."

He opened the kitchen door, went across the yard and into the back lane, creeping along close to the wall. He could smell cigarette smoke, was aware of the man sitting there, the window down. Egan took the can of Mace from his holdall and went forward.

"Excuse me," he said.

The man looked up, startled, and Egan squirted him in the face. The man groaned, his hands went to his eyes and he fell back across the seat. Egan whistled softly and Crowther and Sarah appeared from the shadows.

"Right, let's get out of it," he said, and they hurried away.

FOURTEEN

THE SIDINGS AT VICTORIA Station were a mass of confusion, trains everywhere, lumbering slowly out of the darkness into the occasional patch of light, disappearing again. They had gained access through a hole in the chain-link security fence, and Alan Crowther had led the way with absolute certainty, until they reached the cover of an old disused signal box close to the main line.

He checked his watch. "Here in a second. When it comes, just follow me but don't hang about. It only stops for three minutes here."

"What about the romance of steam?" Egan said.

"Gone, old son." Crowther sighed. "Progress, you see. Mind you, these babies make up for it with speed. You'll be there before you know it. What we don't want is a car transporter. That tends to attract the railway police, as I told you, trying to catch the kids who get on to steal the car radios."

"Can't we ride inside a freight wagon?" Sarah asked.

"I'm afraid not. Security locked. The most we can hope for is a hopper or a flattop, and pray it doesn't rain, of course." Crowther grinned. "Actually, I don't mind that. I like the rain."

At that moment, a train clanked out of the darkness and stopped.

There were several freight cars, then a line of vehicle transporters, carrying not cars but commercial vans.

"Damn!" Crowther said. "Still, it could be worse. Those things aren't much of a target. No radios, nothing to rip out." He grunted in satisfaction as the rear end of the train appeared. "Ah, this is more like it." There were half a dozen flatbed wagons loaded with steel drums and coil. "Burrow in amongst that lot and we'll be fine. Come on."

He scrambled up on the end wagon, turned and gave Sarah a hand as Egan pushed her up and joined them, and at the same moment there was a jolt and the train eased forward.

"Super," Crowther said. "Now let's find a spot and make ourselves comfortable." He sighed contentedly. "You'll find it's the only way to travel."

Ferguson had at one stage in his military career served in Palestine during the period leading to the foundation of the state of Israel. It had left him with an enduring legacy—a liking for Jewish cooking, which meant that his favorite restaurant in the whole of London was Bloom's in Whitechapel High Street. He was sitting at his usual corner table, a bottle of kosher wine at his elbow, working his way through an unbelievably large bowl of *hamishe* barley soup, when Villiers entered.

Ferguson sat back and sipped a little wine. "Tell me the worst, Tony."

"They've disappeared. No phone calls from Alan Crowther's place, so the tap didn't work. Egan led one of my boys a dance which ended with the poor sod sitting in a van with four flat tires."

"I like it." Ferguson returned to his soup. "Really excellent, this. Not just barley, but beans, carrots, peas, potatoes. A meal in itself. Anything else?"

"I had a man at the back of Alan's house. Young Carter. Egan gave him a faceful of Mace."

"Dear me," Ferguson said. "He is a ruthless bastard, our Sean, isn't he?"

Villiers sat down in the opposite chair. "So what do you think?"

"Very much what I thought before. Egan's come up with an alternative route, probably helped by Alan Crowther."

"But what could it be?" Villiers demanded.

A waiter took Ferguson's bowl away. The brigadier said, "That's irrelevant really. All that matters is the destination, and we know what that is."

"So what do we do?" Villiers was very tense. "It's Sarah I'm thinking of. She isn't fit to be out on her own."

"But she isn't, Tony, she has Egan. There is another point. Whatever underground route Egan has chosen will take time. They can't possibly get there until sometime tomorrow." Ferguson helped himself to a slice of rye bread. "You can phone Walsham before you go to bed. Have the Lear Jet ready for a quick flight to Ulster in the morning. Only takes an hour. If we leave at eight, we'll be at Aldergrove by nine. Fifteen minutes by helicopter to the army base at Donaghadee. If I remember my facts correctly, Ballycubbin is only ten miles south." He smiled. "We'll be there by ten o'clock, Tony, thanks to the modern miracle of high technology."

"And then?" Villiers demanded.

"We'll have to see what happens, won't we? But enough of that for now. You must have something to eat. The hot salt beef here is legendary and the potato *latke* quite unbelievable." He kissed his fingers. "Takes me back to Jerusalem in the old days."

"With the odd bomb going off in the distance and the Stern gang lurking in the shadows for a shot at you," Villiers commented.

"Always the cynic, Tony, you never change." Ferguson inhaled with delight as the plate of hot salt beef was placed before him.

Northwest of Birmingham, the train ran on into the night, and Crowther, sitting with his back to an oil drum, produced a thermos from his rucksack and poured coffee, which he passed to Sarah.

"Are you cold?" he asked.

"No, fine," she assured him, and she was. In fact, she hadn't felt so switched on in years as the train roared through the night. It gave her a wild and wonderful sense of freedom. "I think I can understand what you see in this," she told Crowther.

"I've always liked trains from childhood." He smiled. "Very nostalgic things, trains. Railway stations always seemed to have infinite possibilities. All those tracks leading to so many places." He stopped smiling. "And then suddenly you're older."

They roared through a brightly lit station; people crowded the platform. "Warrington," Egan said.

"I know, we're making excellent time. Like I said, we'll be there before you know it," Crowther told him.

At Glasgow airport, Jago just failed to connect with a shuttle to London and had to wait until the next. It was eight-thirty as he walked through the concourse at Heathrow to pick up the Spyder in the car park. An hour later he was parking in Lord North Street and hurrying upstairs to the apartment.

That Sarah's house was unoccupied was obvious, as was the absence of the Mini Cooper. He ran the tape back and then on automatic forward to pick up speech, and took his coat off. As he was going into the kitchen, he heard her voice, returned to the sitting room, lit a cigarette and sat down to listen to what she'd said to Egan earlier. When the conversation was finished he sat there, frowning, then phoned the contact number and went into the kitchen to make coffee. The phone rang about five minutes later.

Smith said, "So you're back."

"Just in," Jago said. "And I've found an interesting conversation on the tape."

He went through it quickly. When he was finished, Smith said, "It doesn't matter."

"Doesn't matter?" Jago said. "Look, I don't know who this Barry she refers to is, but one thing is certain. She and Egan intend to get there in spite of Ferguson blocking all the normal routes."

"They might get there," Smith said. "In fact, I hope they do, but they won't get back, I promise you that. Not ever. Leave it!" he added with grim finality. "You've come to like the lady, that's pretty obvious, but from now on you're off the case."

He put the phone down. Jago sat there for a while thinking about it, then he put his Burberry back on, went down to the basement and got into the Spyder. He dropped the hidden flap, selected a Browning, slipped it into one pocket, the Carswell silencer in the other, and drove away.

"So I'm off the case, am I?" he said softly. "Well, we'll see about that, old stick. We'll see."

The train had passed through Wigan and was well on its way to Preston when Crowther stood up. "I'll just stretch my legs," he said.

He started to work his way forward, straddling the couplings to get from one wagon to the next. After a while he came to a boxcar, went up the ladder and started along the swaying roof, crouching. He heard voices, a burst of laughter, and dropped on his belly at once.

When he inched forward to the edge of the wagon and peered over, he found himself looking down at the line of car transporters with the vans on them. As he watched, two youths got out of one of the vans. There was the sound of breaking glass, more laughter. Crowther turned, went down the ladder and hurried back to Egan and Sarah.

"There's a couple of young bastards vandalizing the vans up there, and they're not being very quiet about it. If there's a railway cop on board we could have trouble."

"What do we do if someone does turn up?" Sarah asked.

Crowther looked over the top of a row of oil drums. There was a two-foot space on the other side, the track below. "Stretch out there and hang on to those steel hawsers, very tight." He smiled. "Oh, and don't forget to pray."

Jago got in through Alan Crowther's door with the assistance of a skeleton key and carefully locked it again. He didn't turn on any lights, simply prowled around each room in turn with the assistance of a tiny pencil flash. He found the computer bank in the study particularly interesting.

"Well now," he said softly, "that explains a great deal."

He went back to the kitchen, opened the fridge and helped himself to a pint of milk, then returned to the sitting room and selected an easy chair. Samson, the Burmese cat, brushed his leg and leaped on his lap. Jago took out the Browning, screwed on the silencer and placed the weapon on a convenient coffee table. He drank his milk slowly as he stroked Samson and waited.

The train passed through Preston and Crowther said, "Lancaster next stop." He checked his watch. "We're ahead of schedule. Should be in by eleven-fifteen."

There was a sudden shout, and they looked along the train to see the two youths on top of the boxcar clearly in the moonlight. The two started down the ladder, and a uniformed policeman clambered onto the roof and went after them.

"That's torn it," Crowther said. "Come on, get moving."

He pushed Sarah forward; she climbed over the steel hawsers and knelt on the narrow strip, hanging on tightly. There hardly seemed room for her knees, and she turned slightly sideways, a bolt digging painfully into her hip as she became aware of Egan's boots in front of her face.

Crowther made for the other side of the wagon and ducked out of sight as the two boys arrived, wailing like banshees. One of them was a punk, his hair cut in a Mohawk. Crowther, peering over the edge, saw that the policeman was almost on them.

The track was steep here, the train starting to slow, and as the youths hit the final wagon, the policeman called, "I've got you now, you bastards!"

"In a pig's ear you have, darling," the Mohawk called, and simply jumped from the moving train as his friend went after him, laughing hysterically. Crowther glanced back, saw one and then the other stand up at the side of the track. The policeman went back up the ladder. He walked across the swaying top of the boxcar and disappeared. Crowther scrambled up, clambered over the steel hawsers and reached for Sarah. He helped her up and back to their original position. They sat down.

"Are you all right?" he asked.

"All right? Do you know something? Most of the time my nose seemed to be about six inches above the track. I know it wasn't, but, Alan," she hugged him tightly, "it was wonderful."

Egan squatted beside them. "If you two have quite finished, you might be interested to know that we're just entering Lancaster."

Ten minutes later, the train slowed to a halt in a freight siding. "Easy one to get out of," Crowther said. "Just follow close."

He hurried across the tracks, ducked up a narrow alley between storage buildings, and came to a high wooden fence. He pulled on one of the planks and it swiveled to one side, leaving a narrow opening. He motioned Sarah through first, then Egan, and he followed, pulling the plank into place behind him. They were standing on the pavement of a main road, the occasional car swishing by.

"This way. Round to the front of the station, the way the people who buy tickets go." They turned the corner, and there was the front of the station, three taxicabs standing at the rank. "There you are, Heysham next stop," Crowther said.

Sarah put her arms around him and kissed him. "I'll never be able to thank you enough, Alan."

"Nonsense." He turned to Egan. "You bring her back safe if you want to break bread with me again."

Egan grinned. "What will you do now?"

"Don't worry about me. Excellent freight train back to the smoke in twenty minutes. Mainly cars, I'm afraid, but it could be fun. Off you go."

They crossed to the taxi rank, Sarah got in the first cab, and Egan gave the man the address of Webster's boatyard. Before getting in, he looked back at the corner, but Alan Crowther had gone.

Webster's boatyard was as run-down a place as Sarah had ever seen, rather like a junkyard with the rusting remains of a number of cars, and here and there the decaying hull of a boat. There was a creek below, which just now contained more black mud than water, a dilapidated jetty extending into it. A line ran out to a motor cruiser sitting on its bottom in a couple of feet of water. There were several smaller boats drawn up on the shoreline.

"You mean someone actually makes a living out of a place like this?" Sarah asked.

Egan nodded. "You'd be surprised. Besides, Webster could never starve. He has his Navy pension. He was Fleet Chief Petty Officer in his day."

A light shone in the window of the old cottage on the side of the hill above the yard. They went up the path and Egan knocked. "Come in!" a voice shouted.

He opened the door and led the way into a long and incredibly cluttered room which took up most of the cottage's ground area. There was a primitive kitchen with a pot sink and a single tap, then a section that was obviously used as an office, with a desk and an old Victorian table awash with files.

The living area was at the far end, a wood fire blazing on a flat stone hearth, an overstuffed sofa and two chairs in front of it. The man who sprawled in one of the chairs, a bottle of whiskey at his elbow, a glass in one hand, a book in the other, was small, with a fierce face, tangled gray hair and beard.

"There you are, you young rogue," he said.

Egan leaned on the mantelpiece. "Sam Webster—Mrs. Sarah Talbot."

Webster looked up at her. "And what's a nice-looking woman like you doing in bad company?"

"Oh, I get by," she said.

He tried to sit up and groaned. "Gout," he said, and she noticed the walking stick on the floor. "The fruits of a misspent life. I hesitate to ask, you women having a great sense of your dignity these days, but would you like to make us all a cup of tea? You'll find everything you need back there."

"I think I can manage that." She filled an old kettle at the single tap, found a match to light the stove and took down three chipped mugs from hooks above the sink.

Sean said, "What about the *Jenny B*? Everything shipshape?"

"Saw to it myself earlier this evening before the leg started playing me up. Everything in apple-pie order. Provisions in the galley, fuel in the tanks. All that's missing is my seven hundred and fifty quid."

"I've got that here." Sarah opened her handbag and produced the money. He counted it carefully, note by note.

Egan lit a cigarette and glanced around with distaste. "Just look at this place. How can you live like this with all the money you've got tucked away?"

"But that's the whole point," Webster told him. "What the tax man can't see won't hurt him. What he sees here just makes him feel sorry for a poor old sailor living alone on his pension."

Sarah brought the three mugs of tea and he poured whiskey into his and drank it noisily. "That's grand." He looked at his pocket watch. "Half-past midnight. You'll not get away for another two hours. The tide's still well out. Are you familiar with boats, Mrs. Talbot?"

"A little."

"Ah, well, it's tricky round here. Sandbanks, quicksand. You can walk two or three hundred yards out to sea in some parts of More-cambe Bay and still be only knee-deep in water."

She idly picked up some of the books on the floor by the chair. Walt Whitman's *Leaves of Grass,* Plato's *The Republic,* novels by Heming-way, Charles Dickens and many others.

"You'll notice I'm a reader," he said. "Forty-five years at sea, Mrs. Talbot, and I sometimes think it was the books that got me through. Education is a wonderful thing. Of course, when I was a lad you didn't get the chances. Something I've never understood about this boy here." He was a little drunk now. "A fine brain, real intellect, a philosopher by nature, and what does he do for a living? He kills people."

"Here we go again." Egan turned to Sarah. "We've had this argu-ment so many times I've lost count."

"Samuel Johnson said you couldn't stand five minutes under a shed in the rain beside Edmund Burke without realizing you were in the company of a great man," Webster said.

"And what in the hell is that pearl of wisdom supposed to mean?" Egan demanded.

"It means that in your company under the shed in the rain," Web-ster said drunkenly, "five minutes, and I know I'm in the company of something special gone wrong." He hauled himself to his feet, swayed there, supported by the stick, and reached for the whiskey bottle. "I'm for my bed. Put the light out when you go."

He lurched up the stairs. They heard him lumbering about for a while and then there was silence.

"An unhappy man," Sarah said.

"Not as long as there's one last bottle of Scotch left in this world."

"And hard on you," she persisted.

"He means well," Egan said. "A bit like the remark on those old school reports: he thinks I could do better." He cut short the discus-sion by standing up. "Let's see if there's anything worth having in the fridge. We might as well eat something before we go."

As the *Jenny B* nosed down the creek on half-engines at two-thirty, the tide was still running in. Visibility was excellent in the bright moonlight and Sarah could see mountains lifting into the night on the far side of the bay.

"That's the Lake District," Egan told her. "Wordsworth country."

Standing there in the wheelhouse beside him with only the small light over the chart table was like being in some private world. She looked at the chart. "The Isle of Man?"

"That's right. We pass the northern tip, the Point of Ayre, and from there it's a clear run to Ballycubbin."

"What time will we get in?"

"Probably about nine o'clock, maybe a little earlier. Depends how the weather works out. I've checked on the radio. It's not too bad. Winds three to four, rain squalls later, and there could be some fog by morning on the Irish coast."

As they moved out to sea, they started to roll, spray drifting against the windows, the masthead light swaying. Egan said, "Here, take the wheel."

She accepted the challenge at once. "This is fun."

"Just keep checking the compass," he said. "Keep on that heading. You'll get the knack."

There were red and green navigation lights in the darkness on the horizon. "What's that?" she asked.

"Probably a ferry. Liverpool to the Isle of Man or maybe a coaster on the run up to Glasgow."

"That's their world and this is ours," she said.

"An interesting way of putting it."

He lit a cigarette, coughing as usual, and opened the side window. She said, "Why don't you care, Sean? You don't, you know. About anything. Oh, you've helped me marvelously, but when it comes to the really important things in life, the things that affect you ..."

Egan laughed. "Webster has a weakness for Plato. There's a bit in *The Republic* where Plato speaks of a man who's lived in a cave all his life. He's never seen the outside world. The people and things of that world are only shadows on the wall of his cave."

"I know the passage well," she said.

"Yes, well, Webster thinks I'm the man in the cave, no links with the real world at all, people only insubstantial shadows to me."

"Is he right?" she asked.

"God knows." He left the wheelhouse and stood at the rail in the prow. She remained at the wheel, hands steady, watching him as they plowed into the night.

It was almost five when Alan Crowther went into the yard at the back of the house and unlocked the back door. He turned on the kitchen light and put his rucksack on the table. Then he switched on the electric kettle. He felt remarkably well. The run down from Lancaster had been excellent, fast and exciting. When it had started to rain, he'd taken his chances, riding right up front in a Ford car, king of the night.

He put a tea bag in a cup, unplugged the kettle and started to pour. There was a slight creak of a floorboard behind him. He put the kettle down slowly and turned to find Jago standing in the doorway, the Browning in his gloved hand, the silencer on the end.

"Do one for me, old boy, while you're at it."

Crowther knew who this must be, of course, but played for time. "Jago, I presume."

"My goodness, we *are* well informed, but then, information is your business, isn't it?" Jago took out a cigarette one-handed and lit it as Crowther got another cup and put a tea bag in it. He reached for the kettle, half-turning, easing the plastic lid, and Jago added, "And speaking of information, old boy, where are they, and don't start giving me problems, otherwise I'll have to be very unpleasant indeed and it is rather early in the morning."

Crowther tossed the boiling water across the table and, as Jago dodged back into the hall to avoid it, turned and wrenched open the kitchen door. As he went through, a bullet burned its way across his left shoulder. In the darkness he presented a poor target. Jago fired again as he saw the back door into the lane open, and went after him.

Crowther turned into the street, rounded the corner on the other side of his house and started to run along the canal toward Camden Lock, alternately in darkness and light as he passed beneath the streetlamps. Jago, very fast, was not far behind him as Crowther, laboring for air now, reached a series of granite steps and lurched up them, hauling on the old Victorian iron rail at his side.

He reached the top, clear for a moment under a streetlamp, and Jago's arm swung up. The silenced Browning coughed twice and Alan

Crowther staggered sideways, pitched headfirst over the low wall and fell into the lock.

Jago went to the wall at the bottom of the steps, but there was no sound, only dark water. He hurried back the way he had come, turned into Water Lane and got into the Spyder. Damn that fool Crowther; the plucky bastard was no use to him dead. So, he was no further forward, would simply have to sweat it out in Lord North Street until she got back.

"That's if you do get back at all from this one, Sarah, my love," he said.

Sarah slept on one of the bench seats in the saloon that doubled as a bed. She came awake slowly and lay there in the darkness, aware of the rolling motion, but still unsure where she was. She went up the companionway. The deck was tilting slightly, there was only darkness all around, the rush of water. When she got the wheelhouse door open, Egan was standing there, his face floating in darkness in the light from the binnacle.

"How are we doing?" she said.

"Fine. The weather's a little rough, but nothing we can't handle. If you look back over your shoulder to port you'll not see the Isle of Man, but it's there."

"What time is it?"

He glanced at his watch. "Six o'clock."

"I'll make some tea."

The wind slashed rain and spray in her face as she crossed the slippery deck and went down the companionway to the saloon and into the galley. She got the stove working and toweled her hair. Her parka was soaked through, but she noticed an old brass-buttoned navy reefer behind the door and tried it on. It was rather large, but warm and comfortable, and there was a blue knitted cap in one of the pockets which she pulled down over her hair. She made the tea, found a thermos jug and two mugs, and when she renegotiated the deck, the rain was driving in with even greater force. She got the door open, lurched inside and slammed it shut.

Egan smiled. "Hey, I like the outfit. The complete sailor."

She put the mugs on the chart table and poured the tea. "Shall I take over?"

"No, I can put it on automatic pilot for a while."

There was no hint of dawn yet, only a slight phosphorescence on the water. She said, "Strange, but I feel as if we're somehow coming to the end of things."

"Nothing ever ends," he said, swinging slightly from side to side in the swivel seat, his hands wrapped around the mug. "Every damn thing you ever did, or was ever done to you, is still around in some form or another, working away."

"But we can cut free from the past, Sean, you must see that. Cut free, start fresh."

"It sounds like an advertising slogan," he told her.

She laughed out loud. "You're damn right, it does."

"Anyway, it's words, just words. Have you cut free from your past?" There was no answer to that and she made no attempt to give one. "Have you, hell. It rides you harder each day and it's changing you. Changing you in every way. The Sarah Talbot who boarded that plane in New York was another person."

My God, it seems a thousand years ago now, she thought, and he's right. I'm not the person I used to be.

She said to Egan, "Suppose I accept what you say as true? What are you suggesting?"

"That you can never go back to anything. I tried it and it didn't work. Home didn't exist any more."

"And you think that will happen to me?" Sarah asked him.

"Oh, yes. Action and passion, they're like drugs that sharpen you up, give you a high. When you're back at your desk in that tall building in Wall Street you'll feel as if that's the dream, and only this was the reality."

She shivered, suddenly cold, reluctantly aware of the truth in his words. "I'm not too sure I want to accept that."

"I can see how you wouldn't, but it's all part of the price you pay, and I did warn you, remember?"

He unlocked the steering wheel and increased speed, racing the heavy weather that threatened them from the northwest.

At the same time, in London at Curzon Street, Ferguson, still in bed, was being gently shaken into life by Kim. The brigadier groaned and came reluctantly awake. "What is it?"

"Colonel Villiers is here, sir."

"What, already?" Ferguson groaned again, threw the bedclothes aside and reached for his dressing gown. When he went into the sitting room Villiers was standing at the window. "Really, Tony, this is outside of enough."

"Sorry, sir." Villiers turned, grim-faced. "There's been a further development."

Kim appeared with coffee and Ferguson accepted a cup gratefully. "All right, tell me the worst."

"I've just been to the Cromwell Hospital. They've got Alan Crowther in intensive care."

Ferguson was immediately alert. "What happened?"

"He was shot twice and fell into Camden Lock. Our friend Jago. Luckily a workman cycling to an early-morning shift along the towpath heard his cries. Found him hanging on to a ladder at the side of the canal."

"And Jago did this?"

"Oh, yes, Alan's just told me. He's in a bad way, but able to talk. Jago wanted him to tell him where Sarah and Sean Egan have gone."

"And did he?"

"No, but he told me. He decided things have gone too far. He escorted them to Lancaster last night. Jumped a freight train, would you believe that?"

"Oh, yes," Ferguson assured him. "At this stage I can believe anything, Tony."

"Anyway, they've hired a motor cruiser from that old rogue Sam Webster at Heysham. Sailing straight across to Ballycubbin."

Ferguson nodded. "I told you young Sean would come up with something."

Villiers said, "But what are we going to do?"

"Do?" Ferguson said. "Well, first, I shall shower, then Kim will provide a traditional English breakfast of scrambled eggs, bacon and tomatoes, with toast and marmalade and a large pot of Indian tea. We will consume this together, Tony, after which we will proceed as planned to Walsham and leave on the Lear at eight o'clock. You do have the helicopter arranged at Aldergrove?"

"Yes, sir."

"Good, and given what we now know, I'd like an escort waiting for us when we arrive at that army base at Donaghadee. One officer, captain rank, I think. Someone experienced, and six paratroopers. I always find it scares the hell out of people rather satisfactorily when they see those red berets." Ferguson smiled. "See to it, Tony."

He turned to the door and Villiers said, "But this could be dangerous, sir, very dangerous for Sarah and Egan. I mean, we're letting them walk straight in on Leland Barry. There's no knowing how he'll react."

"My dear Tony, there's only one way he *can* react. You know it and so do I. He's got to get rid of them, and that, of course, is the reaction we want, because once he makes that sort of move, we've got him."

"Well, all I can say is we'll be cutting it pretty fine," Villiers remarked.

"Don't we always, Tony?"

Just after eight, Sarah caught her first distant glimpse of the Ulster coast through heavy mist and rain. There was light by now, but very murky, gray and mysterious. Somewhere a foghorn sounded.

Egan shivered. "I hate November. It's neither one thing nor the other. Just slap in the middle of autumn and winter."

"I know," she said. "What time will we get in?"

"About a quarter to nine. Here, take the wheel."

She did as she was told. Egan's holdall was on the chart table. He opened it, took out the Walther in its special holster, knelt down and strapped the holster into place just above his right boot. He tested the Walther for ease of movement and pulled down his jeans.

"You Yanks are great believers in an ace in the hole, aren't you?" he said.

"I wouldn't know," she told him. "I don't play cards."

He brought out the Browning, tested it as well, then slipped it inside his leather jacket. He took the wheel back, and at that moment, the wind tore a curtain in the mist and Sarah saw, perhaps a mile away, a small harbor, whitewashed cottages above a jetty.

"Ballycubbin?" she asked.

"The circle of maximum danger," Egan said, and he throttled back and took the *Jenny B* in.

FIFTEEN

THERE WERE FEW FISHING boats in the harbor, but then they had passed most of them on their way in, sailing out to the fishing grounds in search of herring and mackerel.

"It's usual to report to the harbormaster's office when you come in," Egan told Sarah, "but I doubt whether a place like this even has a harbormaster."

He cut the engine as they bumped alongside the lower jetty, and Sarah jumped to the dock with a line. He followed her over the rail to assist and they tied up.

"Well, here we are," she said. "Not much of a place."

"Are you ready with your story?" he asked.

She nodded. "As ready as I'll ever be."

"Good, then let's do it." And he went up the ladder ahead of her.

The Lear Jet landed at Aldergrove at about the same moment and taxied to an area at the far end of the airport that was reserved for military purposes. An Army Air Corps Lynx helicopter was waiting, the pilot already at the controls.

A young lieutenant stood at the bottom of the steps. He saluted. "Everything ready, sir."

"Thank you, Lieutenant," Ferguson said and boarded the Lynx, quickly followed by Villiers.

Villiers leaned forward and tapped the pilot on the shoulder. "How long to Donaghadee?"

"Fifteen minutes, sir."

"Didn't I tell you, Tony?" Ferguson said as he strapped himself in. "You worry too much." And the Lynx lifted off with a roar, drowning any more attempts at conversation.

The street along the front was deserted in the rain, no sign of life, only a small grocery store open. Egan opened its door. A bell tinkled and a young woman reading a magazine on the counter looked up. "Jesus, you startled me."

"Sorry," Egan said. "Just in with my boat. Is there a café? We could do with something to eat and a cup of tea."

"You could try the pub. The Orange Drum. It's a few doors down."

"Isn't it a bit early in the morning for them to be open?"

"Sure, but no one cares in a place like this. Murtagh's always there, he's the publican. He'll see you all right."

"Thanks."

Egan and Sarah continued along the front and stopped under the pub sign. "The Orange Drum," Egan commented. "They don't leave you in any doubts about their politics, do they?"

The door opened to his touch and he led the way into a large, old-fashioned taproom with a low ceiling and a Victorian bar of polished mahogany. It reminded him very much of The Bargee.

The door behind the bar opened and a large, gray-haired man in waistcoat and shirt-sleeves came in, wiping his hands on a dish-cloth. "Good morning," he said genially. "And where did you two spring from?"

"We're just in on a motor cruiser from Bangor," Egan said. "The girl in the shop said you might manage some breakfast."

"No problem." He leaned over the bar and shook hands. "Ian Murtagh."

"My name's Egan."

"Sarah Talbot." She held out a hand. "It's good of you to help us out."

"American?" he said. "We don't get many of your kind round here. The tourist trade isn't what it used to be."

"And isn't that understandable?" Sean said, and to Sarah's astonishment, his voice had changed and he was now speaking with the hard accent of Belfast.

"In the circumstances, one might just wonder why you've chosen Ballycubbin, Mrs. Talbot," Murtagh said.

Egan looked at her. "Go on, tell him, why don't you? He might be able to help."

She leaned across the bar, pushed her knit cap up and turned the full charm of her gray-green eyes on him. "Well, this is in confidence of course, but despite the disguise I'm a journalist for *Time* magazine. There's a man lives somewhere near here, a retired judge called Sir Leland Barry. The IRA tried to blow him up a year or so ago."

"And killed his wife," Murtagh told her, face impassive. "I know Sir Leland well. He's a fine man."

"I was hoping for an interview, but I've heard he doesn't give them. I suppose he's worried about his personal security."

"And why would he have to worry about that in a place like this, with every man in the county on his side?" Murtagh asked. "And in any case, I've always found him a reasonable man. A perfect gentleman with the ladies. Would you like me to phone and explain the situation?"

"Oh, would you?" Sarah said breathlessly.

"No trouble. You make yourselves comfortable by the fire. I'll put the kettle on—my wife's away at her mother's—then I'll phone Sir Leland."

He went out. Sarah stood in front of the fire, warming her hands. "What do you think?"

"Too easy," Egan said. "Much too easy, but let's wait and see."

In the library at Rosemount, Sir Leland Barry sat at his desk. His estate manager, James Calder, stood at his side, a sheaf of papers in his hand. Sir Leland put down the phone.

"They're here, the man Egan I told you about and the American woman."

"We're sure he's IRA?" Calder asked.

"Oh, yes." Barry nodded. "He's been working with their so-called

European battalion, killing unarmed British soldiers in Holland and Germany. She's from some Irish-American organization in New York, and both of them are out to make a name for themselves by shooting me."

"The bastards," Calder said.

"Well, we'll give them their chance, at least on paper. You go down to the village and pick them up. Take one of the gamekeepers with you. Flynn, I think.

He's done well recently. I'm sure he'd like to finish off another Provo gunman. Murtagh can come back with you."

"Fine, sir."

Calder moved to the door. Sir Leland added, "Let's get the timing right, because I'm calling in the RUC now, and we want our friends nicely dead when they arrive."

He picked up the phone and quickly dialed the number of the local RUC headquarters.

The Lynx hovered for a few moments, then settled on the helicopter landing pad at the army base outside Donaghadee. There were three khaki-painted army Land Rovers waiting. The two at the rear of the small column were stripped down. Each one had a driver, three sitting behind, all paratroopers, hard young men in red berets and camouflaged jump jackets, armed with Sterling submachine guns. The front Land Rover still had its housing on. Two officers stood beside it, a paratroop captain and an Army Air Corps colonel. They came forward and saluted as Ferguson and Villiers got out.

"Brigadier Ferguson? Colonel Chalmers, sir, in command here. May I introduce Captain Richard Stacey, Two Para?"

Stacey saluted smartly. Ferguson said, "This is Colonel Villiers, my aide. Time is of the essence, Colonel. I'm obliged to you for your prompt assistance in this matter, but we must move and move quickly. I'll give Captain Stacey his orders as we go."

A few seconds later, Ferguson and Villiers were sitting in the rear of the lead Land Rover, Stacey up front beside the driver, as they led the small convoy toward the gate.

"You know Ballycubbin, Captain?" Ferguson asked as a bar was raised and they sped through.

"Yes, sir," Stacey replied.

"That is our destination. In particular, the home of Sir Leland Barry. You realize, of course, that you are wholly bound by the provisions of the Official Secrets Act?"

"If you say so, sir," Stacey said.

"Good. Then when we get there, you and your men will do exactly as I say, neither more nor less." He turned and smiled at Villiers. "Don't worry, Tony, we'll make it, I promise you."

Egan and Sarah finished the bacon sandwiches that Murtagh had brought them and were into a second cup of tea when he returned. He was wearing a hunter's three-quarter-length parka and a rain hat.

"It's your lucky day, Mrs. Talbot," he said. "I told you Sir Leland was a decent man. He's sent one of the estate cars to pick you up."

"Really?" Sarah said.

"Aren't I telling you? It's waiting for you out back." He lifted the flap of the bar counter. "This way."

Sarah got up, slightly unsure, and Egan said, "Isn't that wonderful, Mrs. Talbot?"

She walked through into the kitchen, and as Egan followed he pulled the zip of his leather jacket down slightly, ready to reach for the Browning if necessary. Murtagh passed them and opened the back door, leading the way into the cobbled yard. There was a large Peugeot estate car standing there, two men beside it.

Murtagh said, "This is Mr. Calder, Sir Leland's factor at the estate, and Malcolm Flynn, head gamekeeper."

Calder smiled charmingly and put out his hand. "A pleasure, Mrs. Talbot. Sir Leland's asked me to take you straight up to the house."

"That's very kind of him," Sarah said, and Calder opened the rear door and motioned her inside.

At the same moment, Murtagh produced an old American army-issue Colt and touched the muzzle to the back of Egan's neck. "But before we go, bucko, let's relieve you of whatever's spoiling the shape of that pretty leather jacket."

Flynn produced a Smith & Wesson thirty-eight revolver from the capacious poacher's pocket of his jacket. Murtagh found the Browning and passed it to Calder.

Calder took it, examined it for a moment, then shook his head sorrowfully and put it in his pocket. "You really can't trust anyone these days, and that means you, sweetheart, so over the car, both of you. Assume the position, isn't that what they say on American TV?"

Sarah turned to Egan, angry and afraid. He said gently, "Just do as they say."

He spread his legs and leaned on the car; she followed suit, aware of hands roughly searching her. Calder said, "Right, the rear seat, both of you."

Flynn got behind the wheel, Calder beside him, and Murtagh sat in the center seat, his back to the door, covering them with the Colt.

"It's not every day we have a couple of Shinners traveling with us and in such style." He glanced at Calder. "Have you ever noticed how you can always tell a Catholic? They look different."

Egan took Sarah's hand and held it tight.

Sir Leland Barry was sitting at the desk in his study, writing, when Calder led the way into the room. He took off his spectacles, looked up and put down his pen. Egan and Sarah stood in front of the desk, Murtagh at the door. He had his gun in his hand as did Flynn, who stood on the opposite side of the room, his back to the library shelves. Calder took out Egan's Browning and laid it on the desk.

"He had this."

Sir Leland picked it up for a moment, weighed it in his hand and put it down. "A journalist, you say, Mrs. Talbot?"

Before she could reply, Egan took out his wallet. As he reached for it, Murtagh and Flynn raised their weapons threateningly. He put up a hand. "A minute only." He tossed the wallet on the desk. "If you check that, you'll find sufficient ID to prove that I'm a serving member of the SAS."

Murtagh laughed harshly. "Bollocks."

"Crude, but adequate." Sir Leland sat back. "That kind of forgery is commonplace with you people."

"And which people would that be?" Egan asked.

"Why, the Provisional IRA, and this lady, I've been given to understand, is an Irish American, a member of a New York-based organization whose sole aim is to cause as much havoc as possible in this province."

"That's nonsense." Sarah leaned on the desk. "My name is Mrs. Sarah Talbot. My son, Eric, was murdered in Paris two weeks ago at the instigation of a man called Smith, with whom I have the best of reasons to believe you have business dealings."

He frowned in apparent bewilderment. "Business dealings?"

"Yes, you've been engaged in the drug trade together."

Flynn, outraged, said, "Jesus, would you listen to that?"

Calder said, "You can cut out the drivel, it's too late for that. We know why you're here. To gain access to this house and assassinate Sir Leland."

"Only it won't work," Barry said, "because I was forewarned." He shook his head gently. "I'm afraid it's you who must pay the price, Mrs. Talbot."

"But that's crazy," she said.

"Not at all. I've been in touch with the RUC. They should be here any moment. They'll find you and Mr. Egan very dead, my life saved by my good friends here."

Egan pushed her to one side. "You can't do this, Barry, she's telling the truth, you know she is."

He made as if to reach across the desk and it provoked the action he'd hoped for. Calder grabbed him by the back of the neck and spun him round and Egan fell back against the couch.

Murtagh moved in and Flynn started across the room. "You bastard!" Murtagh said.

Egan's right hand swung up with the Walther from the ankle holster. He shot Murtagh in the center of the forehead, was already on one knee, grabbing Sarah by the leg and pulled her down, turning and firing again, catching Flynn twice in the heart. Calder scrabbled for the Browning on the desk and was shot in the temple at close range. Egan stood there, very cool, very deadly, feet apart. It was the most terrible and destructive thing she had ever seen, no more than three seconds in the doing.

Sir Leland, still in his chair, said, "For God's sake, no!"

Egan gave Sarah a hand up and pulled her behind him. "Now, I've very little time left before your RUC chums get here so we'll make this brief. I've got three left in this thing." He raised the Walther. "If you don't tell me what I want to know I'll give you all three in the belly. A painful way to go and very slow."

"Anything," Sir Leland said. "Anything you want."

"All right. Smith—who is he? Where do we find him?"

"But I don't know. I can't answer either of those questions." Egan raised the Walther threateningly and Barry cried hoarsely, "It's true, I tell you. I phone a contact number and leave a message. He phones me. It's always been that way."

"I don't believe you."

"It's true, I swear it." There was sweat on Barry's face, blind panic, and then it cleared. "Just a minute. There is something. Let me open the desk drawer."

"All right, but very, very carefully."

Barry opened the drawer and hunted through. "He sent a courier once. She came on the ferry, the Glasgow ferry to Stranraer. Murtagh went to meet her."

"A woman?"

"That's right. She delivered a suitcase."

"Heroin?"

Barry nodded. "Murtagh gave her one in return with the necessary cash and she went back on the next ferry." He laughed in relief. "I've found it, see? Flynn drove Murtagh to Stranraer, stayed out of sight and took a photo of them together." He shrugged. "I thought it might be useful at some stage."

Egan looked down at the photo and Sarah moved forward. "Can I see?"

And then everything happened at once. Sir Leland Barry grabbed the Browning on the desk and got to his feet. Egan fired three times very fast, driving him back through the French windows to the terrace. In the same moment, the outer door burst open and several police constables in the green uniform of the Royal Ulster Constabulary stormed in, submachine guns at the ready. Egan just had time to slip the photo into his pocket before they swarmed all over him.

Egan lay face down on the floor of the Georgian drawing room, his wrists handcuffed behind him. Sarah sat at a table, head lowered. There was one constable on guard by the door, his Sterling ready in both hands. The door opened and a uniformed inspector came in, followed by a sergeant.

The inspector said, "It's like a butcher's shop in there."

The sergeant walked over and kicked Egan in the ribs. "You dirty Provo swine. You killed Sir Leland, you and this Yank bitch."

"Stop that, Carter," the inspector said sharply.

"I'm not a Provo, I'm SAS," Egan said. "And if you're interested, your good friend Sir Leland Barry commanded the Sons of Ulster."

There was a look of anger and disbelief on Carter's face. "You lying bastard."

He kicked him again and the inspector repeated, "Stop that!" He said to Egan, "Can you prove what you say?"

"My wallet's on Barry's desk. My ID is in it."

The inspector said to Carter, "Watch them," and went out.

Carter stood looking down at Egan, touched him gently with the toe of his boot, then he glanced at Sarah, put a hand on her chin and raised her head. "Wait for me outside, Murphy," he told the police constable.

The door closed gently. Sarah said, "What Mr. Egan says is true. You'll see."

"True?" He said, "What do you people know about truth? You butchered Sir Leland's wife, you blow up kids, and you bloody Irish Americans are the worst, coming over here, sticking your noses in what doesn't concern you." He pulled her up. "We'll soon sort you out back at the station, but in the meantime, you need your inspection." She started to struggle and Egan kicked out at him in vain. "Your body inspection. Every nook, every cranny. I mean, we don't know what you're carrying, do we?"

She was back across the table, his knee forced between her legs, his hands on her breasts. As waves of horror and disgust washed over her, she suddenly remembered Jock White's instructions, saw her one chance, and pointed each hand into a perfect phoenix fist and jabbed into each side of his neck. He screamed in agony, and behind him the door was flung open and Ferguson entered, Tony Villiers at his shoulder. Captain Stacey and his paratroopers crowded in behind, weapons ready.

Sergeant Carter backed away, looking dazed, and Sarah sat up as the inspector pushed his way in. "What's going on here?"

Tony Villiers took an ID card from his wallet. "Colonel Villiers, Group Four, and this is Brigadier Charles Ferguson. I think you know who he is."

The inspector saluted at once. "Brigadier."

"I'm assuming full control here under the special powers which, I'm sure you are aware, I hold. All was not what it seemed, Inspector, that's all you need to know for the moment. Now kindly remove the handcuffs from this gentleman."

"Sergeant Carter," the inspector said.

Carter produced a key and released Egan. Villiers put an arm around Sarah. "Are you all right?"

"I am now," she said.

"Let's leave the greetings until later," Ferguson said testily.

They moved to the door. Villiers said, "Excuse me a moment." He turned, crossed the room in two quick strides, kicked Carter between the legs and, as the sergeant keeled over, raised a knee into his face. "When I see rubbish like you at work," Villiers said, looking down at him, "it sometimes makes one think the IRA might have a point."

It was early evening at Aldergrove, darkness falling, rain drifting across the apron where the Lear Jet waited. Sarah stood at the window of the waiting room, a cup of tea in her hand. Egan sat on a seat beside her. The afternoon had passed in a flurry of forms and statements. They hadn't really had time to talk. She was about to speak when the door opened and Villiers and Ferguson entered.

"We'll be off in a couple of minutes," Villiers said.

Ferguson walked across the room and stood beside Sarah. "Are you all right now, Mrs. Talbot?"

"I think so," she said.

"As regards the actions of Sergeant Carter back there, he'll be dealt with appropriately, I can assure you of that. In every barrel there's always at least one rotten apple. The RUC have been on the firing line in one of the dirtiest little wars in modern times for something like fourteen years now. Don't condemn them all because of the actions of one man."

"I'll try not to," Sarah told him.

"Having said that, you'll never come closer to meeting a bad end. A good place to be leaving." Ferguson looked out as rain drummed against the window. "What a bloody awful country. Sometimes I really think we should give it back to the Indians."

SIXTEEN

JAGO, STANDING AT THE window of his apartment on Lord North Street drinking a cup of coffee, saw the Daimler pull up outside Sarah's house at eight o'clock that same evening, and he hurried to turn up the receiver.

In the car, Ferguson said, "I'd like a few words before I go, Mrs. Talbot. May we come in?"

"Is it necessary, Brigadier? I'm very tired."

"Essential, I'm afraid."

"Oh, very well," she said reluctantly, got out of the Daimler, went up the steps and unlocked the front door. Ferguson, Villiers and Egan followed her.

Sarah switched on the light, led the way into the sitting room and turned to face them. "All right, Brigadier, what do you want to say?"

"Some of my superiors in Government will not be pleased," Ferguson said. "But I got what I wanted, Leland Barry's head, and I thank you for that."

"But?" Sarah said.

"Alan Crowther is half-dead in hospital, thanks to our friend Jago, Mrs. Talbot. You didn't know that, did you? Bodies strewn all over the place, Paris, Sicily, Ireland. It's been a Cook's Tour of unmitigated violence. You got everything you wanted, but at a rather heavy price."

"Except Smith."

"We may never know who he is now. If he has any sense, he'll drop out of sight, but one thing is certain. You return to America tomorrow, and I'm prepared to make that a legal directive," Ferguson told her. "It stops here, Mrs. Talbot." He said to Villiers, "You will make yourself personally responsible for seeing Mrs. Talbot gets on that plane in the morning, Tony."

"Yes, sir," Villiers said.

"Good." Ferguson turned to Egan. "And you, young Sean, will present yourself to my flat in Cavendish Place at eleven o'clock in the morning on the dot. We need to have words." He didn't wait for Egan to reply, simply said, "Goodnight, Mrs. Talbot," and walked to the door.

Villiers put a hand on her arm. "I'll see you in the morning, Sarah," he said and went after Ferguson.

The outer door banged, the Daimler started up and drove away. There was silence. Sarah stood there in the old reefer and woolen cap, her face smudged with dirt.

"So that's it?" Egan said.

"No it isn't, Sean. I know it and so do you, but first I need a shower and some clean clothes." She touched his cheek for a moment in genuine affection. "You know something? You're a great guy, or should I say a smashing fella? Isn't that what the cockney girls would say?"

"Something like that."

"All right, smashing fella. Make some tea in the kitchen while I change, and then we'll talk."

She stood under a hot shower for five minutes, then toweled her hair, combed it, still damp, and tied it in a ponytail. She got fresh underwear from the drawer, a cream silk blouse. It was as if she had washed away all that had happened in Ireland, and she felt better already. When she came downstairs and entered the kitchen she was wearing the brown suede trouser suit and high-heeled boots.

"You look nice," he said as he poured the tea.

"Well, I certainly feel better." Rain hammered against the window, and they sat on opposite sides of the table, a curious intimacy between them. "Sean, there's something I've always wanted to ask you."

"What's that?"

"You've never mentioned any girl in your life." She hesitated. "Was that because of Sally? After all, she wasn't your real sister."

"As far as I'm concerned, she was and always will be." He lit a cigarette, coughed a little and paused. "What in the hell am I smoking this thing for?" He stubbed it out. "There was a girl back there in Belfast. Mary Costello. A nice Catholic girl. Naturally, her family didn't approve. In fact, where she lived, nobody approved. It was a very Republican area."

"But you are a Catholic yourself," she pointed out.

"But I was also a soldier in the British Army. Anyway, one night the local women got her. Shaved head, tarred and feathered and left tied to a lamppost. Even her parents didn't dare go out to her. She was found by an army patrol in the morning and taken to hospital." Egan stood up and peered out the window. "She drowned herself in the River Liffey the day they discharged her."

There were sudden hot tears in her eyes. "How could people be so cruel?"

"It's not the people. It's life and what it does to them," Egan said. "The way it provides them with perfectly lousy situations and doesn't give them any choice in the matter."

His face, when he turned, was anguished, and she got up, went around the table and put her arms around him. "Is it that bad?"

"Couldn't be worse," he said.

"Then let's get on with it." She pulled him to the table and they sat down. "That photo Leland Barry gave you when you threatened him, the photo of the meeting at Stranraer. You were just about to show it to me when he grabbed for the gun and then the RUC burst in. You've still got it?"

"Yes."

"But you didn't say anything about it to Tony and Ferguson. Why not?"

"Because it's nothing to do with them, not any more. Now, it's personal."

"The courier Smith sent was a woman, isn't that what Barry said?"

"Oh, yes." Egan nodded. "It was a woman all right."

He took the photo from his pocket and pushed it across the table. It showed Murtagh leaning against a post on the dock at Stranraer. A gray-haired woman in a winter coat talking to him. Ida Shelley.

"Oh, my God!" Sarah said.

Egan's face was unnaturally calm. "She's my cousin, really. Of course, I called her Aunty when I was a kid and she was always Aunty Ida to Sally."

Sarah felt the hurt as much as he, and at the same time was aware of a deep and burning anger, a kind of rage that could become blinding if she let it. "Just take a good long breath, Sean." She held both his hands tightly.

"Sally's Aunty Ida." There were tears in his eyes. "Sally's lovely Aunty Ida." He pulled one hand free and hammered it on the table. "Isn't that the funniest thing you ever heard?"

"No," she said, calm now. "Not really. Actually, I think it's about the worst." She got up. "Wait here for me. I'll only be a minute."

She walked into the sitting room, went to the desk and phoned for a cab, then she opened the drawer in the Sheraton bureau and took out the Walther PPK that Jock White had given her. She checked it very carefully, as he had shown her, then slipped it into her handbag and returned to the kitchen.

"Come on, Sean, I've called a cab. We'll go and see Ida." And she turned and led the way out.

Jago phoned the contact number, at the same time watching the cab move away in the street below. When the phone rang, he picked it up instantly.

"Now what?" Smith demanded.

"If you have tears, prepare to shed them now," Jago said. "Shakespeare, old stick, but very applicable where you are concerned."

"What in the hell are you going on about?" Smith demanded.

"Well, not only have they knocked off your friend Barry and returned in one piece. They also have a photo he gave them—with a little persuasion, I'm sure."

"What photo?"

"Oh, a courier you sent to meet someone at Stranraer, and guess who? Ida Shelley." Jago laughed. "Now don't you think that's rather astounding?"

"No," Smith said. "What I actually think is that it's time you and I got together."

Jago didn't have time to shower, but he did change his shirt for a clean one, crisp white cotton which set off his regimental tie to perfection. Then he opened one of his cases, lifted a false bottom and took out a curious garment. It was a waistcoat of nylon and titanium, manufactured by the Wilkinson Sword Company, and he'd had it for some years. It could stop a .45 bullet at almost point-blank range. He put it on, fastened it neatly, then added his jacket and finally the Burberry. He checked the Browning, slipped it into one pocket, the silencer in the other. He carefully ran a comb through his hair and smiled at his reflection in the mirror. "What a hell of a last act, and definitely not to be missed."

He went out. The door closed softly behind him.

The Mini Cooper was still parked where Egan had left it in the yard at the side of The Bargee. It was busy inside. Through the window they could see the bar crowded with drinkers, Ida and three helpers going at it full blast.

Egan and Sarah slipped in through the kitchen door. He said, "Wait here, I'll only be a minute."

He went up to his bedroom, pulled back the carpet between the bed and the wall and lifted the floorboard. There was another Browning in there somewhere. He found it and a Carswell, got a couple of ammunition clips and went back downstairs.

As he went into the kitchen, the door to the bar opened and Ida hurried in, wiping her hands on a bar cloth. She stared at them in amazement. "Where did you spring from?"

"Just got back," Egan told her.

"Jack was on the phone this afternoon asking after you. He's out of the clinic now. Back at Hangman's Wharf."

"That's good," Egan said. "We met an acquaintance of yours while we were over there in Ulster, Ida, or maybe I should call him a business associate."

She looked puzzled. "What are you on about?" Egan held the photo up in front of her. "This, Ida—this is what I'm talking about." Her face was white, eyes staring. Suddenly she looked ten years older. She took the photo from him, hands trembling, and slumped down at the table. Then she started to cry.

Jago left the Spyder in Wapping High Street and walked the rest of the way in spite of the rain, which was quite heavy now. Finally he turned down the narrow street lined with old Victorian warehouses and came out onto Hangman's Wharf. Smith was standing under a lamp looking out at the river. He was holding a large black umbrella, a raincoat slung over his shoulders.

Jago stood there, hands in pockets. "Mr. Smith? We meet at last."

"And about bleeding time," Jack Shelley said, and turned to face him, smiling, a curiously dashing figure, his left arm in a heavy black sling.

Ida remained at the kitchen table, aware of the roar of the Mini Cooper's engine starting up outside and fading away. She'd stopped crying now; she took out a handkerchief and wiped her eyes. The bar door opened and one of the barmen looked in. "What you up to, Ida? We're run off our feet in here, girl."

"I'll be right in, Bert."

She walked to the mantelpiece and picked up the photo of Egan and Sally, the girl slightly profiled, looking up at him with such love.

"My little Sally," Ida whispered. "I let you down, love, didn't I? I was always too afraid, you see, but not any more."

She put the picture down, picked up the card Tony Villiers had given her and went to the phone.

As the old freight elevator went up slowly, floor by floor, Shelley said, "You've done a great job on your appearance. I wouldn't have known you."

"You knew what I looked like before, then?" Jago asked.

" 'Course I did. Don't be bleeding stupid. I knew more about you than you know about yourself. That's why I picked you."

"But the way you handled things," Jago said. "All those calls. That was brilliant."

"Balls!" Shelley said. "It was easy. The great thing about the telephone is that as long as you're the one making the call, you're in charge. The bleeper alerted me if I was in range and if I wasn't I only had to call the contact number at intervals to see if there was a message."

"Clever," Jago said.

"Not really. If someone phones you and says they're in London, you believe them, but they could be in Paris. That's how salesmen manage their dirty weekends away from home." He laughed coarsely as the lift stopped and he stepped out. "Yes, I could phone you from anywhere and you didn't know where it was coming from. Car phone, when I was lying in bed in that clinic, phone booths. Of course, what really covered my tracks was Paris. You shooting at me like that. Just enough to make it look like I was one of the good guys. I took a big chance on you there, but you handled it just right."

He led the way down the corridor past the kitchen and opened the door into the main room. He reached for a bank of switches, made an adjustment so that there were only a couple of table lamps on at the other end, most of the room shrouded in darkness.

"Don't want too much light."

"What about your usual boys?" Jago asked.

"Frank and Varley? Gave 'em the night off. They do as they're told. To be honest, they've no idea what I've been up to in the last three or four years." He stopped at the drinks cabinet, picked up a brandy decanter and splashed some in two glasses. "No, this is just you and me."

"And our friends."

"Definitely." Shelley laughed. "In fact I'll drink to that. To friends." And he clinked his glass against Jago's.

The lift jolted to a halt. Egan led the way down the corridor. He paused, took the Browning from his pocket and nodded to Sarah.

"Be careful, Eric," she said. "Be very careful."

Egan smiled somberly. "It's Sean, Mrs. Talbot, not Eric."

He opened the door and stepped in. He stood there, the Browning at his side, Sarah at his shoulder. The room was a place of shadows. They started forward.

"Jack, are you there?" Egan called.

"Right here, my old son." The doors to the old freight platform stood open and Shelley moved in, the umbrella in one hand. "Pissing down out there, but I just felt like a breath of air." He peeled off his coat, one-handed, walked a few paces and turned. "Is that a shooter I see in your hand, Sean? Not a very friendly gesture to your old uncle."

"Yes, well, I thought I'd probably need it with Mr. Smith," Egan said. "We've had an interesting conversation with Ida about you, Jack. Jesus!" he said in disgust. "Jack Shelley, the Robin Hood of the East End, a drug baron. Why, Jack?"

"Don't be stupid. You know how much I've got in Swiss bank accounts after four years in this racket? Twenty-two million quid. Twenty-two million. That's serious business."

"And what are you going to do with it, Mr. Shelley?" Sarah asked. "I understood your legitimate business interests are worth that kind of money anyway."

"And what's that got to bleeding well do with it?"

"All that money and no way of spending it," Egan said. "Just like some of your old mates when I was a kid. The blokes who'd knock over a security van and end up with a suitcase full of money under the bed that they couldn't spend because that's what the coppers were waiting for."

"Leave it out," Shelley said. "You're talking crap."

"But never mind all that," Sean said. "Bad enough, but not as bad as what Ida told us. How she came back to The Bargee unexpectedly one afternoon and found you in bed with Sally. How the kid seemed like another person, totally changed. How she was never the same again."

"And we know why, Mr. Shelley," Sarah said. "Scopolamine and phenothiazine, otherwise burundanga."

"You keep out of this, you snotty bitch. You've caused enough grief." Shelley turned back to Egan. "So what? She was a little slag. I caught her at it with a fella when I called in there one morning when Ida was out. Anyway, she wasn't family, was she?"

Egan raised the gun. It shook in his hand, but he didn't fire. Instead he allowed the Browning to swing down again and Shelley laughed triumphantly. "I knew you couldn't. I know you better than you know yourself, my old son." He raised his voice. "All right, Jago!"

Jago stepped in through the open windows from the freight platform and struck Egan across the back of the neck with the barrel of his Browning. Egan fell to the floor and lay there.

Jago looked across at Sarah and smiled. "A pleasure to see you again, Mrs. Talbot."

Shelley looked down at Egan. "Went soft on a skirt, the silly young bastard." He glanced up at Sarah. "And it's all your fault, coming around here, sticking your nose in, upsetting everybody. Well, not any more." He turned to Jago. "See her off then. Put her over the rail into the river."

Jago looked at Sarah and he wasn't smiling now. The Browning wavered slightly, lowered. "I don't think I want to do that, Mr. Shelley."

"Another one of you gone soft on a bleeding bird," Shelley said contemptuously.

He fired twice very fast, the bullets thudding into Jago, knocking him back through the windows against the railing of the freight platform. He tried to get up and Shelley's left hand came out of the sling holding a snubnosed revolver. He fired twice more at close quarters and Jago rolled on his back, limbs twitching.

Shelley laughed coldly. "Looks like I'll have to take care of this myself after all." He bent down to pick up Egan's Browning and stirred him with his toe. "Family, you see, Mrs. Talbot. I knew he couldn't shoot me when it came down to it."

And then the rage, the loathing for this monster and every terrible thing he had ever done, exploded inside her. Her hand came out of her pocket holding the Walther PPK. When she extended her arm, the muzzle touched him between the eyes.

"But I can, you bastard!" she cried, and pulled the trigger.

The final expression in his eyes was not so much fear as astonishment and then the back of his skull disintegrated, blood and brains spattering across the white wall as he was hurled backward.

She fell on her knees, still clutching the gun and a voice called, "Sarah." She looked up and saw Jago standing in the open window. He looked ghastly. "That's my girl," he said. "I'm proud of you." And then he lost his balance, staggered back against the rail and toppled over, down into the river below.

The door burst open behind her. She got to her feet, dropped the Walther and turned, swaying, and Tony Villiers caught her as she started to fall.

Sarah sat on the couch drinking hot tea with brandy in it. Three young men in parkas and jeans holding Sterlings stood in the shadows. Tony was on the telephone; Ferguson sat in a chair opposite, watching her.

She heard Tony say, "I need the disposal team now at the following address."

She said, "The disposal team?"

Ferguson said, "Jack Shelley, well-known City businessman, albeit with a rather colorful background, died of a heart attack tonight. No need for an autopsy as he's been receiving treatment for his condition from a prominent Harley Street specialist. No trouble with an adequate death certificate."

"You people can do anything, can't you?" she said. "CIA, KGB, SIS, you're all the same, when it really comes down to it."

"Yes, well, passing over the histrionics, Mrs. Talbot, Jack Shelley will leave here within the next half-hour and proceed to a crematorium in North London.

By midnight he will be five pounds of gray ash, and by midnight, you will be winging your way to America."

Egan came out of the shadows as Villiers put the phone down. Sarah said, "Are you all right, Sean?"

"I wasn't much good to you."

"Understandable in the circumstances."

He gave her a strained smile. "So, Jock was wrong. When it really came down to it, you were able to pull the trigger."

"I'm not going to apologize," she said. "He deserved to die and I killed him. I'm not proud, but I'm not sorry. It's something I've got to learn to live with."

"A season in hell," he said. "I warned you."

Ferguson said, "Tony, I think Mrs. Talbot should be leaving now."

Villiers walked toward her. "Come on, Sarah."

She took Egan's hands in hers. "What will you do, Sean?"

"Get by," he said. "I'll get by."

She put her hands on his shoulders. "You've come to mean a great deal to me. But then I think you know that."

"Me, Mrs. Talbot? Or Eric?"

"Oh, you, Sean. Very definitely you."

She held him close for a long moment, then walked away very quickly. And Villiers hurried after her.

Egan crossed to the drinks cabinet and poured a Scotch. He walked to the open window, ignoring Shelley's body under the blanket, and stood on the freight platform, looking down at the river.

Ferguson said, "And what now, young Sean?"

"God knows."

"Well, then, there's nothing for it. You'll just have to come and work for me at Group Four."

"Like hell I will," Egan said.

"My dear Sean, the Inland Revenue will recover your uncle's ill-gotten gains from Switzerland, but it will still leave you sole heir to a business empire in excess of twenty million pounds." Ferguson smiled. "Now what on earth would a chap like you want with that kind of money?"

Sean Egan put down his glass, turned and walked into the shadows. Ferguson called, "You'll be back, Sean. Nowhere else to go."

The river moved on, drifting under heavy rain and fog. A boat eased down toward the sea, sounding its foghorn. By the long-disused wharves all was quiet, and then, at King James's Stairs, something moved below the wharf and a shadow hauled itself up a ladder.

There was a streetlamp on top of the deserted wharf and Jago stood underneath it, streaming with water, and unbuttoned his Burberry. The rounds Shelley had fired at him were embedded in the bulletproof vest. He pulled them out, one by one, tossed them into the river, and belted the Burberry again. High above, a plane lifted from Heathrow and passed over the city. It could be Sarah. Probably not but that didn't matter.

He looked up at the night, arms wide, smiling, then he turned and walked into the darkness. Was gone.

A BIOGRAPHY OF JACK HIGGINS

Jack Higgins is the pseudonym of Harry Patterson (b. 1929), the *New York Times* bestselling author of more than seventy thrillers, including *The Eagle Has Landed* and *The Wolf at the Door*. His books have sold more than 250 million copies worldwide.

Born in Newcastle upon Tyne, England, Patterson grew up in Belfast, Northern Ireland. As a child, Patterson was a voracious reader and later credited his passion for reading with fueling his creative drive to be an author. His upbringing in Belfast also exposed him to the political and religious violence that characterized the city at the time. At seven years old, Patterson was caught in gunfire while riding a tram, and later was in a Belfast movie theater when it was bombed. Though he escaped from both attacks unharmed, the turmoil in Northern Ireland would later become a significant influence in his books, many of which prominently feature the Irish Republican Army. After attending grammar school and college in Leeds, England, Patterson joined the British Army and served two years in the Household Cavalry, from 1947 to 1949, stationed along the East German border. He was considered an expert sharpshooter.

Following his military service, Patterson earned a degree in sociology from the London School of Economics, which led to teaching jobs at two English colleges. In 1959, while teaching at James Graham College, Patterson began writing novels, including some under the alias James Graham. As his popularity grew, Patterson left teaching to write full time. With the 1975 publication of the international blockbuster *The Eagle Has Landed*, which was later made into a movie of the same name starring Michael Caine, Patterson became a regular fixture on bestseller lists. His books draw heavily from history and include prominent figures—such as John Dillinger—and often center around significant events from such conflicts as World War II, the Korean War, and the Cuban Missile Crisis.

Patterson lives in Jersey, in the Channel Islands.

Patterson as an infant with his mother, grandmother, and great grandmother. He moved to Northern Ireland with his family as a child, staying there until he was twelve years old.

Patterson with his parents. He left school at age fifteen, finding his place instead in the British military.

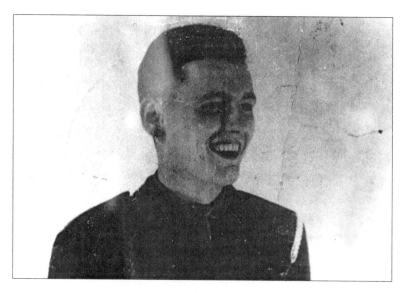

A candid photo of Patterson during his military years. While enlisted in the army, he was known for his higher-than-average military IQ. Many of Patterson's books would later incorporate elements of the military experience.

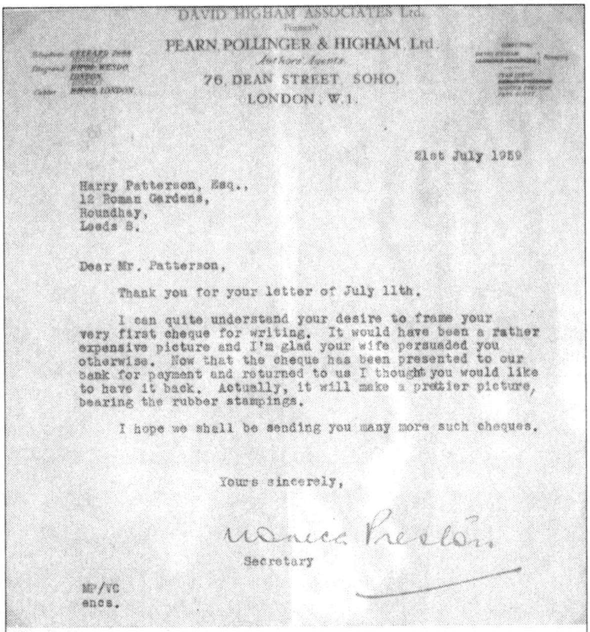

21st July 1959

Harry Patterson, Esq.,
12 Roman Gardens,
Roundhay,
Leeds 8.

Dear Mr. Patterson,

Thank you for your letter of July 11th.

I can quite understand your desire to frame your
very first cheque for writing. It would have been a rather
expensive picture and I'm glad your wife persuaded you
otherwise. Now that the cheque has been presented to our
bank for payment and returned to us I thought you would like
to have it back. Actually, it will make a prettier picture,
bearing the rubber stampings.

I hope we shall be sending you many more such cheques.

Yours sincerely,

Monica Preston
Secretary

MP/VC
encs.

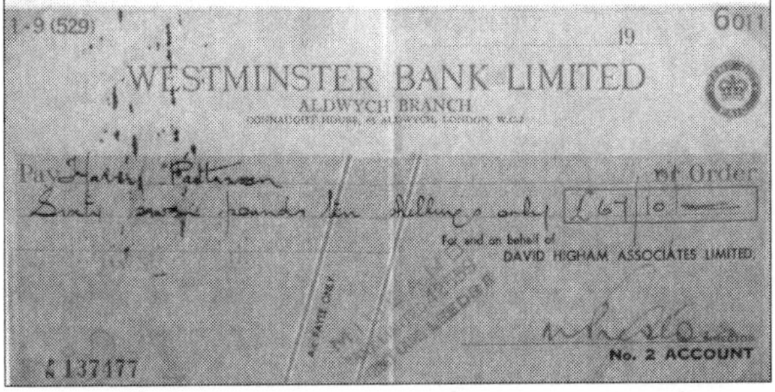

WESTMINSTER BANK LIMITED
ALDWYCH BRANCH

Patterson's first payment as an author, a check for £67. Though he wanted to frame the check rather than cash it, he was persuaded otherwise by his wife. The bank returned the check after payment, writing that, "It will make a prettier picture, bearing the rubber stampings."

Patterson in La Capannina, his favorite restaurant in Jersey, where he often went to write. His passion for writing started at a young age, and he spent much time in libraries as a child.

Patterson visiting a rehearsal for *Walking Wounded*, a play he wrote that was performed by local actors in Jersey.

Patterson with his children.

Patterson in a graveyard in Jersey. Patterson has often looked to graveyards for inspiration and ideas for his books.

copyright © 1989 by Jack Higgins

cover design by Elizabeth Connor

ISBN: 978-1-4532-9411-6

This edition published in 2012 by Open Road Integrated Media
180 Varick Street
New York, NY 10014
www.openroadmedia.com

EBOOKS BY JACK HIGGINS

FROM OPEN ROAD MEDIA

A PRAYER FOR
THE DYING

BLOODY
PASSAGE

CRY OF THE
HUNTER

DILLINGER

THE EAGLE
HAS LANDED

EXOCET

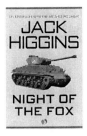

NIGHT OF
THE FOX

A SEASON
IN HELL

THE
VALHALLA
EXCHANGE

Available wherever ebooks are sold

OPEN ROAD

INTEGRATED MEDIA

OPEN ROAD
INTEGRATED MEDIA

Open Road Integrated Media is a digital publisher and multimedia content company. Open Road creates connections between authors and their audiences by marketing its ebooks through a new proprietary online platform, which uses premium video content and social media.

Videos, Archival Documents, and New Releases

Sign up for the Open Road Media newsletter and get news delivered straight to your inbox.

Sign up now at
www.openroadmedia.com/newsletters

FIND OUT MORE AT
WWW.OPENROADMEDIA.COM

FOLLOW US:
@openroadmedia and
Facebook.com/OpenRoadMedia